COLD WAR LIBERATION

THE NEW COLD WAR HISTORY
Odd Arne Westad, editor

This series focuses on new interpretations of the Cold War era made possible by the opening of Soviet, East European, Chinese, and other archives. Books in the series based on multilingual and multiarchival research incorporate interdisciplinary insights and new conceptual frameworks that place historical scholarship in a broad, international context.

A complete list of books published in The New Cold War History is available at www.uncpress.org.

Cold War Liberation

The Soviet Union and the Collapse of the
Portuguese Empire in Africa, 1961–1975

Natalia Telepneva

THE UNIVERSITY OF NORTH CAROLINA PRESS

CHAPEL HILL

© 2022 The University of North Carolina Press
All rights reserved

Set in Garamond Premier Pro by PageMajik
Manufactured in the United States of America

The University of North Carolina Press has been a member of the
Green Press Initiative since 2003.

Library of Congress Cataloging-in-Publication Data
Names: Telepneva, Natalia, author.
Title: Cold War liberation : the Soviet Union and the collapse of the
Portuguese empire in Africa, 1961–1975 / Natalia Telepneva.
Other titles: New Cold War history.
Description: Chapel Hill : University of North Carolina Press, [2021] |
Series: The new Cold War history | Includes bibliographical
references and index.
Identifiers: LCCN 2021052598 | ISBN 9781469665856 (cloth) |
ISBN 9781469665863 (paperback) | ISBN 9781469665870 (ebook)
Subjects: LCSH: Revolutionaries—Angola. | Revolutionaries—Mozambique. |
Revolutionaries—Guinea-Bissau. | Soviet Union—Relations—Angola. |
Angola—Relations—Soviet Union. | Soviet Union—Relations—Mozambique. |
Mozambique—Relations—Soviet Union. | Soviet Union—
Relations—Guinea-Bissau. | Guinea-Bissau—Relations—
Soviet Union. | Angola—History—Revolution, 1961–1975. |
Mozambique—History—1891–1975. | Guinea-Bissau—History—Revolution,
1963–1974. | Portugal—Colonies—Africa.
Classification: LCC DT1402 .T45 2021 | DDC 967.3/03—dc23/eng/20220107
LC record available at https://lccn.loc.gov/2021052598

Cover illustration: Viktor Kobelev, "At Luanda Airport. Electrician Juan Garcio."
Used by permission of Sputnik News.

To the loving memory of my grandfather,

Moisei Slutskii (1920–2005)

CONTENTS

ILLUSTRATIONS AND MAPS

ACKNOWLEDGMENTS

I have accumulated many debts whilst finishing this book, intellectual and otherwise. I am grateful to Arne Westad, who has been a consistent champion of this project, giving the much-needed encouragement and important feedback over the years. He has pushed me to see the bigger picture and his own work has provided a source of inspiration. This book started as a project, which focused primarily on the Cold War and high politics, but it has evolved in other directions, partly under the influence of the very talented people I have collaborated with over the past years. In particular, I would like to thank David Anderson for encouraging me to think about African politics and Kristin Roth-Ey for inspiring me to conduct oral history interviews. Vladimir Shubin has been extremely helpful, providing important contacts, advice and support over the years. He has been an insightful critic, urging me to question assumptions as well as filling the gaps on some of the key protagonists in this story. The generous British Academy Postdoctoral Fellowship grant provided the crucial basis for conducting research for this book.

My collaboration with Daniela Richterova in putting together the "Secret Struggle for the Third World" workshop at the University of Warwick in September 2018 allowed me to think broader about the role of secret intelligence in the Cold War. I have learnt a great deal about East-Central Europe whilst working on the edited volume "Warsaw Intervention in the Third World" with Philip Muehlenbeck, as well as through discussions with colleagues on the "Socialism Goes Global" project. Jan Koura and Mikuláš Pešta helped me understand the role of Czechoslovakia in this story and organized a useful workshop at Charles University, Prague. In Portugal, I have greatly benefited from participating in the "Amilcar Cabral project" and from discussions and support from Julião Soares Sousa, José Neves, Aurora Almada e Santos, and Catarina Laranjeiro. Rui Lopes has been a wonderful critic and a great friend, whose enthusiasm for this work was uplifting in what was a long journey.

I am deeply indebted to Vladislav Zubok, Artemy Kalinovsky, Jeremy Friedman, Alexander Hill, Eric Burton, Mustafah Dhada, Nathaniel Powell, and Allen Isaacman, who read and gave useful feedback on earlier drafts and chapters from the book. My cousin Andrei Frolov gave extremely useful advice on certain military aspects of this story, spending long hours looking at old photos and explaining to me the technical specifications of Soviet weaponry. I also want to thank George Roberts, James Brennan, Radoslav Yordanov, Alessandro Iandolo, William Minter, Yusuf Adam, Nick Rutter, Irina Filatova, Elizabeth Banks, Corina Mavrodin, Hans-Georg and Ilona Schleicher, Helder Fonseca, Sergei Radchenko, and Iva Cabral for sharing tips on sources and expertise. I am grateful for the book's anonymous reviewers who forced me to sharpen the arguments, and to the team of the University of North Carolina Press, especially Debbie Gershenowitz and Andrew Winters, and to Ihsan Taylor of Longleaf Services, in seeing the project through.

While the book has benefited from excellent scholarships and published sources, I relied on extensive archival research and conducted oral history interviews in many corners of the globe to complete the story. I am grateful to the archivists, especially at the Russian State Archive for Contemporary History and the Archive of Foreign Policy of the Russian Federation in Moscow, and the Security Services Archive in Prague who offered good advice and helped in processing requests for sources. In Maputo, I want to thank Clinarete Munguambe and Carlos Jorge Siliya at Centro de Pesquisa da História da Luta de Libertação Nacional for helping me getting around and introducing me to ex-combatants. In Cape Verde, Tatiana Neves at the Fundação Amílcar Cabral provided contact details, while Saidu Banguru and Dominika Swolkien gave crucial logistical assistance and made me feel welcome during my trip to Praia and Mindelo. My research trip to Guinea-Bissau would have been a very different experience without the enthusiastic support from Sana Baldé and information on ex-guerrillas received from Quentino Napoleon dos Reis at Museu Militar da Luta de Libertação Nacional and João Paulo Pinto Có and Papis Sadjo Turé at Instituto Nacional de Estudos e Pesquisas. Joana Sousa and Liam Carney translated oral histories from Kriol to English and Kim Friedlander helped improve the readability of the manuscript.

A very special thanks goes to the men and women who agreed to be interviewed for this book. Due to the nature of this project, I could not spend any significant length of time in the countries I visited. They thus had to take a chance on me, a person who waltzed in without much introduction, and trust me enough to share their stories. I was particularly impressed with the generosity of Vasilii Solodovnikov who, at the age of ninety-seven years old when I met him, not only agreed to an interview, but also offered to work with his personal papers, sharing his meals in the process. I was sad to learn about his death in 2018, and that he would not see the book.

The final year of writing this book coincided with the Covid-19 pandemic. My colleagues at the University of Strathclyde provided me with a safe harbor and I have benefited from discussions with them, as well as with my students. Meanwhile, my friends have provided me with warm companionship, and a much-needed space not to talk (or think) about the book during rare moments of relaxation. I am particular grateful to Natalia Lapotko, Adela Gjorgjioska, Bosiljka Kozomara, Daria Aitmatova, Vladimir Dobrenko, Elizaveta Tikheeva, Irina Maslenkova and Oleg Goriunov for being there for me when I need them.

None of this would have been possible without the love and support of my family. Hussain Mehdi has been a true comrade-in-arms, taking over daily chores, offering psychological counselling and last-minute proofreading. This book is also his. I want to thank my father Evgenii who translated documents from Czech and Polish and my mother Irina whose unconditional love sustains me. They will forgive me for devoting this book to the memory of my grandfather, Moisei Slutskii. A devoted husband, father, grandfather and a talented scientist, he weathered the ups and downs of Russia's turbulent 20th century with his integrity and passion for life intact. His deep-seated belief in the equality of all men and women irrespective of their gender, race, and ethnicity was what inspired me to write this book in the first place.

ABBREVIATIONS IN THE TEXT

AAPSO	Afro-Asian People's Solidarity Organization
ANC	African National Congress
BCP	Bulgarian Communist Party
CC CPSU	Central Committee of the Communist Party of the Soviet Union
CCP	Chinese Communist Party
CEI	Casa dos Estudantes do Império (the House of Students from the Empire)
CIA	Central Intelligence Agency (U.S.)
CIR	Centro de Instrução Revolúcionário (Centre for Revolutionary Instruction)
CMEA	Council for Mutual Economic Assistance
CONCP	Conference of Nationalist Organizations of the Portuguese Colonies (Conferência das Organizações Nacionalistas das Colónias Portuguesas)
COREMO	Comité Revolucionário de Moçambique (The Revolutionary Committee of Mozambique)
CPC	Communist Party of Czechoslovakia
FAPLA	Forças Armadas Popular para Libertação de Angola (Popular Armed Forces for the Liberation of Angola, MPLA)
FARP	Forças Armadas Revolúcionarias do Povo (Revolutionary Armed Forces of the People, PAIGC)
FLEC	Frente para a Libertação do Enclave de Cabinda (Front for the Liberation of the Enclave of Cabinda)
FLN	Front de Libération Nationale (National Liberation Front, Algeria)
FNLA	Frente Nacional de Libertação de Angola (National Front for the Liberation of Angola)
FRELIMO	Frente de Libertação de Moçambique (Mozambique Liberation Front)

GRAE	Governo Revolúcionário Angolano no Exílio (Revolutionary Angolan Government in Exile)
GRU	Glavnoe Razvedyvatelnoe Upravlenie (Main Intelligence Directorate, USSR)
KGB	Komitet Gosudarstvennoi Bezopasnosti (Committee for State Security, USSR)
KUTV	Komunisticheskii Universitet Trudiashchikhsia Vostoka (Communist Institute of the Toilers of the East, USSR)
MAC	Movimento Anti-Colonialista (Anti-Colonialist Movement)
MANU	Mozambique African National Union
MFA	Movimento das Forças Armadas (Armed Forces Movement, Portugal)
MLG	Movimento de Libertação da Guine (Movement for the Liberation of Guinea)
MO	Mezhdunarodnyi Otdel (CC CPSU International Department, USSR)
MPLA	Movimento Popular de Libertação de Angola (Popular Movement for the Liberation of Angola)
MUD	Movimento de Unidade Democrática (Movement of Democratic Unity)
NESAM	Núcleo dos Estudantes Africanos Secundários de Moçambique (Center for African Secondary-School Students of Mozambique)
OAU	Organization of African Unity
PAIGC	Partido Africano da Independência da Guiné e Cabo Verde (Party for the Independence of Guinea and Cape Verde)
PCA	Partido Comunista Angolana (The Angolan Communist Party)
PCP	Partido Comunista Português (Portuguese Communist Party)
PIDE	Polícia Internacional e de Defesa do Estado (International and State Defense Police, Portugal)
PRC	People's Republic of China
PUWP	Polish United Workers' Party
RENAMO	Resistência Nacional Moçambicana (The Mozambican National Resistance)
SADF	South African Defence Force

SKSSAA	Sovetskii Komitet Solidarnosti so Stranami Azii i Afriki (Soviet Afro-Asian Solidarity Committee; USSR)
StB	Státní Bezpečnost (State Security, Czechoslovakia)
SWAPO	South West African People's Organization
TANU	Tanganyika African National Union
TASS	Telegrafnoe Agentstvo Sovetskogo Soiuza (Telegraph Agency of the Soviet Union)
UDENAMO	União Democrática Nacional de Moçambique (National Democratic Union of Mozambique)
UNAMI	União Africana de Moçambique Independente (African Union for Independent Mozambique)
UNITA	União Nacional para a Independência Total de Angola (National Union for Total Independence of Angola)
UPA	União das Populações de Angola (Union of Peoples of Angola)
UPNA	União das Populações do Norte de Angola (Union of the Peoples of the North of Angola)

A NOTE ON TRANSLITERATION

I have followed the simplified version of Library of Congress (ALA-LC) system for the romanization of Russian names and places. Thus, I have omitted soft signs, apostrophes, and diacritical marks throughout the text.

COLD WAR LIBERATION

Introduction

We are approaching Luanda, but nobody is at the airport. Our AN-12 lands. I walk out. In front of me, I see an Angolan soldier standing ten to fifteen feet away. He carries an American automatic rifle hanging on a piece of rope. His eyes are blank. Holding his finger on the trigger, he aims at my stomach. It's not clear who's in charge. I can't reach him because he will open fire and riddle me with bullets. He stares at me menacingly, and I assume that he doesn't know Portuguese. I was rescued by the chief of airport security, an Angolan who knew me well. He ran towards me for about a hundred and fifty meters, shouting, "Boris." This helped me. Then we were accompanied to our hotel.[1]

— Boris Putilin

THIS IS HOW BORIS PUTILIN recalls arriving at Angola's capital, Luanda, on November 11, 1975. Putilin was a Soviet Chief Intelligence Directorate (GRU; Glavnoe Razvedyvatelnoe Upravlenie, military intelligence) officer whose job had been to coordinate arms transfers from the Soviet Union to the Popular Movement for the Liberation of Angola (MPLA; Movimento Popular de Libertação de Angola). The MPLA had been fighting for control over Luanda in the run-up to Angola's independence on November 11. The previous day, celebrations in the capital had begun with a symbolic torchlight procession to commemorate the beginning of a popular uprising against Portuguese colonial rule in Luanda on February 4, 1961. Near midnight, crowds crammed into Luanda's stadium, cheering and firing weapons into the night sky as the red and black flag of independent Angola was raised to the sounds of the new national anthem, *"Angola Avante!"* ("Forward Angola!").[2]

Putilin flew to Luanda to attend the inauguration of the MPLA's leader, Agostinho Neto, as the first president of independent Angola. He arrived with other dignitaries, including Evgenii Afanasenko, the Soviet ambassador to the Republic of the Congo (hereafter "Congo-Brazzaville"). After landing in Luanda, they were escorted to a hotel and then to city hall for the ceremony. Putilin recalled that Afanasenko was the first foreign dignitary to address the crowds from the balcony of city hall. Standing next to Neto, he read out a short greeting from the Soviet government to the cheering crowds.[3] That day, November 11, 1975, Portuguese colonialism in Africa came to an end.

The Portuguese Empire in Africa began to crumble after a group of military officers overthrew the Portuguese dictatorship in a military coup in Lisbon on April 25, 1974. Spurred in part by fourteen years of colonial wars, the coup brought to power a coalition of political forces that initiated a series of fundamental changes to democratize Portuguese society, known as the "Carnation Revolution." The new government also moved swiftly to negotiate independence for the Portuguese colonies in Africa. In 1974, the Portuguese government negotiated transfers of power to the Party for the Independence of Guinea and Cape Verde (PAIGC; Partido Africano da Independência da Guiné e Cabo Verde) in Portuguese Guinea (hereafter "Guinea-Bissau") and to the Mozambican Liberation Front (FRELIMO; Frente de Libertação de Moçambique) in Mozambique. The PAIGC and FRELIMO had dominated the military struggle against Portuguese colonial rule in Guinea-Bissau and Mozambique, respectively, and thus transitions to independence were relatively smooth.

The situation was markedly different in Angola, where the collapse of the Portuguese dictatorship intensified a power struggle between the MPLA and rival nationalist movements that had gained support from Zaire (today the Democratic Republic of the Congo), the Republic of South Africa, and the United States. By June 1974, their rivalry turned into a full-scale civil war. As independence approached, the MPLA's rivals launched an assault on Luanda. Armed with Soviet weapons and backed by a contingent of the Cuban Special Forces, the MPLA managed to retain control of the capital. Afanasenko's symbolic appearance next to Neto on November 11 was no coincidence: it signified the Soviet role in enabling the MPLA to hold onto the capital during the crucial transition to independence.

This book argues that Soviet policy toward anticolonial movements in the Portuguese colonies was primarily shaped by the interactions between the Soviet middle-level bureaucratic elite—that is, men and women like Boris Putilin—and African revolutionaries. Their contacts began in the 1950s when the Soviet Union first attempted to win over the "hearts and minds" of Third World elites. As the anticolonial campaigns in Angola, Mozambique, and Guinea-Bissau started in the 1960s, the Soviets began to provide cash, training, and weapons for the MPLA, FRELIMO, and PAIGC. This assistance was managed by a small group of Soviet bureaucrats and military officials. This book explores the evolution of the relationship between the Soviet elite and African revolutionaries to explain the Soviet role in the collapse of the Portuguese Empire in Africa. As such, the book makes three major contributions to the new histories of the Cold War. First, the book establishes the importance of African agency in the process that led to the collapse of the Portuguese Empire. Second, it highlights the role of ideology and the contribution of the Soviet bureaucratic and military elite in the conduct of foreign policy. Finally, it provides a fresh interpretation of Soviet involvement in Angola in 1974–75, substantially revising existing scholarly accounts.

Power, Agency, and African Diplomacy during the Cold War

The most popular conception of the Cold War, the conflict that pitted the Soviet Union against the United States after 1945, invites a binary understanding of power in international society. Since both the United States and the Soviet Union were the only "superpowers" during the Cold War, power, by implication, must have resided solely with the two giants. The end of the Cold War led to a substantial rethinking of the definition and geographic context of the conflict. In one trend, scholars have shifted their attention to examining the agency of what Tony Smith has called "junior members in the international system" and their role in "expanding, intensifying, and prolonging" the titanic struggle.[4] While many early studies that adopted the "pericentric" framework focused on U.S. and Soviet allies in Europe, the publication of Odd Arne Westad's *The Global Cold War* inspired a plethora of new research emphasizing the role of local actors in shaping Cold War struggles in Africa, Asia, and Latin America.[5]

The final dissolution of European empires coincided with the onset of the Cold War. By the mid-1960s, most European powers had given up de jure control of their colonies in Africa. Portuguese rule in Africa was widely considered a relic of the past, yet Portugal managed to hold onto its colonies until the 1970s amidst armed opposition from the liberation movements. One reason for the prolongation of Portuguese rule was the Cold War. Portugal was a member of the North Atlantic Treaty Organization (NATO) and controlled the Azores archipelago, which hosted a crucial military base in the middle of the Atlantic. Portugal's prime minister, António de Oliveira Salazar, skillfully used access to the Azores as a bargaining chip to resist Western pressure for decolonization. Portuguese colonial rule was also sustained by an unofficial alliance with its powerful neighbors: Southern Rhodesia (later Zimbabwe) and the Republic of South Africa. By the mid-1960s, however, Portugal came into violent conflict with anticolonial movements in Angola, Mozambique, and Guinea-Bissau, all of which demanded independence. In each case, military support for armed struggle was available mainly from socialist countries. Portugal's delayed decolonization thus embedded struggles against colonial rule within the international context of the Cold War.

The first generation of African studies scholars had little to say about the liberation movements' international alliances. Their primary task was to revive the history of resistance to colonialism, but these accounts often confirmed metanarratives drawn up by African elites to legitimize their nationalist projects.[6] When the Cold War ended and archives opened up, a number of historians began to subvert the narratives of "national liberation" to explore connections among the liberation movements, African host states, and international allies.[7] The extent to which the Soviet Union was able to influence the African National Congress (ANC) in its struggle against the apartheid regime in South Africa has in particular attracted significant controversy.[8]

While the literature on South Africa is substantial, historiographies of anticolonial movements in the Portuguese colonies—Angola, Mozambique, and Guinea-Bissau—are much fewer by comparison. Studying nationalist movements in Portuguese-speaking (Lusophone) Africa is no less important than examining English-speaking movements for numerous reasons. First, they were engaged in guerrilla campaigns against the Portuguese through the 1960s and 1970s, in contrast to the ANC, which had limited opportunities to engage in active combat at that time. Second, they were led by influential African leaders who were inspired by Marxist thought. Recent years have seen a proliferation of studies on Amílcar Cabral, the leader of the PAIGC who fought for the independence of Guinea-Bissau and Cape Verde.[9] However, only a fraction of this work considers his ideas in conjunction with diplomatic strategies.[10]

After the Portuguese Empire collapsed, the liberation movements that came to power in Angola, Mozambique, and Guinea-Bissau adopted socialist-inspired modernization projects, which were arguably much more inspired by Soviet socialism than the strategies embraced by the first generation of African leaders.[11] By looking at the international connections of the liberation movements in the Portuguese colonies, we can better understand why certain elites would come to dominate political life in Lusophone Africa after independence.

This book highlights the agency of African anticolonial nationalists in the Cold War. Nationalist activism in the Portuguese colonies took off in the aftermath of World War II, and the first organizations campaigning against Portuguese rule were set up in the 1950s, mainly among émigré communities in neighboring states. Initially, there were many groups with competing agendas and strategies for liberation. As the Portuguese stepped up their repression of nationalist activism in the late 1950s, it became clear that whichever group could successfully mobilize resources for armed struggle would be able to capture the "national liberation" movement title.

Specifically, this book looks at a set of African intellectuals from the Portuguese colonies, many of whom grew active in anticolonial nationalist movements while studying in Portugal in the 1950s and would come to dominate the liberation movements in Angola, Mozambique, and Guinea-Bissau. It explains how these African intellectuals managed to obtain assistance in the aftermath of the Angolan uprising in 1961 and details the varied diplomatic strategies they employed to obtain military support from the Soviet Union and other socialist countries. The narrative follows the cast of characters into 1975, as it reexamines how the MPLA leadership drew the Soviets into increasingly deeper commitments in Angola in 1974–75. For better or worse, the Africans in this story were agents of their own liberation.

Ideology, Foreign Policy, and the Soviet Bureaucratic and Military Elite

The role of ideology on both sides of the Cold War divide has attracted substantial attention among historians and observers alike. In the 1950s and 1960s, Western observers often pointed toward the expansionist nature of Marxism-Leninism to explain Soviet foreign policy during the Cold War.[12] With the relaxation of superpower tensions in the 1970s, many began to emphasize "national interest" and security concerns. Subsequently, the end of the Cold War has led to the rediscovery of ideology as the key to understanding both sides of the conflict.[13] In *The Global Cold War*, Odd Arne Westad has argued that both the Soviet Union and the United States espoused universalist ideologies, driving interventions in the Third World.[14] Friedman's study of Sino-Soviet competition in the Third World has added another substantial dimension to the debate, reinforcing the importance of ideology.[15] Today, this debate continues, and it is fundamentally tied to a larger question about the essential nature of the Soviet Union: was it a continuation of Imperial Russia, a revolutionary state, or a blend of the two?[16]

This book follows in the path of scholars who have highlighted ideology as the key motivating factor in Soviet foreign policy. The very definition of "ideology" has been subject to debate. If authors like Arthur Schlesinger tended to define ideology as a "body of systematic and rigid dogma," new studies operate with a more flexible and nuanced understanding of the term.[17] Instead of judging my cast of characters on the basis of a strict set of dogmatic beliefs, I prefer to define ideology as a particular lens through which individuals processed and understood events around them. To the Soviets, the lens was the ideology of Marxism-Leninism, which entailed a particular reading of human history and progress.

This book studies the role of ideology by following a group of people at the forefront of Soviet policy in Africa: the Soviet bureaucratic and military elite. Above all, these were the experts in international relations or *mezhdunarodniki* (literally, "internationalists") who staffed the various departments of the Central Committee of the Communist Party of the Soviet Union (CC CPSU) and the Ministry of Foreign Affairs. Some of them were international journalists and members of the Soviet academe. These were also officers of intelligence services, the KGB (Committee for State Security) and the GRU, who were often responsible for the practical implementation of policy.

The importance of this bureaucratic elite is not new to students of Soviet foreign policy. Oded Eran's *Mezhdunarodniki* was the first comprehensive study of the group and their roles in training personnel, producing knowledge, and legitimating foreign policy decisions.[18] In his analysis of Soviet cultural relations with Latin America, Tobias Rupprecht has called *mezhdunarodniki* "desk revolutionaries" to underscore the idealism of those who staffed Soviet academic institutes.[19] In *Hot "Cold War,"* Vladimir Shubin has described the Soviet officials as "unsung heroes" for their dedication to the cause of African liberation.[20] Still, we know relatively little about the roles that the bureaucratic and military elite played in the conduct of Soviet policy in Africa.

Studying the bureaucratic and military elite has broad implications for our understanding of Soviet policy in Africa. This book argues that the Soviet "interventionism" in Africa during the 1970s was deeply rooted in the prior decade. Rather than a product of strategic parity with the United States, the roots of Soviet involvement in Africa stretched back to the bureaucratic changes that took place under Nikita Khrushchev, the first secretary of the CC CPSU who succeeded Joseph Stalin in 1953. While Stalin prioritized relations with the West after World War II, Khrushchev began to pursue a much more active policy in Asia, Africa, and Latin America, expanding the bureaucratic and foreign policy apparatus in the process. The primary party organ empowered to forge policy toward the liberation movements in the 1950s was the CC CPSU International Department. Responsible for providing support to international communist and anticolonial movements worldwide, the International Department staff and notably its Africa section forged personal relationships with

African revolutionaries, which often proved instrumental in determining policy choices.

The KGB and GRU acted in crucial supportive roles. They often served as liaisons with African revolutionaries, aiding allies in their struggles with local rivals, gathering information and producing analyses for decision-makers in Moscow. As the anticolonial wars in Angola, Mozambique, and Guinea-Bissau escalated in the 1960s, the GRU and the Soviet military also became increasingly involved in the practical side of support for the liberation movements: delivering arms, training soldiers, and advising on military strategy. The book reveals that the Soviet military believed that limited hit-and-run guerrilla tactics were no substitute for large-scale military operations against the Portuguese. Therefore, they often advocated the expansion of military operations and supplied African revolutionaries with increasingly "advanced" Soviet weapons. Such interactions contributed to what I call the "militarization" of Soviet interactions with African allies, which was in itself a product of frustrated hopes for rapid revolutionary transformation throughout the continent and the rise of African militaries as political actors in their own right.

Prior to the second half of the 1970s, the Soviet Union often lacked hard power in sub-Saharan Africa, especially compared to Western powers with a history of presence on the continent. Thus, the Soviets often used secret intelligence to conduct what I call "Cold War on the cheap." This book uncovers the clandestine relationships that the Soviet and Czechoslovak intelligence officers forged with African revolutionaries as a way to level the playing field. By reconstructing these secret contacts, I show that Africans often used them for personal advantage. This book thus contributes to a growing body of work that aims to revise our understanding of the role of secret intelligence during the Cold War.[21]

The study of the Soviet bureaucratic and military elite also helps explain how ideology functioned in practice. Ideological affinity was essential to develop trust on a personal level between African anticolonial nationalists and the Soviet bureaucrats, spies, journalists, and diplomats who supported them. African nationalists from the Portuguese colonies like Angolan Mário de Andrade, Cape Verdean Amílcar Cabral, and Mozambican Marcelino dos Santos were well-known in leftist European circles. Their ideological "credentials" helped forge their initial contacts with the Soviets and allowed them to receive the first aid packages for their organizations. Meanwhile, the Soviets were highly skeptical of FRELIMO's first president, Eduardo Mondlane, because of his U.S. education and high-profile contacts in Washington. Ideological affinity also meant that the Soviets continued to support the MPLA, even though relations with its president,

Agostinho Neto, were often conflictual. In each of these cases, ideology was the prism through which Soviet officials looked at their allies as the 1960s transitioned into the 1970s. Relations with the African countries never topped the agenda of the Soviet leadership, who were primarily preoccupied with relations with the United States, Western Europe, Eastern European allies and China. Thus, Soviet middle level bureaucrats often played particularly important roles in shaping relations with African allies.

The Soviet Union and the Internationalization of the Angolan Civil War, 1974–1975

Soviet involvement on the side of the MPLA in the Angolan Civil War has captivated scholars since the 1970s. The majority of early works analyzed Soviet policy from a political science perspective, giving weight to factors such as the importance of ideology vs. strategic interests and competition with China vs. the United States.[22] In line with the general trend, the end of the Cold War led scholars to re-emphasize ideology. John Lewis Gaddis argued that Soviet interventions in the 1970s were shaped by "reasons more sentimental than rational."[23] Jonathan Haslam has gone even further to suggest that Moscow pursued an aggressive strategy toward revolutionary goals.[24] Vladislav Zubok has explained Soviet policy in terms of the "revolutionary-imperial paradigm," a mix of Stalin's *realpolitik* and Marxism-Leninism. As the Soviet leadership under Leonid Brezhnev grew increasingly myopic, he argues, they became "prisoners" of dynamic leaders like the Cuban Fidel Castro or the Angolan Agostinho Neto, thus allowing them to be dragged into the African gambit.[25] These studies have offered broad interpretations but do not focus on Angola in much detail.

To date, the new narrative of Soviet and Cuban involvement in Angola was based on accounts written by Arne Westad and Piero Gleijeses, both of whom had unique access to archival sources. Westad has depicted the Soviets' relatively limited and reluctant delivery of arms to the MPLA before switching gears to support the Cuban operation once South Africa intervened in autumn 1975. Gleijeses, like Westad, emphasized Cuba's key role in pulling the Soviets into supporting the MPLA. However, the authors differ in their analysis of the buildup of Cuban military presence in Angola in September–December 1975, with Gleijeses arguing that Castro was only able to convince the Soviets to support the airlift of Cuban troops in early 1976.[26] Although these narratives still dominate, Vladimir Shubin's partly eyewitness account has added some critical details, especially about the role of Soviet personnel on the ground.[27]

This book offers a revised assessment of Soviet policy in Angola within the broader context of developments in Portugal after the coup that overthrew the dictatorship on April 25, 1974. It reinforces the role of ideology in how the Soviets perceived events in Portugal as closely interlinked with events in the colonies. It differs from existing accounts to show that the Soviets prioritized revolutionary developments in Portugal and feared that putting too much pressure on Lisbon to decolonize could jeopardize the role of the Portuguese Communist Party and left-wing members of the military who had assumed an important role in government after the coup. It reveals how Agostinho Neto and the MPLA leveraged his close relationship with military officers in Portugal to seek support from the Soviet Union amid increasingly violent competition with his rivals in 1974. The book provides details of the Soviet logistical operation to supply the MPLA with weapons and resolves the debate about the timing of Cuban involvement in Angola. The new narrative also reconstructs the role of Soviet liaisons, "men on the ground" who were fundamental in shaping perceptions of the changing situation in Angola. It shows how pressure from these actors and a broader ideological framework shaped Soviet decision-making on Angola.

Organization, Sources, and Limitations

The book is divided into seven chapters. Chapters 1 and 2 review the backgrounds, formative experiences, and worldviews of key protagonists: African nationalists from the Portuguese colonies and Soviet bureaucratic and military elites. Chapter 1 shows how Nikita Khrushchev's turn to the Third World in the 1950s gave rise to a new stratum of Soviet military and bureaucratic elite with vested interests in developing relations with newly independent African nations. Chapter 2 outlines the key tenets of Portuguese colonialism and recounts the rise of African nationalism, focusing on the life stories of key protagonists— Amílcar Cabral, Mário de Andrade, Agostinho Neto, and Viriato da Cruz. Chapter 3 centers on the 1961 Angolan uprising as the key moment when the two groups forged their first alliances. Specifically, it explains why the Soviets and Czechoslovaks provided their first assistance packages to the nationalists from Lusophone Africa in 1961 and the long-term implications of these decisions.

Chapters 4, 5, and 6 discuss how the MPLA, FRELIMO, and the PAIGC tried to dominate their respective nationalist movements and the limits of their endeavors. Chapter 4 examines the politics of liberation movements in exile in the context of the Sino-Soviet split. It illustrates how African revolutionaries used diplomacy to obtain support from their African host states and international patrons and tackle local rivals. Chapter 5 concentrates on guerrilla strategy and the role of Soviet military assistance in the context of the "militarization" of the Cold War in Africa. It traces discussions over guerrilla warfare strategies and how these conversations shaped relations between African revolutionaries and their international patrons. Chapter 6 follows the evolution of anticolonial campaigns in the 1970s, placing them in the context of superpower détente. It argues that détente had a minimal impact on Soviet policy in Africa. Chapter 7 reveals Soviet views of revolution in Portugal and the decolonization process, especially in Angola. Finally, the conclusion discusses the broader implications of Soviet involvement in Portuguese colonies within the Cold War context.

This book is based on extensive research in Russian and Eastern European archives. When I first began studying this topic almost ten years ago, access to Russian sources was minimal. I had to consult archives in the Czech Republic, Bulgaria, Poland, and Germany to construct a partial picture of what had transpired. In a few instances, the need to consult East European archives produced astounding results, as I discovered the depth of Czechoslovak involvement, especially with the PAIGC. Since then, access to Russian archives has markedly improved. In a significant development, the Russian State Archive of Contemporary History (RGANI) has declassified thousands of documents pertaining to Soviet foreign relations. I was often the first to see the records of the CC International Department and its Africa desk, including reports from Soviet embassies, press agencies, and analytical overviews written by the KGB and GRU. Some of these files were available only for a brief period in the 1990s before access was closed in the early 2000s.[28]

Major gaps remain. The declassification has not been completed, as many files remain unavailable. Further, there is still no access to the records of the Soviet intelligence services. Therefore, any operational details relating to the activities of the KGB and GRU remain a black box. This lack of access contrasts sharply with the situation in the Czech Republic, which has released almost all the files of its security service (StB; Státní Bezpečnost). I have tried to fill the gaps with information acquired through memoirs and interviews with key protagonists in the story. Here too, the source base is uneven. Readers will notice that the amount of detail is particularly rich when it comes to the PAIGC and the context of anticolonial campaigns in Guinea-Bissau. This is because I was able to conduct extensive interviews with dozens of former participants in Guinea-Bissau and Cape Verde. I also conducted interviews in Maputo. A similar opportunity did not present itself in Angola, mainly for practical reasons.

Other omissions are deliberate. The book is fundamentally a study of the USSR's foreign policy in Africa, written mainly from the perspectives of the

Soviets and their African interlocutors. With the exception of military training in the Soviet Union, it does not generally address the perspectives of the
rank-and-file members of the liberation movements. It also does not address the
perspectives of their regional rivals or of those African men and women who did
not fit into the narrative of the "national liberation struggle."

There are several reasons for this. When I started to conduct interviews with
some rank-and-file members, I realized that the material was too rich to fit into
one book. I also recognized that these perspectives would distract from the main
focus of the book, which is a history of relations between the Soviets and the
African elites who came to dominate liberation movements in Angola, Mozambique, and Guinea-Bissau. However, I did not want to deliberately privilege elite
perspectives over other voices, and I have benefited immensely from a growing
literature that looks at nationalism, decolonization, and conflict in Portuguese
Africa from the perspective of nonelites.[29]

I have thus made an explicit choice to focus on the perspectives of those who
occupied positions of leadership in the liberation movements because they were
the ones who communicated with international patrons. Thus, their strategies
shaped relationships with the Soviets and Moscow's view of the anticolonial
movements as a whole. Also, for reasons of space, I have decided to limit the
discussions of East German, Bulgarian, Czechoslovak, and Polish support for
the liberation movements in Lusophone Africa except when they are directly
relevant to the main story. *Cold War Liberation* is, therefore, a starting point
in the journey toward understanding the true extent of the Soviet impact on
liberation struggles in Angola, Mozambique, and Guinea-Bissau.

Telling the story of Soviet relations with liberation movements in the Portuguese colonies brings to the fore some understudied aspects of the Cold War
while offering a new perspective on such much-debated events as the 1974–75
Angolan Crisis. The anticolonial wars in the Portuguese colonies shaped the
Soviet Cold War in Africa in ways that have not yet been appreciated. The story
told here offers insights into the Soviet decision-making process and the people involved in it. It also provides a comprehensive overview of the diplomacy
of the African liberation movements and helps explain their durability as the
often-dominant political forces in modern-day Angola, Mozambique, and
Guinea-Bissau. What follows is the story of fourteen years of colonial wars, the
African nationalists who would come to dominate the campaigns against Portuguese rule, their supporters and rivals, and the international environment in
which they operated. Before going any further, we need to look at the inception
of Soviet policy in Africa and the *mezhdunarodniki* who came to occupy important roles as "mediators of liberation" in this story.

CHAPTER ONE

Mediators of Liberation

Nikita Khrushchev, the Soviet Bureaucratic Elite, and the Cold War in Africa

T HE PRINCIPLE OF WORKING-CLASS solidarity or *proletarian interna-tionalism* is fundamental to Marxist thought. According to the German philosophers Karl Marx and Friedrich Engels, humankind developed in stages. These took the form of a series of revolutions in the modes of production, starting from tribal society and eventually reaching capitalism in the nineteenth century. Class struggle was the key driving force of such revolutions. Under capitalism, the industrial working class (the proletariat) engaged in class struggle against the property-owning class (the bourgeoisie). This clash would inevitably lead to revolution, the overthrow of capitalism, and eventually the creation of a new, classless society or "communism." In their *Manifesto of the Communist Party* (1848), Marx and Engels urged workers to act in solidarity worldwide to defeat the bourgeoisie—a call embodied in the document's famous final words: "Workers of all lands, unite!"[1] Thus, the principle of *proletarian internationalism* became a fundamental means of achieving the goal of international revolution.

Marx and Engels, however, did not provide a blueprint for waging revolutionary struggles, and many debates emerged about how to carry this out in practical terms. One dispute centered on how to square the goal of socialist revolution with demands for national self-determination in the largely agrarian and multiethnic empires of the nineteenth century. One key contributor to the debate was the leader of the Bolshevik faction of the Russian Social Democratic Labor Party (RSDRP, Rossiiskaia Sotsial-Demokraticheskaia Rabochaia Partiia)—Vladimir Ilyich Ulyanov (Lenin). In *Imperialism, the Highest Stage of Capitalism* (1916), Lenin postulated that imperialism led to a division of the world into "oppressor" and "oppressed" nations, competition, and, inevitably, war—World War I. In Lenin's eyes, the movement for national liberation was imperialism's weakest link and was, therefore, an accelerating force on the road to socialism and world peace. Even though nationalist movements in "oppressed nations" were bourgeois—the majority of colonial subjects were peasants—self-determination was a necessary stage in the inevitable merging of nations. Consequently, Lenin advocated self-determination up to the point of "separation from the empire."[2] Lenin's radical anti-imperialist agenda attracted many Third World nationalists, disillusioned with U.S. president Woodrow Wilson's promise of self-determination in the aftermath of World War I since it seemed to apply only to Europe.[3]

After coming to power in Russia in October 1917, Lenin and the Bolsheviks believed that a worldwide socialist revolution was both imminent and essential for the survival of the first workers' state. In 1919, the Bolsheviks institutionalized their revolutionary agenda by establishing the Third International (the Comintern), an organization dedicated to spreading socialist revolution. The Comintern embraced anti-colonial and anti-imperialist agenda, and established policy on the "Negro Question," as issues related to the liberation of men and women in Africa and the Diaspora were referred to at that time. The Comintern thus made attempts to bring men and women of color into trade unions, launched the first African studies program in the USSR, and organized mass antiracist campaigns, bringing attention to the discrimination against African Americans in the U.S. In the 1920s, Moscow became a "Red Mecca" for many African and African American activists who arrived to witness the socialist experiment.[4]

However, by 1934, the Comintern had scaled back its commitment to anti-colonial agenda in the face of the threat from Nazi Germany. The zigzags in Comintern's support for the anti-colonial cause, including only lukewarm defense of Ethiopia in the face of Italian aggression in 1935, and finally Soviet non-aggression pact with Nazi Germany in 1939 left many anti-colonial activists deeply disappointed in the Comintern. The Stalinist purges during the Great Terror decimated the organization, which was formally dissolved in 1943. Although World War II greatly increased Soviet prestige internationally, Stalin remained relatively uninterested in Africa after World War II.[5]

This chapter charts the revival of Soviet interest in Africa under Stalin's successor, Nikita Khrushchev. Khrushchev's time in office between 1953 and 1964 coincided with the quickening pace of decolonization in Africa. By the mid-1960s, the European colonial powers—Britain, France, and Belgium—had given up control of empire either via "negotiated exits" after pressure from the colonized subjects or as a result of prolonged military campaigns, such as in Algeria. The first summit meeting of leaders from Asia and Africa in Bandung, Indonesia, in April 1955, heralded the advent of the "Third World," a political project, a "third way" in world politics which was to unite countries in Africa, Asia and Latin America, bound by common experience of foreign domination.[6] In Africa, leaders like Ghana's first prime minister, Kwame Nkrumah, advocated the policy of non-alignment and pan-African unity as a way to achieve full liberation of the continent.[7] Khrushchev saw these developments as opportunities for the Soviet Union to gain new allies in Asia, Africa and Latin America, but also to revive Soviet socialism in line with revolutionary ideals, which coincided with his agenda on de-Stalinization.

The men and women who carried out Khrushchev's new policy in the Third World were primarily members of the Soviet bureaucratic and military elite— cadres in the various departments of the CC CPSU apparatus diplomats, jour- nalists, and intelligence officers. Coming from different backgrounds and with distinct personal experiences, they would become what I call "mediators of liberation" between African anticolonial nationalists and the top Soviet deci- sion-makers. This chapter examines Khrushchev's view of Soviet aims in Africa in the context of his broader foreign policy goals. It also provides an overview of the key Soviet institutions and paints the profiles of several key figures who became involved in supporting anticolonial movements in the Portuguese colo- nies in the 1960s and 1970s.

Nikita Khrushchev and the Cold War in Africa

Nikita Khrushchev seemed an unlikely candidate to succeed Joseph Stalin in 1953. Born in 1893 in the Russian-Ukrainian border town of Kalinovka, he was the son of poor peasants and received only a rudimentary education, working in various jobs in the mining towns of Ukraine during World War I. He joined the Bolshevik Party in 1918 and volunteered for the Red Army during the Russian Civil War. Khrushchev's career skyrocketed during the interwar period. From a party boss in the Donbas region in Ukraine, by the early 1930s, he was trans- ferred to Moscow and made responsible for overseeing the construction of the Moscow-Volga Canal and the Moscow metro system. In 1939, he became a full member of the Politburo of the CC CPSU, the highest decision-making organ in the USSR. Although a talented organizer and a shrewd politician, Khrush- chev had no foreign policy experience and little formal education, especially in contrast to more experienced colleagues.[8] However, he would soon emerge as the undisputed leader, partly due to his bold foreign policy initiatives.

Stalin's successors all agreed there should be a relaxation of tensions with the West, but debates raged as to how rapprochement could be squared with maintain- ing the stability of the Eastern Bloc. The critical issue was the status of divided Ger- many. In response to an economic crisis in East Germany, in 1953, the Politburo proclaimed a "New Course" for Eastern Europe to reverse some of the Stalin era's most heavy-handed policies, such as collectivization. They even contemplated the prospect of a unified Germany in exchange for a pan-European security arrangement that would, in essence, end the Cold War in Europe. However, Khrushchev was unwilling to jeopardize socialism in East Germany. In response to West Germany joining NATO, Khrushchev backed the formation of the Warsaw Pact in May 1955. He continued to pursue détente with the West but also reaffirmed Moscow's commitment to the Eastern Bloc.[9]

Khrushchev also wanted to pursue a more active policy in the Third World. In October 1955, he went on a highly publicized tour of India, Burma (today Myanmar), and Afghanistan. Khrushchev argued that with the advent of nuclear technology, a military confrontation was inconceivable, and thus the USSR should adapt to new, peaceful forms of competition with the West, which were possible in the Third World. In India, Khrushchev challenged the West: "We say to the leaders of the capitalist states: Let us compete without war."[10]

The Soviet Union thus started forging new diplomatic, commercial, and cultural links with countries in Asia, Africa, and Latin America, as well as providing loans and developmental assistance. In newly independent Ghana, Guinea-Conakry, and Mali, the Soviets promoted a "socialist model of development." The model included a state-led program of establishing mechanized agriculture based on state farms and investment in infrastructure and industry.[11] Soviet academics also resuscitated the concept of "noncapitalist development," which premised Third World countries could skip the "capitalist stage of development" and move directly to socialism with the support of the state and the Soviet Union. That way, the Soviet Union could pursue an increasingly close relationship with radical nationalist leaders like Egypt's Gamal Abdel Nasser and Ghana's Kwame Nkrumah.[12]

Soviet allies were also supposed to pursue more active policies in the Third World. On September 27, 1955, Nasser announced the purchase of weapons worth $45.7 million from Czechoslovakia. While the Czechoslovak-Egyptian arms deal was negotiated on an initiative emanating from Prague, the agreement was seen as the symbol of a bold, new Soviet policy on the African continent, historically a playing field for European colonial powers.[13] The Soviet foreign ministry memorandum from January 1956 argued that China's role at Bandung, the Czechoslovak-Egyptian arms deal, and Khrushchev's trip to Asia in 1955 all proved that there were substantial opportunities for socialist countries to work together to expand ties with the Third World.[14] That same month, Khrushchev inaugurated what Csaba Békés has termed Soviet "active foreign policy doctrine," encouraging Eastern European allies to take action and develop their own economic and diplomatic relations with countries in Africa, Asia and Latin America.[15]

Khrushchev's boldest move came shortly afterward when he took on Stalin's legacy at the Twentieth Congress of the CPSU in February 1956. Khrushchev opened the Congress by asserting that a new world war was not inevitable and that different countries could take their own peaceful roads to socialism. In fact, the new policy of "peaceful coexistence" dovetailed with his attack on Stalin, which he made at the closed session of the Congress on February 25. In a four-hour speech, Khrushchev condemned Stalin for unlawfully persecuting party members during the purges and for his mistakes during World War II. He also promised to eliminate Stalinism's excesses and revive socialism in line with "Leninist principles."[16]

The transcript was quickly leaked to the West, and an abridged version of the speech soon became available to Soviet citizens. Although the speech was received with highly mixed reactions, it accelerated the so-called cultural Thaw that had begun shortly after Stalin's death. Soviet artists, theater directors, and writers were now permitted a never-before-seen degree of discussion and openness. Cultural exchanges between the Soviet Union and the West proliferated, with crowds queuing at the Pushkin Museum of Contemporary Art in 1956 to see the first Soviet exhibition of the Spanish Cubist painter Pablo Picasso.[17]

Although Khrushchev wanted to establish more equitable relations with Warsaw Pact partners, the secret speech unleashed a major crisis. It started in Poland, where popular protests over living standards strengthened reformists who sought to redefine the relationship with Moscow. In October 1956, the Polish leader, Władysław Gomułka, managed to negotiate a new relationship with the Soviets and avoided intervention. However, the situation turned out very differently in Hungary, where the newly appointed leader, Imre Nagy, was unable to calm street protests. On November 4, Soviet tanks rolled into Budapest, crushing the Hungarian revolution. Nagy was arrested and later executed.[18] Although events in Hungary showed the limits of de-Stalinization, Eastern Europeans continued to pursue "national roads to socialism" and retained relative autonomy in foreign policy.[19]

While the Soviets were dealing with the consequences of the secret speech, a major international crisis was developing over access to the Suez Canal. In July 1956, President Gamal Abdel Nasser of Egypt proclaimed the nationalization of the Suez Canal Company, which had been controlled by a conglomerate of Western companies. After failed talks, Israel, Britain, and France intervened militarily to retake control of the Suez in October. The Soviets were initially slow to respond, but in November, Moscow issued a stark warning to end intervention, threatening a world war if there was no withdrawal. Under pressure from the United States, the British government announced a ceasefire. France and Israel followed. While the outcome of the Suez Crisis actually hinged on U.S. unwillingness to support key allies, the Soviets scored a major public relations victory.[20] The Suez Crisis showed that the Cold War had moved to the periphery and that both the Soviet Union and the United States would be central players.

In 1960, the Cold War in Africa was heating up, mainly because of events in the former Belgian Congo (hereafter referred to as "Zaire").[21] A resource-rich country two-thirds the size of Western Europe, Zaire became independent on June 30, 1960, after hasty negotiations between the Belgians, the former colonial power, and the main nationalist parties. However, only five days after the proclamation of independence, Zaire's army mutinied over low pay and the continuing presence of Belgian officers in high-level positions. A workers' and a general strike followed, unleashing widespread chaos and sporadic violence. On July 11, Brussels sent in paratroopers, ostensibly to restore law and order, and the following day, Moïse Tshombe, the leader of Katanga province, announced the secession of the resource-rich province.

Zaire's first democratically elected prime minister, Patrice Lumumba, believed the Belgian intervention was a neocolonial coup and appealed to the United States, the United Nations, and the Soviet Union for military support against the secessionists in Katanga. By August, Washington believed that Lumumba was dangerously close to the Soviets and started scheming for his removal. The crisis reached its crescendo on September 5 when Lumumba was ousted from power in a U.S.-backed plot concocted by the army's chief of staff, Joseph-Désiré Mobutu. Lumumba was arrested, while Soviet and Czechoslovak diplomats were ordered to leave the country in forty-eight hours.[22]

Events in Zaire frustrated Khrushchev. He became exasperated with what he believed was collusion between U.S. president Dwight Eisenhower and UN Secretary General Dag Hammarskjöld and frustrated he could not help Lumumba.[23] When Khrushchev heard about Mobutu's coup while crossing the Atlantic on his way to speak at the UN General Assembly in New York, he became angry and spent the rest of the trip working on proposals to reform the UN General Secretariat.[24] Western actions in Zaire undermined Khrushchev's belief that "peaceful competition" in the Third World was possible. It also revealed Soviet weakness since Moscow was neither capable of providing military assistance quickly over long distances nor willing to risk a world war over Lumumba's plight.[25]

One consequence of the Zaire debacle was that the Soviets would increasingly use clandestine means to support local allies. In 1961, Soviet and Czechoslovak intelligence services would cooperate to support Lumumba's loyalist Antoine Gizenga, who fled to Stanleyville (now Kisangani), Eastern Zaire, after the coup. The use of clandestine means in the African context was a way to fight the Cold War "on the cheap" since it did not require substantial material investments nor headstrong collision with the superpowers.[26] As subsequent chapters show, the Soviets and Czechoslovaks would often use clandestine means, including the recruitment of African collaboration, to achieve their aims.

Khrushchev's motivations for launching a new "offensive" in the Third World have become the subject of substantial debate. Was he a pragmatist or an idealist who placed spreading socialist revolution above domestic goals? The interplay of pragmatic and ideational motivations was deeply bound up with Khrushchev's background and formative years. His peasant upbringing gave him a strong sense of social justice, and he believed that the Soviet Union had a duty to help newly independent nations and revolutionary movements that leaned towards socialism. Khrushchev's son Sergei recalled: "There, in the colonies, the almost forgotten dream of revolution was reborn. It seemed to my father that the world was beginning to stir, that with only a small effort there would be progress."[27]

Khrushchev was also a product of the Comintern of the 1930s. The interwar period was a peak of antiracist campaigns in the USSR. Like other Soviet officials, he internalized internationalist ideals and learned to "speak antiracism."[28] To Khrushchev, the dream of revolution was bound up with the mythologized figure of Lenin, which was at the heart of his de-Stalinization campaign. If only the USSR could adhere to "Leninist principles," Soviet socialism could be revived and overcome the Western system on a global scale.[29] His support for national liberation movements was thus necessarily interwoven with his domestic agenda.[30]

Khrushchev's enthusiasm for the Third World resonated with many Soviet citizens who were tired of years of imposed isolation, drawn to foreign cultures and peoples, and eager to participate in the scaling-up of the socialist experiment. The discussion below examines the two generations of Soviet party cadres who played influential roles in Soviet Africa policy. One group was made up of former Comintern functionaries (hereafter "the Cominternians"). Another was the so-called "war generation," younger people who began to occupy posts in the party and state bureaucracy, academia, and journalism during World War II. The sections below highlight how their formative experiences informed their worldview and came to shape their attitudes toward policy in Africa.

The "Cominternians": Key People and Institutions

In the 1950s, the Cominternians were a small yet influential group of people in the party apparatus. These were mostly men of modest backgrounds in their sixties and seventies who had joined the Bolsheviks before or shortly after October 1917. Many of them had participated in the Russian Civil War, building up their careers and networks when the Comintern was carrying out large-scale antiracist campaigns. They were the rare survivors of the Stalinist purges of the 1930s who remained committed to socialist internationalism and welcomed Khrushchev's policy in the Third World.[31]

The one man among the Cominternian generation who possessed the most expertise on Africa was Ivan Potekhin. He was born in 1903 in the village of Krivosheino, central Siberia, into a family of Old Believers. After finishing school, he joined the Bolsheviks, working as a party organiser. He was then mobilized into the Red Army and in 1929, served as a political commissar during an armed conflict with China over control of the Eastern Railroad in China's northeast. In 1930, he enrolled at Leningrad's Institute of Oriental Studies, first studying Arabic, before developing an interest in African politics.[32]

In the 1930s, Potekhin and several fellow Africanists at Comintern-affiliated Communist Institute of the Toilers of the East (KUTV) launched their first academic program, which was intended to analyze the prospects for "noncapitalist development" in Africa. However, in 1936, he was accused of "Trotskyism" and expelled from KUTV with party sanctions—a relatively light punishment compared to the terror unleashed only a year later. After Stalin's death, Potekhin became actively involved in reviving Soviet engagement with Africa. He used connections from the interwar period to develop informal links with African leaders and pushed for the establishment of the Institute of African Studies as an independent research body within the Academy of Sciences. In 1959, he became the institute's first director.[33]

Throughout his life, Potekhin remained a committed supporter of African liberation. As he told Basil Davidson, a British journalist and historian of Africa whom he first met in the early 1950s: "I am a scholar. My job is to do research and teach. But should it be necessary, I will exchange that for arms—I will drop my pen and take up a rifle instead—to fight for justice as I did more than 40 years ago during the October Revolution."[34] Potekhin was also a prolific writer, continuing to work on concepts such as "noncapitalist development" and writing opinion pieces about the prospects of socialism in Africa until he succumbed to a tropical disease in 1964 after a research trip to Ghana.

While Potekhin was among a handful of Soviet Africa experts with any kind of international standing, the most influential "Cominternian" in the party apparatus was Boris Ponomarev. Only twelve years old in 1917, Ponomarev claimed to have started his party career at fourteen, first serving as a party activist at a local textile factory in his native Zaraisk, near Moscow. Then, he continued his education at Moscow State University (MGU) and the elite Institute of Red Professors. In the mid-1930s, he helped produce the *Short History of the Bolshevik Party*, a famous text commissioned by Stalin as the official guide to party history. In 1936, Ponomarev became a personal assistant to Georgii Dimitrov, the new head of the Comintern. At the height of the Stalinist purges in 1937, Ponomarev was accused of harboring "Trotskyist" sympathies and was questioned about his connections to high-ranking colleagues who had been purged. However, he managed to shake off the allegations, probably due to Dimitrov's patronage.[35]

In 1957, Ponomarev was appointed the head of the International Department of the CC CPSU (hereafter "MO" or "International Department"). A successor to the Comintern, the International Department was fairly insignificant in the postwar period. However, after Khrushchev's turn to the Third World in the mid-1950s, the International Department was entrusted with several crucial functions. Its cadre collected and processed information from papers drafted by Soviet academic research institutes and reports from diplomatic, press, and intelligence sources abroad. The International Department also maintained regular contacts with the leaders of foreign communist parties, processed their requests for assistance, and made policy recommendations to the CC CPSU. The department was also responsible for allocating cash allowances for communist parties and liberation movements from the International Trade Union Fund for Assistance to Left Workers' Organizations.[36]

This is not to say that the International Department was without bureaucratic rivals. Ponomarev was a protégé of the party ideologue Mikhail Suslov, but he had a notoriously contentious personal relationship with Andrei Gromyko, the longtime minister of foreign affairs. In fact, the priorities of the Foreign Ministry and the International Department did not always coincide, and many conflicts ensued. However, the International Department still retained the final say on policy vis-à-vis African anticolonial movements.[37] Ponomarev's colleagues saw him as a "true believer" in socialist internationalism, albeit somewhat "dogmatic" in his views. According to Karen Brutents, a senior official at the International Department in the 1970s, Ponomarev possessed a "Cominternian mindset" and tended to "preach" to foreign dignitaries who came to Moscow

seeking assistance. At the same time, he was also a "true anti-Stalinist" who supported people who had been persecuted during the 1930s.[38] One of these was
Rostislav Ulianovskii.

Ulianovskii had a unique career for his time. Born in 1905 in Vitebsk, a city in
modern-day Belarus, he joined the Red Army in 1920 and moved to Tashkent,
in Soviet Uzbekistan. In 1922, he was dispatched to Moscow and enrolled at the
Institute of the Far East. After graduation, he joined the Comintern-affiliated
International Agrarian Institute, eventually becoming the head of the Far East
and the Colonies section. His life took a sharp turn on January 1, 1935, when
he was arrested, charged with belonging to a Trotskyist organization, and dispatched to the Gulag. Ulianovskii spent almost twenty years in labor camps and
was only rehabilitated in 1955, during the Thaw. In 1961, Ponomarev appointed
him as his deputy responsible for Afro-Asian affairs.[39]

As the functions of the International Department expanded in the late 1950s,
it was also entrusted with coordinating the work of the so-called public organizations, including the Soviet Afro-Asian Solidarity Committee (hereafter SKS-
SAA or "Soviet Solidarity Committee"). The Soviet Solidarity Committee was
established in 1956 as the Soviet branch of the Afro-Asian People's Solidarity
Organization (AAPSO) on the heels of the Bandung conference. Its goals were
to represent Soviet agenda at AAPSO's Permanent Secretariat based in Cairo
and develop links with the so-called "progressive, democratic" forces in the colonies and newly independent countries. In Moscow, the presidium of the Soviet
Solidarity Committee consisted of prominent academics, cadres at relevant government ministries, and public figures who debated Third World policies during
regular meetings. The cadre of the Soviet Solidarity Committee also served as
the first point of contact and the official hosts for non-state actors from Asia, Africa, and Latin America during their trips to the Soviet Union. Thus, the Soviet
Solidarity Committee served as a conduit for the agenda and an informal think
tank for the International Department.[40]

Meanwhile, the Soviet intelligence services worked to implement policy priorities by clandestine means. One was the First (intelligence) Directorate of the
KGB. A much-feared institution closely associated with the Stalinist purges, the
KGB was overhauled in the wake of the Twentieth Congress of the CC CPSU.
Many cadres were forced to resign, while new, younger officers were promoted
in their wake. Khrushchev wanted to direct the KGB's activities abroad, a task
he entrusted to his protégé Aleksandr Shelepin. Under Shelepin, the KGB's First
(intelligence) Directorate became increasingly active in the Third World, setting
up a network of intelligence stations (known as *rezidentury*) in Asia, Africa,

and Latin America.[41] Although the KGB and the International Department did not always see eye to eye, intelligence officers had to implement decisions made in Moscow.[42]

No less important was the role of the GRU. The chief of the GRU was directly responsible to the minister of defense, and thus its aims were shaped by the priorities of the Soviet military. Its efforts entailed gathering intelligence on Western weapons systems via a network of clandestine human contacts, as well as from signals intelligence. GRU analyses also fed into reports for the CC CPSU and the International Department. When it came to African liberation movements, the GRU was often more closely involved than the KGB—its officers often advised on military strategy, reviewed the requirements for weapons, and were involved in military training.[43]

In 1963, the CC CPSU appointed Petr Ivashutin the new chief of the GRU. Born in 1909 as the son of a railway worker in Brest (contemporary Belorussia), Ivashutin trained as a military pilot. During World War II, he worked for the Red Army's military counterintelligence branch, rising to the rank of lieutenant general. After the war, he was recruited by the KGB, becoming deputy chairman in 1954. In this capacity, he was involved in the violent crackdown on protests in the Soviet city of Novocherkassk in June 1962. However, he made his most significant mark at the GRU, expanding its capacity to collect signals intelligence, and would dominate the organization until his retirement in 1986. Much has been said about the long-standing institutional rivalry between the KGB and the GRU, which often produced drastically different assessments of developments on the ground. Ivashutin did little to foster cooperation with the KGB and apparently favored the "less politicized" nature of his job. The GRU was arguably more professional and more selective in its recruitment practices than the KGB, but in general, the two intelligence services operated on the same turf, often using similar contacts and methods.[44]

Hierarchies mattered among the members of the Cominternian generation. As the head of the International Department, Ponomarev was much more powerful than Potekhin, who was largely dependent on the party for resources and permission to do academic work abroad. Recommendations and policy papers drafted by the Institute of African Studies could easily be rejected by middle-ranking desk officers of the International Department.[45] However, men like Potekhin still played a crucial role in reviving Soviet African studies and reengaging with African elites. They were also sources of inspiration, patronage, and ideas for the younger generation that would come to dominate Soviet Africa policy.

The War Generation: The Soviet Bureaucratic Elite and Their Environment

The younger generation was quite different from the Cominternians. Born in the interwar period, they did not participate in or witness the Russian Revolution or the Civil War. However, a lack of direct experience of 1917 did not mean that these young people were devoid of revolutionary ideals. Growing up during the height of the Soviet antiracist campaigns in the early 1930s, many sympathized with the plight of African Americans and colonial subjects. However, their core formative experience was World War II, in which they participated as combatants in the Red Army or as civilians working for the war effort. Some experienced the war and its harsh deprivations as children or teenagers, and many lost family members and friends. As a result, this generation shared an overwhelming sense of pride in their country. This sense of patriotism was compounded by postwar Soviet advances in science and technology: the 1957 launch of Sputnik, the first artificial satellite, and cosmonaut Iurii Gagarin's first space flight in 1961.[46]

This younger generation reacted to Khrushchev's denunciation of Stalin in varying, often conflicting ways. Some abhorred the Great Terror and welcomed Khrushchev's secret speech, but their break with Stalin did not imply disillusionment with socialism. Many believed Stalin had perverted the so-called "Leninist principles," a mythologized concept that, in their imagination, contrasted the early Bolsheviks' democracy and idealism with the privilege and terror unleashed by Stalin. Georgii Mirskii was part of the team at the Institute of World Economy and International Relations in Moscow, working on theorizing such concepts as "noncapitalist development" in the 1950s. He later wrote that he and his colleagues genuinely believed that capitalism could not offer solutions to the problems facing developing countries: "We felt like innovators, working against Stalin's dogmatism, one cannot understand this outside the historical context of the Twentieth Party Congress which changed the situation in the country within days."[47]

Not all men and women of the younger generation supported Khrushchev's denunciation of Stalin, however. To some, Stalinism was synonymous with the massive surge of upward social mobility that allowed many men and women from modest peasant backgrounds to obtain an education and achieve a social standing that would never have been possible before 1917. Many others resented the belittlement of Stalin's role in the victory over Nazism.[48]

Whatever their attitudes to Stalin, Khrushchev's opening to the Third World offered new opportunities for the younger generation. With foreign travel restricted for Soviet citizens, Soviet *mezhdunarodniki* had an opportunity to see the world and experience foreign cultures. They also gained access to Western consumer goods on trips abroad. For all these reasons, studying to become a foreign policy expert was highly competitive. The Soviet Ministry of Foreign Affairs and the foreign intelligence services recruited students from the prestigious Moscow State University of International Relations (MGIMO) and the Military Institute of Foreign Languages. Entry required high academic achievement, and enrollment was also limited on the basis of one's gender and ethnicity. Women were rarely accepted for foreign postings and generally did not exceed 10–20 percent of the MGIMO student body. The main outlets for women area studies experts were either to enter academia to work as university professors or to be interpreters, translators, and foreign language instructors. Soviet Jews would also generally not be accepted for posts at the Ministry of Foreign Affairs or the foreign intelligence service, reflecting state-sanctioned postwar anti-Semitism.[49]

Other hierarchies reflected differences in student backgrounds. At MGIMO in the 1950s, the student body was divided between the children of the party elite, the Red Army veterans (they were accorded certain privileges upon enrollment), and a large group of young people from outside Moscow whose parents did not have much influence. The latter group was at the bottom of the ladder and eager to accept less prestigious jobs upon graduation.[50] These hierarchies were often reflected in language specialization. European languages were considered the most prestigious, followed by Arabic, Hindi, and African languages. Students from outside Moscow were often assigned non-European languages, considered difficult.[51] African languages thus remained at the "bottom of the pile" in terms of prestige for the majority of graduates. However, the continent also offered career opportunities, particularly for graduates from modest backgrounds who had niche skills. The biographies of select cadres who came to occupy important roles in Soviet relations with the anticolonial movements in Portuguese Africa illustrate these points.

One of them was Petr Manchkha, the head of the Africa section at the International Department. Of Greek origin, Manchkha was born in modern-day Ukraine, where he spent his childhood working in the countryside. He had some naval experience before moving to Moscow, where he eventually became the chief of the Albania section at the International Department. One of his tasks was maintaining relations with left-wing groups in Albania and Greece, for which he had to cross the Albanian–Greek border to meet Greek partisans, often on horseback. When Soviet-Albanian relations faltered, Manchkha moved on to become the first head of the newly established Africa section in 1961. According to Vladimir Shubin, Manchkha was a "cheerful and life-loving man, a big patriot of the African continent."[52] However, he was not a trained Africanist, and rumor had it he had never visited the Lenin Library, a must for research work.[53] The Africa section was small and staffed with middle-ranking officials with specific regional specializations who were known as *"referenty."*

The man who became the key *referent* on Portuguese Africa was Petr Evsiukov. Born on January 3, 1921, in Harbin, China, Evsiukov moved to Moscow at an early age. He served in the Red Army during World War II and was wounded twice. After the war, he studied and then taught at the Military Institute of Foreign Languages. After its dissolution in 1956, Evsiukov went to work at the Foreign Languages Publishing House. He was brought in to work under Petr Manchkha as the desk officer for the Portuguese colonies in 1961 because he was fluent in Portuguese, a rare skill in the USSR at that time.

He was not an expert on Lusophone Africa, but he fairly quickly became well-informed since it was his job to filter and analyze information coming to the International Department from the Soviet press agencies, embassies, and the intelligence services. He also became one of the regulars who would "meet and greet" the leaders of the African liberation movements in Moscow and process requests for assistance. Like many men and women of his generation, Evsiukov believed that decolonization was an inevitable process and that the socialist countries had an internationalist duty to support national liberation movements. His military background also helped Evsiukov find affinity with African revolutionaries and facilitated collaboration with the Soviet military.[54] These younger intelligence officers often had very similar backgrounds to their peers in the party bureaucracy and academia.

Vadim Kirpichenko's biography is characteristic in this respect. Born in 1922 in Kursk, he volunteered for the Red Army during World War II, serving in a paratrooper battalion. After the war ended, Kirpichenko enrolled at the Moscow Institute of Eastern Studies, where he specialized in Arabic, graduating in 1952. At the university, he was spotted by recruiters from the KGB, and after a year's training at the Higher Intelligence School, he joined the KGB's First (intelligence) Directorate in 1953. In memoirs written shortly after the collapse of the Soviet Union, Kirpichenko criticized the lawlessness of the security organs under Stalin. However, he was ambivalent about de-Stalinization since it was undertaken by the same people, like Khrushchev, who had participated in the Great Terror. After his first foreign posting to Cairo in the late 1950s, he became the first head of the Africa section at the KGB's First Directorate.[55]

Kirpichenko recalled great optimism among the officers who joined the Africa section in the early 1960s. First, the continent seemed to offer good prospects for spycraft. Second, the aims of Soviet intelligence in Africa—to contribute to decolonization, support national liberation movements, obtain "friends and allies," and analyze American policy—also seemed "noble." In general, the First Directorate's Africa specialists believed that the newly independent African nations would soon choose the socialist path, but they also realized the continent was "riddled with problems," including poverty and instability. To Kirpichenko, these dilemmas were encapsulated in the title of a 1955 bestselling book by two Czechoslovak travelers, Jiří Hanzelka and Miroslav Zikmund, *Africa: The Dream and the Reality*.[56] Like others in his generation, Kirpichenko was optimistic about the prospects of socialism in the Third World.

There was no other single event that better encapsulated the optimism of the 1950s than the Sixth World Festival of Youth and Students. Held a year after Khrushchev's secret speech, the festival was designed to celebrate the new era of de-Stalinized socialism. In preparation for the celebration, tourist infrastructure was upgraded, and Soviet citizens were encouraged to learn foreign languages and engage in conversations with foreigners. Meanwhile, the Soviet youth organization, the Komsomol, put together an impressive program of sports, cultural, and artistic events to project the image of a modern Soviet Union. The festival, which opened in July 1957, exceeded all expectations. The streets of Moscow turned into a carnival for two months, as several million Soviet citizens and thousands of foreigners exchanged gifts, embraced, danced, talked, and shared romantic encounters in the spirit of the relative openness and permissiveness that permeated the festival.[57] The African delegates enjoyed great popularity among Soviet citizens, and their hotel quickly became a vibrant social spot in the city.[58] The festival was the first encounter between significant numbers of Africans and Soviet people, and it made a lasting impression.[59]

In sum, the younger-generation cadres who worked for the foreign intelligence service, the International Department, and the Ministry of Foreign Affairs all shared some core experiences and characteristics. Educated at the most prestigious universities, they belonged to the Soviet elite. They knew foreign languages, regularly met foreigners, traveled, and often lived abroad as government employees. They were all profoundly shaped by World War II, both the traumas and the victory, which instilled in them a sense of pride and optimism about the socialist system. Many had direct experience of combat, which would prove significant in their future dealings with African guerrillas. However, few were trained Africanists, and most knew little about the continent or its people. What they lacked in regional expertise they came to compensate for in personal relationships with Africans, which they started developing in the late 1950s. This development does not mean they were free from prejudice or personal biases, but the majority did believe in the ideals of socialist internationalism. As the following chapters show, men (there were very few women) like Kirpichenko, Manchkha, and Evsiukov became "mediators of liberation" precisely because Africa would remain a relatively low priority for the Soviet leadership over the long term.

Conclusion

The late 1950s saw a profound transformation of Soviet policy toward the Third World. Highly ambitious yet at the same time personally insecure, Khrushchev used foreign policy pragmatically as a tool to raise his domestic and international profile. After members of Stalin's "old guard" made a failed attempt to remove Khrushchev in June 1957, he became the prime trendsetter in foreign policy. However, his hopes for socialist revolution in the Third World and his belief in "peaceful competition" cannot be dismissed as simple pragmatism in the battle for supremacy after Stalin's death. Like many men and women in his generation, Khrushchev was convinced that socialism was superior to capitalism. If only socialism could be purged of Stalinism and revived around "Leninist principles," then its power and strength could also be restored on the international stage.

The revival of socialist internationalism was thus irrevocably connected to Khrushchev's domestic program of de-Stalinization. Because he promised to revive socialism around an idealized notion of "Leninist principles" (however ephemeral the actual meaning of that phrase may be), Soviet internationalism in the Third World could not (and would not) be reversed by his successors. However, Khrushchev's belief in "peaceful competition" in the Third World was undermined by events in Zaire. In fact, the crisis in Zaire would also prove a sobering experience for younger party cadres entering the service in the early 1960s.

Another long-term legacy of Khrushchev's turn to the Third World was the expansion of the bureaucratic apparatus. If only a handful of experts had a stake in the Third World in the mid-1950s, by the early 1960s, hundreds of young men and women would take up new jobs available in Soviet academia, the bureaucracy, and the intelligence services. The profiles and personal experiences of the Soviet bureaucratic elite who would come to specialize in African affairs differed. Men like Potekhin, Ponomarev, and Ulianovskii—the Cominternians—had had a long-standing belief in proletarian internationalism and some experience of supporting an international revolution. The Cominternians were at the forefront of the Soviet outreach to the Third World in the 1950s, often due to their long-standing contacts with foreigners and international experiences.

Still, they were very few in number, and when it came to those involved in foreign policy, only Potekhin had any considerable expertise of Africa.

The new generation was different in many ways. These were young, ambitious men and women who were keen to seize the opportunities opening up in the 1950s. However, they were not immune to idealism and held a genuine belief in the superiority of the socialist system. Africa was not the most desirable destination for most young and ambitious cadres who joined the bureaucratic elite in the 1950s and 1960s. However, those who did become involved would quickly establish contacts with African revolutionaries, travel around the continent, and often become keen (long-term) lobbyists on behalf of their clients. Both the Cominternians and the younger generation thus became important "mediators of liberation," playing a pivotal role in fostering contacts with African revolutionaries, including those from Portuguese Africa. The next chapter investigates the development of these initial contacts in the context of the 1950s.

CHAPTER TWO

Revolutionaries

The Portuguese Empire and the Rise of African Nationalism

"PORTUGAL IS NOT A SMALL COUNTRY," read an inscription on a map displayed at the First Colonial Exhibition in Porto, held in 1934. The map showed the Portuguese colonies—Angola, Mozambique, Guinea-Bissau, Cape Verde, São Tomé and Principe, and Macau—superimposed on the political map of Europe. A chart attached to the map showed the surface area of Portugal and its colonies: 2,168,077 square kilometers, which was greater than the combined total area of continental Spain, France, England, Italy, and Germany—then totaling 2,091,639 square kilometers. Designed by Henrique Galvão, the curator of the exhibition, the map was supposed to represent the revival of Portugal's status as a great European power. With over five hundred pavilions displaying various aspects of Portuguese colonization and attracting one million visitors, the Exhibition was truly a major propaganda feat for the newly established authoritarian regime, led by Portugal's prime minister António de Oliveira Salazar.[1]

The discussion that follows opens with an overview of the Portuguese presence in Africa, which began in the fifteenth century, and describes its transformation into more formal colonial rule by the early 1900s. It analyzes the role of African labor in the Portuguese colonies and examines the key components of Salazar's vision, enshrined in the ideology of Estado Novo ("New State") in the 1930s. The chapter then turns to the rise of nationalism in Portuguese Africa during the interwar period. The core of the discussion is the analysis of the formative experiences of a select number of African intellectuals from Portuguese colonies—Amílcar Cabral, Agostinho Neto, Mário Pinto de Andrade, Viriato da Cruz, and Marcelino dos Santos—who would come to dominate the leadership of the anticolonial movements in the 1960s.

This chapter situates these future African leaders in a sociocultural milieu of urban centers across the Portuguese Empire. It charts their transition from student activists inspired by experiments in cultural self-expression in the late

1940s to revolutionaries dedicated to the violent overthrow of Portuguese colonial rule. It also traces their personal stories and ideological influences, following them on their first trips to socialist countries in the 1950s. Finally, this
chapter highlights the origins of the Cold War alliance that would define the
international dimension of anticolonial movements in Angola, Mozambique,
and Guinea-Bissau as rooted in the Soviet cultural diplomacy of the 1950s.

Trade, Labor, and Race in Portuguese Africa

The small kingdom of Portugal was at the forefront of European maritime explo-
ration during the "Age of Discovery" in the fifteenth century. Driven by the pursuit of economic profit and the search for the legendary ruler Prester John (who
was rumored to reside in northeastern Africa), Prince Henrique (1394-1460)
supported the development of the caravel—a highly maneuverable, light, and
powerful vessel that could make long-distance voyages. In the 1440s–60s, the
Portuguese ventured beyond the Saharan littoral, reaching the rivers of Upper
Guinea (modern-day Guinea-Bissau). The uninhibited Cape Verde archipelago
was discovered in 1455–56. In 1482, Diogo Cão reached the mouth of the Zaire
River and established the first European contact with the Kingdom of Kongo,
which stretched across northern Angola and southwestern Zaire at the height of
its influence. In 1497, Vasco da Gama rounded the continent, stopping at port
cities along the eastern coast of Africa before sailing to India.[2]

In Africa, the Portuguese used a combination of infiltration, persuasion, and
coercion to extend their influence. They co-opted the rulers of Kongo, who adopted Christianity and welcomed Catholic missionaries. However, further to the
south, the Ndongo were more suspicious of the Portuguese. In 1576, Paulo Dias de
Novais arrived to subdue the Ndongo by force in a quest to find silver, unleashing a century of wars, most notably against Queen Nzinga (c. 1583–1663). The
Portuguese did not find any silver and eventually settled for slaving in the vast
interior of the territory they called "Angola." On the eastern coast of Africa, the
Portuguese gradually replaced Arab, Persian, and Swahili traders and established
a garrison at Mozambique Island, which became the central point for exporting
ivory, gold, and slaves to Portuguese India. By the nineteenth century, the Portuguese dominated a network of trading posts from Lisbon to Nagasaki in Japan.
However, Portuguese control did not extend much beyond coastal areas, and they
relied on intermediaries to obtain slaves for the lucrative trans-Atlantic trade.[3]

The abolition of slavery and the onset of the Industrial Revolution in the
nineteenth century led to the beginning of more formalized colonial rule. The

competition between European powers for a sphere of influence in Africa led to a partition of the continent at the Berlin Conference in 1885. Partly with British support, Portugal managed to secure control over Angola, Mozambique, and Guinea-Bissau. Lisbon harbored plans to connect its possessions in East and West Africa into a central African empire. However, the plan clashed with British ambitions to establish a protectorate, stretching from Cape Town to Cairo. In 1890, Britain gave Portugal an ultimatum: withdraw from the contested territories or face military action. Lisbon had little choice but to accede, but national humiliation contributed to the downfall of the monarchy in 1910. As one of the poorest European countries, Portugal ended up on the losing side in the "scramble for Africa."

The extension of formal control beyond the coastal areas was also closely connected to the need to acquire cheap African labor. Laborers were required to work in coastal fisheries, on agricultural plantations, and to build roads and railways. In the late nineteenth century, Angola began exporting coffee, sugar, and rubber, while Cadbury Brothers started importing cocoa from the plantations of São Tomé. The Portuguese also started constructing railways, connecting oceanic ports to mining centers in neighboring countries. In Angola, the Benguela railway carried copper from Zaire to the ports of Beira and Lobito on the Atlantic coast. In Mozambique, railway lines connected copper mines in neighboring Southern Rhodesia (Zimbabwe), British Nyasaland (Malawi), and South Africa to the ports of Lourenço Marques (Maputo), Beira, and Nacala (see maps 6.1 and 7.1). Lisbon also struck a deal with London, allowing the British to recruit Mozambican laborers for the gold mines of Transvaal, South Africa, in exchange for paying taxes for the use of port facilities at Lourenço Marques. Although slavery was officially abolished, in reality, the practice persisted. The treatment of plantation workers in São Tomé was so dire that the international scandal even caused Cadbury to suspend cocoa imports in 1909.[4]

After the Portuguese monarchy collapsed in 1910, the rulers of the First Republic wanted to rationalize the exploitation of the empire. They stamped out slavery, imposed taxation, reduced protectionist tariffs, and gave colonial high commissioners a great deal of freedom to engage in developmental schemes. They also wanted to move toward wage labor, but demand was too high. They thus formalized a colonial hierarchy, dividing the African population into "native" and "civilized." All "natives" who had no income from cash crops were subject to at least three months of compulsory labor, known as *chibalo*. The term referred to low-paying or unpaid work that included prison labor, forced contracts or recruitment, and compulsory service on public works such as railways or road building. The labor requirements were rationalized as part of Portugal's "civilizing mission." However, the abusive practices did little to revive Portugal's economic fortunes. By 1926, colonial finances were in disarray, while the share of colonial trade remained consistently low.[5] On May 28, 1926, a group of military officers launched a coup that brought down the First Republic.

In 1928, the military appointed António de Oliveira Salazar finance minister, assigning him a brief to solve Portugal's economic crisis. Salazar was born on April 29, 1889, into a religious peasant family in Vimieiro, in northern Portugal. He received his primary education at a seminary before studying law and economics at the University of Coimbra. An ultraconservative Catholic known for his ascetic lifestyle, Salazar rose rapidly, becoming prime minister in 1932. One year later, he enshrined his vision for Portugal in the new constitution of the Estado Novo. Portugal became a "unitary and corporatist republic," and Salazar's União Nacional (National Union) became the country's only political party. Unions were suppressed, and the police were given new powers to stamp out criticism of the regime. The patriarchal nuclear family became institutionalized, and women faced restrictions on suffrage and discrimination in the labor market. Salazar would come to dominate Portugal's political life until a debilitating stroke in 1968.[6]

Empire was fundamental to Salazar's vision for Portugal, and he believed it was crucial to safeguarding Portugal's status in Europe. The colonies were also supposed to serve as a source of cheap raw materials for Portuguese industry and a market for its imports, thus driving economic recovery.[7] In 1930, Salazar sponsored the Colonial Act, which ended colonial autonomy, centralized control over finances, and took steps to diminish the role of foreign capital in the colonies. Prices and quotas were set to drive the production of raw materials, including cotton, coffee, tea, rice, sugar, and maize. In the effort to rapidly expand trade with the empire, Salazar introduced the compulsory cultivation of certain crops, such as cotton, to fuel Portugal's textile industry. Economic autarky seemed ever more urgent with the onset of the Great Depression in the 1930s because Portugal's regular trading partners, Europe and Brazil, imposed protectionist tariffs and capital controls, depriving Lisbon of its traditional sources of income. Still, economic reality lagged far behind Salazar's vision. In 1939, only 10 percent of Portugal's imports came from the colonies.[8]

Japan's entry into World War II created shortages and stimulated demand for colonial goods, rapidly increasing the demand for African labor. In 1942, the colonial authorities announced that Africans were obliged not only to pay taxes but also to cultivate an area of land or work for an employer. Lisbon also instructed local administrators to assist with the allocation of labor. Local Portuguese *chefes de posto* (chiefs of post) were assigned a quota to deliver a specific number of contract workers, which usually fell on African *regulos* (chiefs). If a *regulo* failed to deliver, he could be fined or even punished. Unsurprisingly, the system perpetuated abuses because chiefs would often use coercive methods to fill their labor quotas.[9]

The availability of cheap African labor was key to Salazar's dream of economic autarky. The 1930 Colonial Act codified the division of all colonial subjects into two groups: *indígenas* (indigenous) and *não indígenas* (nonindigenous). The latter category included white Europeans and the so-called *assimilados* (assimilated), who were either *mestiço* (biracial or multiracial) Afro-Portuguese or Black Africans who fulfilled certain conditions. "*Assimilado*" status granted full Portuguese citizenship, which meant freedom from forced labor and "native taxes," the right to vote in local elections, and better access to welfare and job opportunities. However, there were many roadblocks to obtaining *assimilado* status, including the requirements to speak Portuguese, have a certain level of income, and show loyalty to the regime. Unsurprisingly, the number of *assimilados* remained extremely low. Out of a combined 10,388,360 inhabitants of Angola, Mozambique, and Guinea-Bissau in 1953, only 235,629 persons, or 2.7 percent of the population, were considered "civilized."[10]

One of the critical roadblocks to achieving *assimilado* status was the highly restrictive educational system. There were very few government schools, and these were reserved for Europeans, *mestiços*, and *assimilados*. There were also Protestant mission schools run by Baptists, Methodists, and Swiss Presbyterians. In 1940, Lisbon placed all "rudimentary" primary education for the indigenous population in the hands of the Roman Catholic Church, partly to counter the influence of the Protestant missionary schools, which, as Salazar suspected, were transmitting foreign influences and ideas to the African population.[11] The Portuguese clergy did not conceal the fact that the main purpose of the primary schooling provided by the Roman Catholic Church was to produce a docile population of farmers loyal to the state.[12] At the end of the 1950s, only 8 percent of school-age children in Angola, 2.4 percent in Mozambique, and 7.3 percent in Guinea-Bissau were engaged in any kind of formal education.[13]

Among the African colonies, Cape Verde was something of an exception. An archipelago located around 500 km off the Senegalese coast, the Cape Verdean islands were uninhabited when first discovered in 1460. The islands lacked rainfall and thus were unsuitable for cultivating Portuguese staple crops. The crown therefore granted special trading rights and tax exemptions to propertied settlers on Santiago Island. They acquired slaves to sell to the Americas or to cultivate cotton on local farms. The presence of African slaves created an overwhelmingly multicultural population akin to that of northeastern Brazil.[14] In a 1950 census, out of a population of 148,331, 2.06 percent were recorded as "white," 69.09 percent as "*mestiço*," and 28.84 percent as "black."[15] All Cape Verdeans were designated as *não indígenas*, and as a result, enjoyed better access to educational opportunities, which enabled many to take up lower-level administrative posts across the empire.

However, their special status did not spare Cape Verdeans from hardship. The arid archipelago had been affected by droughts for centuries, and islanders often resorted to immigration as a way to escape starvation. When the rains failed again in 1939, common migration routes were disrupted by World War II. The only solution Lisbon proposed involved public works and encouraging people to migrate to São Tomé—but both measures were inadequate and came too late. As a result, almost 24,643 people lost their lives in the famine that struck between 1941 and 1943.[16] Very little was done in the immediate aftermath to develop access to water or prevent soil erosion. Portugal's neglect of the archipelago led to another devastating famine in 1947–48.[17]

The transition to formal colonialism in the nineteenth century required the kind of investment and capital that Lisbon did not have. Successive Portuguese administrations used human exploitation to extract profits from Empire, but these strategies failed to produce the desired results. Only the exceptional circumstances during World War II brought Salazar's dream of economic autarky closer to fruition—at Africans' expense. However, the war also accelerated a general crisis of colonialism, as subjects of Empire demanded equal rights for their sacrifice. Abusive colonial practices encountered criticism, even from ardent supporters of colonial rule. In a closed session of the Portuguese National Assembly in 1947, Henrique Galvão, the curator of the 1934 Colonial Exhibition, argued that the brutality of forced labor in Angola impelled many people to migrate to neighboring countries. Rather than "civilizing" and "educating," the reality of labor practices was a "colossal lie."[18] While Portuguese dictatorship adopted a developmentalist rhetoric to placate its critics after the war, abusive practices, including the existence of forced labor, remained a fact of life in the colonies until the 1960s. This was the context in which, by the late 1950s, opposition to Portuguese rule crystallized among the young men and women growing up under Salazar's rule.

African Intellectuals in Portuguese Africa: Coming of Age under Salazar

While similar to its European counterparts, Portuguese colonialism had developed some distinctive characteristics by the early twentieth century. The Portuguese were the first to explore all of Africa's coasts, leading to the emergence of so-called "creoles" or "Luso-Africans," who often spearheaded colonization with little direction from Lisbon. Luso-Africans were a heterogeneous group of Black Africans and *mestiços*, who were born in the colonies. Their European ancestors included *conquistadores*, soldiers, merchants, and criminals who had been banished from Portugal. Luso-Africans aspired to be "white" in cultural terms: they spoke Portuguese or local creole languages, adopted Christianity, and wore European clothing and shoes.[19]

The changes in colonial rule in the late nineteenth and early twentieth centuries often marginalized creoles. One problem was the expansion of white settlement, which grew from 13,000 in 1913 to 43,000 in 1927 in Angola and increased from 11,000 to 175,000 in 1928 in Mozambique.[20] Creoles thus faced increasing competition with European settlers, often for the same jobs as civil servants, skilled workers, soldiers, or priests.[21] Another issue was the bureaucratization of the hierarchical racial order, which privileged white Europeans. These grievances found expression in the so-called "nativist movement," which saw notable creole intellectuals form associations and spearhead campaigns protesting racist laws and abuses committed by the colonial administration. The republican administration initially tolerated the nativist movement but then tried to put it under government control by deporting particularly outspoken critics to Portugal.[22]

The new generation of urban Africans who grew up during the interwar period shared many similarities with their parents. In some ways, they occupied positions of privilege in colonial society. As already discussed, those designated as *assimilados* constituted a tiny proportion of the overall population, had citizenship rights, and were spared the harsh realities of forced labor. Their parents were educated government employees or small business-owners who were often critical of the colonial administration. Growing up mainly in urban areas, they had better access to educational opportunities, and some received scholarships to pursue further studies in Portugal. Nevertheless, they were not a homogenous group, and many differences remained because of their varying ethnic, socioeconomic, and educational backgrounds. Unlike some of their parents or grandparents, who valued Portuguese culture, the new generation—as we will see—considered themselves African. The biographies of Amílcar Cabral, Marcelino dos Santos, Mário Pinto de Andrade, and Agostinho Neto provide insight into the early formative experiences of some of the key protagonists in this story.

Amílcar Cabral's early years were fairly typical of many Cape Verdeans growing up during the interwar period. Born on September 12, 1924 in Bafatá, Central Guinea-Bissau, Cabral was the son of Juvenal António da Costa Cabral and Iva Pinhel Évora. Like thousands of Cape Verdeans who found employment in neighboring Portuguese colonies, Cabral's parents met in Guinea-Bissau, where Juvenal was a schoolteacher, and Iva owned a small hotel.[23] When Cabral was nine years old, the family moved back to Cape Verde. His parents separated, and his mother was compelled to take up a succession of low-paying jobs to feed her children. Still, Cabral attended the prestigious Liceu Gil Eanes, the only high school in the archipelago, located in the port city of Mindelo.[24]

Cabral's student days in Mindelo coincided with a literary renaissance movement known as the *Caboverdenidade*. Developed around a new journal, *Claridade*, the movement sought to break with the sterile traditions of Portuguese literature and focus on Cape Verdean problems in the "nativist" tradition. Like other young men and women at the time, Cabral in his early writings expressed outrage at the isolation and living conditions on the islands and spoke of hope and optimism for the future. He was also profoundly affected by the plight of Cape Verdeans dying of famine.[25] In 1945, Cabral received a scholarship to study agronomy at the University of Lisbon, where he would meet other students from Portuguese colonies.

One of them was Marcelino dos Santos. Santos was born on May 20, 1924 in Lumbo in northern Mozambique, the son of Firmindo dos Santos and Teresa Sabina dos Santos. In 1938, his family moved back to the colonial capital, Lourenço Marques (now Maputo). Traditionally, Mozambique was "farther and freer" from Portugal than other colonies, and therefore the locus of a vibrant nativist movement.[26] His father, a mechanic, was a member of Associação Africana (African Association), a *mestiço* organization that pressed for reform within the framework of the state. In 1947, Marcelino dos Santos left to study in Lisbon, where he shared an apartment with Cabral.

Another member of their circle was the Angolan Mário Pinto de Andrade. He was born on August 21, 1928 in Golungo Alto in northern Angola, to Ana Rodrigues Coelho and José Cristino Pinto de Andrade. In 1930, the family moved to Angola's capital, Luanda. The educated society in interwar Luanda was socially complex. There were "old *assimilados*," mainly Black Catholics with roots going back to the seventeenth century and few links to the countryside.

"New *assimilados*" retained links to the countryside and spoke both Kimbundu and Portuguese at home. Many of them were educated by the Methodist missionaries who dominated Luanda and its surroundings. The third group comprised *mestiço* families, the product of steady and predominantly male immigration to Luanda.[27]

Mário de Andrade's lifestyle during his early years resembled that of "old *assimilados*" in many ways. His father was a bank worker and an activist in the nativist movement. Mário attended the Catholic Seminário de Luanda and the Colégio das Beiras, two prestigious secondary schools that were accessible to both Luanda's white inhabitants and *assimilado* Africans. As he recalled much later, he developed a taste for Russian literature from a young age, with the works by Lev Tolstoy, Nikolai Gogol, and Maxim Gorky evoking the struggles against injustice.[28]

However, even distinguished families like Mário de Andrade's felt pressure from incoming European immigrants. During the interwar period, the family lived in Ingombotas, a historically African neighborhood that was also home to many *assimilado* families. However, their house was leveled after World War II to accommodate Portuguese immigrants, and the family had to move to a neighborhood close to the *musseques*, Luanda's shantytowns. There Mário spent his days socializing with other young men of his age, watching U.S. cowboy films, listening to jazz and Brazilian music, playing soccer, and writing poetry.[29] In 1948, he received a scholarship to study classics at the University of Lisbon.

Another Angolan in their group was António Agostinho Neto. Like Mário de Andrade, Neto belonged to the Mbundu ethnic group. Born in 1922 in Catete, Ícolo e Bengo, near Luanda, Neto was the son of Pedro Neto, a Methodist pastor, and Maria da Silva Neto, a schoolteacher. In Luanda, Neto managed to enroll at the Liceu Salvador Correia, one of the few government-sponsored high schools. He also supplemented his income by working as a secretary for a colleague of his father's, the Methodist bishop Ralph Dodge. As Dodge later recalled, Neto was a "very serious lad, very studious and very intelligent," one of the "very few blacks" who completed the lyceum, which allowed him the rare opportunity to apply for a place at the university.[30]

After graduating, Neto obtained a job in the colonial healthcare administration in Malange, a large agricultural center in northern Angola. There, he came into regular contact with contract laborers, an experience that opened his eyes to the violence inherent in Portuguese colonialism.[31] Neto's early poetry illustrated his indignation at the violence and poverty of everyday life in Luanda's *musseques*. In 1947, the year he left Angola for Portugal to study medicine at the

University of Lisbon, Neto wrote "Adeus A Hora de Largada" (Farewell at the Time of Parting), a poem that called for a change in the status quo:

> My Mother
> (all black mothers whose sons have gone away)
> you taught me to wait and hope
> as you hoped in difficult times
> But life
> killed in me that mystic hope
> I do not wait now
> I am he who is awaited[32]

All the key protagonists in this story—Marcelino dos Santos, Agostinho Neto, Mário de Andrade, and Amílcar Cabral—shared similar socioeconomic backgrounds, coming from *assimilado* or *mestiço* families in urban centers across the Portuguese Empire. Each belonged to a relatively privileged stratum of society, but they were by no means the colonial elite. Many were quite impoverished and faced increasing pressure from the influx of European immigrants after World War II. Recent research has also emphasized the role of Protestant missionaries and other religious networks in fostering a sense of national identity.[33] Above all, these were young men who all either bore witness to or directly experienced discrimination and injustice in their youth.

The memory of Portuguese abuses remains a key starting point for the generation who would later rebel against colonial rule. In 2017, I visited Praia, Cape Verde, to talk to men and women who had participated in the liberation struggle. Two of my interviewees were Amélia Araújo and her daughter Teresa. Amélia was born in Luanda in 1933, the daughter of Felisbela Rodrigues de Sá, an Angolan, and João Baptista Andrade Sanches from Cape Verde. Her father was an accountant and her mother a housewife. Her family was not wealthy but was still better off than the majority of Black Angolans. As someone who became involved in the nationalist struggle as an adult, Amélia was keen to emphasize the injustices she had witnessed in her childhood. She was distressed to see that Black people walking barefoot were not allowed to walk on the pavement. There were also several specific incidents that repelled her.

One such confrontation occurred when her aunt took her to enroll in a state-run primary school in Luanda. The room, she recalls, was full of "scruffy, dirty, and barefoot children," waiting to be enrolled. Then the coordinator approached her and started firing questions at her and her aunt: "Does the girl speak Portuguese or Kimbundu? Does she sit at the table to eat, or does she eat

Left to right: Agostinho Neto, Amílcar Cabral, José Araújo, Mário Pinto de Andrade and Marcelino dos Santos at the OAU summit in Accra, October 1965. Fundação Mário Soares e Maria Barroso/Arquivo Mário Pinto de Andrade.

on the floor? Does she sleep on a bed or on a mat?" Amélia refused to be enrolled, appealing to her father, who promised that she and her siblings would attend a private school, but the experience marked her for life: "It was then that I realized that those boys standing there did not stand a chance of being admitted to that school. Not a chance at all ... I have never been able to forget that man's face and those boys who were unable to attend that school." Another incident involved witnessing elderly agricultural workers being beaten as punishment for failing to pay taxes to the colonial authorities. Amélia detested such discrimination, but she was not involved in political affairs. Her brothers were "handing out fliers," but girls generally "stayed out of politics." Her life would change dramatically in 1956 after she joined her fiancé and future husband, José Araújo, in Portugal, unaware that he was involved in nationalist activism.[34]

Like Amélia, the African students who went to Portugal to study in the late 1940s were repulsed by neglect and racial injustice in the colonies. Their level of participation in the cultural and political life in urban centers differed, but most did not dream about revolution. Like elsewhere in Africa after World War II, many entertained reformist agendas and sought equal rights with the Europeans within the imperial context.[35] This would change in the course of the 1950s, as young Africans studying in Portugal and those in the urban centers across the colonies were increasingly exposed to radical ideas.

The Rise of African Nationalism: From Cultural Self-Discovery to Independent Statehood

World War II and its aftermath was a moment of crisis for Salazar's regime. Portugal remained neutral during the war and thus escaped the physical destruction of other European countries. However, the spiraling costs of living and problems with rationing resulted in food shortages and hunger in the countryside. Across Europe, wartime devastation and the Red Army's role in defeating fascism increased the appeal of Soviet socialism and fueled the rise of communist parties. In Portugal, the wartime shortages increased the attraction of the illegal Portuguese Communist Party (PCP) and other opposition parties that coalesced around a broad anti-Salazarist front, the Movimento de Unidade Democrática (MUD; Movement of Democratic Unity). In 1945, Salazar allowed the opposition parties to contest parliamentary elections and implemented several measures to speed up economic development in the metropole and the colonies. Only three years later, however, MUD was banned as the extent of opposition to Salazar's rule became apparent. In the colonies too, the majority remained without citizenship rights, and government-sponsored investment programs were curtailed.[36]

These developments notwithstanding, Portugal remained largely immune to international criticism. The key reason was the strategic value of the Portuguese-controlled Azores archipelago, conveniently situated in the middle of the Atlantic. During World War II, the British and the Americans used the Azores as a refueling and resupplying station. As the Cold War gained traction in the late 1940s, continuity of access to the Azores was one of the main reasons why Portugal was invited to join NATO in 1949. The U.S.-Portugal Lajes Base Agreement of 1951 stipulated that NATO could use the Azores as a military base and, in return, the United States would provide the country with military aid. A secret clause allowed Lisbon to make use of U.S. aid in Africa.[37] As massive campaigns for independence were underway in the British, French, and Belgian empires in the late 1950s, Salazar used the concept of "Lusotropicalism" to argue that the Portuguese people were uniquely suited to live in the tropics due to their multiracial heritage. He also maintained that harmonious racial relations prevailed across Portuguese Africa.

Beneath the veneer of stability, the 1950s would serve as a crucial decade for the formation of various clusters of nationalist activity in Portugal and across the empire. One cluster formed among African students in Portugal—a group that was supposed to become the new colonial elite. In Lisbon, the social life of students from the colonies revolved around Casa dos Estudantes do Imperio (CEI; House of Students of the Empire). The CEI was a self-help organization with a canteen, a medical center, and a social club, which became a convenient spot for students from the Portuguese colonies to socialize. Amílcar Cabral, Agostinho Neto, Mário de Andrade, and Marcelino dos Santos belonged to a politicized group of students who were actively involved in the social life at the CEI.[38]

When the authorities began to restrict open expression, they organized a clandestine group, Centro de Estudos Africanos (Center for African Studies). The group functioned as a colloquium that intended to analyze the problems of the colonies.[39] Inspired by the Francophone African writers of the Négritude movement such as Aimé Césaire and Léopold Senghor, African students explored their cultural roots and what it meant to be an *"assimilado"* in the context of the Portuguese empire. By studying and reconnecting to specifically African culture, these students rejected the concept of "Lusotropicalism," arguing it was a convenient extension of a fundamentally exploitative and racist colonial order.[40]

Other clusters of nationalist activity would form in urban centers across the Portuguese empire. In Angola, Luanda's *musseques* were the focal point for the formation of a specific national culture. As Marissa Moorman has argued, music was particularly significant in the development of Angolan consciousness, often to a greater extent than political nationalism. Music and dance intersected with political activism in critical ways. In the late 1940s, several civil servants formed a band called Ngola Ritmos, which performed in Kimbundu and other Angolan languages, using local instruments. The music was supposed to awaken people to colonial oppression, and many of its members were politically active. The band and its music became popular and were well known to African intellectuals at the time.[41]

Literature was another medium for expressing cultural nationalism. In Luanda, a group of politicized youths calling themselves Novos Intelectuais de Angola (New Intellectuals of Angola) published *Mensagem*, a journal dedicated to the rediscovery of Angola's politics, culture, and history. The editor of *Mensagem*, Viriato da Cruz, was a childhood friend of Mário de Andrade. Although Cruz did not get a scholarship to study in Portugal due to his political activism, the two stayed in touch via correspondence. As Mário de Andrade later argued, Cruz and *Mensagem* inspired their group in Portugal to start the journey to "rediscover" African problems. The authorities considered *Mensagem* subversive and banned the publication after only two issues.[42] As oppression intensified during the 1950s, many African intellectuals in the colonies and those studying in Portugal started to embrace more radical ideas. Increasingly, their attention was drawn to Marxism.

Marxist ideas were popular among African nationalists after World War II. In the postwar period, many African leaders preferred socialism to capitalism for several reasons. To them, capitalism in the African context was associated with colonial exploitation. The majority of African economies relied on the export of agricultural goods, leaving them vulnerable to fluctuations of the global economy. Socialism was attractive for many African leaders who wanted to overcome the colonial legacy and achieve rapid economic development upon independence. However, many African leaders of the first post-independence generation did not believe their economies or societies were suited to a socialist transformation along the lines of the Soviet Union. Many thus embraced "African socialism" to combine state-led development initiatives with the coexistence of private capital.[43]

In Portugal, the Portuguese Communist Party was influential in the underground anti-Salazarist movement and dominated its youth wing, MUD-Juvenil. As a result, many African students in Portugal, including Andrade, Santos, Neto, and Cabral, forged contacts with the PCP upon their arrival. Mário de Andrade recalled distributing Marxist literature, and all of them participated in the PCP-sponsored Soviet Peace Campaign launched by the USSR in response to the escalation of the Cold War in Europe.[44]

Still, relations between the PCP and African students in Portugal were often strained. The PCP's policy on the colonial question was often contradictory. African students resented that the Portuguese Communists prioritized struggle against the dictatorship over the liberation of the colonies. These disagreements were resolved only when the PCP formally approved support for the independence of the colonies at its fifth congress in 1957.[45] One way or another, the PCP provided a vehicle for African students to gain experience of underground activism, with some, like Neto, forming long-term contacts that would prove vital in the long run.

Marxist ideas also gained some traction in urban centers across the Portuguese colonies. In Angola, Marxist literature was fairly readily available through the clandestine publications and documents of the Portuguese, Uruguayan, and Brazilian Communist Parties, which had been smuggled to Angola, often by sailors who traveled between Portugal, Brazil, and Africa. In 1955, Viriato da Cruz and others associated with Novos Intelectuais de Angola established the

Angolan Communist Party (PCA; Partido Comunista Angolana).[46] Shortly afterward, Cruz and his followers realized that the party would not have broad appeal. Therefore, in 1956, they published a manifesto, calling for the people of Angola to create "thousands and thousands" of organizations under the banner of the Popular Movement for the Liberation of Angola (MPLA). The manifesto envisioned a future independent Angola run by a popular government with the "working class at the forefront."[47] It is unclear whether the PCP had any input in forming the PCA or drafting the manifesto.

The 1950s were a period of profound ideational transformation for African intellectuals, as they started to analyze the concepts of race and racism in the context of the Portuguese Empire. Inspired by the Négritude movement, their early activities centered on efforts to "rediscover" their "Africanness." However, they would soon abandon cultural nationalism in favor of a fundamentally Marxist analysis of Portuguese colonialism. As Branwen Gruffydd Jones has argued, these young people abandoned Négritude because they concluded that the narrow *assimilado* culture of urban areas could not be connected with the experiences of the vast majority of people living under Portuguese rule. The main enemy was not the "white man," but the global imperialist system.[48] In short, contacts with Portuguese communists helped politicize African students, but these did not determine their politics.

These Marxist intellectuals differed significantly from African leaders like Julius Nyerere in Tanganyika (later Tanzania) or Léopold Senghor in Senegal, who advocated "African socialism." As Neto and Cabral argued, "African socialists" underplayed the importance of class struggle in Africa and the Marxist laws of historical development. Cabral specifically distinguished his "revolutionary nationalism" from the "bourgeois nationalism" of African socialists, which he argued would not lead to any profound transformation of society.[49] Such critiques of "African socialism" emerged gradually throughout the 1960s, but some of the fundamental differences were visible from the outset.

By the mid-1950s, it became clear that it would be challenging to engage in anticolonial activism in Portugal. Any association with the PCP, in particular, was dangerous. In November 1951, Andrade, Santos, and Neto, among others, were arrested while laying flowers at the monument to fallen soldiers in Lisbon as part of their involvement with the PCP-sponsored Peace Campaign.[50] Marcelino dos Santos left for Paris shortly afterward. Mário de Andrade soon followed. Cabral continued to work as an agricultural expert, first in Guinea-Bissau and then Angola. Neto graduated with a medical degree but was in and out of prison for most of the 1950s because of his activism and association with the PCP.

The repression in the colonies also intensified. By 1957, most nationalist activists in Angola were either in prison or in exile. In 1957, Viriato da Cruz fled Luanda to join the others in Paris, fearing arrest. At a meeting in Paris in November, Cabral, Santos, Andrade, and Guilherme do Espírito Santo decided to establish a common platform for the struggle against Portuguese colonialism, which would be known as the Anticolonial Movement (MAC; Movimento Anti-Colonialista). The move signified that the center of political activism had to move outside of Portugal into exile.[51] In the following years, the Paris-based activists—Mário de Andrade, Viriato da Cruz, and Marcelino dos Santos—would form a close-knit group and engaged in international travel, forging initial contacts with socialist countries, including the USSR.

First Contacts: Tashkent, Beijing, and Exile Activism in the 1950s

From the outset of the interwar period, Paris served as a hub for nationalist activity for African intellectuals. When Mário de Andrade arrived there, he started working for *Présence Africaine*, an influential journal founded by Alioune Diop, a famous Senegalese writer and a key figure in the Négritude movement. Andrade's association with the journal led to the development of contacts with other Francophone nationalists based in Paris and raised awareness of Portuguese colonialism. However, disagreements between Francophone and Lusophone activists about the direction of political nationalism also emerged. These became clear when Marcelino dos Santos, Viriato da Cruz, and Mário de Andrade were invited to attend the "First Conference of African and Asian Writers," held in Tashkent, Soviet Uzbekistan, from October 7–13, 1958.

The Tashkent conference was a landmark event in Soviet cultural diplomacy designed to offer Moscow an opportunity to interact closely with noncommunist anticolonial elites.[52] Bringing together 196 writers and poets from fifty countries in Asia, Africa, Europe, and the Americas, the conference provided a broad platform to denounce colonialism and economic exploitation. Nikita Khrushchev set the tone in his opening speech when he underlined the importance of writers in developing the nationalist consciousness of people struggling against imperialism. Behind the scenes, though, the conference was marred by the delegates' many competing agendas.[53]

Alioune Diop was among those who clashed with the Soviets in the lead-up to the conference. According to the Soviet version of events, the conflict began during preparatory meetings, where Diop insisted that the Soviets not participate in the proceedings. He then withdrew his participation and that of *Présence Africaine*. In an internal report, the Soviet Writers' Union blamed Diop for trying to undermine the conference, branding him a "hostile bourgeois nationalist."[54] There is also evidence that the Soviets refused to invite Diop because they were uncomfortable with Négritude as a movement explicitly focused on racial, rather than social, justice.[55]

The incident caused some controversy during discussions at the Presidium of the newly established Soviet Solidarity Committee, with some Africanists like Alexander Zusmanovich arguing there should have been more "patient" engagement with Diop. Although not everyone agreed with such a proposal, other members of the Presidium noted that many people in Diop's circle did not share his views.[56] In an interview with Michael Laban conducted much later, Mário de Andrade recalled he clashed with Diop about attending the conference and claimed he was even forced to quit his job at *Présence Africaine*.[57] As Rossen Djagalov has argued, the Tashkent conference was divided among those writers who favored strong connections between literature and politics and those who wanted literature to maintain its independence.[58]

Andrade belonged to the former group. He made his mark on the conference with a passionate speech condemning Portuguese colonialism, arguing that artistic expression cannot flourish without freedom, independence, and national sovereignty.[59] He also met many prominent writers, among them the Turkish Nâzım Hikmet. Andrade recalled that he was particularly impressed to meet W. E. B. Du Bois the ninety-year-old founder of the Pan-Africanist movement.[60] Back in Paris and writing under a pseudonym, Andrade described Tashkent as a "Literary Bandung" and expressed thinly veiled criticism of the African delegates who had refused to attend.[61]

Andrade made a very positive impression on the Soviet conference organizers. In an internal report, the Soviet Writers' Union named Mário de Andrade among a dozen other writers whose actions coincided with the union's agenda: "The efforts of these people helped defend our [Soviet] line at the conference and achieve the correct decisions."[62] Viriato da Cruz and Marcelino dos Santos were not listed in the reported, even though they both attended the Tashkent conference.

Andrade also established correspondence with Ivan Potekhin, the first director of the Institute of African Studies. In June 1959, Potekhin notified Andrade about the creation of the Soviet Friendship Association with the African Peoples and asked Andrade to put him in touch with "cultural figures, mass and youth organizations in their country."[63] In turn, Andrade asked Potekhin for

Mário Pinto de Andrade (right, wearing a tie) with W. E. B. Du Bois (center) at the "First Conference of African and Asian Writers," held in Tashkent, October 7–13, 1958. Department of Special Collections and University Archives, W. E. B. Du Bois Library, University of Massachusetts Amherst.

scholarships for students from the Portuguese colonies. Potekhin had to decline since the Friendship Association still did not have the capacity to offer such scholarships.[64] Andrade thus emerged as the central figure representing African writers from the Portuguese colonies after Tashkent.

Cultural exchanges remained an important part of the engagement between the Soviets and their new African allies. In 1959, a collection of poems by Marcelino dos Santos was published in the USSR in Russian translation.[65] In the early 1960s, Pavel Shmelkov was given responsibility for sub-Saharan Africa at the Association for Friendship and Cultural Ties with Foreign Countries. He recounted meeting Marcelino dos Santos, Mário de Andrade, and Agostinho Neto at a poetry reading in Moscow: "A small hall in an old building of the library at Razin Street was filled to capacity. There gathered the library staff, readers, and simply young people who had found out there would be a meeting with the Africans gathered there. The guests did not expect such a lively interest in their art, and they read poetry in Portuguese and French. A famous translator, Lidiia Nekrasova, read their poetry in Russian. The evening lasted into the night. Nobody wanted to leave."[66]

Such meetings fulfilled some crucial functions. They showed the domestic audience that the revolution was still alive, with poetry reading serving as a way to connect African intellectuals with the Soviet public. They also raised the prestige and increased the international exposure of African writers. Thus, the Soviet cultural diplomacy of the 1950s was important for fostering personal contacts and connections between African revolutionaries and local intermediaries.

The Soviet Union was not the only actor interested in capturing the "hearts and minds" of Third World elites due to the rise of China as a formidable regional power with global ambitions in the 1950s. The People's Republic of China (PRC) was established in 1949 after the Chinese Communist Party (CCP) defeated its rival, the nationalist Kuomintang, in a long and bitter civil war. Initially, the Chinese leadership forged a close alliance with the Soviet Union. However, the CCP's leader, Chairman Mao Zedong, was not happy with the pace of modernization and decided to pursue a "national road to socialism" after Khrushchev's denunciation of Stalin. In 1958, he launched the "Great Leap Forward," a scheme that aimed to increase industrial production and agricultural output at breakneck speed.[67] China also started to pursue a more assertive foreign policy in the Third World. The Chinese leadership believed that their revolution could provide a model for "colonial and semi-colonial countries" and started inviting Africans to visit China.[68]

Three of our protagonists—Mário de Andrade, Marcelino dos Santos, and Viriato da Cruz—grew infatuated with the Chinese Revolution during the 1950s. The first to visit China was Marcelino dos Santos. He had already gone to Bucharest, Romania, for the Fourth World Festival of Youth and Students with Agostinho Neto and was impressed with the warm reception, which contrasted sharply with the reality of daily racism in Portugal. However, his trip to China in 1954 made a distinct impression. He traversed the country, visiting factories, speaking to leaders of trade unions, women's groups, and youth organizations. He remembered being impressed with the massive scale of industrial construction, with all the work done through sheer physical labor. As he later recalled: "The time spent in China was a real school in Marxism-Leninism."[69] Like Santos, Andrade and Cruz were impressed by the Chinese revolution when they visited in 1958—the height of the Great Leap Forward. Andrade romanticized his experience in China as he recollected the highly visible production of steel, the slogans advocating manual labor plastered all over the walls, and the people's enthusiasm for the new society.[70]

Their first experience of state socialism would be significant for African intellectuals from the Portuguese colonies. Growing up under a racist social order, those who traveled to the Soviet Union and Eastern Europe were positively impressed by the explicit antiracism of their hosts. Although such expressions of socialist solidarity were often ritualized, the lack of any (visible) racial and ethnic hierarchies demonstrated what socialism could achieve, even in multiethnic societies. The experience of the Chinese Revolution in the 1950s was particularly influential for African intellectuals because it offered a model of state-led mass mobilization for a non-white, non-Western country with a history of suffering from imperialism. Although the Great Leap Forward would end in disaster and mass starvation in China, the perceived mobility and grandeur of the experiment that Africans witnessed during the often carefully choreographed tours left a profound and long-lasting impression.

In the USSR, the majority of these encounters were part of Soviet cultural diplomacy, an attempt to capture the "hearts and minds" of Third World elites. The contacts forged through these early encounters, such as with Mário de Andrade, were significant—they placed the Paris-based African intellectuals in contact with central Soviet figures and organizations that were involved in establishing these personal contacts. These international travels contributed to a radical vision of a just society that many African intellectuals from the Portuguese colonies would come to share by the late 1950s. However, theirs was not the only one, and a number of local rivals would emerge in the 1950s and 1960s in urban centers across the Portuguese Empire and the neighboring countries. In Angola, the Luanda-based intellectuals would be challenged by a group of people based in Zaire who sought inspiration and support from the United States.

Alternative Visions: Holden Roberto, Bakongo Nationalism, and the United States

Various regions of the Portuguese Empire had long-standing links to neighboring countries, as people moved in search of better job opportunities or to escape the compulsory labor requirements that tightened under Salazar. Masses of migrants traveled from Mozambique to work in the mines and on the railways of Southern Rhodesia (later Zimbabwe) and South Africa. Thousands migrated from Cape Verde to São Tomé, Senegal, Guinea-Bissau, and Angola to escape famine. Angola had historical links with the Belgian Congo (later Zaire) to the north and Northern Rhodesia (later Zambia) to the east. By the late 1950s, migrants had started to set up self-help organizations to support members of their communities.

One such organization was based in Léopoldville (later renamed Kinshasa), the capital of Zaire. Angolans living in Léopoldville were rooted in the

5,000-strong Bakongo community, which had traditionally inhabited northern Angola and southwestern Zaire. Those who settled in Zaire spoke fluent French rather than Portuguese and were well integrated into the local politics and culture. These were key features of the so-called "Léopoldville group" of Angolans, initially dedicated to the restoration of the Kongo kingdom. Unlike the Luanda-based intellectuals, the Léopoldville group was opposed to communism and derived their inspiration from the United States. In 1956, they established the Union of the Peoples of the North of Angola (UPNA; União das Populações do Norte de Angola).[71]

The man who would come to dominate the Léopoldville group was Holden Roberto. Born in 1923 in São Salvador (now Mbanza-Kongo), northern Angola, Roberto's family moved to Zaire when he was only two years old. He studied at a Baptist missionary school and then worked as an accountant for the Belgian colonial administration in Léopoldville. In 1958, Roberto represented the UPNA at the First All-African People's Conference in Accra where he encountered many influential African leaders who advised him to broaden the organization's appeal. He thus renamed the group the Union of the Peoples of Angola (UPA; União das Populações de Angola). By dropping the narrow regional focus from the title, Roberto wanted to show the UPA aspired to represent all Angolans. Roberto stayed in Accra after the conference, where he met and became inspired by Frantz Fanon, the Martinican philosopher and ideologue of a violent revolution in Algeria.[72]

Although Roberto began to entertain ideas about the violent overthrow of colonial rule, he fashioned himself as a staunch anticommunist and established relations with U.S. officials. In late 1955, Roberto first met with the U.S. Consulate in Léopoldville. He managed to impress the Consul General so much that the CIA station allocated him $6,000 in direct monthly payments.[73] Much later, Roberto claimed that when Soviet officials, including Ivan Potekhin, approached him during his time in Accra, he refused all attempts to turn him to their side.[74] His model was the United States, and in 1959 he departed for New York to present a case against Portuguese colonialism at the United Nations and make contacts with U.S officials.

The timing was opportune, since Washington was in the process of revising its policy on Africa in the late 1950s. Although the United States had a long-standing anticolonial tradition, many U.S. politicians saw Africans through a racial lens because of the bitter history of segregation in the southern United States. U.S. president Dwight Eisenhower was not particularly interested in Africa during his first term in office (1953–57) because he preferred slow-paced decolonization under European patronage. However, this policy started to change, especially after Vice President Richard Nixon made an extended tour of Africa in 1957 and came back convinced that the continent would become the next battlefield between the West and the Eastern Bloc. Eisenhower and Secretary of State John Foster Dulles agreed to a policy review, and on August 23, the National Security Council approved their final report, NSC 5719/1. The report recommended that the United States "combat Communist subversive activities" and support "constructive non-Communist, nationalist, and reform movements" in Africa.[75]

The Eisenhower administration also faced substantial criticism of its Africa policy. One of the critics was John Fitzgerald Kennedy, a young Democratic senator at that time. Kennedy believed that one had to engage with African nationalist leaders—or risk having them fall under the spell of communism. On July 2, 1957, Kennedy shocked the Senate when he denounced U.S. support for the French colonial war in Algeria. The speech scandalized Washington and Paris but earned the respect of many African leaders.[76] When Holden Roberto journeyed to New York for the first time in 1959, he reportedly met Kennedy. According to Roberto, the two talked "for hours" and agreed it was necessary to prevent the communists from taking over Angola.[77] Holden Roberto thus established himself as a reliable "noncommunist nationalist," which put him on a path of long-term collaboration with Washington.

The major differences between the Luanda and Léopoldville-based Angolan nationalists have attracted significant attention from historians. Both groups represented educated elites, but they were distinct in terms of ethnic background, culture, and education. While Luanda-based intellectuals embraced Marxism as a form of identification that stood above race largely due to their multiethnic background, Holden Roberto and the UPA identified predominantly with the Bakongo. What is more, the Léopoldville-based group was exposed to a much more racially segregated form of (Belgian) colonialism, and they were uneasy around people of Portuguese origin.[78]

The difference in the way the two groups understood race was compounded by variations in religion and occupation. As David Birmingham has argued, the UPA embraced a "capitalist ethos" because it was rooted in Bakongo-dominated Northwest Angola, a major coffee production center. Although white farmers often occupied the best land, there was also substantial coffee planting among Africans. Aspirations to engage in free enterprise were fostered by a "Protestant ethic," which was encouraged by the Baptist missionaries who dominated education in northern Angola.[79] More generally, these divisions were reflective of how "Angola" was put together, cutting across ethnocultural divides. By 1960, the

UPA emerged as a powerful rival to the Luanda-based intellectuals, as Holden Roberto managed to mobilize the Bakongo of northern Angola and started to develop a network of international patrons.

From Paris to Conakry: Toward an Armed Struggle

As the 1950s drew to a close, it became increasingly evident that Salazar was not willing to relinquish Portugal's empire in Africa. In 1959, violent protests broke out in Zaire. Fearing that the same would happen in Angola, the colonial administration arrested and jailed fifty Angolans suspected of involvement in nationalist agitation. In Guinea-Bissau, the police shot at peaceful protesters at the Pidjiguiti docks in Bissau, killing fifty people and injuring many more, on August 3, 1959.

The man who would connect this act of police brutality to the nationalist narrative was Amílcar Cabral. After graduating from the University of Lisbon with a degree in agronomy, Cabral took a job at an agricultural research station near Bissau. There, he conducted the country's first agricultural census and developed a critique of colonial land exploitation.[80] He combined this work with social activism, organizing a sports and recreation club for young people. He also acquired connections among the Cape Verdean community in Bissau.[81]

The Portuguese secret police, the PIDE, treated such activities with suspicion. Cabral was forced to leave Guinea-Bissau, coming back only occasionally to see his family. According to the official party history, in 1956, Cabral established a party that came to be known after several name changes as the PAIGC. However, as Julião Soares Sousa has discovered, Cabral actually set up the PAIGC after the events at the Pidjiguiti docks in August 1959. He then left Bissau for Paris with a number of his followers.[82]

The building pressure for violent action became apparent at the Second All-African People's Conference, held on January 25, 1960, in Tunis. The Tunis conference was very different from the first such meeting in Accra in 1958. By 1960, the Algerian War had become a rallying point for the Non-Aligned Movement and inspired other Third World revolutionaries.[83] Frantz Fanon personified the militant mood in Tunis, calling upon delegates from the Portuguese colonies to launch an armed struggle against the Salazar regime in solidarity with the Algerian National Liberation Front (FLN), who were fighting against French rule in Algeria.

In 1959, Fanon had proposed to Mário de Andrade, Viriato da Cruz, and Lúcio Lara that the FLN provide military training to eleven young Angolans recruited in the colonies. Cabral then went to Luanda but failed to find any recruits because of the repression. In fact, Cabral's trip showed that the conditions for armed rebellion were not right, but Fanon disagreed. He branded the MPLA "people from the city" and instead offered the FLN's support to Holden Roberto, who, he believed, was "connected with the masses."[84] The lesson was striking: Paris-based activists had to move to Africa to mobilize support on the ground or lose out to regional rivals embedded in local politics. In early 1960, Amílcar Cabral, Viriato da Cruz, and Mário de Andrade moved from Paris to Conakry, the capital of the newly independent Republic of Guinea (hereafter "Guinea").

Guinea provided an ideal "launching pad" for armed action in Guinea-Bissau. The two countries share a long and porous border, which is difficult to control because of the long-standing movement of goods and people. In the early 1960s, Conakry became a critical hub for African revolutionaries due to the patronage of Ahmed Sékou Touré, Guinea's first president. Touré's name hit the international headlines in 1958 when Guineans voted to reject French president Charles de Gaulle's proposal of continued membership of the French community. Although the referendum result was very much an outcome of pressure from below, Touré used it to construct an image of himself as an uncompromising, radical nationalist leader, and he pledged support for African liberation.[85] When Amílcar Cabral, Mário de Andrade, and Viriato da Cruz relocated to Conakry in early 1960, they formally established the headquarters for the PAIGC and the MPLA and started approaching the embassies of the socialist countries, looking for support. China was among them.

China's interest in Africa picked up in 1960 because of competition with the Soviets. Sino-Soviet disagreements had been brewing for some time for many reasons. The CCP's chairman, Mao Zedong, wanted Moscow to treat Beijing as an equal partner. He was unhappy when the Soviets criticized the Great Leap Forward and failed to support China in its border conflict with India. As Sino-Soviet competition intensified, China started to challenge the USSR openly for leadership in the Third World. Beijing stepped up its support for anticolonial movements in Africa and began offering cash and military training to these movements.[86] As Mário de Andrade recalled much later, during their first encounters with representatives of the socialist countries in Conakry, the Chinese were the most "forthcoming" and invited him, Cabral, and Cruz to visit Beijing.[87]

Their trip to China took place in August 1960. Apparently, Cabral, Andrade, and Cruz made a good impression on their Chinese hosts, securing $20,000 in financial assistance for the MPLA and the PAIGC.[88] Cruz, who had been appointed general secretary of the MPLA, returned to Conakry with some of the cash tucked away in his overcoat in $20 bills. In addition to receiving the cash, Cabral and Cruz took some practical lessons in "guerrilla warfare" in China. Some of their notes from the course were allegedly preserved on microfiche and transported secretly to MPLA supporters in Angola. Cabral also negotiated with the Chinese to send recruits from Guinea-Bissau for a short training course at the Nanjing Military Academy. As Anrade later recalled, the trip showed that the Chinese were much more willing to support armed struggle than the Soviets.[89]

The Soviet stance on armed struggle in 1960 has given rise to some controversy. In the case of South Africa, Stephen Ellis has argued that the Soviet Union was instrumental in providing "tacit approval" and backing the policy of armed struggle in conversations with the members of the South African Communist Party (SACP) in the summer of 1960.[90] Then, the argument goes, the SACP influenced members of the African National Congress (ANC) to engage in violence against the apartheid regime. This led to the formation of its armed wing, Umkhonto we Sizwe (Spear of the Nation), in 1961. However, the central role of the USSR as "backing" the violent option has been disputed by several authors. According to Hugh Macmillan, the transition to violence was the product of an internal debate within the ANC. Simon Stevens has argued that the turn to violence was hastened by pressure "from below" after police opened fire on peaceful protesters in the Sharpeville township in March 1960.[91]

Similarly, there is no direct evidence that the Soviets encouraged a violent anticolonial uprising in the Portuguese colonies. We know that Andrade, Cruz, and Cabral visited the Soviet Union in the summer of 1960, but the details of conversations they had there are unknown. In fact, Andrade does not mention the trip in his otherwise detailed interview with Michel Laban. One Soviet Foreign Ministry report from 1963 stated that both Andrade and Cruz came to Moscow in 1960, where they "declared that armed struggle was necessary and were preparing for it."[92] However, the files of the Soviet Solidarity Committee do not mention armed struggle.[93] We also do not know whether Andrade and Cruz made any requests of their Soviet hosts.

Soviet inaction could also be explained by the fact that Portuguese colonialism was nowhere near the top of the Politburo agenda in 1960. In fact, even if such requests were filed, the Soviets lacked the organizational capacity to process them. During their early trips to Moscow, African anticolonial activists were usually hosted by members of the Soviet Solidarity Committee. Although staff of the various "public organizations" were important intermediaries, the International Department was only building up a designated Africa desk at that time. While the Chinese took a highly personalized approach, the Soviet bureaucracy was cumbersome and often slow, with minimal access to high-level decision-makers. It would take some time—and some exceptional circumstances—for the Soviets to truly notice developments in the Portuguese colonies.

By 1960, it had become clear to African revolutionaries that they had to harness support for armed struggle quickly—or lose out to local rivals. Although violence was never their preferred option, African intellectuals realized that they had to demonstrate the ability to challenge the Portuguese by the force of arms. In Angola's case, the rivalry between the Luanda-based intellectuals and the Léopoldville group emerged early on, with both vying for leadership in the anticolonial movement. Speaking at the London Conference for Nationalist Leaders from the Portuguese Colonies on December 6, 1960, Mário de Andrade declared that the liberation movements would resort to "direct action" if faced with continued Portuguese intransigence. The MPLA would later claim this was a signal for the Angolan underground to launch preparations for armed struggle.[94] However, as the next chapter shows, there was no such concrete plan, especially in the short term.

Conclusion

The 1950s were a crucial period in which the men and women who would later preach revolution in Angola, Mozambique, and Guinea-Bissau came of age. Initially, these were young people who expressed their frustration with the colonial regime in ways that had been common in interwar Paris, London, and Brussels—through cultural production and self-discovery. However, they eventually abandoned Négritude in favor of a more radical approach. Specifically, they would come to understand the Portuguese colonial system in terms of class rather than race. Their vision of the future came to rest on socialism as a way to ensure total liberation from colonialism. Thus, they were quite different from "African socialists," who often opted to combine state-led modernization with the preservation of what they called "African culture and traditions."

Andrade, Cabral, and Neto envisioned a radical transformation of society. By the late 1950s, they had adopted a Marxist framework to analyze colonialism and forged close connections with European left-wing circles and officials across the Eastern Bloc. Their trips to the socialist countries were impactful, as they reinforced the belief in the mobilizing potential of socialism and fostered personal links with key people and institutions that would be significant once the anticolonial wars began in the early 1960s.

While intellectuals from Lusophone Africa preferred peaceful transition to independence, by 1960, it became clear that Salazar was unwilling to negotiate. As a result, leadership of the liberation struggle hinged upon the ability to prepare and ultimately lead armed uprisings in the colonies. In the years that followed, they would have to compete with many local rivals who also claimed ownership of the nationalist project in Angola, Mozambique, and Guinea-Bissau. Such divisions were evident early on in Angola because Luanda-based intellectuals were challenged by a group with a very different nationalist vision. Thus, the mobilization of resources from African and international patrons became particularly pertinent. However, African revolutionaries were running out of time.

In 1961, Angola was in the midst of a recession. A few years earlier, world prices for coffee, Angola's most significant export commodity, had dropped, leading to wage cuts in the coffee-producing areas of the north. In addition, 1960 was not a good year for the cotton farmers of the Kassange (Malanje) region. In January 1961, wage cuts in Kassange spurred a wave of protests, which were soon answered by arrests. This crisis led to a full-blown rebellion against the system of forced cotton growing in the area. The Portuguese responded with massive reprisals, killing thousands.[95] This revolt and the reprisals, known as "Maria's War," passed relatively unnoticed by the world press, mainly due to strict censorship. In 1960, developments in the colonies still did not feature in international headlines—but this would change on January 23, 1961, when the *Santa Maria*, a Portuguese luxury liner, was hijacked by a group of political activists led by sixty-six-year-old Henrique Galvão.

CHAPTER THREE

Cataclysm

The Angolan Uprising and Its Aftermath, 1961

O N JANUARY 23, 1961, international headlines captured what seemed like an unbelievable story: a group of political activists opposed to Salazar's rule had hijacked the *Santa Maria*, a Brazilian luxury liner. Their leader was none other than Henrique Galvão, the curator of the 1934 Colonial Exhibition in Porto. Galvão had been a staunch supporter of the regime, but turned against Salazar after his criticism of abusive labor practices in the colonies fell on deaf ears, eventually leading to his arrest. He spent some time in prison before fleeing to Venezuela, in 1959. However, it was the hijacking that would become the most dramatic event in Galvão's career. The hijacking attracted widespread attention, and rumors spread that his ship was sailing toward Luanda, the capital of Angola, to launch a coup. Reporters thus flocked to the capital, awaiting the ship's arrival.[1] After ten days navigating the Atlantic, the *Santa Maria* docked in Recife, Brazil. The journalists who remained in Luanda bore witness to events that would shatter Salazar's myth of harmonious racial relations in Portuguese Africa.

The events known as the "Angolan uprising" started with a series of violent incidents in Luanda on February 4, 1961. Then, on March 15, a major uprising swept across northern Angola. Although the uprising allegedly began after a dispute at the Primavera coffee plantation near São Salvador (Mbanza-Kongo), northern Angola, it was actually initiated by Holden Roberto's UPA. In the north, local Bakongo joined the UPA, attacking farms, destroying property, and killing European farmers. The Angolan uprising was a violent rebellion against the forced labor system, and the scale of the violence was unexpected—even among the nationalist leaders.

The events in Angola were a significant challenge to Salazar's rule. In April, Minister of Defense Júlio Botelho Moniz demanded urgent reforms in Angola and called for Salazar's resignation. However, the coup failed, and Salazar resolved to crush the uprising in the north with overwhelming terror. On orders from Salazar, the Portuguese army bombed and raided entire villages looking for suspects, killing thousands on the spot and arresting many more. By the end of the year, about 50,000 Africans had been killed in the conflict, and 300,000 Angolan refugees had crossed the border into Zaire. The number of European casualties ranged between several hundred and two thousand according to different estimates.[2]

The Angola uprising raised questions regarding the salience of Portuguese colonialism. Portugal's colonial policy was condemned in the press and discussed at the United Nations.[3] In Washington, the newly elected John F. Kennedy broke the pattern by siding with the Soviet Union to condemn Portugal at the UN Security Council. He also used diplomatic channels and the promise of economic aid in an attempt to convince Salazar to proceed toward self-determination. However, Washington's response was constrained by the fact that Portugal controlled access to the Azores archipelago, which hosted a NATO military base at Lajes. Lisbon made it clear that it would not hesitate to terminate the lease if Washington continued to exert pressure over its colonial policy. The State Department was split on the response, with "Africanists" arguing for a tougher stance on colonialism and "Europeanists" advocating against any measures that might alienate Salazar.[4]

Then, during the first meeting between Kennedy and Nikita Khrushchev in Vienna on June 4, 1961, the first secretary astounded the president with an announcement that the Soviet Union would sign a peace treaty with the GDR and terminate Western access to West Berlin. Khrushchev's attempt to force a solution to the status of West Berlin backfired.[5] Kennedy refused to relinquish Western access and ordered a military build-up to defend the city. Over the summer, tensions rose as thousands of East Germans streamed to the West, leading to the construction of the Berlin Wall in August. The Lajes military base in the Azores was used heavily during the Berlin airlift in the summer of 1961, thus strengthening the arguments of State Department and Pentagon officials who warned against alienating Salazar. Kennedy continued to press Salazar for reforms but refrained from any measures that would deny continued U.S. access to the base.[6]

Although Washington's reaction to the Angolan uprising is well known, this chapter discusses the reactions of the USSR and Czechoslovakia to events in Angola in the context of the Berlin Crisis. Beyond supporting resolutions to condemn Portugal's actions at the UN, the Soviets were initially slow to respond to events in Angola. It was not until the heating up of the Cold War in the summer of 1961 that the Soviets offered their first assistance package to the MPLA.

The Soviet and Czechoslovak intelligence services also came up with a plan for Angola, which entailed sustained support for the MPLA and outlined their intention to help establish a "common front" with the UPA. Czechoslovakia also emerged as an important patron of the MPLA and PAIGC, forging a special relationship with Viriato da Cruz and Amílcar Cabral. This chapter charts the largely unknown story of how the interplay between the Angolan and Berlin crises led Moscow and Prague to approve the first aid packages for the MPLA and the PAIGC, detailing the important role key officials—*mezhdunarodniki*—played in such responses.

The Angolan Uprising, the MPLA, and the Soviet Plan for Angola

On February 4, 1961, around 150 Black men armed with clubs and knives attacked the police station, São Paolo prison, the military detention barracks, the radio station, and the airport in Luanda. By evening, six white policemen, one African army corporal, and fourteen so-called rebels had been killed. The next day, interracial violence erupted again at the large public funeral of those who had been killed on the previous day. The prison was attacked again on February 10, leaving seven dead and seventeen wounded. Colonial authorities responded with punitive sweeps of Luanda's slums. They were joined by vigilante groups, who harassed, attacked, and shot at Black residents.[7]

As Dalia and Álvaro Mateus have discovered, neither the MPLA nor the UPA orchestrated these events in Luanda. The attackers wanted to express a desire for independence and free political prisoners, which was timed to coincide with the arrival of foreign journalists who came to Luanda to report on the hijacking of the *Santa Maria* liner.[8] In fact, the violence in the Angolan capital took the MPLA by surprise. In a communiqué released on February 5, the MPLA's steering committee condemned the Portuguese response to events in Luanda but did not mention any involvement.[9] Mário de Andrade later admitted that they first heard about these events on the radio in Conakry.[10]

Meanwhile in Zaire, Holden Roberto was preparing to launch an armed struggle in northern Angola. Although he advocated nonviolence in public, in private, he was frustrated with the failure of peaceful protest and was preparing for armed action. In March, he went to the United States and spoke about Angola at the United Nations. In a carefully crafted international strategy inspired by the FLN in Algeria, the timing of the UPA's invasion of northern Angola on March 15 coincided with a vote on Angola at the UN Security Council. As details of the attacks fully emerged, Roberto publicly condemned the violence before returning to Léopoldville.[11] Still, he managed to secure some support from Washington, allegedly after a meeting with Attorney General Robert Kennedy. In April, the CIA put Roberto on an annual retainer of $6,000, which was subsequently raised to $10,000. Nonetheless, the State Department insisted the agency make sure such payments were made under deep cover to avoid alienating Salazar.[12]

The Angolan uprising and Salazar's brutal response drove home the importance of a coordinated response. In April, leaders of the Lusophone nationalist movements gathered in Casablanca, Morocco, to establish a new umbrella organization, the Conference of Nationalist Organizations of the Portuguese Colonies (CONCP; Conferência das Organizações Nacionalistas das Colónias Portuguesas). Its organizers—Amílcar Cabral, Mário de Andrade, and Marcelino dos Santos—envisioned that the new organization would raise the international profiles of the MPLA and the PAIGC and allow them to capture the leadership of the nationalist movement. For the MPLA, the meeting also presented an opportunity to accomplish their long-sought-after objective of establishing a common front with the UPA. However, Holden Roberto continued to deny any association with them and refused to attend the Casablanca meeting.[13] On June 9, 1961, the MPLA released a statement that retroactively proclaimed February 4 as the beginning of the armed struggle in Angola and publicly appealed for international support.[14]

The first country to provide an assistance package to the MPLA was Czechoslovakia. Starting in the 1950s, Czechoslovakia had been pursuing an active policy in the Third World. One of the most industrialized states in Eastern Europe, Czechoslovakia boasted an advanced arms manufacturing industry that had been famous since the interwar period. It also maintained a network of commercial and diplomatic contacts with many countries in Africa, Asia, and Latin America. The communist takeover in 1948 saw a temporary decline in Czechoslovak commercial and diplomatic engagement with Africa, Asia, and Latin America, but the 1955 Czechoslovak-Egyptian arms deal once again put Prague on the map as the "go-to" capital for Third World leaders looking for arms. Thus, the Czechoslovak leadership wanted to profit from arms sales, but also to gain prestige among members of the Warsaw Pact.[15]

These considerations often matched the personal ambitions of the top leadership. The first secretary of the Central Committee of the Communist Party of Czechoslovakia (CC CPC), Antonín Novotný, was an unpopular figure in the party, and he staked his claim to leadership on his close collaboration with

The photo shows African villagers in Northern Angola lining up before a contingent of Portuguese troops. Although Portuguese propaganda claimed the colonial forces provided security for the local population, in reality the army often engaged in punitive sweeps of African villages, trying to weed out so-called "terrorists." More than half of the Portuguese colonial army consisted of African troops, mainly rank-and-file soldiers under direction of European officers. Bettmann/Getty.

Moscow. His immediate rival was Rudolf Barák, the minister of the interior, who oversaw the Czechoslovak state security (StB, *Státní Bezpečnost*) and its foreign intelligence branch, the First (intelligence) Directorate.[16] A rising star in the party, Barák expanded the activities of the First Directorate in the Third World and often supported requests for assistance as a way to forge new clandestine contacts with revolutionary movements.[17]

In January 1961, the MPLA's Viriato da Cruz and Matias Miguéis arrived to Prague to discuss their requirements for scholarships, placements for military training, financial aid, and weapons. In conversations with Czechoslovak officials, Viriato da Cruz emphasized the MPLA aspired to establish a common front of all the Angolan movements. The only impediment, argued Cruz, was the UPA, which was "founded and supported by the United States." Cruz stated he did not believe in nonviolent liberation of Angola, but argued that the situation was not "not ripe for armed struggle at the moment."[18] The statement seems somewhat ironic in hindsight, since it was made on the eve of events in

Luanda, confirming the MPLA did not have any immediate plans to launch armed struggle.

The Angolan uprising probably accelerated the timetable on Prague's decision to approve the MPLA's requests. On April 18, 1961, CC CPC granted the MPLA a monthly allowance of 3,000 Czech crowns koruna (Kč), allocated twenty annual university scholarships, and twenty placements for military training in Czechoslovakia. Prague also agreed to discuss the possible delivery of arms with their Soviet colleagues. The overall assistance for the MPLA in 1961 amounted to 965,000 Kč.[19] In support of the decision, the CC CPC argued that the MPLA's leadership had substantive knowledge of Marxism-Leninism and envisioned the construction of a "socialist-style society." However, if the MPLA did not obtain assistance, it would be outdone by the "reactionary" UPA, which received support from the USA.[20] Ideology clearly mattered for the CPC leadership who emphasized ideational affinity with the MPLA and internalized Cruz's politically charged Cold War identification of the UPA as essentially a foreign, U.S.-sponsored organization.

In comparison to Czechoslovakia, the Soviets were initially slow to respond to events in Angola. The Soviet Union supported all the UN resolutions condemning Portugal's action in the colonies, but did not actively engage with nationalist activists until May, when the Soviet Solidarity Committee offered to commandeer one of their staff, Valentin Ivanov, for a three-week reconnaissance trip to Morocco, Ghana, and Guinea. The International Department supported the initiative and petitioned the CC CPSU to authorize the trip so that Ivanov could obtain more information about the situation in the Portuguese colonies, especially in Angola.[21]

Around the same time, the Soviet ambassador to China sought contact with Pascoal Luvualu, the Angolan trade union organization leader affiliated with the MPLA, and invited him for talks in the Soviet Union. In Moscow on June 8, the Soviet Solidarity Committee informed Luvualu that they could offer "money, medicines, and food" to the MPLA in Conakry. They also considered supplying weapons but asked him to explore ways to transfer arms to Angola—perhaps using African troops stationed in Léopoldville who were there under the auspices of the UN peacekeeping mission in Zaire. Luvualu then wrote to Viriato da Cruz, informing him of the conversation and advising him to get in touch with the Soviet Solidarity Committee.[22]

These developments indicated that Moscow was stepping up its support for the Angolan nationalists. On May 27, the Soviet daily *Pravda* published a strongly worded statement on its front page, "The Situation in Angola: The

Declaration of the Soviet Government," which outlined crimes committed by the Portuguese army in Angola and declared that the Soviet Union "will not remain indifferent to Angola's fate."[23] In a meeting with Kennedy in Vienna on June 3, 1961, Khrushchev mirrored the mood of the declaration. He challenged Kennedy on U.S. policy in Angola, Algeria, and the Congo, and reaffirmed Soviet support for the "national wars of liberation," which he defined as a "sacred war."[24] Besides, the Soviets also buffed up the fairly new Africa desk at the International Department by appointing Petr Evsiukov as the desk officer responsible for Portuguese colonies. As one of only few cadres in the party apparatus who could speak fluent Portuguese, Evsiukov would become a regular participant in meetings with lusophone anticolonial activists from the Portuguese colonies.

Once the Berlin Crisis erupted over the summer, the KGB and the Czechoslovak StB worked out the first set of measures that would guide their policy on Angola. The first reference to a strategy on Angola comes from a lengthy document—the outcome of a joint high-level coordination meeting chaired by Rudolf Barák and KGB chairman Aleksandr Shelepin in Prague on June 26–30, 1961. Among the myriad proposals against the "main enemy—the United States and its allies," the KGB and the StB agreed to recruit "progressive agents" among the leaders of the liberation movements. They also drafted joint action plans on Zaire, India, Indonesia, and Egypt. As for Angola, Moscow and Prague pledged to support a publicity campaign to draw attention to Portuguese colonialism, identify "progressive forces," and assist them in creating a common anticolonial front.[25]

The StB's First Directorate pretty quickly proceeded to implement the plan. In Guinea, the task of developing contacts with representatives of the African liberation movements fell to a young and ambitious StB intelligence officer named Miroslav Adámek (codenamed "Alter"). He arrived in Conakry in 1960 and forged contacts with leaders of the African liberation movements based there, including with Amílcar Cabral and Viriato da Cruz. In late June 1961, Adámek proposed recruiting Cabral and Viriato da Cruz to collaborate with the StB. In his pitch to Barák, Adámek argued he had already developed a very close relationship with those African leaders and that they had already shared information on a range of topics.[26]

Prague quickly approved Adámek's proposal, which is unsurprising given the KGB-StB plan to recruit "progressive agents" among the liberation movements. On July 14, 1961, Adámek met Viriato da Cruz at his house in Conakry and proceeded to talk about Czechoslovak assistance for the MPLA, pointing out that their goals were the same and that both sides would benefit from closer cooperation. As Adámek reported to Prague, Cruz agreed that they shared the same goal—"fighting imperialism in Africa"—and promised to use his position as the MPLA's secretary general to share information. The two even agreed on a way to communicate in secret. From then on, the StB would refer to Viriato da Cruz by the new code name, "Kříž" (Cross). He would be classified as their "confidential contact" (*důvěrný styk* or "D.S." in Czech).[27]

The Soviet-Czechoslovak plan for Angola was thus in the making by the time Viriato da Cruz and Mário de Andrade arrived in Moscow for talks in late July 1961. The details of their trip to the Soviet Union are scant. In a series of meetings with the cadre from the Soviet Solidarity Committee, Petr Evsiukov at the International Department, and CC CPSU Secretary Nuritdin Mukhitdinov, the Angolans discussed the prospects for armed struggle and their disagreements with the UPA. They also asked for financial assistance, humanitarian aid for Angolan refugees, training for party cadres in the USSR, and arms. The Soviets at least partially fulfilled these requests, as they allocated yearly financial assistance to the MPLA, starting with $25,000 in 1961 and 1962. They also began delivering medicine and other humanitarian aid and allocated scholarships for party cadres.[28] There is no evidence to suggest that the Soviets agreed to supply arms or if any promises about the subject were made. The MPLA was still based in Conakry, unable to move to Léopoldville because of the crisis in Zaire, so questions of logistics must have taken center stage.

There is both indirect and direct evidence to suggest that the Berlin Crisis hastened the intensification of support for African nationalist movements. First, the timing—the Soviets stepped up their efforts to support the Angolan nationalist movement only toward the end of May and in particular after Khrushchev's June meeting with Kennedy in Vienna. The other piece of evidence is more direct. Specifically, as Vladislav Zubok has discovered, on July 29, the KGB chief Shelepin sent Khrushchev a "mind-boggling set of proposals" for intelligence action in various parts of the world aimed at distracting the United States during the settlement of the Berlin Crisis. These proposals included measures to "help organize mass anticolonial uprisings" in Kenya, Northern and Southern Rhodesia, and Guinea-Bissau by arming rebels and training military cadres. On August 1, the CC CPSU approved the measures.[29] Shelepin's proposals seem as ambitious as the joint KGB-StB coordination plan from July and likely were part of the same strategy. Surely, the Angolan uprising was a crucial factor motivating the Soviets to act, but the Cold War context also played an important role in accelerating attempts to develop a plan for Angola.

Amílcar Cabral and Czechoslovakia:
The Birth of D.S. "Sekretář"

When the Angolan uprising took place, Amílcar Cabral was still establishing the PAIGC's primacy in Conakry, Guinea. That was no easy task because he faced substantial local competition. There had always been considerable cross-border movement in Guinea-Bissau, with men and women leaving for neighboring Senegal and Guinea to seek job opportunities, escape forced labor, or avoid political persecution. By the time Cabral arrived in Conakry in 1960, several nationalist organizations had already started recruiting members among the immigrant community. One such Conakry-based organization was led by Luiz da Silva and Belarmino Gomes. There were also a number of nationalist organizations based in Dakar, the capital of Senegal. One of them, the Movement for the Liberation of Guinea (MLG; Movimento de Libertação da Guiné), managed to find support among the Manjako ethnic group in northern Guinea-Bissau and gained backing from the Senegalese authorities. Most of these organizations opposed Cabral's binationalist vision and advocated independence for Guinea-Bissau alone.[30]

Cabral used a variety of tactics to counter his local opposition. Settled in Conakry, he organized a leadership election, mobilizing Balante émigrés from Guinea-Bissau in support.[31] When Cabral learned that the Soviet embassy in Conakry maintained contacts with Luiz da Silva and Belarmino Gomes, he complained to Valentin Ivanov at the Soviet Solidarity Committee in Moscow, arguing the men had been excluded from the movement "by the masses" and had escaped Conakry.[32] The Soviet Solidarity Committee wrote back, confirming that they had formed a similar view of Belarmino Gomes during his "one-day stay" in Moscow.[33] In Conakry, Cabral also met Miroslav Adámek who supported his request to visit Prague.[34]

In March, Cabral went to the Soviet Union, followed by a visit to Czechoslovakia. It was not Cabral's first trip to the Soviet Union—one year earlier, he traveled to Moscow on his way to China with a group of recruits from Guinea-Bissau and Cape Verde.[35] In March 1961, however, he stayed longer, visiting Moscow and Leningrad by invitation of the Soviet Solidarity Committee. Cabral positively impressed his hosts, as he was "highly critical" of U.S. policies on Africa, criticized the concept of "African socialism" on the grounds that there was only "scientific socialism," and marveled at Soviet achievements.[36] However, it is unclear whether assistance to the PAIGC was discussed seriously during the trip, and there is no evidence that the Soviets offered any support for the PAIGC at that point. Most likely, Guinea-Bissau was not a priority for the Soviet leadership.

Cabral's trip to Czechoslovakia with his right-hand man Aristides Pereira was much more fruitful. In Prague, Cabral was received by several high-ranking officials. One of them was the Czechoslovak Deputy Interior Minister Karel Klima, whom Cabral and Pereira asked for weapons, financial assistance, experts who could provide security training, and instructors in "subversive activities."[37] Another was allegedly Rudolf Barák, the interior minister. As Pereira recalled much later, Barák was impressed with Cabral and promised to deliver arms if they received the go-ahead from Guinea—the host country for the PAIGC.[38] Although there is no record of Cabral's meeting with Barák, the StB indeed supported Cabral's requests on the grounds that the PAIGC was an "anti-imperialist and an anticapitalist organization," led by a "Marxist-oriented" politician.[39]

The timing also worked in Cabral's favor. Over the summer, the Soviets stepped up their rhetoric condemning Portuguese colonialism and offered assistance to the MPLA. In July, the KGB and the StB worked out a plan for Angola, and the StB proceeded with "recruitment" of MPLA's Viriato da Cruz. It is thus unsurprising that on August 1, the Politburo of the Czechoslovak Communist Party approved an assistance package to the PAIGC: monthly assistance worth 2,500 Czech crowns and a shipment of light weapons for 500 guerrillas. The Ministry of the Interior also pledged to organize a six-month course for a dozen recruits. In total, the package added up to 1,210,000 Czech crowns.[40] Prague also approved Adámek's proposal to "recruit" Cabral for collaborate with the StB.

Adámek's "recruitment" meeting with Cabral on August 13, 1961 was similar to the one with Viriato da Cruz a month earlier. Adámek informed Cabral that Prague had just approved his request for assistance to the PAIGC and then proceeded to talk about their aligned goals, which entailed "fighting imperialism and colonialism." He also asked Cabral to share information about people and the political situation throughout Africa. According to Adámek's report to the StB, Cabral promised to help, but also warned that his options were limited since he was often critical of the Guinean authorities. Although Cabral was noncommittal, Adámek presented the recruitment as a win for the StB. In the same way as Viriato da Cruz, the StB classified Cabral as their "confidential contact" and assigned a code name, "Sekretář" (Secretary).[41]

While Adámek presented the meeting as a professional success, Cabral's "recruitment" was a bit more ambiguous than the case of Viriato da Cruz since it is not clear whether Adámek broke his diplomatic cover or if any papers were signed. The category "confidential contact" was flexible enough to allow no formal commitment on either side, and Cabral never became an "agent." In the following years, the StB would try to employ "Sekretář" for various tasks, yet

Cabral managed to shape the relationship to further his interests without compromising his integrity.[42] In fact, as we will see, Czechoslovak support for the PAIGC would be more substantial and more durable than that for the MPLA.

Julius Nyerere, Eduardo Mondlane, and the Foundation of FRELIMO

Meanwhile, political activity was on the rise among Mozambican migrants in East Africa. The Makonde of northern Mozambique were particularly important in the history of the nationalist movement. In the 1950s, many Mozambican Makonde emigrated to neighboring countries in British East Africa—Tanganyika, Zanzibar, and Kenya—to work on sisal plantations and escape the forced labor still in place in Portuguese Africa. In the 1950s, a number of Makonde associations appeared in Tanganyika, including in Dar es Salaam, the capital, and Tanga. The Dar es Salaam association consisted of a small group of politicized Makonde who spoke English and knew very little Portuguese. In the 1950s, many joined Tanganyika's African National Union (TANU), a nationalist front campaigning for the independence of Tanganyika, a territory held under British trusteeship. In March 1960, TANU supported the transformation of the Dar es Salaam group into the Mozambique Africa National Union (MANU), with the 25-year-old Tanganyika-born Makonde Matthew Mmole as president.[43]

The events leading up to what is known in the Mozambican nationalist historiography as the "Mueda massacre" started with a grievance rooted in the rural Makonde community. In 1960, the Tanga association petitioned the Portuguese administration at Mueda, northern Mozambique, for permission to return to their home country. That was the subject of a meeting on June 16, 1960, as crowds gathered at the office of the local authorities in Mueda. However, the meeting quickly degenerated into violence when the police opened fire after people reacted angrily to the arrogant speech of the governor, who announced that their leaders had been arrested. While the interpretation of the event—including the number of victims—has since been substantially revised in recent years, police brutality politicized the Makonde and reaffirmed their belief in the need for armed struggle in Mozambique. One consequence was that many Makonde joined yet another nationalist grouping—the National Democratic Union of Mozambique (UDENAMO; União Democrática Nacional de Moçambique).[44]

While MANU was rooted in Dar es Salaam, UDENAMO started as an association of Mozambican migrants in Southern Rhodesia (later renamed

Zimbabwe). The organization quickly managed to attract members from several regions, including Portuguese-speaking Makonde. One of its founders was 22-year-old Adelino Gwambe, a former employee of the south Rhodesian railways from Inhambane in southern Mozambique. In April 1961, Gwambe and MANU's president Matthew Mmole represented the Mozambican liberation movement at the CONCP meetings in Casablanca. Upon returning to Dar es Salaam, Gwambe used his new international connections to start building up UDENAMO. In July 1961, Gwambe publicly announced to the press in Dar es Salaam that he stood for immediate armed struggle. As the claim was too radical for the local authorities, he was expelled from Tanganyika and moved to Ghana with support from President Kwame Nkrumah.[45] From Ghana, Gwambe continued harnessing international support.

In September, Gwambe visited the Soviet Union. In his memoirs, Petr Evsiukov wrote that Gwambe did not impress him. Evsiukov disapproved of Gwambe's general behavior, noting that he "marveled at the swords and maces" on display at Moscow's Armory Museum and refused to eat anything except the Russian type of sour yogurt, called *kefir*, in memory of his "hungry comrades." Evsiukov noted he and his colleagues were also suspicious of Gwambe's travels to the United States, describing him as a "petty political adventurer, whose main goal was to misinform us and receive more money."[46] However, it is difficult to say whether the Soviets were as critical back then. In fact, the International Department allocated $3,000 for UDENAMO in 1961.[47] The role played by Marcelino dos Santos, who joined UDENAMO and moved to Dar es Salaam after Gwambe was expelled in 1961, might have been the reason for the allocation of funds.

UDENAMO's main rival, the Dar-es-Salaam-based MANU, also appealed to the Soviets for assistance. In February 1962, MANU's chairman, Matthew Mmole, and its secretary-general Lawrence Millinga, approached the Soviet ambassador in Ethiopia, asking for financial assistance and scholarships. In their pitch, they claimed that MANU had already developed a considerable following inside Mozambique and enjoyed support from TANU. Mmole and Millinga also claimed that Gwambe's UDENAMO was a movement of "assimilated" (*assimilado*) Mozambicans who had, in fact, made a secret deal with the Portuguese.[48] As indicative from the meeting, various Mozambican organizations started to compete in the wake of the Angolan uprising, which did not bode well for the unity of the nationalist project. In June 1962, representatives from a number of Mozambican nationalist organizations gathered in Dar es Salaam to discuss unification in a common front under the auspices of TANU's leader and the first president of Tanganyika, Julius Nyerere.

Nyerere's role would be critical for the future of the Mozambican nationalist movement. Alongside many African leaders of his generation, Nyerere believed that liberation would not be complete until all of Africa was free. Since the 1950s, Nyerere had expressed staunch opposition to South Africa's apartheid and was among the founders of the Britain-based Anti-Apartheid Movement. After Tanganyika gained independence on December 9, 1961, Nyerere allowed exiled liberation movements from the Portuguese colonies, South West Africa (Namibia), and South Africa to establish their offices and training camps in the country. However, Nyerere did not approve of Gwambe's militant rhetoric, which was one reason why he was expelled from Dar es Salaam in July 1961. He was also concerned about the support that Gwambe received from Kwame Nkrumah, Nyerere's rival.[49] The candidate whom Nyerere favored for the leadership of the Mozambican nationalist movement was the U.S.-educated Mozambican Eduardo Chivambe Mondlane.

Mondlane certainly had the proper credentials for the job. Born on June 20, 1920, he was the son of a Tsonga chief from Gaza province in southern Mozambique. Educated by Swiss missionaries, he moved to Johannesburg to study at the University of Witwatersrand. In South Africa, he became involved in political campaigning, for which he was expelled from the country. Back in Mozambique's capital, Lourenço Marques (later renamed Maputo), he cofounded the association for Black students in Mozambique (NESAM; Núcleo dos Estudantes Africanos Secundários de Moçambique), which spoke out against Portugal's racist policies. He then continued his education, first, briefly, in Lisbon, before moving to the United States to study sociology and anthropology at Oberlin, Northwestern, and Harvard. While living there, he married Janet Rae Johnson, a white woman from Indiana.

In 1957, Mondlane started work as a research officer at the Trusteeship Department of the United Nations, where he met Nyerere. In 1961, he embarked on a tour of Mozambique, campaigning for reform. Back in the United States, he established contacts with the Kennedy administration, urging them to put pressure on Salazar.[50] Nyerere later claimed he was the one who urged Mondlane to come to Dar es Salaam and participate in liberating his country.[51] With the support of the Tanganyikan authorities, on June 25, 1962, Mondlane became the first president of the newly founded common front—the Mozambican Liberation Front (FRELIMO; Frente de Libertação de Moçambique).

Fundamentally, FRELIMO represented an alliance between UDENAMO and MANU.[52] UDENAMO's Uria Simango was appointed as vice president, Marcelino dos Santos became the secretary for foreign affairs, while MANU's Matthew Mmole became treasurer and David Mabunda the general secretary.

According to a nationalist narrative, FRELIMO represented a genuine union of ethno-nationalist organizations rooted in distinct communities of Mozambican émigrés. As Michel Cahen has argued though, the FRELIMO base was made up of the Makonde-based UDENAMO, which had already become a "pluriethnic organization with a modernist program" by 1962.[53]

Mondlane's election as president proved immediately controversial. In July 1962, David Mabunda, Fanuel Mahluza, and Matthew Mmole came to Moscow to participate in the International Congress for Peace and Disarmament. Only one month after the formation of FRELIMO, they expressed concern about Mondlane's election. Mabunda questioned Mondlane's "political affiliation" and declared that UDENAMO could withdraw from the union at any time.[54] Mmole asked for military training, scholarships, and financial assistance but refused to answer if he represented FRELIMO or MANU.[55] In August, Adelino Gwambe accused Mondlane of being a U.S. agent and officially withdrew UDENAMO from the front.

The Soviet reaction to Mondlane's election is difficult to establish. In his memoirs, Evsiukov recalled that Mondlane impressed him during his first visit to the USSR in early 1962 as someone who was well educated and knew the situation in his country well. He was also not in a hurry to begin an armed struggle, a decision that the Soviets understood.[56] Nonetheless, as the next chapter explains, the Soviets were actually very suspicious of Mondlane's connections with the Kennedy administration and often sided with his critics.

"The Great Escape": Student Activists Flee Portugal

The Angolan uprising brought home the urgency of establishing a political and military organization in Africa. While the most high-profile anticolonial nationalists had already left Portugal by 1961, many remained in the country and continued to engage in underground activism. However, staying in Portugal became too dangerous, since the authorities increased their surveillance of African students and ramped up their recruitment drive for the colonial army. The Portuguese had always used African troops to provide security, which usually accounted for 50–75 percent of its colonial armies. By 1960, out of 8,000 troops in Angola, 5,000 were African.[57] In the aftermath of the Angolan uprising, African student activists feared they could be arrested or drafted into the Portuguese army. Many also believed that they could best serve the anticolonial cause by joining the nationalist movements rather than continuing with underground activism in Portugal.

Therefore in 1961, many African activists in Portugal decided to flee and join the struggle from new bases in Guinea, Léopoldville and Dar es Salaam. A number of African students got in touch with the World Council of Churches in Geneva who connected them to the CIMADE, a French ecumenical organization that had smuggled Jewish children out of occupied Europe during World War II. CIMADE developed a daring escape plan, which involved driving several groups of students to Porto, northern Portugal, before using boats to smuggle them to the border and across the Minho River to Spanish territory. After they reached Spain, a group of young Americans drove them across the country to France. Overall, fifty-eight people escaped Portugal in the first group.[58]

One of the escapees was Amélia Araújo from Luanda, who had moved to Portugal in the late 1950s to join future husband José, who was involved in nationalist activism. In 1961, Amélia fled Portugal with her three-month-old daughter Teresa. José was to follow shortly afterward via a different route. However, when reaching France, she heard that her husband was among the group of escapees who had been arrested and imprisoned in Spain. Then, they were suddenly released, allegedly on orders from Madrid, for reasons that are still not entirely clear. Amélia remembered that the next time she saw her husband, his hair had turned white: "Why is your hair white?" she asked. "Can you imagine what would have happened to you if they had sent us back to Portugal?" he replied.[59] After staying in France for several months, the group left for Accra, Ghana.

Those students who escaped Portugal became the core of the Western-educated, cosmopolitan elite who would take over critical functions in the administration of the anticolonial movements. The Araújos joined the PAIGC at their headquarters in Conakry, where José worked closely with Cabral. Cape Verdeans Maria da Luz "Lilica" Boal and Pedro Pires were dispatched to Senegal to recruit among the Cape Verdean community. Lilica Boal would become the director of the PAIGC's Escola-Piloto, an experimental school established in Conakry to educate the future national elite. The Mozambican Joaquim Chissano continued his studies in France before joining FRELIMO's leadership in Dar es Salaam. The Angolan Henrique "Iko" Carreira became a member of the MPLA's first executive committee, responsible for security, after undergoing training in Czechoslovakia. Many of the cadres trained in Portugal continued their education in the Soviet Union and other socialist countries.

Training and educating recruits became a central component of the Soviet and Eastern European support programs for the MPLA, FRELIMO and PAIGC. In the 1950s, the Soviets increased the number of scholarships available for African students in the battle for the "hearts and minds" of Third World elites. In 1960, the CC CPSU opened the Peoples' Friendship University (later known as Patrice Lumumba University), specifically to cater to students from Asia, Africa, and Latin America. Although the Soviets did not expect that Third World students would necessarily turn into communists during their studies, they hoped that those students would appreciate the benefits of socialist modernity and, most importantly, return to their home countries as "sincere friends" of the USSR.[60]

The MPLA, FRELIMO, and PAIGC also used scholarships to reward loyal followers. The majority of the recipients trained at professional technical colleges while the elite cadres studied at universities. In 1962, Mário de Andrade's wife, Sara Ducados, received a scholarship to study at the prestigious All-Union Institute of Cinematography in Moscow. Cabral's brother Fernando studied medicine at Lumumba University in Moscow. Amélia Araújo went to study radio broadcasting in the USSR before returning to lead Rádio Libertação (Liberation Radio) in Conakry. The children of the party leadership, including Cabral's daughter Iva and Araújo's daughter Teresa, were sent to "Interdom," the boarding school for the children of elite foreign communists in Ivanovo near Moscow.[61] However, as discussed in the next chapter, the reality of students' daily lives often undermined the Soviet educational program. As a result, internal conflicts and schisms within the movement frequently played out among students in the USSR.

Conclusion

The Angolan uprising was a significant catalyst for the Portuguese colonies' entry into the Cold War. The events in Angola offered significant opportunities for both Moscow and Washington, but the international environment shaped their actions in very different ways. While the Berlin Crisis limited the effectiveness of Kennedy's anticolonial policy, rising Cold War tensions encouraged the Soviets to formulate a strategy on Portuguese Africa. The timing of the Berlin Crisis helps explains why Soviet decision-making on Angola accelerated over the summer, which resulted in the first assistance package for the MPLA. The story shows that the Soviet response to events in Angola was initially slow, and the initiative came from middle-ranking cadres in the Soviet bureaucracy, the *mezhdunarodniki*. In due course, men like Petr Evsiukov would emerge as an increasingly important liaisons for day-to-day relations with African revolutionaries.

The involvement of the intelligence services with the liberation movements is not surprising. As discussed in chapter 1, the Zaire crisis demonstrated that the

Soviets lacked the hard power to compete with the established European powers in Africa. After that, secret intelligence became a way to fight the Cold War "on the cheap." The KGB and the StB played an important role in devising a plan for Angola in 1961. The clandestine relationship that the StB developed with Viriato da Cruz and Amílcar Cabral also helps explain the reasons behind Czechoslovak support for the MPLA and PAIGC. From the perspective of Czechoslovakia, a country with limited resources, these secret contacts offered a good opportunity to influence the Cold War in Africa to Prague's advantage. As the following chapters show, the intelligence officers would play key roles as liaisons with the African anticolonial intellectuals, trying to establish the dominance of their allies over the nationalist movement.

While Cold War considerations certainly mattered, the choice of partners was closely tied to ideological considerations. By 1961, Viriato da Cruz, Mário de Andrade, and Marcelino dos Santos were already known to the Soviets as African intellectuals influenced by Marxism. A sense of ideological affinity mattered to the Soviets and Czechoslovaks, who saw the world in terms of class struggle. The Soviets and the Czechoslovaks explicitly underlined Cabral's criticism of "African socialism" and praised him for what they described as his preference for "scientific socialism." However, these ideological interpretations were not rigid, and they could be reconsidered based on shifting realities.

Overall, support from the socialist countries in 1961 was fairly limited. By the end of the year, the brutal suppression of the Angolan uprising showed that Salazar would not give up the empire without a fight. The nationalist movements would have to organize in exile, mobilize and train recruits, and supply them with weapons if they wanted to launch an armed struggle. They would thus need to find additional assistance from international donors, while maintaining support from their African host states and overcoming internal rivalries. As we will see, these tasks were often closely interlinked. The next chapter addresses how our key protagonists used diplomacy to establish dominance over the nationalist movements in Angola, Mozambique, and Guinea-Bissau.

CHAPTER FOUR

Diplomacy of Liberation

Exile Politics, International Alliances, and
Maoism in Africa, 1961–1964

FTER CRUSHING THE Angolan uprising in 1961, Salazar announced a series of reforms. Lisbon granted colonial subjects equal rights, abolished labor requirements, attempted to improve essential services, and opened up the colonies to foreign direct investment. While the colonial elites welcomed these reforms, the measures were piecemeal at best, and there was no discussion of self-determination. In the 1960s, Lisbon rapidly expanded the size of the colonial armies, including the share of European troops, at an estimated cost of $120 million a year.[1] By 1974, there would be 70,000 troops in Angola, 43,000 in Guinea-Bissau and 60,000 in Mozambique.[2]

In December 1961, India seized the momentum occasioned by events in Angola and invaded the Portuguese-controlled Goa. Salazar ordered the vastly outnumbered contingent of Portuguese troops in Goa to resist at all costs and court-martialed the officers who (sensibly) surrendered without much resistance. Although Salazar had to accept the loss of Goa, his treatment of the officers was a clear sign that he was comfortable in sacrificing human lives and resources to defend the empire.[3]

The international environment helped Salazar. Although Kennedy had tried to put pressure on him in the aftermath of the Angolan uprising, the Cuban Missile Crisis in 1962 once again raised the importance of continued access to the Lajes military base in the Portuguese-controlled Azores. On November 22, 1963, Kennedy was assassinated in Dallas. His successor, Lyndon Johnson, initially continued his predecessor's balancing act but eventually normalized relations with Portugal.[4] Lisbon also acquired modern military equipment from France and West Germany to fight its colonial wars.[5]

The discussion that follows explores the diplomacy of the key protagonists of this story—Agostinho Neto, Amílcar Cabral, Eduardo Mondlane, and Marcelino dos Santos—as they sought to mobilize recruits and resources for guerrilla campaigns from African "hubs of decolonization," such as Accra, Cairo, Conakry, and Dar es Salaam.[6] As explored in chapters 2 and 3, by 1962, the ability to wage armed struggle became fundamental to establishing a claim to leadership of the nationalist movement. On May 25, 1963, thirty-two African leaders founded the Organization of African Unity (OAU) as a forum for collective action on the continent. The OAU confirmed that violent struggle would follow if a colonial power was unwilling to accept self-determination, and the organization established the Liberation Committee in Dar es Salaam to fund nationalist movements.[7] However, the process of obtaining international support often proved problematic for the MPLA, PAIGC, and FRELIMO.

The key challenge that all three organizations faced was internal. In 1961–64, the MPLA, the PAIGC, and FRELIMO all confronted internal critics and local rivals that, for the most part, formulated alternative visions of anti-imperialism based on race and ethnicity. After Agostinho Neto joined the MPLA in Léopoldville in 1962, he clashed with Viriato da Cruz and others, who argued against the preponderance of *mestiços* (men and women of multiracial heritage) in leadership positions. In Conakry, Cabral faced challenges from local rivals who opposed his binationalist project and criticized the role of Cape Verdeans in the PAIGC. As the newly elected president of FRELIMO, Mondlane had to answer to charges that Mozambican "southerners" like himself occupied key posts in the organization. What made things even more complicated was that the internal dynamics of liberation movements in exile was closely connected to the politics of their African host states that frequently maintained relationships with competing nationalist organizations.

China's growing competition with the Soviet Union further complicated the internal dynamics of the liberation movements. As Sino-Soviet disagreements burst into the open in the early 1960s, Beijing started to aggressively promote its model of a peasant-based, popular revolution that emphasized race and nation over class—in direct opposition to the Soviet model. Sino-Soviet wrangling started to dominate the proceedings of major Afro-Asian forums, such as the Afro-Asian People's Solidarity Organization (AAPSO). China's ideas on race deepened factionalist struggles within liberation movements since critics often used Mao Zedong's ideas to bolster their claims and often found an ally in Beijing. The conflicts over race and privilege coincided with discussions of political strategy, thus complicating relationships with international patrons and African hosts. While Cabral and Mondlane managed to secure their positions in Guinea and Tanzania, respectively, by 1964, the MPLA under Agostinho Neto was evicted from Zaire.

This chapter shows how the dynamics of local and international patronage were closely interlinked, with our key protagonists using international support to solidify their position in host states and vice versa. It also demonstrates that the politics of African host states often shaped Soviet policy toward Lusophone liberation movements in the context of the Cold War and Sino-Soviet competition. Based on their 1961 plan for Angola, the Soviets sought to establish a "common front" of all Angolan organizations, which would ensure continuous MPLA access to Zaire, a key "launching pad" for guerrilla action in the neighboring Angola. As the new documents reveal, a substantive part of the plan included the Soviet and Czechoslovak intelligence services infiltrating Holden Roberto's UPA in Zaire. In 1962, Moscow established a close relationship with Amílcar Cabral, but the provision of arms was delayed by the dynamics of its relationship with Guinea. The Soviet interest in FRELIMO picked up in 1964 after what the Soviets perceived to be revolutionary changes in East Africa, following a left-wing revolution in Zanzibar. The Soviets were still suspicious of Eduardo Mondlane, but they began to provide limited support due to advocacy from key individuals such as Marcelino dos Santos and the increased importance of Tanzania in the Cold War in Africa.

In an influential thesis, Jeremy Friedman has argued that Sino-Soviet competition in the Third World pushed Moscow to embrace militant, anti-imperialist struggles.[8] This chapter shows that competition with China was only one factor in an otherwise complex web of considerations for the Soviets, including the politics of African host states and personal relations they developed with anticolonial nationalists from the Portuguese colonies. As we will see, African revolutionaries played a fundamental role in sustaining the Soviet commitment to their struggles in the aftermath of the Angolan uprising.

Agostinho Neto, Viriato da Cruz, and the Crisis in the MPLA: Race, Ideology, and the Struggle for Zaire

The political fortunes of Angolan nationalists centered on the shifting political landscape in Zaire. In October 1961, the MPLA finally moved its headquarters from Conakry to Léopoldville (Kinshasa). There, they established a center to support Angolan refugees, set up a newspaper, and organized a recruitment drive. The move was highly significant for the MPLA since it opened up easy access to northern Angola. As Mário de Andrade recalled, the move was a small victory because Léopoldville was "Holden's fiefdom."[9] Indeed, Roberto had good relations with key politicians in the country, and the UPA had a strong presence

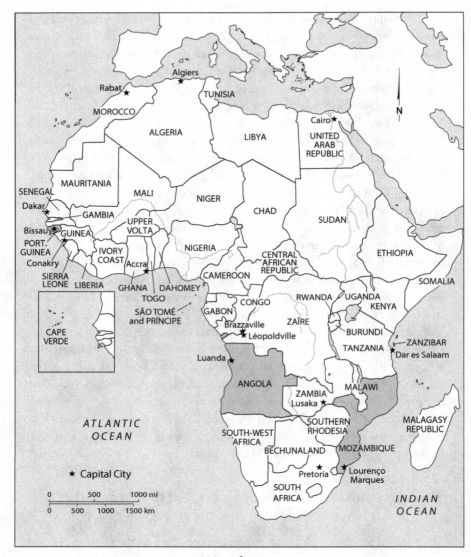

MAP 4.1. Africa in 1965

among the Bakongo émigré community in Zaire. The MPLA was keenly aware of the UPA's advantage and hoped to pursue a "common front" strategy to solidify their position in the country. As the MPLA's Lúcio Lara explained to East German representatives in September 1961, their goal was to establish a "common front" in order to draw the "progressive forces" within the UPA to their side and gradually isolate Holden Roberto, who was the "Americans' man."[10] The MPLA continued to use Cold War logic to "Americanize" Roberto, thus ensuring continued support from the socialist countries.

The task of securing a "common front" in Angola fell to Soviet and Czechoslovak intelligence officers stationed in Zaire. The Soviet embassy staff and the KGB *rezidentura* had been expelled from Zaire after the coup d'état that brought down Patrice Lumumba in September 1960. Then, the Soviets tried to transfer funds and weapons to Antoine Gizenga, who had fled to Stanleyville (Kisangani) following the coup in an attempt to challenge the new government in Léopoldville. By the summer, it became clear, though, that Gizenga's plan to restore power by military means had failed. The Soviets thus encouraged a power-sharing agreement between Lumumba loyalists like Gizenga and members of the conservative Binza group (a group of Mobutu's Congolese allies named for the prosperous suburb in Léopoldville where its members lived). On July 22–23, a new power-sharing agreement was negotiated at Lovanium University, 20 km from Léopoldville. According to the arrangements, several Lumumba followers entered the new government and Gizenga was elected deputy prime minister in absentia (he refused to attend). Still, members of the Binza group retained the most powerful positions, and a U.S-favored candidate, Cyrille Adoula, became the new prime minister. The Soviet Union recognized Adoula's government, which allowed the embassy and the *rezidentura* to return to Léopoldville in September 1961.[11]

One member of the KGB team who returned to Léopoldville in 1961 was Oleg Nazhestkin. A young Soviet intelligence officer in 1961, Nazhestkin first went to Léopoldville in August 1960. From the start, he was assigned to establish contacts with Angolan nationalists based in Zaire. His mission was cut short because of the coup in Léopoldville, only to be revived a year later. As Nazhestkin recalled in his memoirs, the KGB and the International Department wanted him specifically to target what he called "pro-Western" organizations like Holden Roberto's UPA to facilitate the establishment of a "common front."[12] Although the UPA was fundamentally an ethno-nationalist organization representing the aspirations of the Angolan Bakongo rather than being specifically "pro-Western," Nazhestkin clearly internalized the Cold War rhetoric employed by the MPLA against its local rivals.

The Soviet-Czechoslovak intelligence plan for Angola was quite elaborate, at least on paper. The centerpiece of the Czechoslovak strategy for Angola from January 1962 involved infiltrating Holden Roberto's UPA using various means. One option included training an MPLA cadre for this purpose. Another involved the StB's First Directorate working with its *rezidentura* in Brazil to send "one of their men" to join the UPA's military leadership under cover. The StB also pledged to continue supporting the MPLA. Such assistance included Operation codenamed JISKRA, in which, among other things, weapons would be shipped to the MPLA. Prague specified that they relied mainly on Viriato da Cruz—their "confidential contact" for regular communications and to "oversee" the activities of the MPLA's president Mário de Andrade.[13] The ultimate goal was to establish a common front between the MPLA and UPA, using clandestine means if necessary.

Meanwhile, Holden Roberto also made moves to claim leadership over the Angolan nationalist movement. In December 1961, the MPLA accused the UPA of capturing and executing a group of their men, who were on an exploratory mission to northern Angola, fueling fears that the competition was turning violent. Then, in March 1962, the UPA united with a number of Bakongo-based nationalist groups to form the National Front for the Liberation of Angola (FNLA; Frente Nacional de Libertação de Angola). Shortly afterward, Roberto announced the creation of an Algerian-inspired front, the Revolutionary Angolan Government in Exile (GRAE; Govêrno Revolucionário de Angola no Exílio). The formation of GRAE was a significant propaganda success and legitimized Roberto's leadership beyond his core Bakongo base. The MPLA was excluded from the front, showing that Roberto was unwilling to treat them as an equal partner.[14]

The MPLA's position in Zaire remained precarious. Members of the Binza group continued to dominate the government; and in early 1962, key MPLA ally Antoine Gizenga was detained and placed under house arrest. In conversations with Soviet interlocutors during his trip to Moscow in August 1962, Mário de Andrade complained that the Zairean authorities were harassing the MPLA because of pressure from the U.S. State Department.[15] In fact, the reasons for such an attitude toward the MPLA were internal. Roberto was an asset to the Binza group since they could rely on his men to intercept the Katangese gendarmes who had escaped to Angola after the fall of Moïse Tshombe's secessionist state. Adoula was friendly with Roberto (the two had played semi-professional football together before getting involved in politics) and permitted the FNLA to establish representation in Katanga. The Zairean authorities even assisted Roberto by allocating land for a military base at Kinkuzu, near Léopoldville, and helped to intercept the MPLA raids across the border into Angola.[16]

Then, on June 29, 1963, Adoula announced that his government would extend de jure recognition to GRAE as the only representative of the Angolan liberation movement. The decision was a significant blow to the MPLA because it meant the Zairean government would no longer provide safe haven for the organization. Shortly afterward, the OAU confirmed this decision, concluding that the MPLA had grown ineffective as an armed anticolonial movement because of an ongoing internal conflict.[17]

The OAU were not wrong—in 1963, the MPLA was in the midst of its first major crisis. In July 1962, Agostinho Neto arrived in Léopoldville after escaping prison with the support of the anti-Salazarist underground in Portugal.[18] His prestige and international credentials made Neto a natural candidate for the leadership position, and at the MPLA's first conference in December 1962, he was elected president. Neto then abolished the position of secretary-general, occupied by Viriato da Cruz, setting the two men on a collision course. Cruz left Léopoldville, but when he returned in 1963, he found the MPLA stripped of official recognition by the Zairean authorities. In response, he and a group of about fifty supporters dismissed the MPLA steering committee and declared their intent to join the FNLA. On July 7, the conflict culminated in a physical fight for control over the MPLA office in Léopoldville. After the incident, Cruz and his followers like Matias Miguéis were formally expelled from the MPLA and joined the FNLA. However, the alliance failed, and Cruz later moved to China to spend the rest of his days in exile.[19]

The root causes of the schism have been the subject of much speculation. On the surface, the crisis had all the features of a power struggle between Cruz and Neto. However, others have emphasized fundamental differences, which centered on issues of race, ideology, and the Cold War. Some have argued that Cruz, an avowed Marxist, had initially fallen victim to Neto's strategy of creating the image of a nonaligned MPLA. In October 1962, Neto had approached the U.S. embassy in Léopoldville, looking to establish contacts. He later went to the United States, seeking support.[20] Others have argued that at the center of the conflict lay disagreements over the hierarchical relationship between the Black rank-and-file membership and its predominantly *mestiço* leadership. Although himself a *mestiço*, Cruz argued that the MPLA had been overtaken by a multiracial leadership like Neto's right-hand man Lúcio Lara who had underestimated the importance of race, as opposed to class, in the struggle.[21]

Cruz's views on race might have been influenced by the ideas of Mao Zedong. He was inspired by the Chinese revolution after his trip to China in 1958 and often participated in Beijing-sponsored events. After his break with the MPLA in 1963, Cruz tried to discredit Neto by calling him "pro-Soviet" and started to echo Beijing's criticism of Moscow for prioritizing "peaceful coexistence" over anticolonial struggle.[22] While the Sino-Soviet split might have added to the intensity of these debates, the fundamental disagreement centered on a political strategy that mapped onto Cruz's views on race. According to Edmundo Rocha, who worked for the MPLA in Léopoldville, Cruz believed that the "main enemy" was colonialism rather than the FNLA or "American imperialism." He thus preferred compromise, opting to join the FNLA with a view to ultimately changing its "pro-American stance."[23]

Cruz was not the only one who disagreed with Neto's political strategy. Mário de Andrade initially supported Neto. However, when in 1963 Neto announced he would establish a "common front" with a number of small Bakongo nationalist organizations, Andrade was among many who opposed the decision, citing their dubious connections to the Portuguese authorities. He did not break with Neto, but moved away from the center of exile politics in Léopoldville, moving to work for the nationalist movements in Rabat, Morocco.[24] He remained part of the MPLA, but continued to be critical of Neto and his leadership style.

Although Cruz branded Neto as "pro-Soviet," the International Department did not necessarily back Neto in his struggle with Viriato da Cruz, at least not initially. Viriato da Cruz was well known to the Soviets, while Neto had spent the previous decade in and out of prison and was thus a relatively new figure. As Petr Evsiukov recalled in his memoirs, they viewed the schism between Cruz and Neto in highly negative terms: "The break-up of relations between these people caused a rather negative reaction among MPLA members and was beyond our understanding."[25]

One of Neto's regular Soviet contacts in Léopoldville was Oleg Nazhestkin. After returning to the Zairean capital in 1961, Nazhestkin acted as Neto's regular liaison in Léopoldville, handing over cash and relaying messages from Moscow. As Nazhestkin recalled in his memoirs, he had been intrigued by Neto since their first clandestine meeting in Léopoldville, in 1962. Neto seemed a gentle, intelligent, and kind man—an image that did not quite correspond to Nazhestkin's idea of a leader determined to wage an armed struggle. Nonetheless, he was impressed with his inquisitiveness and realism. Neto did not simply "blame Americans or imperialism" for everything, argued Nazhestkin, and did not insist that the whole population was already behind the MPLA. Nazhestkin liked that Neto had his "own philosophy," as well as integrity. He was also impressed by Neto's Portuguese wife, Maria Eugénia.[26]

His positive impression of Neto did not quite match with those of the International Department members, though. As Nazhestkin recalled, Moscow frequently instructed the KGB to investigate Neto's contacts in the United States, even if the International Department actually advised African leaders to find allies among U.S. officials who opposed Washington's policy on Portugal. Nazhestkin believed that his superiors in Moscow disliked Neto because of his independence and un-willingness to kowtow to Soviet demands.[27] Although the sources do not tell us exactly how and why Neto's relationship with the International Department soured, the schism in the MPLA might have contributed to this division.

Czechoslovakia was also critical of Neto during the schism. When the crisis unfolded in 1963, Prague continued to maintain relation with both Neto and Cruz, but cut all financial assistance to the organization. As a result, relations with Neto soured, and at some point, the MPLA leadership even suggested that it was Czechoslovakia who wanted to split the organization via its "informant"— Viriato da Cruz—and others. In an internal report from 1966, the StB insisted they had nothing to do with Cruz's decision to join the FNLA and that he had acted "independently." The StB also developed a clandestine relationship with the MPLA's Henrique "Iko" Carreira (codename "Konik") who first came to Czecho-slovakia for training in internal security in January 1963. However, Czechoslovak relationship with Neto never fully recovered after his break with Cruz.[28]

In November 1963, the Soviet presence in Léopoldville ended abruptly be-cause of the renewed political crisis in Zaire. The power-sharing agreement negotiated at Lovanium had been eroding for some time, and in late 1963, the followers of Patrice Lumumba crossed into neighboring Congo-Brazzaville to organize an armed uprising against the central government, known as the "Simba rebellion." As the Simba rebellion gathered strength in eastern Zaire, the Soviet embassy was once again expelled from Léopoldville. The crisis in re-lations was precipitated by a humiliating incident, which involved Joseph Mobu-tu's troops arresting and beating up a member of the Soviet embassy and chief of the KGB *rezidentura* in Léopoldville, Boris Voronin, as the pair returned from Brazzaville where they had met members of the opposition.[29] Having lost their foothold in Zaire for the second time in three years, the Soviets engaged in a last-ditch attempt to enact their plan for Angola. In a surprising twist, in late 1963, Holden Roberto approached the Soviets, seeking assistance.

Holden Roberto, Jonas Savimbi, and the Disintegration of the Soviet Plan for Angola, 1963–1964

As 1963 drew to a close, Holden Roberto grew increasingly impatient with the lack of support from Washington. Roberto had been pleading for increased assistance for his FNLA/GRAE since 1961. In the aftermath of the Cuban Missile Crisis in 1962, Roberto twice wrote personally to Kennedy, criticizing the U.S. voting record at the UN, the continued use of NATO weapons in Angola, and the lack of support for refugees in Zaire. Roberto warned that he did not want to publicly embarrass Washington, but he would not hesitate to turn to the socialist countries if such a policy continued.[30]

Kennedy's assassination removed the constraints on Roberto. In late 1963, he publicly attacked the United States for its policy in Angola and approached representatives of the Soviet Union and China, seeking support. In his conversations with Soviet representatives on December 4, 1963, Roberto admitted that his contacts with Moscow had so far been limited because he did not want to become a "second Lumumba" and feared losing access to Zaire. He also asked Moscow for arms and cash to buy weapons from the West.[31]

The Soviets were eager to engage with Roberto. On December 17, a group of Soviet officials met him at Nairobi's Ambassadeur Hotel. According to a report by secretary of the Soviet Solidarity Committee Dmitrii Dolidze, Roberto seemed "visibly worried and nervous" as he relayed his requests for weapons, medicine, and provisions for Angolan refugees. He also insisted that the FNLA controlled 75 percent of Angolan territory, that he was not "pro-American," and that he intended to go to China. Over the course of the conversation, however, it became clear that Roberto was not open to the idea of any common front with the MPLA in which the two organizations would be equals. Instead, he charged Neto with collaborating with the Portuguese secret police and the colonial administration. Although the Soviets were clearly concerned about Roberto's stance on the MPLA, they invited him to the Soviet Union.[32] For the moment, the Soviets adopted a wait-and-see approach, advising their allies to maintain relations with both the FNLA and the MPLA.[33]

In Washington, Roberto's challenge spurred the new president, Lyndon B. Johnson, to act. Johnson's administration recognized that Roberto's move was a pressure tactic designed to extract additional support from Washington. Therefore, in early 1964, the CIA, Attorney General Robert Kennedy, and the Africa Bureau of the State Department pushed to expand funding. The Zairean prime minister Cyrille Adoula also lobbied Washington on Roberto's behalf, claiming the FNLA was under threat from a "leftwing takeover."[34] Meanwhile in the State Department, George Ball opposed the initiative and instead argued Washington should engage with Portugal in order to proceed with a negotiated settlement in the colonies. On May 21, 1964, both sides reached a compromise solution: Washington approved political funding for the FNLA but withheld

military assistance.[35] In the meantime, opposition to Roberto's leadership crystallized around the figure of thirty-year-old Jonas Malheiro Savimbi.

Savimbi was very influential in the FNLA. Born in 1934 in Munhango, Eastern Angola, Savimbi belonged to the Ovimbundu, Angola's largest ethnic group.
He was educated in Protestant and Catholic mission schools before receiving
a scholarship to study medicine in Portugal. In Lisbon, he became involved in
nationalist politics and got to know many student activists, including Neto.
His original plan was to enter the MPLA, but, apparently under the influence
of some Kenyan politicians, in 1961, he joined the UPA on the grounds that
it represented "black people" rather than "*mestiços*." Intelligent and ambitious,
Savimbi had a substantial Ovimbundu following, which added credence to the
Bakongo-dominated UPA. He was also primarily responsible for reorganizing
the UPA into the FNLA/GRAE and harnessing African support. However, by
1963, Savimbi had become increasingly critical of Roberto for favoring his own
Bakongo ethnic group, his dictatorial leadership style, and his failure to take
military action in Angola. Savimbi also argued that the FNLA should seek assistance from the socialist countries in order to obtain arms for armed struggle.[36]

Savimbi first forged contacts with the socialist countries via Cairo. In early
1964, he approached representatives of Czechoslovakia, the Soviet Union, and
the GDR there. In his pitch to the Czechoslovak ambassador to Egypt, František
Zachystal, Savimbi emphasized his left-wing views and contacts with Portuguese
and French Communists, and he praised Neto for enjoying popular support
in Angola.[37] Savimbi also held regular discussions with Latip Maksudov, the
representative of the Soviet Solidarity Committee at AAPSO's headquarters in
Cairo. The East German ambassador Ernst Scholz was particularly impressed
with Savimbi and even advised East Berlin to extend formal recognition to the
FNLA/GRAE without necessarily asking for permission from Moscow.[38] In
April 1964, Savimbi set off for a trip to Prague, Moscow, and East Berlin.

Savimbi's pitch for assistance from the socialist countries rested on his willingness to establish a common front with the MPLA. In conversations with the
staff of the International Department in Moscow on April 17, Savimbi claimed
to have founded a group inside the FNLA/GRAE that was in favor of a common
front with Neto's MPLA. Once the common front was established, Adoula's
government would have no choice but to support it. Savimbi also compared his
revolutionary stance with that of Holden Roberto, who never intended to go to
either China or the Soviet Union and maintained close contact with U.S. officials. In responding to a question from his Soviet interlocutors, Savimbi argued
that Moscow should not give unilateral assistance to Roberto since it would

allow him to get rid of the "progressive forces" inside the organization. He also cautioned against recognizing the FNLA/GRAE because it would strengthen Roberto. Another target of criticism was Viriato da Cruz, who had undermined the movement by joining the FNLA. In the end, Savimbi requested financial aid and scholarships for training in the USSR and Czechoslovakia for his followers.[39] Savimbi's message in East Berlin and Prague was similar.[40]

The Soviets were clearly interested in Savimbi's proposal. Since 1961, the Soviet plan for Angola had been to establish a "common front" of Angolan forces and to support "progressive forces." Savimbi neatly presented himself as both a man who shared left-wing views and someone willing to ally with the MPLA. His opening thus presented an opportunity for the Soviets to enact their plan. As Oleg Nazhestkin recalled, when Savimbi started to criticize Roberto in order to take over the FNLA/GRAE, the KGB intensified its efforts to "tear him away from Roberto."[41] However, it is not fully clear how far Moscow was willing to go. As Savimbi later claimed, the Soviets were only interested in recruiting new members for the MPLA.[42] In fact, the Soviet flirtations with Roberto and Savimbi presented a significant challenge for Neto.

The MPLA was in dire straits in late 1963. The organization had lost support from Zaire and the OAU and was reeling from the split between Neto and Cruz. On November 2, the Zairean authorities ordered the MPLA to leave the country. The ban on activities in the Zaire presented a major problem because it denied the MPLA access to the crucial territory of northern Angola—the center of the 1961 uprising. As a CIA assessment of November 5 put it, "Once a strong contender for pan-African support, the MPLA faces an uncertain future and, possibly, political oblivion."[43]

The MPLA's remaining option was to establish a new center of operations in neighboring Congo-Brazzaville, a former French colony. Although Congo-Brazzaville had no direct access to Angola proper, it bordered on the Angolan enclave of Cabinda, which Neto picked as a new target for military operations against the Portuguese. The timing of the (forced) move to Congo-Brazzaville was opportune. In August 1963, the first president of Congo-Brazzaville, the defrocked priest Abbé Fulbert Youlou, was deposed in a coup d'état after three days of street riots. His successor, Alphonse Massamba-Débat, promised to fight corruption, proclaimed his adherence to scientific socialism, and established relations with socialist countries. With support from Massamba-Débat, in January 1964, Neto gathered his supporters in Brazzaville for a conference, which reconstituted the MPLA under his leadership. The MPLA then went on a diplomatic offensive to restore recognition from the OAU and discredit Roberto and Savimbi.[44]

The MPLA's diplomacy was nearly derailed when, during one of Neto's trips to Moscow in 1964, he discovered that the Soviets had decided to extend official recognition to the FNLA/GRAE. As Petr Evsiukov recalled, the decision came directly from Nikita Khrushchev upon his learning that many African countries had already recognized Roberto's FNLA/GRAE. Apparently, Khrushchev made the decision impulsively and without consulting the International Department. Evsiukov was often critical of Neto, but on that occasion, he believed it would be a mistake to recognize the FNLA, even a betrayal of what he called "our friends." He thus urgently advised Neto to talk to the leader of the Portuguese Communist Party, Alvaro Cunhal, who had escaped from prison and was living in Moscow at that time. According to Evsiukov, Cunhal used his connections with the Soviet leadership, and the decision was reversed.[45]

Another source of support for Neto came from Oleg Nazhestkin. Although Nazhestkin was forced to leave Léopoldville in November 1963 with other embassy staff, he continued to monitor the situation among the Angolan liberation movements. In late April 1964, Holden Roberto formally admitted Viriato da Cruz and his followers into the FNLA. In a brief from June 1964, Nazhestkin sharply criticized Cruz for his "factional" activities, arguing that by joining with the FNLA, he had proven that he was motivated solely by personal ambition. Meanwhile, Roberto's decision to admit him to the FNLA further undermined the chances of a reconciliation between the MPLA and FNLA.[46]

In July 1964, Savimbi officially resigned from the FNLA, citing the decision to accept Viriato da Cruz as a member. In a conversation with Latip Maksudov in Cairo on July 30, Savimbi warned the Soviets against engaging in any more "flirtations" with Holden Roberto. He argued that official recognition of the FNLA/GRAE would severely damage the prospects of the "progressive forces" and that Roberto was only using the prospect of visiting China or the USSR as a bargaining chip to extract more support from the United States. He also warned about Cruz's close links with the Chinese, highlighting the fact that Beijing had advised him to agree to join the FNLA/GRAE with the prospect of taking over the movement.[47] Having resigned from the FNLA, Savimbi traveled to Congo-Brazzaville to discuss the possibility of joining the MPLA. However, talks with Neto failed, and Savimbi left Angola for training in China only to reemerge three years later as a major challenger to the MPLA in southeast Angola.[48]

The fate of the Soviets' flirtation with Roberto was sealed by yet another twist in the Zaire crisis. By mid-1964, the Simba rebellion in Eastern Zaire was gaining ground. In July, the rebels quickly approached Léopoldville, and Moïse Tshombe, the former leader of the Katanga secessionists, was recalled from exile and replaced Cyrille Adoula as the new prime minister in the hopes he could provide strong leadership in crisis. While Adoula was an ardent supporter of Roberto's, Tshombe pursued a hostile policy toward the FNLA/GRAE as he reengaged with South Africa and Portugal, bringing in a mercenary army to fight the Simbas. He thus asked Washington to cut support to Roberto. Eager to counter a "communist onslaught" in Zaire, Lyndon Johnson's administration acquiesced.[49]

The Soviets were well aware of these developments. Along with information coming from interlocutors like Neto and Savimbi, the Soviets received regular reports from their Czechoslovak counterparts, who still had a diplomatic presence in Léopoldville. According to the Czechoslovak journalist Dušan Provazník, Roberto's fortunes were declining following Adoula's departure, while the MPLA's were on the rise because of increased support from Massamba-Débat. As a result, argued Provazník, Prague should continue contacts with both the MPLA and the FNLA/GRAE.[50]

The Soviets, however, had decided to cut all contact with FNLA/GRAE. One reason might have been Roberto's declining fortunes. Another was surely Tshombe. The Soviets must have calculated that engaging seriously with the FNLA/GRAE in Zaire under Tshombe was unrealistic and could bring about reputational risks rather than benefits. On December 16, 1964, *Pravda* published an article by Evsiukov's immediate superior, Veniamin Midtsev, who lashed out at Roberto for allegedly colluding with Tshombe in a military campaign against the Simbas.[51] The rhetoric showed that Moscow was done with Roberto.

Soviet policy was fundamentally shaped by the changing realities in Zaire, as seen through the prism of their Marxist-Leninist worldview. The rationale for the "common front" strategy rested on the MPLA's need to establish a foothold in Zaire. While the incident involving Soviet near-recognition of the FNLA/GRAE has been often cited as an example of "pragmatic" policy, ideology mattered in complex ways.[52] From the start, the Soviets were frustrated with the schism in the MPLA and perhaps hoped Cruz could provide the leadership for the new "common front." The same held for Jonas Savimbi, who flaunted his left-wing credentials and his willingness to create a "common front" with Neto. In the end, Neto's continuous diplomacy and interventions from allies like Alvaro Cunhal "saved" the MPLA from the ad-hoc withdrawal of Soviet recognition. Although the Sino-Soviet split intensified the schism in the MPLA, Cruz's contacts with China did not seem to be a problem for the Soviets, at least initially, and breaking the bond between Roberto and the United States remained the primary target for Moscow.

One way or another, the Soviets and their Czechoslovak partners tried to undermine Roberto's influence in the movement and establish a common front, using clandestine means if necessary. Although we do not know if the Soviets or the Czechoslovaks were successful in "infiltrating" the FNLA/GRAE, the goal of creating a "common front" was not achieved. The MPLA lost access to Zaire and would strive to stake a claim to national leadership from a new base in Congo-Brazzaville in the following years. Over the long term, expulsion from Zaire deepened the divide between the MPLA and FNLA and solidified ties with their respective regional and international patrons.

A Quest for Arms: Amílcar Cabral, Petr Evsiukov, and the Rivalry for Primacy in Guinea, 1961–1964

While the Angolan nationalists' fortunes hinged on access to Zaire, the PAIGC relied on access to Guinea. In 1961 Cabral secured cash, guns, and scholarships for military training from Czechoslovakia for the guerrilla campaign against the Portuguese. Cabral claimed the Guinean authorities were behind him. As he conveyed to his StB contact in Conakry, Miroslav Adámek (code name "Alter") in November 1961, the PAIGC was "finishing off preparations for armed struggle," and the Guinean Ministry of Defense had even agreed to provide trucks to transport arms to the border with Guinea-Bissau.[53] When Cabral's half-brother Luís visited the Soviet Union the following month, he claimed the PAIGC was ready to begin armed action with weapons they had received from Czechoslovakia. As for Soviet assistance, continued Cabral, his older brother Amílcar was planning to visit the USSR to discuss the requests in person.[54]

Amílcar Cabral's trip to the USSR in early 1962 was significant—it was then that he made a lasting impression on Petr Evsiukov. Although Cabral had visited the Soviet Union several times, this was his first meeting with Evsiukov, who greeted him at the Sheremetyevo airport in Moscow. Cabral made an excellent first impression by telling Evsiukov he should be addressed as "Comrade" rather than "Señor."[55] Cabral's choice of address was significant since "comrade" indicated to Evsiukov that he was speaking to a fellow Marxist. In his memoirs, Evsiukov shared his high regard for Cabral, whom he described as "physically attractive," "erudite," and a man who could debate complex issues in a way that would not offend his interlocutors. Evsiukov marveled at Cabral's ability to "charm everyone," including the staff at the Hotel Oktiabrskaia, where he often stayed during his trips to Moscow.[56]

In the aftermath of Cabral's trip, the USSR extended support to the PAIGC. A significant part of this support was financial in nature. In 1962, the International Department allocated $35,000 to the PAIGC, rising to $50,000 in 1963.[57] The PAIGC also received additional scholarships for study in the Soviet Union. By 1967, seventy-four PAIGC members were studying at universities and technical schools in the USSR.[58] However, it is not clear whether the Soviets provided arms for the PAIGC at that point. One reason cited for the lack of Soviet military support was the absence of a clear logistical route to transfer arms to Guinea.[59]

Indeed, Cabral's timetable for hostilities ran into problems in late 1961 when the Guinean authorities seized a shipment of arms from Prague upon arrival in Conakry. In conversations with Czechoslovak interlocutors, Cabral argued that the main cause was his conflict with the Guinean minister of defense, Keita Fodéba. Allegedly, Fodéba did not like it when Cabral, who worked as an agricultural adviser to the Guinean authorities upon his arrival to Conakry, criticized the army for not cultivating their peanuts themselves. Another reason for the conflict was Cabral's independence. The Guinean authorities entertained the idea of a union between Guinea and Guinea-Bissau and initially treated the PAIGC as a branch of the ruling Democratic Party of Guinea (PDG; Parti Démocratique de Guinée). When Cabral expressed staunch opposition to the plan, they started putting obstacles in the PAIGC's way. In fact, continued Cabral, Fodéba was among the foremost supporters of the union.[60] As Cabral's right-hand man, Aristides Pereira, argued in an interview much later, Fodéba did not want to spoil relations with the Federal Republic of Germany by supporting an armed uprising against one of their NATO allies—Portugal.[61]

Under such circumstances, it is unsurprising that the Soviets were reluctant to ship arms to the PAIGC. The Soviet Union had established a close relationship with Sékou Touré after the Guineans famously rejected membership in the French Community in a 1958 referendum. However, in 1961, Soviet-Guinean relations were in disarray. The crisis was precipitated by a wave of strikes involving students and teachers protesting against poor working conditions, with some voicing left-wing criticism of the government. Touré responded by crushing the opposition and expelling Soviet ambassador Daniel Solod for allegedly encouraging the "Teachers' Plot." Although there was no indication that Solod had directly participated in opposition activities, the Soviets were eager to restore relations with Guinea. In 1962, it took the personal diplomacy of the chairman of the USSR Council of Ministers, Anastas Mikoian, to mend relations with Touré.[62] Since Soviet-Guinean relations remained fragile, it is likely that Moscow was not willing to ship arms to Conakry without official authorization from Touré. While Cabral continued to lobby the Guinean authorities to release the Czechoslovak arms, he also engaged in hectic diplomacy to find alternative routes to smuggle weapons into the country.

The foci of Cabral's efforts were Morocco and Algeria. Newly enthroned Moroccan King Hassan II wanted to continue his father's legacy and support liberation movements. When Cabral arrived in Rabat, the king offered Moroccan arms and allegedly even dispatched a special mission to ask Sékou Touré for permission for Moroccan aircraft to land matériel in Conakry. Hassan also allowed Morocco to be used as a transportation hub for arms from Algeria and elsewhere but refused to help with illegal smuggling. Cabral also held successful talks with the Algerian president Ben Bella, who promised to either airlift a shipment of arms or smuggle them to Conakry by boat.[63] As a result, the PAIGC arranged for arms of Moroccan, Algerian, and Czechoslovak origin to be loaded in Morocco and then smuggled to Conakry on small boats.[64]

Cabral also sought support from Guinean politicians in anticipation of the PDG's Sixth Congress in December 1962. The congress was an important event for Cabral because it represented an opportunity to assert his primacy over the nationalist movement. However, as he discovered, a number of his rivals had been invited to attend. Cabral thus sought support from Saïfoulaye Diallo, a cabinet minister and a long-time supporter of the PAIGC. As the congress began, Diallo convinced his colleagues to let Cabral attend and make a speech.[65] Much later, Cabral would underline the symbolic importance of the congress to the Soviet journalist Oleg Ignatev: "That was one of our major victories. My statement showed everybody that the Republic of Guinea supported our party."[66]

Nonetheless, logistical problems continued. In late January, Guinean customs officials at the Conakry docks discovered a shipment from Morocco of a dozen automatic rifles and walkie-talkies labeled "fish conserves." The Guinean authorities responded by arresting four high-ranking members of the PAIGC for illegal smuggling. In conversation with StB officers in Rabat, Morocco, Cabral argued that the incident was no mistake. Guineans had long known about the illegal shipments and that the "discovery" was initiated by Keita Fodéba, who wanted to strengthen his position when the fear of coups in Africa was on the rise.[67] The men were soon released after some back-channel communication. However, only after the PAIGC started its military operations in January 1963 did the Guinean authorities fully allow the uninterrupted flow of weapons through the port of Conakry.

Although the PAIGC would soon emerge as a dominant nationalist movement in Guinea, there was still no firm backing from Senegal—another important "launching pad" for military operations in northern Guinea-Bissau. As discussed in chapter three, Senegal had provided support for numerous local lusophone nationalist organizations with links to the political establishment. In August 1962, several of those groups formed an umbrella organization, the Front for the National Independence of Guinea (FLING; Frente de Luta pela Independência Nacional da Guiné). As the name suggests, FLING opposed Cabral's binationalist vision and contested the PAIGC's national leadership on racial grounds, arguing against the presence of Cape Verdeans in the movement. In 1963, FLING conducted some military operations at the northern border, and it would later receive some assistance from China. In some ways, the FLING/PAIGC juxtaposition on racial grounds paralleled the MPLA/FNLA competition in Angola.[68] However, FLING would never gain international patronage nor be able to obtain exclusive support from Senegal. As the PAIGC grew to dominate the guerrilla campaign, the importance of FLING diminished.

Cabral's diplomacy in this period was closely entangled with the politics of its main host state—Guinea. To claim leadership of the liberation movement, which was still contested by local rivals like FLING, the PAIGC needed to launch an armed campaign against the Portuguese. Thus, much of Cabral's early politics involved finding ways to smuggle arms to Conakry. In contrast to the MPLA, the PAIGC emerged as the dominant nationalist movement in Guinea, partly due to Cabral's diplomatic skills and international connections. He also established a close personal relationship with Petr Evsiukov, which proved fundamental to the PAIGC's long-term success in establishing itself as the dominant nationalist movement. The Soviet support in the meantime was limited to financial assistance and scholarships, mainly due to the complicated logistics of arms supplies via Guinea. The Mozambican nationalist movement would face similar problems in its early years.

From Crisis to Recognition: Eduardo Mondlane, Marcelino dos Santos, and Revolution in East Africa, 1962–1964

On June 25, 1962, Mozambican activists established a new anticolonial front, FRELIMO, with Eduardo Mondlane as its president. The front was supposed to represent a "union" of smaller regional parties: UDENAMO, MANU, and UNAMI. However, the election of Eduardo Mondlane proved controversial. A native of the southern Gaza province, Mondlane received better access to socioeconomic and educational opportunities than those Mozambicans living in the rather remote and underdeveloped north of the country. Mondlane's educational background, comfortable lifestyle, and the fact that his wife Janet Mondlane (née Johnson) was a white American solidified his image as a privileged "southerner." The first FRELIMO Congress, held from September 23–28, 1962, reinforced the perceived dominance of what John Marcum has called the "*mestiço-assimilado*" group in the leadership. Only three former MANU members were elected to the new eleven-man Central Committee, which was dominated by former UDENAMO activists from the south. A few also objected to the election of Marcelino dos Santos, a *mestiço*, to the post of the Secretary for Foreign Affairs and his central role in the drafting of the FRELIMO constitution along Marxist-Leninist lines.[69]

To make matters worse, controversy surrounded the appointment of Leo Milas as the Secretary for Information and Culture. Mondlane had met Milas in the United States. He was impressed by Milas's educational background (he had an M.A. from UCLA) and invited him to join FRELIMO. Although Milas claimed to have been born in Mozambique, he did not speak Portuguese or any African languages, and suspicions about his true identity and contacts with the CIA arose upon his 1962 arrival in Dar es Salaam.

On January 5, 1963, a number of high-ranking members of FRELIMO accused Milas of being a CIA agent and physically attacked him. However, vice-president Uria Simango and Marcelino dos Santos backed Milas, and the Central Committee thus issued orders to expel David Mabunda, Paulo Gumane, and Fanuel Mahluza for their alleged role in the incident. They were subsequently denied access to Tanganyika and moved to Cairo. Mondlane was in the United States for much of the infighting and continued to trust Milas, even placing him in charge of planning military operations. Only after making inquiries, Mondlane found out that suspicions were justified, since Milas was actually born in the United States and that his real name was Leo Clinton Aldridge. He was subsequently expelled from FRELIMO.[70]

In the meantime, Mondlane's critics sought support from Moscow, painting the internal conflict in Cold War terms. On October 2, 1962, speaking to the Soviet ambassador to Tanganyika, Andrei Timoshchenko, David Mabunda argued that Mondlane and his supporters had eradicated the "progressive elements" from FRELIMO's executive committee and replaced them with people who had been bribed by "the Americans"—a thinly veiled reference to Milas. Mabunda also warned Timoshchenko that he was already being called a "red agent and a traitor" and would probably be expelled soon.[71] Mondlane's critics also approached the Czechoslovak embassy in Cairo, requesting arms.[72] Although neither the Soviets nor the Czechoslovaks responded to such a request, they believed such criticism was justified and that it might be worthwhile to maintain contact with the Cairo-based opposition.[73]

As the Soviets tried to understand the nature of the crisis, Marcelino dos Santos played a critical role in backing Mondlane's leadership. In several conversations between Marcelino dos Santos and Latip Maksudov, the Soviet representative to the AAPSO secretariat in Cairo, Santos argued that the schism in the movement had nothing to do with ideological differences or Mondlane's pro-U.S. orientation. The real reason that David Mabunda had left for Cairo, Marcelino dos Santos argued, was because he could not handle the hardships of life in Dar es Salaam. He admitted that Mondlane may have been an "American," but emphasized that his education, contacts in the United States, and skin color made him the only person who could act as a unifying force for the liberation movement in Mozambique: "We have decided from the very beginning—let Mondlane be at the head of the movement and we will work inside and direct it along the correct path." In turn, Maksudov reassured Santos that he was an "old friend" whom they trusted and whose opinion would be considered.[74]

Another important figure who provided support for Mondlane was Oscar Kambona. One of the most influential politicians in Tanganyika, Kambona had regular contact with representatives of the socialist countries in Dar es Salaam as Tanganyika's first minister of foreign affairs. Czechoslovaks and their Soviet colleagues believed that Kambona was a "progressive person," an evaluation they had apparently received from various sources, including the Communist Party of Great Britain (CPGB).[75] In 1963, Kambona was appointed the first head of the OAU's Liberation Committee, based in Dar es Salaam. Kambona's assessment of Mondlane as a "sincere and honest person" must have also worked to his advantage.[76]

Tanganyikan politics in 1963 were conducive to FRELIMO's mobilization for armed struggle. Portuguese colonialism was one of the central topics at the founding meeting of the OAU, where all the delegates signed a charter pledging to support the liberation of the entire continent. For his part, Julius Nyerere formally declared that safe havens for guerrillas should be established along the Mozambique-Tanganyika border. Nyerere also intensified his efforts to convince Washington and London to pressure Portugal and South Africa to accept majority rule. However, Nyerere's diplomatic overtures to the Kennedy administration did not bring the desired results.[77] As Nyerere increasingly lost faith in the possibility of a negotiated settlement, pressure was building for FRELIMO to prepare for a guerrilla war.

Having consolidated their position in Tanganyika, Eduardo Mondlane and Marcelino dos Santos spearheaded a campaign to raise funds from international patrons for FRELIMO. In February 1963, Mondlane met Attorney General Robert Kennedy in Washington. Kennedy found Mondlane a "terrifically impressive fellow" who could ensure a peaceful solution to the Mozambique problem. Kennedy then arranged for the Ford Foundation to give $99,700 to the Mozambican Institute in Dar es Salaam, which Mondlane had established to cater to refugees who had fled to Tanganyika. The CIA also extended a $60,000 subsidy to Mondlane. Although the Ford Foundation would later cut the funding, rumors of Mondlane's clandestine dealings with the United States and the cash he obtained would haunt him until his assassination in 1969.[78]

Meanwhile, Marcelino dos Santos provided a link with the socialist countries. One was China. Having been inspired by the Chinese revolution, Santos was keen to establish a close relationship with Beijing. When he visited China in 1963, he met Chairman Mao Zedong himself and allegedly received an offer of financial assistance. On his return, Santos urged Mondlane to also go to Beijing to seal the deal. However, Mondlane's trip to China in early 1964 was more disappointing since the Chinese apparently would not offer aid unless FRELIMO ceased contact with the Soviet Union and the United States.[79]

Santos also lobbied the Soviet embassy in Dar es Salaam, submitting a request for military training, humanitarian assistance and financial assistance, and the treatment of wounded soldiers in the Soviet Union. These efforts had some effect. In a letter to the Soviet Solidarity Committee from Dar es Salaam on November 15, Andrei Timoshchenko reiterated concerns about internal divisions but recommended that Moscow provide scholarships for military training and invite a FRELIMO delegation to the USSR since the organization contained "healthy, progressive forces."[80]

However, FRELIMO's plans were delayed by a general crisis that swept East Africa in 1964. The crisis started on the island of Zanzibar, a former British colony with close connections to mainland Tanganyika. On January 12, 1964, a group of revolutionaries overthrew the sultan, set up a revolutionary council, and proclaimed the People's Republic of Zanzibar. The events spurred antigovernment protests in Kenya, Uganda, and Tanganyika. In Dar es Salaam, soldiers mutinied over low pay and the retention of European officers in top positions.

As the rebellion spread, Nyerere requested help from the British government, which successfully crushed the mutiny. Convinced that events in Zanzibar and elsewhere in East Africa were linked, Nyerere exploited the power struggle in Zanzibar to push for unification with the mainland. On April 24, the agreement was signed, and the new state was named the United Republic of Tanzania. The turmoil in East Africa put a temporary stop to FRELIMO's military preparations. Tanzanian authorities confiscated a consignment of Algerian weapons for FRELIMO, releasing them only in May.[81]

The Zanzibari revolution thrust East Africa into the Cold War. The Soviet Union and other socialist countries applauded events in Zanzibar, extended diplomatic recognition, and offered economic assistance. Zanzibar was the first country in Africa to grant diplomatic recognition to the GDR, leading to an inflow of East German aid. Thus, British intervention and the union agreement were a major disappointment for the Soviets, who believed it represented a backlash against the revolution. The Soviets and Czechoslovaks were particularly disappointed with Oscar Kambona, who had a pivotal role in negotiating with the mutineers in Dar es Salaam and supported Nyerere.[82]

It was against this background that Mondlane and Santos journeyed to Moscow and Prague in May 1964. From Czechoslovak documents, we know they asked for scholarships and humanitarian assistance since there was no reliable route to transport arms to Dar es Salaam. Still, Czechoslovakia denied these requests, citing internal divisions within FRELIMO.[83] Their trip to Moscow was more successful, as the Soviets granted humanitarian assistance and forty scholarships for military training.[84]

The full details of Soviet decision-making on FRELIMO in 1964 are still buried in the archives. Although Evsiukov writes in his memoirs that Mondlane's prestige was "unquestionable," we do know that Moscow was suspicious of Mondlane and supportive of what they called "progressive" critics of the party.[85] Mondlane believed that the Soviets accepted FRELIMO's relations with Washington as a counterweight to China's influence.[86] The "China factor" might have contributed to the decision, but it was unlikely the main consideration for the Soviets since Beijing did not establish a close relationship with FRELIMO until a few years later. In fact, events of 1964 in East Africa must have played a key part in Soviet calculations. Although the union of Tanganyika and Zanzibar frustrated Soviet hopes for an "African Cuba," the revolution raised the region's importance in Cold War terms. As the head of the Africa desk at the International Department, Petr Manchkha, argued during deliberations of the presidium of the Soviet Solidarity Committee on October 13, 1964, the Soviets still had "friends" in the leadership of the union who deserved "multisided help."[87] By providing support for FRELIMO, an organization supported by Nyerere and Kambona, Moscow would potentially strengthen its alliances in an increasingly important region. In any case, Soviet assistance was quite modest. We do not know if the FRELIMO received any weapons from Moscow, but there would be no financial assistance, in contrast to Soviet support for the MPLA and PAIGC.

In *The Struggle for Mozambique*, published in 1968, Mondlane argued that the Mozambicans who gathered in Dar es Salaam in 1962 represented "every region of Mozambique and every sector of the population."[88] In reality, the organization was highly fractured from the start. The "Leo Milas" controversy complicated matters further, especially since Mondlane was only rarely present in Dar es Salaam before 1964. Although the Soviets sympathized with Mondlane's critics, they extended limited support to FRELIMO due to lobbying from Marcelino dos Santos and the realization that the organization enjoyed exclusive support from Nyerere. In June 1965, those expelled from FRELIMO established a rival Zambia-based organization, the Revolutionary Committee of Mozambique (COREMO; Comité Revolucionário de Moçambique). Although COREMO mounted no significant challenge to FRELIMO, power struggles and debates over race, class, and privilege among Mozambicans in Dar es Salaam continued to center on the figure of Eduardo Mondlane and his wife Janet.

Students in Revolt: Racism in the USSR and the Chinese Challenge in Africa

In the early 1960s, the Chinese launched a massive propaganda offensive to spread their revolutionary model in Africa. Books by Mao Zedong became widely available in urban centers such as Léopoldville, Conakry, and Dar es Salaam. The Chinese also used radio broadcasts, cultural events, and film screenings to spread their ideas to a wider local audience.[89] Another source of propaganda came in the form of military training. In the case of the PAIGC, men who were trained in China were the first to be infiltrated to southern Guinea-Bissau to mobilize the population, train recruits, and eventually begin armed action.[90]

Some of the men who were trained in China in the 1960s were inspired by the Maoist model of guerrilla warfare, which was based on peasant mobilizations. One of them was the Cape Verdean Silvino da Luz. Having escaped the Angolan military in 1961, he joined the PAIGC in Conakry in 1963. Later, he was sent for military training in China. As Silvino da Luz recalled, Maoist ideas appealed to him because of the conditions in Guinea-Bissau, where the majority of recruits were subsistence farmers. In retrospect, he admitted, "I was pro-Chinese."[91] As previously discussed, the Chinese challenge manifested itself in leadership struggles in the MPLA and FRELIMO, especially as Sino-Soviet disagreements intensified in the early 1960s. These debates also resonated among anticolonial activists studying in the USSR.

By 1964, there were ninety-two men and women from the Portuguese colonies studying in the Soviet Union. One of them was the Cape Verdean Osvaldo Lopes da Silva. He first arrived in the Soviet Union as a student after escaping Portugal to join the PAIGC in 1961. After a year at the preparatory faculty at the Kiev State University, he was enrolled to study economics at the prestigious Plekhanov Institute of the National Economy in Moscow. He was also one of Cabral's trusted men who represented students from Guinea-Bissau in the USSR. Silva remembered that Moscow in the early 1960s had the euphoric atmosphere of a utopia in the making, a sense that the country was rapidly advancing toward communism: "The bread was free. Also, the transport. The underground was free. You entered and did not have to pay."[92]

His time in Moscow did not turn Silva into a communist, however. It was clear it would not be possible to provide free bread for everybody, and one of his professors even warned international students against blindly emulating the Soviet experiment. As for daily experiences, Silva recalled it was still "novel" for Soviet citizens to see an African person on the streets of Moscow. Some people would approach students of color, touch their skin, and ask "startling questions." Over time, Silva argued, the students discovered that these attitudes were not a product of racism but instead came from a lack of awareness.[93]

Not all African students shared Silva's assessment. As the scholarship program expanded in the early 1960s, interactions between Soviet citizens and Africans multiplied, often in little-controlled environments such as student dorms, cafes, and discos. The reactions of Soviet citizens to African students varied, ranging from expressions of friendship to overt hostility. Soviet citizens often resented African students for what they considered "positive discrimination": relatively better access to housing and higher scholarships. Tensions also emerged over African students' romantic relationships with Soviet women. African students often complained to the authorities about abuse, discrimination, and sometimes instances of physical violence, but the Soviet authorities regularly dismissed their concerns.[94] When a Ghanaian student was found dead in Moscow in 1963, African students staged unprecedented protests on Red Square against what appeared to be a racially motivated murder.[95] Similar incidents and protests against racial discrimination occurred across Eastern and Central Europe.[96] In the context of the Sino-Soviet split, the ideas of Mao Zedong gave students ammunition for expressing opposition to what many perceived as Soviet racism as well as power imbalances in their own countries.

The case of the so-called *complot anti-Partido* (antiparty plot) among PAIGC students in the USSR provides a good example. In the highly charged atmosphere of 1963, the Congress of the Federation of African Students in the USSR adopted a pro-Chinese stance. The students from Angola and Guinea-Bissau sided with the Maoists. However, many students from Guinea-Bissau went further. In December 1963, a PAIGC student enrolled at the preparatory faculty at the University of Kiev, Soviet Ukraine, fell victim to a racially charged, violent attack. In the aftermath, a number of students from Guinea-Bissau attacked not only the Soviet Union but also Amílcar Cabral and the presence of Cape Verdeans in the PAIGC leadership.[97]

The fact that the students targeted Cape Verdeans was particularly dangerous since the PAIGC was dedicated to a binationalist vision of unity between the mainland and the archipelago. Thus, the PAIGC charged the rebellious students with involvement in an "antiparty plot" and suspended their scholarships. Although Osvaldo Lopes da Silva had previously complained to the Ukrainian authorities about racially charged acts of violence, faced with a direct challenge to Cabral and the status of Cape Verdeans, Silva helped put down the revolt. Students were told to adhere to the party line, and in 1965 the MPLA and the PAIGC voted against the Maoists in the Federation of African Students. Silva confirmed that the rebellious students basically expressed their opposition toward Cabral's binationalist project. He also had his own "doubts," recalled Silva with hindsight, but explained they had to "maintain unity" in front of Soviet authorities.[98]

In fact, African students in China faced similar issues to their counterparts in the Soviet Union and Eastern Europe. In 1963, Ghanaian Emmanuel John Hevi published a highly critical account of his time in China, highlighting the strict control, poor living conditions, and discrimination experienced by African students. When a Zanzibari student in China was beaten in March 1962, African students staged a protest, and the majority ended up leaving the country.[99] Although Hevi's claims were quickly dismissed due to allegations of bias, subsequent investigations found that the Chinese indeed saw Black Africans from the position of deep-seated cultural superiority.[100] It is not clear if African students in the Soviet Union were aware of these allegations or how they perceived them. However, it is likely that African students professed their allegiance to China not solely because of Soviet racism but as a proxy expression of grievance against racial hierarchies in their own countries.

As much as the MPLA, PAIGC, and FRELIMO tried to control students' behavior, these attempts often proved problematic. Students sometimes defied party orders and caused problems by marrying local women, failing to return to their countries of origin, or, worse, defecting to the West. FRELIMO became particularly suspicious of international students and their commitment to revolution, so much so that they limited the number of scholarships requested from socialist countries. As the story of the "antiparty plot" showed, students did not necessarily share the class-based definition of imperialism propagated by the largely cosmopolitan, European-educated leadership of the nationalist movements.[101]

The Soviets would not tolerate a Maoist challenge on their own soil. In the context of an open conflict with China, Moscow carefully monitored all expressions of "pro-Chinese" sentiments among African students. Those who continued to support the Maoist line openly would be expelled. However, these incidents notwithstanding, the Soviets continued to believe that education could turn Third World youths into "friends of the USSR." In fact, Moscow suspected that the low enrollments of Mozambican students in Soviet universities and colleges indicated a degree of mistrust on FRELIMO's part since the assumption was that Soviet-educated students would adopt a pro-Soviet, "Marxist" stance when they returned home.[102]

Conclusion

Neto, Cabral, and Mondlane used international connections to gain ascendancy over local and internal rivals and acquire support from their host states with varying levels of success. The MPLA leadership sought to establish a "common front" with Roberto's FNLA in order to gain access to Zaire and ultimately take over the movement. As new evidence shows, the Soviets backed the MPLA's plan by trying to subvert Holden Roberto's FNLA through clandestine means. However, Roberto was a formidable rival, who likewise used international diplomacy successfully to bolster his claim to national leadership. While Neto's contacts with the Portuguese Communists helped him maintain support from the Soviets at a time of intense internal infighting within the MPLA, his diplomatic effort failed to prevent the MPLA's expulsion from Zaire.

While the MPLA faced stiff competition in Zaire, the PAIGC's local competition in Guinea was much weaker. Amílcar Cabral used diplomacy to forge exclusive relationships with a number of African states and international donors in order to smuggle weapons into Guinea. In 1962, he established a close relationship with Petr Evsiukov—a testimony to Cabral's well-known diplomatic skills. However, Moscow erred on the side of caution regarding providing weapons, mainly because of a delicate relationship with Touré's Guinea. Among the socialist countries, Czechoslovakia remained the key ally, providing cash, arms, and training for Cabral. As we will see in the following chapter, it was only after the PAIGC began guerrilla warfare in early 1963 that the movement would secure its dominant position in Guinea.

Meanwhile, Tanzanian support was fundamental to FRELIMO's claims to nationalist leadership. Mozambican early nationalist politics were highly fractured and dominated by disagreements over Mondlane's election as president. The Soviets were highly suspicious of Mondlane for ideological reasons and initially doubted FRELIMO's long-term viability. The Soviets provided only limited material support for FRELIMO in 1964 in the context of what they considered revolutionary developments in Zanzibar, which raised the importance of Tanzania more generally. However, the relationship would remain complicated because of uncertainty around Mondlane's allegiance and, starting in the mid-1960s, increasing concerns about a burgeoning relationship with China.

The Sino-Soviet split was damaging to the nationalist movements not only because it potentially ensconced the African revolutionaries in a tug-of-war between Beijing and Moscow but also because it undermined internal unity. For the MPLA's and the PAIGC's multiracial and largely *assimilado* leadership, Chinese claims of unity based on nonwhite identity risked exacerbating existing divisions based on ethnic, linguistic, and racial lines. The same was true for FRELIMO, which was open to the charge of being an organization dominated by "southerners." As the schisms within the MPLA and FRELIMO and among PAIGC students in the Soviet Union showed, leaders of the liberation movements were susceptible to challenges on ethnic or racial grounds. Since China's ideas of anti-imperialism based on race could be employed to mount a critique to national leadership, it is not surprising that Cabral in particular, but also Mondlane and Neto to an extent, grew skeptical of Maoism.

In the following years, as we will see, China would curtail its assistance to the MPLA and PAIGC and would only maintain a strong connection with FRELIMO because of Beijing's close connection with Tanzania. However, critics of racial and ethnic-based privilege among the leadership did not disappear. In fact, in the course of the anticolonial struggle, they would frequently resurface during moments of crises. In the immediate term, though, the early schisms lead to the greater centralization of the leadership around

Neto, Cabral, and Mondlane. The continuous ascendancy of their moderniz-ing visions would depend on the African revolutionaries' ability to obtain the "means of war" to fight against the Portuguese. Overall, Soviet support for lib-eration movements during this period was limited to financial assistance and scholarships. The onset of guerrilla campaigns meant a much greater commit-ment was required, especially from the Soviet military. The next chapter thus turns to the militarization of Soviet involvement in Africa in the mid-1960s.

CHAPTER FIVE

From the Barrel of a Gun

Weapons, Training, and Strategy of Guerrilla Warfare, 1964–1970

O N OCTOBER 14, 1964, Nikita Khrushchev was ousted from his position by senior members of the Politburo, which was led by Leonid Brezhnev. The organizers of the palace coup—all of whom were Khrushchev's protégés—were unhappy with his leadership style and his domestic and foreign policy. They criticized Khrushchev for trying to find accommodation with the United States, spoiling relations with communist leaders like Mao Zedong, Cuba's Fidel Castro, and Romania's Gheorghe Gheorghiu-Dej, and decried his nuclear brinkmanship during the Cuban Missile Crisis. Overall, the coup signified a conservative turn in Soviet foreign policy, with the new collective leadership initially adopting a more confrontational stance with the United States over the Vietnam War.[1]

Most scholarly accounts have argued that Soviet policy in Africa became much more pragmatic and disinterested in revolution after Khrushchev's departure.[2] Relying on new archival documents, this chapter demonstrates that rather than disengaging from Africa, Moscow in the mid-1960s redirected its energies to develop relations with the security and military services of its African allies. The mid-1960s saw a revision of Soviet foreign policy as a result of the "coup contagion," which led to the downfall of the first generation of Africa's post-independence leaders: Patrice Lumumba in Zaire (1960), Abbé Fulbert Youlou in Congo-Brazzaville (1963), Ben Bella in Algeria (1965), Kwame Nkrumah in Ghana (1966), and Modibo Keïta in Mali (1968). The Soviets believed they underestimated the role of armies and thus increasingly used supplies of arms and training to strengthen relations with key African allies, drawing the military and intelligence services into deeper involvement on the continent.

The chapter also shows how the Soviets became the key supplier of military equipment and training to Lusophone nationalist movements. By 1965, the Soviet Union would replace Czechoslovakia as the key provider of arms, cash, and training to the PAIGC—an alliance based on close personal connections and ideological affinity between Cabral and his Soviet liaisons. Moscow also started providing arms and training to Neto's MPLA. However, the extent of Soviet involvement would be limited due to the MPLA's logistical problems after their expulsion from Zaire. The Soviet relationship with FRELIMO once again proved particularly complex. Although Moscow supplied arms and material support for the organization, the Soviets were continuously distrustful of president Mondlane. In 1966–1968, FRELIMO plunged into an internal crisis, culminating in Mondlane's assassination in Dar es Salaam in 1969. The Soviet intelligence services closely followed FRELIMO's rivalries through a variety of clandestine sources, eventually adopting a rather critical view of its leadership. Still, the Soviet military held high hopes that their training programs would win African revolutionaries over to their side. As the oral histories in this chapter will show, African soldiers saw Soviet military technology as a symbol of modernity and a practical tool of their own liberation.

As the anticolonial wars began, the strategy of guerrilla warfare also became a contested subject. In Guinea-Bissau, Cabral opted for a "cautious approach" toward military operations in order to limit casualties. The MPLA suffered from logistical and supply problems in eastern Angola and Cabinda, while FRELIMO's guerrilla operations were hampered by an internal crisis. New evidence shows the Soviet military were frustrated by the lack of progress and, in the case of the MPLA, believed that Neto was not doing enough to forge broad political alliances. Thus, this chapter recovers the role of military strategy in understanding how the relationship between the Soviets and the Lusophone nationalist movements developed and evolved in the 1960s.

Of Coups and the Military: Soviet Policy in Africa after Khrushchev

The collective leadership that took over from Nikita Khrushchev was well aware that early Soviet optimism about a quick revolutionary transformation of the African continent was premature. In the late 1950s, Moscow believed that by following the "Soviet model of development" and benefiting from Soviet assistance and advice, newly independent African countries would achieve fast economic growth and move toward socialism.[3] The unpublished "Polianskii report" that the collective leadership had prepared as a record of Khrushchev's policy failings criticized his policy in Africa. Leaders like the Guinean president Sékou Touré, argued the report, reaped the benefits of Soviet aid but gave little in return. This did not mean scaling down commitments to revolutionary movements around the world, but being more careful about choosing friends based on class and political affiliation.[4]

In practical terms, there were many continuities with the pre-Khrushchev period. The cadres at the International Department and its Africa desk—the head of department Boris Ponomarev, his deputy Rostislav Ulianovskii, the head of the Africa section Petr Manchkha, and Petr Evsiukov—all stayed at their posts. The International Department probably became even more prominent after Khrushchev's departure since Brezhnev preferred a collegiate decision-making style and increasingly left each department to make decisions in their own domain. Once Khrushchev was ousted, the CC CPSU approved the construction of a large training facility for mainly African revolutionaries at the village of Perevalnoe in Crimea, Soviet Ukraine. In addition to Perevalnoe, the Soviets also continued to provide specialized military training at multiple locations, including at Skhodnia, near Moscow, as well military academies such as the naval academy at Poti, a seaport on the Black Sea in Georgia.[5]

Meanwhile, the "coup contagion" in Africa stimulated a discussion about policy implications. In consultations with his Czechoslovak colleagues in late April 1966, the Soviet deputy foreign minister Iakov Malik stated that the socialist countries faced a double bind. On the one hand, they had to overcome the general distrust of "whites" and the "flawed perception" that the world was divided into the "rich North" and "poor South." On the other hand, they had to face the continuous assault of the "neocolonial and imperialist" forces, which exploited internal problems in newly independent states. Malik highlighted that Moscow would "no longer support the megalomania" of African leaders, but he also cautioned against being "overly pessimistic." He argued that the socialist countries should become more attuned to was happening with the army and police and continue cooperation, especially in the military sphere. His Czechoslovak colleagues agreed.[6]

The KGB shared a similar view. As KGB Chairman Vladimir Semichastnyi admitted to his Bulgarian counterparts on March 18, 1966, the security services had underestimated the value of clandestine work among the military forces in Africa. From then on, he continued, Africa should become a more important focus for the intelligence services.[7] The Soviets believed the coups represented a temporary setback and that socialist countries should strengthen alliances with African military and the security services.[8]

Not all Soviet allies shared a similarly optimistic assessment. The situation in Africa became a hotly debated topic during the first coordination meeting of solidarity committees from the Warsaw Pact countries in June 1966. The

challenge came from the head of the Polish Solidarity Committee, Lucjan Wolniewicz, who questioned whether African countries would "ever join the socialist camp" since the Cold War enabled them to take advantage of both sides. He
also lambasted the leaders of liberation movements based in Dar es Salaam for
their "bourgeois lifestyle." Dmitrii Dolidze of the Soviet Solidarity Committee
pushed back. Although one could witness a "slowdown in revolutionary progress" in Africa, one could not generalize, and "progressive" organizations like the
Angolan MPLA had a "big future."[9] While Wolniewicz's skepticism made sense
in view of Poland's overall limited involvement in Africa in the 1960s, a number of Eastern European countries also started to move away from unaffordable
commitments in the Third World.[10]

One country seeking to limit the costs of involvement in Africa was Czechoslovakia. Although Prague was among the first to pursue an active Africa policy
since the 1950s, by the mid-1960s, many among the bureaucracy were starting to
reevaluate their commitments. The main reason was economic. While the economy grew at an impressive rate after World War II, Czechoslovakia experienced
a significant downturn in the early 1960s and shortages of foreign cash. As a
result, Czechoslovakia increasingly focused on ways to make a profit, especially
on arms sales.[11] In June 1968, at the peak of a period of the liberalizing reform
known as the Prague Spring, the Ministry of Foreign Trade actually proposed
far-reaching reforms aimed to place the Czechoslovak arms trade on sure economic footing free from political constraints.[12]

The lively debates stimulated by the Prague Spring ended abruptly after the
Warsaw Pact invaded Czechoslovakia to crack down on liberalization in August
1968. As Soviet tanks rolled into Prague, thousands of Czechoslovak citizens
protested the invasion. Many Czechoslovak intelligence personnel supported
the Prague Spring, and some defected from their posts following the intervention. In response, Czechoslovak authorities withdrew embassy staff for "debrief-
ings" and momentarily reduced overseas commitments.[13]

The intervention in Czechoslovakia was a public relations disaster with long-
term consequences for the communist movement, but in Africa, official reactions were mixed. Mali's Modibo Keïta voiced his support, while others—like
the president of Congo-Brazzaville, Alphonse Massamba-Débat—maintained
a calculated silence.[14] Zambia's Kenneth Kaunda and Tanzania's Julius Nyerere
openly condemned the invasion. In a private conversation with the Soviet ambassador to Guinea, Alexander Startsev, President Sékou Touré reacted to the
justification for the invasion "with understanding." Using the invasion as a point
of comparison, Touré chastised the Soviet government for not doing more to

support the North Vietnamese and suggested the socialist countries dispatch troops to Vietnam to "end the imperialist war."[15]

The public reaction to events in Czechoslovakia was particularly dramatic in Tanzania. On August 23, TANU's Youth League led anti-Soviet protests in Dar es Salaam, vandalizing the grounds of the Soviet embassy in the process.[16] These events were indicative of growing Chinese influence in Tanzania, with militants in the Youth League finding inspiration in the "Great Proletarian Cultural Revolution." In 1968, the Youth League spearheaded a number of policing campaigns, including "Operation Vijana," which were designed to eliminate all signs of "imperialist behavior" and dress. Their practices elicited comparisons with the "Red Guards" of the Chinese Cultural Revolution.[17]

Elsewhere in Africa though, the Cultural Revolution prevented Beijing from capitalizing on events in Czechoslovakia. While China had been an active player in Africa since the early 1960s, the Cultural Revolution ushered in a period of self-imposed diplomatic isolation, as Beijing recalled many of its ambassadors and scaled down overseas commitments. The Chinese also started to pursue more aggressive anti-Soviet tactics in the Third World, pressuring African liberation movements to break contact with Moscow. In response, the Soviets launched their own campaign to counter the Chinese, including in international forums. In 1965, attendees at the fourth AAPSO conference in Winneba, Ghana, agreed to hold the subsequent, fifth, conference in Beijing. The decision risked completely sidelining the Soviets from the AAPSO, and the Soviet Solidarity Committee mobilized its contacts to reverse the decision.

One such contact was Amílcar Cabral. At the meeting of the AAPSO Presidium in Nicosia, Cyprus, on March 15, 1967, Cabral was one of the delegates who successfully pushed for the motion to reverse the decision made at Winneba. The Nicosia meeting also purged the AAPSO of pro-Chinese liberation groups. In response, China de facto withdrew from the organization. Cabral's role at Nicosia and his unwillingness to cease contact with Moscow angered the Chinese, and relations between the PAIGC and Beijing broke down.[18] China then proceeded to channel funds toward splinter organizations: FLING in Guinea-Bissau, UNITA in Angola, and COREMO in Mozambique. Only FRELIMO received Chinese support, mainly because of Mondlane's close relationship with Tanzania's Julius Nyerere, who continued to obtain substantial assistance from Beijing.[19]

In January 1969, the AAPSO hosted an International Conference in Support of the Peoples of Portuguese Colonies and Southern Africa in Khartoum, Sudan. The Soviet Solidarity Committee, the primary sponsor of the event, hoped that it would help revive the AAPSO after China's withdrawal and improve Soviet public relations after the invasion of Czechoslovakia.[20] Although countries like Zambia and Tanzania refused to participate, the conference still drew representatives from fifty-six countries and twelve international organizations. The conference also bolstered the prestige of the Soviet-backed liberation movements, including the MPLA, FRELIMO, and PAIGC, since they were declared the only "authentic" representatives of the liberation struggle in their respective countries.

On February 19, 1969, the deputy of the CC CPSU International Department, Rostislav Ulianovskii, spoke about his impressions of the conference to the Presidium of the Soviet Solidarity Committee. Ulianovskii argued the Vietnam War showed African revolutionaries that it was "impossible to defeat imperialist racism" without Soviet military assistance. He also pointed to positive developments in the liberation movements. In particular, leaders like Eduardo Mondlane and Agostinho Neto had come to understand the utility of scientific socialism and the value of the Soviet approach to questions of ethnicity and race. Thus, the conference demonstrated that Soviet influence in Africa had increased.[21]

By the late 1960s, the Soviets believed they had managed to restore their prestige in the Third World. The collective leadership that took over from Khrushchev shared much of the same commitment to proletarian internationalism, and there was no bureaucratic overhaul, ensuring many continuities. The Soviets continued to be preoccupied with challenges on the "right" and "left," especially those emanating from China. The most significant change involved the reevaluation of the importance of African army and security services. Starting from the mid-1960s, the Soviets sought to strengthen their alliances with African allies by providing weapons and military training. The discussion below will explore the dynamics of military cooperation with the PAIGC, MPLA, and FRELIMO.

The War Begins: Czechoslovak Advisers and Soviet Instructors for Cabral's Guerrillas

On January 23, 1963, the PAIGC launched its armed struggle by attacking the Portuguese garrison at Tite, in southern Guinea-Bissau. The official PAIGC narrative, now firmly rooted in the literature, credits the PAIGC leadership with preplanning the attacks. Among the small group that was involved in the attacks was Dauda Bangura. He was an early convert to the nationalist cause whilst working as a mason in Bissau, and part of the first group to go to China for military training in 1960 before being dispatched to mobilize the population in the southern

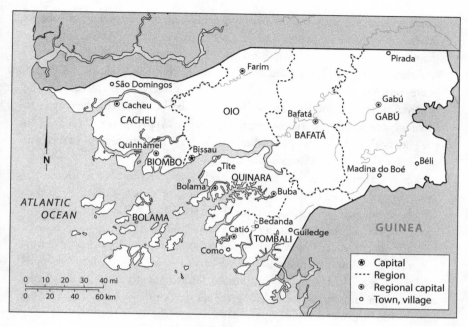

MAP 5.1. Guinea-Bissau

Guinea-Bissau province of Tombali (see map 5.1). In my interview with him in 2019 Bangura claimed that the order to fire the "first shots" did not come from the PAIGC in Conakry; the decision was instead taken on the local group's own initiative. Once Cabral heard about the operation, Bangura recalled, he authorized the beginning of guerrilla war.[22] In a detailed study of Cabral's correspondence, Julião Soares Sousa confirms Bangura's account. The attacks on Tite were not planned, and Cabral was not even present in Conakry at that time.[23]

Nonetheless, preparations for armed action had been ongoing since 1961, with Czechoslovakia the one actor that was actively involved. In 1961, the StB decided to support Cabral's bid for dominance over the nationalist movement. Some of the measures included the StB helping the PAIGC design and spread anti-war propaganda among the Portuguese garrisons, assisting in infiltrating one of its Senegal-based rivals, and shipping arms to Conakry.[24] However, in December 1961, the Guinean authorities detained a shipment of Czechoslovak arms, and thus, no armed action was possible—a cause of growing concern for Prague. During a conversation with Cabral on October 13, 1962, his new StB contact in Conakry, code name "Václavic," pressed Cabral to engage in "acts of sabotage" in Guinea-Bissau in order to gain access to Portuguese weapons, positively influence world opinion, and show the Guinean authorities that the party could still obtain matériel without their permission. The StB also feared the PAIGC could lose momentum in competition with local rivals if they further delayed hostilities.

Cabral disagreed. He argued that "sabotage" could only alarm the Portuguese, pushing them to reinforce their military presence, which would make it harder to launch guerrilla action. Instead, Cabral insisted that he engage in diplomacy to find an alternative route for weapons via Algeria or Morocco. In the end, both sides agreed that Cabral would draft an "action plan" in order to proceed with the new, active stage of armed action.[25]

When Cabral secured a route to smuggle arms via Morocco in December 1962, the StB decided to deliver another shipment of weapons. The new load of Czechoslovak arms was signposted for "Operation BETA," which involved 150 men attacking a Portuguese military post at Bedanda. The StB also dispatched a military expert, Major František Polda, who was to provide logistical advice on the ground.[26] While Operation BETA was later canceled, Czechoslovak weapons clandestinely reached Conakry via Morocco. One shipment contained thirty-two machine guns, 100 pistols, hand-held grenades, and ammunition.[27] The machine guns would be distributed among the first recruits who joined the PAIGC.

One of those young recruits was Sae Breia Na Nhakpba. He was twenty years old in December 1961 when PAIGC guerrillas came to his village to mobilize people. Among them was Domingos Ramos, a charismatic commander who apparently convinced the villagers to join the struggle. In most cases, the process involved moving the whole village to the bush under the control of the guerrillas. Young people would be organized to patrol villages, make shelters, and recruit others while simultaneously receiving basic military and political instruction from more experienced combatants. Sae Breia recalled that by the end of 1962, he had received his first *patchanga* (machine gun). Armed with the new weapon, he would patrol the villages and talk to people, convincing them to join the fight. The message was for Africans to follow the example of Guinea and take back their land from the colonizers. The weapons served as "encouragement" to show that they had the means to fight the Portuguese army.[28] This example is not to say that the process of mobilization was always voluntary, and at least some young people joined the struggle to protect their families from guerrillas.[29]

Once armed attacks against the Portuguese began in January 1963, the rebellion quickly spread. The center of the uprising was southern Tombali province. The province bordered on Guinea, and Cabral's guerrillas had reasonably easy access to Tombali by land and sea. Another advantage was the province's lush, subtropical climate, which meant dense vegetation provided cover for guerrillas in hit-and-run attacks. By the end of the year, the Portuguese minister of defense General Manuel Gomes de Araújo confessed that the PAIGC had gained control over a significant portion of Guinea-Bissau.[30]

In early 1964, the guerrillas mounted a concerted resistance against a large-scale Portuguese operation to retain control over the island of Como. The fight over the rice-growing marshy island in southern Guinea-Bissau saw the Portuguese deploy 3,000 ground troops to the island, backed by aerial support. Both sides suffered casualties, and the Portuguese eventually withdrew, having lost the support of the local population. The PAIGC declared Como a "liberated area," which was a significant psychological victory since it showed the insurgency could not be easily crushed.[31]

While the battle over Como was in full swing, Cabral faced a major challenge to his authority. By 1964, reports had emerged that many regional military commanders were abusing the civilian population for personal gain. Although the PAIGC stood for a modernizing platform, these regional commanders often used deep-set beliefs to attack local rivals. Witchcraft was a common charge, and people accused of being *futseru* (sorcerers) could be attacked or killed, especially since these were often accompanied by accusations of espionage and betrayal. Some guerrillas used their status to take away girls and women and subject them to sexual violence.[32] Another problem emerged when some local commanders refused orders from Conakry to extend the war into the Fula-dominated Gabú region of eastern Guinea-Bissau.[33] To resolve these issues, Cabral called an all-party meeting at Cassaca in February 1964.

The so-called Cassaca Congress became a turning point in the history of the PAIGC. Insubordinate military commanders were ordered to attend, and those who refused were arrested and imprisoned. Some were allegedly executed. The Congress also pledged to establish a network of essential social services for the civilian population—basic health facilities, "people's stores," and bush schools—in order to harness support from the population and effect socio-cultural transformation in the countryside. Another set of measures included putting the guerrillas under centralized control. Cabral set up the *Conselho de Guerra* (War Council), which would supervise all military operations. The Congress also approved the establishment of a regular armed force, the Revolutionary Armed Forces of the People (FARP; *Forças Armadas Revolucionarias do Povo*).[34] To support the decisions taken at Cassaca, on May 26, 1964, Cabral appealed directly to Nikita Khrushchev, asking for "urgent assistance" in terms of matériel, goods, and large-scale training to support a "new stage" in the liberation struggle.[35]

After the Cassaca Congress, Czechoslovakia remained important to the PAIGC. One role it played was advisory. In September 1964, Czechoslovakia dispatched an StB officer, František Polda (codename "Peták"), to counsel Cabral in Conakry. Polda's task was to organize the FARP general staff and train recruits, especially in intelligence and security matters. Naturally, he would report back on his conversations with Cabral and share his opinions about the military situation and political developments in the organization. He was also to provide advice on operations.[36] Polda was actually well known as Cabral's adviser at PAIGC headquarters in Conakry and often instructed groups of young recruits.[37]

As the anticolonial war unfolded, the Czechoslovak Ministry of the Interior increasingly took on the role of providing security and intelligence training for Cabral's guerrillas. In August 1961, eleven men arrived for training at the Felix Dzerzhinsky Central School (Ústřední Škola Felixe Edmundoviče Dzeržinského) in Prague to receive generalized instruction in "guerrilla warfare" and "sabotage."[38] From 1963 onwards, though, Prague would offer training solely in security and counterintelligence. Czechoslovak instructors taught the recruitment of agents and collaborators, operative techniques like wiretapping, the basics of investigation and interrogation, and the fundamentals of criminalistics. The graduate of the 1963 course, Otto Schacht, soon became the head of PAIGC security.[39]

While Prague offered instruction in intelligence and security, the Soviets started training the bulk of the armed force, the FARP. The first group of recruits from Guinea-Bissau arrived in June 1964 for a six-month training course in Leningrad.[40] However, it was only after the construction of specialized facilities at Perevalnoe in 1965 that the Soviet training program for the PAIGC—and other African liberation movements, including the MPLA and FRELIMO—truly expanded. While early courses could accommodate no more than several dozen men from each organization, Perevalnoe was a large training facility that could host several hundred men at the same time. Its secluded location off the main road between Simferopol, the capital of Crimea, and Alushta, a famous vacation destination on the Black Sea, was to protect the guerrillas' identities and limit unsupervised contact with the local population. Other measures included flying recruits to Simferopol with several transit stops and driving them to the school on a special bus with drawn curtains.[41]

Outside of the extra secrecy, Perevalnoe functioned like a regular Soviet military school. Trainees' daily lives were governed by the strict rules of military discipline and hierarchy. They woke up at a specific time, marched to the canteen in a military formation, and observed rank. Soviet instructors (many of them World War II veterans) delivered training under three principal specializations: artillery, mines and explosives, and anti-aircraft defense. The leadership of the liberation movements selected trainees for particular specializations and reviewed performance reports. Those in anti-aircraft defense initially practiced how to operate Soviet heavy machine guns (KPVT and DShK) designed to hit low-flying targets—Portuguese aircraft—at close range.[42] Military training became closely tied to the provision of Soviet arms since new systems would have to be first introduced to by guerrillas at Perevalnoe.

Soviet instructors also devoted much time to so-called "political training." These involved informal "cultural events" ranging from outings to popular tourist sites and model communal farms to film screenings. The formal political training classes included an introduction to Marxism-Leninism, the history of slavery and colonialism in Africa, and discussions of current events. In many internal reports, Soviet instructors heralded the political training program as a success, reporting that exposure to the combination of discussions and sightseeing tours convinced the cadets of the benefits of the socialist system.[43]

Memoirs show that at least some Soviet instructors believed in the transformational impact of training programs on the cadets. One political instructor who arrived at Perevalnoe in 1966, Iurii Gorbunov, wrote that he witnessed how training in the USSR turned the cadets, often "shy and illiterate people," into men who became convinced of the "righteousness of their struggle."[44] Overall, Gorbunov's memoirs are tinged with a certain paternalism toward common soldiers, also evident in other similar recollections.[45]

It is difficult to evaluate whether military training in the USSR actually had such a significant impact on the trainees, as Gorbunov suggests. Sae Breia was among the first group of twenty-five recruits to go for military training in the USSR in June 1964. He recalled that the time he spent in Leningrad was transformative because what they learned about slavery and the Russian Revolution made them angry and even more convinced they should fight the Portuguese.[46] Some trainees from Guinea-Bissau also seemed impressed by the Soviet system of communal farming. The screenings of World War II films, with their stories of personal sacrifice—showcasing the role of the USSR in the defeat of Nazism— were also memorable for many cadets.[47]

At the same time, the majority of the trainees at Perevalnoe had already shared ideas about social justice they derived through their own experiences and peer-to-peer teaching at "centers for revolutionary instruction" established by the PAIGC in Guina-Bissau. When those men arrived at Perevalnoe, many saw their

PAIGC combatants during military training in the Soviet Union, most likely at Perevalnoe, Soviet Ukraine. The trainee is operating a Soviet heavy machine DShK gun, which became a common weapon of guerrilla warfare in the Portuguese colonies in the 1960s. Fundação Mário Soares e Maria Barroso/Arquivo Amílcar Cabral.

classes as a continuation of their studies.[48] To some, staying at Perevalnoe was revelatory in other ways. The Cape Verdean João Pereira Silva arrived at Pereval-noe in 1971. As he recalled in 2017 his experiences in Perevalnoe exposed to him hierarchies inherent in the Soviet system. Still, he argued that training forged group solidarity through discipline, thus bridging regional divides.[49] Although trainees' experiences of Perevalnoe differed depending on their prior experience, level of education and pre-conceived ideas, the majority appreciated the skills they acquired, which they could put to use upon their return to Guinea-Bissau.[50]

The extent of Czechoslovakia's involvement with the PAIGC during the early stages of armed struggle was extraordinary. Prague was the first to offer a comprehensive assistance package to the PAIGC and, as we know now, pushed Cabral to proceed with "acts of sabotage" to maintain dominance over its local rivals. Nonetheless, Cabral resisted StB's "advice," and it is clear that the initiative for armed action came from local activists rather than being dictated from abroad. As the war progressed, Perevalnoe increasingly became a critical contact zone for interaction between African revolutionaries and their Soviet instructors. Nevertheless, the Czechoslovaks retained a vital function as the providers of security and intelligence training. Moscow and Prague hoped that arms and training would allow the FARP to put mounting pressure on the Portuguese to negotiate. However, the prospect of a quick military breakthrough would prove fleeting.

Enter Cuba: Fidel Castro, Amílcar Cabral, and the Debates over Military Strategy in Guinea-Bissau

The years following the Cassaca Congress were exceptionally fortuitous for the guerrillas in Guinea-Bissau. Having secured training and military support from the Soviet Union and Czechoslovakia, in 1965, Cabral planned to move to a new stage of the war to eliminate Portuguese fortified posts. The leadership had also decided to start armed struggle on the Cape Verde archipelago. As Cabral conveyed to Czechoslovak Minister of the Interior Josef Kudrna during a visit to Prague in May 1965, he had decided to expand operations across the whole country and start liquidating the garrisons.[51] Prague believed that prospects of a breakthrough were good and allocated $1.85 million worth of arms to the PAIGC in 1965. The Soviets also contributed additional arms to support the plan.[52]

Cabral also obtained support from Cuba. In late 1963, the Argentinean-born revolutionary Ernesto "Che" Guevara visited Conakry as part of his Africa tour to find volunteers to join the Simba rebellion in Zaire. Although Guevara failed to convince Cabral to support his venture, he was impressed with the PAIGC. Back in Havana, Guevara pressed the Cuban leader Fidel Castro to provide military training for Cabral's men, especially Cape Verdeans, since he believed conditions for armed struggle in the archipelago were good. Castro agreed. In July 1965, a handful of Cape Verdeans journeyed to Cuba for military training.[53]

Guevara's trip to Conakry set the stage for Cabral's first trip to Havana to participate in the Tricontinental Conference and the founding of the Organization of Solidarity with the People of Asia, Africa and Latin America in January 1966.[54] At the conference, Cabral made a passionate speech on revolution in Africa, emphasizing the role of the "petite bourgeoisie" as the vanguard in the national struggle.[55] The speech impressed Castro, and after several days of conversations with Cabral and a trip to the Escambray mountains, the Cuban leader pledged to send military experts who would provide support for FARP. Cuba also provided goods—sugar, cigars, uniforms, and transport vehicles.[56] As Cabral's right-hand man Aristides Pereira recalled, donations from the socialist countries would contribute to the PAIGC's internal economy, as they would sell excesses of goods like Cuban sugar and Soviet diesel in Guinea for cash.[57]

Although the FARP had become much better equipped and supplied than at the beginning of the war, by 1967, it became clear there would be no easy victory against the Portuguese. The PAIGC faced a particular problem in expanding its operations in the Gabú region in Eastern Guinea-Bissau. One reason for these difficulties was that the region was dominated by the Fula. While the Balanta generally provided the bedrock of support for the PAIGC in the south, the Fula were often resistant to the nationalist drive, and many had been co-opted to serve in the Portuguese army. The Fula saw the Portuguese had much more advanced weapons than the PAIGC, recalled Dauda Bangura, and thus did not believe it would be possible to defeat the colonial power.[58]

The Portuguese counter-insurgency strategy compounded these difficulties. When the first attacks began, the Portuguese launched a major propaganda campaign in the east, urging the local Fula population to flee to so-called "protected villages." When the war escalated in 1966, the majority of the population fled to such villages near Portuguese posts at Madina de Boé and Beli. In the eastern Gabú region, the guerrillas thus could not rely on the local population to provide food or shelter and often faced shortages of basic necessities.[59]

Much of FARP activity in Gabú focused on the Portuguese post at Madina do Boé. Located close to the border with Guinea, the fort blocked the guerrillas' access to the eastern hinterland. When the PAIGC launched a major attack against Madina do Boé on November 11, 1966, the operation failed tragically, resulting in multiple casualties. Cabral was particularly distraught by the death of Domingos Ramos, who was hit by a mortar shell during the failed operation. Ramos was a charismatic leader and an effective mobilizer who became the commander of the eastern front after the Cassaca Congress. He was also Cabral's close friend.[60]

The disaster at Madina do Boé made Cabral rethink his military strategy. As he informed the head of the Africa desk at the StB, Josef Janouš, on February 13, 1967, the operations in the Gabú region would continue, but these would have to be much more carefully planned to avoid significant losses. He also shared his objections to Cuba's advice to launch a number of large-scale operations, including an attack on the capital, Bissau, since these could lead to significant loss of life, which would be demoralizing and harmful to the movement's prestige.[61] While Cabral preferred a war of attrition to avoid high casualties, the Cubans argued in favor of more extensive operations. However, as Piero Gleijeses has noted, the Cubans never tried to impose their opinions on Cabral, who possessed ultimate authority on military strategy.[62]

New documents show that the Soviets and Czechoslovaks were also concerned about the lack of military progress in Guinea-Bissau. In November 1966, the Soviets and their Czechoslovak counterparts gathered to discuss the war in Guinea-Bissau. They acknowledged that the guerrillas' morale was low, and their military reconnaissance was lacking. As a result, the operations resembled a "war game" rather than an actual "armed struggle." The solution was to "work out a strategic and tactical plan" for the PAIGC in consultation with the Cubans and then "choose and teach a few qualified men" who could carry it out.[63]

Although the full details of the plan are unclear, the Czechoslovak adviser František Polda believed FARP should be organized into larger military units capable of "preplanned" military operations. His Cuban interlocutors in Conakry agreed.[64] During a conversation with Cabral and Aristides Pereira in Conakry on March 5, 1967, Polda stressed that by establishing larger military units, the FARP would be able to destroy the Portuguese forts and ultimately win the war. Cabral pushed back, arguing that the commanders did not yet have the proper training.[65]

Polda remained wedded to his advice, Cabral's opposition notwithstanding. On February 8, 1968, he pressed Cabral to intensify ongoing attacks at Madina do Boé. Cabral again argued for caution since the FARP lacked anti-aerial defense and feared retaliatory bombings; he hoped that the new 122mm mortars he had obtained from the USSR would lead to a breakthrough. In a tense exchange, Polda countered that the liberation struggle increasingly resembled a "war game," to which Cabral replied that was precisely part of the "psychological warfare" to put pressure on the Portuguese. In a clear sign of disagreement, Polda responded that history would judge Cabral as a "great political strategist" but a "poor military commander."[66]

In 1968, a group of thirty Cape Verdean recruits arrived for advanced weapons training in Skhodnia, near Moscow. The majority of the men in the group—Pedro Pires, Silvino da Luz, Olívio Pires, Osvaldo Lopes da Silva, Antonio Leite, and Júlio de Carvalho, among others—had arrived in Moscow from Cuba, where they had been undergoing training for a clandestine mission to launch an armed struggle in Cape Verde. However, in 1967, the plan was abandoned because the leadership decided it was high risk.[67] In Cuba, military preparation involved "basic guerrilla training," while in Skhodnia, the group learned to operate advanced artillery, including 120mm mortars. Once they returned to Guinea-Bissau, the Cape Verdeans were deployed in the mortar units that engaged in attacks against Madina do Boé. The FARP finally seized the fort in February 1969.[68]

Unlike trainees at Perevalnoe, who were subject to strict military discipline and political instruction, the Cape Verdeans enjoyed a sense of political autonomy at Skhodnia, opting out of compulsory political classes. In fact, the group included men of varied persuasions. Júlio de Carvalho recalled he was inspired by the Cuban Revolution.[69] Silvino da Luz was influenced by the Chinese model of peasant-based revolt during their time in training.[70] However, most seemed to share an appreciation of Soviet military technology. Pedro Pires, the head of the group, recalled with hindsight: "Every guerrilla, from South America to Africa, passing through Asia, used this weapon. The great weapon of the guerrillas was the automatic machine gun AK of the Kalashnikov [AK-47]. That is the great contribution of the Soviet Union to the national liberation struggles."[71]

Meanwhile, Cabral continued to seek additional advanced weapons from the Soviet Union. Petr Evsiukov recollected that the GRU's chief Petr Ivashutin acted as a champion of Cabral's struggle. In his memoirs, he described at least one occasion when Cabral came to Moscow with his second wife, Anna Maria, with a request for additional heavy weapons. Ivashutin believed the Soviets should help, but the minister of defense, Marshal Andrei Grechko, rejected his request. Ivashutin and Evsiukov thus agreed that the former would introduce Cabral and Anna Maria to Grechko at a state reception, hoping a personal interaction would reverse the decision. The plan succeeded. Evsiukov recalled that Grechko was quite "excited" and in a "good mood" during the state reception. He greeted Cabral in a friendly way and promised to approve his request for arms.[72] Although Evsiukov does not provide a date, the anecdote shows that by the late 1960s, the Soviet Military and the GRU were heavily involved with the PAIGC.

It is more challenging to determine Soviet views about Cabral's military strategy. Osvaldo Lopes da Silva became an artillery commander on the eastern front after finishing military training in the USSR in 1969. In an interview from 2017, he argued that the Soviets were always more "in tune with us than the Cubans," advising them to "proceed with your own strength."[73] However, some archival documents indicate the Soviet military and GRU were also critical of the lack of military progress. In August 1969, Aleksandr Predvechnov (most likely of the GRU) relied on Cuban assessments to claim that "so-called liberated areas" were little more than hard-to-reach, swampy, or forested parts of Guinea-Bissau with "minimal importance." Predvechnov also criticized Cabral's strategy of relying too much on acquiring advanced weapons from the USSR to boost morale. Instead, he advised that FARP should focus on carrying out a number of "significant operations" to destroy Portuguese garrisons after acquiring new heavy weapons from the USSR. Such a strategy would allow the PAIGC to launch a "realistic propaganda campaign" to strengthen confidence and boost morale.[74]

The new weapons that Predvechnov referred to was Grad-P (Partisan), a system that the Soviets made available to the FARP in 1969. A lightweight version of the BM-21 "Grad" weapons system, Grad-P was developed in the 1960s for the North Vietnamese where it was known as 122mm DKZ-B rocket launcher. The weapon soon became a popular means of guerrilla warfare because of its transportability and ability to withstand humid conditions. The offer of Grad-P was significant, since unlike the heavy machine guns from World War II that had dominated Soviet deliveries before that, Grad-P could be operated individually and was lighter than a mortar. In 1969, a group of recruits went to Perevalnoe to train how to operate Grad-P.[75]

To sum up, the lack of military progress in Guinea-Bissau led to the emergence of debates over military strategy. Cabral was well aware that the guerrillas might have claimed vast "liberated areas," but the Portuguese still commanded the skies. He thus wanted to move cautiously and continuously pushed the Soviets to provide additional weapons systems, including anti-aerial defense. It is not fully clear how the Soviets evaluated such a strategy, but there are indications that Prague, Moscow, and Havana shared similar criticisms of Cabral's tactics. In 1968, Polda was recalled to Prague. While it is unclear whether this move was connected to the Prague Spring or any disagreements with Cabral, debates about military strategy would continue. In the meantime, similar conversations about military strategy in Angola would emerge in the mid-1960s.

Searching for Alternatives: The MPLA and Guerrilla War in Cabinda and Southeast Angola, 1964–1970

Back in west-central Africa, the MPLA faced tremendous logistical challenges in starting military operations in Angola. Having lost access to Zaire in 1964, Neto and his followers crossed the Zaire River from Léopoldville to the neighboring Congo-Brazzaville. From their new base in Brazzaville, the MPLA had three main options. One included starting guerrilla operations in Cabinda, an Angolan enclave that bordered on Congo-Brazzaville. The party could also smuggle men and weapons across Zaire to northern Angola, but it was a treacherous path where the guerrillas risked capture by Mobutu's troops. The final possibility involved moving the center of operations to southeast Angola. The MPLA tried all the three options with varying degrees of success.

After the move to Brazzaville, Agostinho Neto first attempted to start operations in Cabinda with Cuban support. The relationship between the MPLA and Cuba was forged after Che Guevara's talks with Neto in early 1965 in Brazzaville. The Cubans provided protection for Massamba-Débat's government in Congo-Brazzaville and also advised Neto on military strategy. In May 1965, after the first Cuban advisers arrived in Brazzaville, MPLA guerrillas ventured across the border to Cabinda and engaged in minor hit-and-run skirmishes with the Portuguese patrols. As was the case in Guinea-Bissau, the MPLA leadership disagreed with the Cuban advisers about the need to launch larger-scale operations to attack Portuguese forts. One such MPLA-Cuban operation, entitled "Operation Macaco," involved a plan to engage about one hundred guerrillas and a few pieces of 75mm artillery in an attack on the Portuguese fort of Sanga Planicie in northeast Cabinda. The MPLA did not want to proceed, arguing that the proposed size of the unit was too large and the operation too risky. The Cubans insisted. However, only two days after entering Cabinda, the Portuguese ambushed the column, causing the guerrillas to disperse in a panic.[76]

Neto was also keen to restart operations in northern Angola—the heartland of the rebellion in 1961. However, that involved trekking almost 400km through thick jungle and across Zairean territory. What was even more perilous than the journey itself was the attitude of the Zairean authorities. In November 1965, the powerful chief of the Zairean army, Colonel Joseph Désiré Mobutu seized, power in a bloodless coup d'état. While Mobutu's predecessor, Moïse Tshombe, was hostile to Roberto as he collaborated with white minority regimes to crush the Simba rebellion, Mobutu ramped up support for the FNLA. That involved denying the MPLA access to northern Angola via Zaire.

In 1966–67, the MPLA dispatched three expeditions of about 100 men each to northern Angola via Zaire, but only the first expedition reached its destination. The others were apprehended by the Zairean authorities, arrested, and imprisoned. Many of those men and women were never seen again. By June 1967, the MPLA had run out of weapons and realized the futility of the enterprise. The Cubans, who provided the training for the columns, ended their support for the MPLA in June 1967. Havana claimed their mission in Congo-Brazzaville was over, but there was clearly no love lost between the two sides. Fidel Castro was critical of the MPLA's performance, while Neto resented the Cubans' attempts to take charge of operations in Cabinda.[77]

Starting in 1966, the MPLA began to infiltrate southeast Angola from a new base in Zambia. Bordering Angola to the west, Tanzania to the east, and Southern Rhodesia (Zimbabwe) to the south, Zambia had become independent on

October 24, 1964. Zambia's first president, Kenneth Kaunda, was initially reluctant to allow liberation movements to operate from Zambia since the country was landlocked and relied on neighboring Southern Rhodesia to transport its copper. However, things changed after November 11, 1965, when Southern Rhodesia announced a Unilateral Declaration of Independence (UDI) to preserve white minority rule. In opposition to the UDI, Kaunda allowed liberation movements to open offices in Zambian territory. In early 1966, the MPLA started transferring recruits from Congo-Brazzaville to Zambia to prepare for a campaign in southeast Angola.[78]

The MPLA faced significant challenges when trying to launch an armed struggle in southeast Angola. Most weapons for the liberation movements in Eastern Africa arrived at the port of Dar es Salaam in Tanzania. Then, they had to be transported on a long journey to Zambia. Moreover, Zambia initially refused to allow arms that were transported from Tanzania. Beyond the logistical challenges, Jonas Savimbi's UNITA had reemerged as a rival to the MPLA in southeast Angola. Savimbi was an Ovimbundu, an ethnic group that dominated southeast Angola. He and his organization, UNITA, thus gained local followers and support from the Zambian authorities. As the MPLA's representative in Lusaka, Anibal de Melo, complained to Soviet ambassador Sergei Slipchenko, the Zambian authorities wanted to strengthen UNITA, presenting it as the most effective liberation movement in southeast Angola.[79] Only in October 1966 did Lusaka lift an unofficial ban over the movement of men and arms across the Zambia-Tanzania border. According to Slipchenko, Kaunda reacted against the Portuguese soldiers launching a cross-border raid across the Angola-Zambia border yet remained reluctant to support the liberation movements wholeheartedly.[80]

The Soviets were initially quite optimistic about the MPLA's prospects. Soviet financial assistance jumped from $50,000 in 1963 to $100,000 in 1965, and Moscow began providing the MPLA with weapons.[81] In a conversation with the Polish delegation on the sidelines of the Twenty-Third Congress of the CPSU on April 2, 1966, Petr Manchkha argued that Neto was a "doctor and a Communist" who commanded authority among the "progressive forces" in Africa. He confirmed that Moscow had fulfilled "all of the MPLA's requests" for assistance which included, uniforms, medicine, equipment for the printing press, hospital equipment, cash, and arms via Dar es Salaam.[82] In 1966, financial assistance to the MPLA increased to $145,000.[83]

Soviet journalists also started to support the MPLA's effort to construct its image as the only liberation movement dedicated to armed struggle in Angola.

In 1965, Mikhail Domogatskhikh, a journalist with the Soviet daily *Pravda*, traveled to Cabinda, accompanied by MPLA guerrillas. He came back with field notes that he published in a series of articles in *Pravda* between May and June 1965. He was followed by Tomas Kolesnichenko, one of *Pravda*'s leading foreign correspondents, known for his lively writing style and flair for adventure. In early 1966, Kolesnichenko published a series of reports for *Pravda*, in which he depicted scenes from the "liberated areas" and featured conversations with popular guerrilla commanders, like the MPLA's Hoji Ya Henda. These romanticized reports from the "liberated areas" served several purposes. They helped the liberation movements construct heroic metanarratives of anticolonial struggle for international consumption. By invoking the struggle for justice and socialism in faraway lands, they were also meant to validate the socialist experiment and increase the prestige of the Soviet Union.[84]

The journalist who became the most frequent Soviet reporter on anticolonial struggles in the Portuguese colonies was Oleg Ignatev, who also worked for *Pravda*. Ignatev's interest in Guinea-Bissau in particular was shaped by a close personal relationship that he developed with Amílcar Cabral, whom he first met in November 1965. Upon Cabral's suggestion, Ignatev ventured to Guinea-Bissau for the first time the following year. He became a regular visitor to Guinea-Bissau, returning in 1968 to shoot a film about the PAIGC, followed by trips in 1970 and 1973. Ignatev also went to Angola and Mozambique and would often serve as a go-between for the leadership of the liberation movements and Soviet officials, providing firsthand information about developments on the ground.[85]

Although the MPLA was lauded in the press, the Soviets became increasingly critical about the lack of military progress in Angola. The Soviet embassy in Congo-Brazzaville argued in February 1967 that the MPLA had failed to win over the local population in Cabinda since the majority of guerrillas had come from around Luanda and northern Angola. As a result, the Portuguese managed to co-opt Alexander Taty, a former member of Roberto's FNLA and a Cabinda native who had organized the local people to resist the MPLA. Since the MPLA had moved its center of operations to southeast Angola, only 250 guerrillas remained active in Cabinda, mainly engaging in hit-and-run attacks across the border from Congo-Brazzaville.[86]

The Soviet embassy in Tanzania also criticized the MPLA for a lack of political work among the population in southeast Angola. In particular, the movement needed to develop "clear and attractive slogans" to pull different groups, especially the peasantry, into fighting the Portuguese. The MPLA's famous

Agostinho Neto (center, glasses) and commander Hoji Ya Henda shaking hands with the editor of *Pravda*, Mikhail Zimianin. Ignatev/Sputnik.

rallying cry, "*Vitória ou Morte!*" (Victory or Death!) simply was not enough to gain support among the local population. The people needed to have a clear understanding of the benefits of independence. As for military operations, the embassy acknowledged the logistical problems of moving guerrillas and weapons via Zambia. The MPLA had experienced leaders and organizers who were united around Neto, the embassy continued, but military operations were still scattered. There was little coordination of military operations and no radio contact between small groups of guerrillas.[87]

It is not clear where the embassies obtained information about military developments. For the most part, the Soviets had to rely on conversations with different MPLA representatives and, most likely, Cubans who were closely involved in guerrilla operations. In general, access to what the Soviets termed "reliable information" about military progress would become an important issue for Moscow and would often determine the level of assistance. In late 1966, Zambia's permission to transfer arms across the border opened up new opportunities for the anticolonial campaign in southeast Angola.

In early 1967, an intradepartmental Soviet team set off for Congo-Brazzaville, Zambia, and Tanzania to investigate the situation on the ground. The mission included: Genadii Fomin, the head of the Third African Department at the Ministry of Foreign Affairs; Vadim Kirpichenko, the head of the Africa desk at the KGB's First Directorate; and Petr Evsiukov and Petr Manchkha from the International Department. Kirpichenko recalled that their primary focus was Angola, and their task was to "find anybody" who had firsthand evidence of military operations. Apparently, at the MPLA's main base at Dolisie in Congo-Brazzaville, they met a Soviet doctor who confirmed that guerrillas had been arriving at the hospital on a daily basis. Kirpichenko also recalled that Neto made a good impression since he did not exaggerate the MPLA's achievements and had realistic expectations of Soviet assistance.[88]

The trip was, in many ways, a turning point because it confirmed that the MPLA was actively engaged in armed struggle. As Fomin shared with the GDR's consul at Dar es Salaam, Gottfried Lessing, the Soviet delegation was impressed by the "unity and political clarity" of the MPLA's leaders. In addition, the opening of the new route for weapons to reach Angola through Tanzania and Zambia created possibilities for increasing pressure on the Portuguese in southeast Angola.[89] As Petr Evsiukov recalled, the Politburo decided to provide "all-around support to the militant nationalists in Portuguese colonies" following the trip.[90] In 1968, the bulk of MPLA cadres and their families would be airlifted from Congo-Brazzaville to Tanzania on Soviet planes.[91]

However, Soviet relations with Neto soon grew strained. Starting in 1965, Neto started receiving assistance from Yugoslavia, which he preferred to the countries of the Eastern Bloc because of its nonaligned status. Yugoslav assistance was modest at first, but in January 1968, Belgrade decided to increase its financial contribution to $15,000 and started shipping arms for the MPLA. In October 1968, Neto met the Yugoslav leader Josip Broz Tito. The two discussed military strategy in Angola, and Tito strongly criticized the Soviet intervention in Czechoslovakia. Initially, the Soviets did not seem to have a problem with Neto's relationship with Tito. However, when Neto continued his connection to Belgrade even after Yugoslavia openly criticized the Soviets for the invasion, Moscow allegedly suspended assistance to the MPLA. As Jovan Čavoški has discovered, the Yugoslavs stepped up their support in response, providing more than $270,000 in aid, including arms, medicine, and cash.[92]

Relations with Neto in 1969 indeed appeared rocky. When the MPLA's Anibal de Melo met Ambassador Slipchenko in Lusaka on September 4, 1969, he shared his frustration about his recent trip to Moscow. While meetings at the

CC CPSU were generally friendly, Melo said that he and Neto were "shocked and surprised" about the attitudes of the two Soviet military experts who first "interrogated" them about the progress of guerrilla warfare in Angola and, in the end, made accusations that the MPLA did not have any active military operations, despite extensive Soviet assistance. Melo also insisted that the Soviets were also misinformed about the activities of UNITA and Jonas Savimbi, who had "betrayed the MPLA." Slipchenko, in turn, reassured Melo that the Soviets had not "turned away" from the MPLA but instead wanted to make sure they understood the scope of military operations to provide adequate assistance and advice.[93]

Neto and Melo were right to detect the Soviets' frustration with the lack of military progress in Angola. In a note for the CC CPSU from June 1970, the KGB made a scathing critique of the MPLA's progress in southeast Angola, arguing that the efficacy of armed action had decreased. The MPLA's leadership had "underestimated the value of underground work" in big cities like Luanda, and they had no clandestine cells in urban areas. The MPLA was further hindered by "tribal" tendencies in southeast Angola, which were exacerbated by arbitrary attitudes toward the local population. The KGB also argued the MPLA leadership was wrong to avoid any contact with Savimbi, who had acquired substantial support in the southeast.[94] In effect, the Soviet evaluation of progress in southeast Angola mirrored their view of what the Cubans believed went wrong in Cabinda: the MPLA had failed to mobilize the people because they did not have an appropriate strategy. As a result, the MPLA was losing out to its local rivals.

Soviet relations with the MPLA at least partly revolved around disagreements over military strategy. Although we do not know how often the Soviets consulted with the Cubans, their general assessments of Neto's military strategy in Cabinda were similarly critical. The Soviets believed that the MPLA was not doing enough to embed themselves in the local population. Although Moscow was well aware of the MPLA's logistical limitations and increased support in 1967, new documents show that the Soviet military was quite critical about what they perceived as a lack of military progress. While the full extent of Soviet conversations with Neto is not available, the evidence we do have suggests that the relationship was often conflictual and that military and political strategy was subject to much debate. Personalities mattered since, in contrast to Cabral, Neto never really established a close relationship with his Soviet liaisons. As we will see, the Soviets also developed a skeptical view of the FRELIMO leadership.

Mondlane's Diplomacy of Liberation and China's Influence in Tanzania

In late 1964, the Portuguese authorities woke up to another front in the colonial war: Mozambique, East Africa. The first attack claimed by FRELIMO
took place on September 25, 1964, when a number of guerrillas attacked the
post of the *chefe do posto* (colonial administrator) in the small town of Chai
in Cabo Delgado, a northern Mozambican province bordering Tanzania. The
chefe do posto was killed, along with six other men. As FRELIMO's president
Eduardo Mondlane admitted in his 1968 book, *The Struggle for Mozambique*,
in 1964, FRELIMO had only "250 men trained and equipped" who engaged in
hit-and-run attacks against the Portuguese. Two years later, Mondlane claimed,
the insurgency spread into the sparsely populated Niassa province, and the size
of FRELIMO's army had reached 8,000 men.[95]

While Mondlane argued that armed action was the only option because the
Portuguese were not ready to accept self-determination, he knew he could no
longer delay violent action because of pressure from activists, the Tanzanian
authorities, and local competitors. In June 1964, a rival organization, MANU,
had staged an attack in the northern Cabo Delgado province and killed Father
Daniel Boorman. Although the murder of the popular Dutch missionary did
not elicit local support and led to massive repercussions against MANU, Mondlane realized that FRELIMO had to take the initiative.[96]

Once FRELIMO started its campaign in late 1964, Mondlane engaged in
hectic diplomacy to obtain further military support from the socialist countries.
In April 1965, he toured southeastern Europe, receiving weapons and financial
assistance from Czechoslovakia and Bulgaria.[97] Mondlane also requested additional financial support from Moscow. The Soviets provided weapons and
ammunition, as well as medical supplies and other types of humanitarian assistance.[98] However, Soviet support remained limited and included no cash—in
contrast to the MPLA and the PAIGC. At a meeting with Soviet embassy staff
in Dar es Salaam on March 16, 1965, Mondlane claimed that "eighty percent of
Mozambicans" had been equipped with Soviet weapons, but FRELIMO also
required financial assistance.[99] However, the Soviets continued to deny such requests because of Mondlane's connections to Washington.

In 1966, the CC CPSU International Department refused Mondlane's bid
to attend the Twenty-Third Congress of the Party in Moscow. As Rostislav
Ulianovskii explained the decision in an internal memo, Mondlane received

regular cash handouts from U.S. organizations and was connected to the government in Washington. Furthermore, Mondlane "lacked trust" from the leaders of the MPLA, the PAIGC, the South African Communist Party, and FRELIMO's deputy president the Reverend Uria Simango. Allegedly, the head of the KGB's First Directorate, Aleksandr Sakharovskii, also supported Ulianovskii's decision to deny Mondlane an invitation to the Congress. The Soviet ambassador in Dar es Salaam was thus instructed to find an excuse to politely refuse.[100]

The special mention of Uria Simango in Ulianovskii's memo is telling. Born in 1926 to a peasant family in Sofala province, central Mozambique, Simango was educated by Protestant missionaries in Mozambique and Southern Rhodesia and was ordained as a Church of Christ pastor in 1956. After Simango was elected vice president of FRELIMO in 1964, he became involved in diplomatic missions to socialist countries.[101] Toward the mid-1960s though, Simango became unhappy with what he saw as the role of "whites"—more specifically, Janet Mondlane, João Ferreira, Fernando Ganhão, and Jacinto Veloso—who joined the movement, working in Dar es Salaam in various roles, including as teachers at the Mozambique Institute.[102] Ulianovskii's memo seems to suggest that the Soviets considered Simango to be more trustworthy than Mondlane.

The Soviets distrusted Mondlane because they were worried that the U.S. funds he was receiving were tied to the CIA. In fact, Moscow took Mondlane's contacts with Washington seriously, especially since they believed British influence in Tanzania was still strong. As the KGB argued in early 1966, the conservative wing in the Tanzanian government wanted to eliminate "progressives" like Oscar Kambona, and it was likely that a right-wing coup in the country was imminent.[103] Rumors around Mondlane and his private fortune continued to circulate, and in 1965, the Soviet journalist Mikhail Domogatskhikh was approached by two separate Mozambicans who complained about Mondlane's unwillingness to engage in armed struggle and issued a warning about his close contacts with U.S officials.[104]

At the same time, the Soviets worried about growing Chinese influence in Tanzania, which became increasingly prominent after the revolution in Zanzibar. After Tanganyika and Zanzibar signed an act of union in 1964, a number of Marxist politicians, among them Abdulrahman Mohammed Babu, moved from Zanzibar to the mainland and joined Julius Nyerere's cabinet. Babu's diplomacy paved the way for Nyerere's first highly publicized visit to China in February 1965, after which Beijing committed to training Tanzania's army and investing in development projects. In 1967, Beijing announced that it would construct a railway linking the copper mines of landlocked Zambia to the port of Dar es Salaam and committed a $401 million, interest-free loan to finance the project. China also became an essential source of assistance to FRELIMO and other liberation movements in Dar es Salaam, providing small arms, cash, and training for guerrillas in Tanzania.[105]

China's influence in Tanzania extended beyond developmental assistance. A longtime proponent of "African socialism," Nyerere was inspired by the Chinese revolution. On February 5, 1967, he outlined a radical development program based on collective hard work, agrarian transformation, and an anti-imperialist stance that he termed *ujamaa* ("brotherhood" in Swahili). In the words of Priya Lal, the Cultural Revolution and Nyerere's *ujamaa* "shared imaginaries" such as a dedication to self-reliance, discipline, hard work, and commitment to rural transformation. As Beijing flooded Tanzania with propaganda materials and Mao Zedong's ideas spread widely via a network of bookstores and the radio, many urban intellectuals were inspired by China's transformation.[106] Since FRELIMO was deeply embedded in Tanzanian politics, China's influence was prominent among the members of the anticolonial movements based in Dar es Salaam.

One such member was a FRELIMO military commander named Samora Moisés Machel. Born in 1933 in southern Gaza province to a wealthy peasant family, Machel received his primary education at a mission school before training and working as a nurse at the hospital in Lourenço Marques (Maputo). After attracting attention because of his outspoken views on Portuguese colonialism, he fled to Dar es Salaam in 1963. From there, he was dispatched for military training in Algeria. In 1965, he was sent on a mission to open a new front in Niassa province. He was also responsible for training recruits at a base in Nachingwea, where he became quite popular with the rank-and-file recruits. In Nachingwea, Machel was first introduced to Mao Zedong's ideas by Chinese instructors who worked at the camp. As Machel often claimed, his Marxism resulted from his own experiences of colonialism and racial discrimination. His interest in Mao's ideas of collectivism and solidarity with the peasantry also did not necessarily mean he supported China's racially-based definition of anti-imperialism.[107]

It is not clear whether the Soviets understood such details. In his memoirs, Evsiukov wrote of Machel in hindsight as someone who was a "naturally talented leader," but also of someone who "lacked education." Evsiukov also believed that Machel embraced "leftist extremism," often speaking favorably about China's Cultural Revolution and admiring Joseph Stalin.[108] The Soviets closely monitored China's aid to FRELIMO and the so-called "pro-Chinese" sentiments among the leadership and Mozambican trainees at Perevalnoe.[109] Naturally, it was not always easy for the Soviets to establish exactly who was "pro-Chinese" since the Mozambicans were inspired by a variety of African, Third World, and European "socialisms," often rooted in their own experiences. As Elizabeth Banks has argued, Machel adopted an "explicitly European and Soviet form of socialism" after independence.[110]

Mondlane tried to play on Soviet sensibilities during his trip to Moscow in November 1966. In conversations with Soviet interlocutors, he acknowledged the achievements of Soviet socialism in Kazakhstan and Azerbaijan and complained about China's "anti-Soviet tactics," especially the way they played out at international conferences. However, FRELIMO could not openly express their attitude toward China, he continued, because they could not alienate their hosts—the Tanzanian government—which had a close relationship with Beijing.[111]

To an extent, Mondlane's tactics worked. As Dmitrii Dolidze of the Soviet Solidarity Committee argued in a conversation with an East German diplomat on November 26, Mondlane showed he was positively inclined towards the USSR because he had been "pushed to the left by the progressive forces." Although Mondlane was "not entirely our man," Dolidze continued, the people around him were "quite in order."[112] However, not everyone was fully convinced. As Genadii Fomin shared with Gottfried Lessing in Dar es Salaam in February 1967, Mondlane did not seem to have "political clarity" and exhibited "opportunistic tendencies" during his trip to Moscow. The Soviet Union would continue to supply weapons to FRELIMO, but in a "limited way."[113]

By 1968, the Soviets believed Mondlane had "moved left" in terms of his views, but they would never trust him completely. They seemed to have developed a more favorable view of Simango and maintained clandestine sources within FRELIMO, who informed the Soviets about internal developments. As we will see, the juxtaposition of the pro-U.S. and pro-China lines within the organization would continue to preoccupy the Soviets, as they tried to make sense of the crisis that would thrust FRELIMO into internal turmoil in 1966–70.

FRELIMO in Crisis: The View from Moscow

The crisis that enveloped FRELIMO in 1966–69 consisted of an interconnected series of intraparty conflicts, culminating in the murder of Eduardo Mondlane in 1969. Since FRELIMO's inception in 1962, conflicts inside the organization

Eduardo Mondlane (second on the right, top hat) with Pascoal Mocumbi
(first right) on Red Square, Moscow, 1966. Noskov/Sputnik.

had been defined by struggles between "northerners," predominantly Makonde
rank-and-file members, and "southerners," *mestiço-assimilado* elites epitomized
by such figures as Eduardo Mondlane and Marcelino dos Santos. The north-
south divide also correlated with the growing ideological rift between capitalist
and socialist modernizers inside FRELIMO. Debates around race, class, and
ideology were closely intertwined with rivalries over access to political power.
The crisis was further complicated as warring factions sought supporters in
TANU, Tanzania's ruling party. The Soviets acted mainly as observers in this
process as they tried to untangle the shifting political alliances to determine
which "side" reflected their interests.

    The first rumblings of a crisis began in 1966. On October 10, Filipe Magaia,
FRELIMO's first chief of defense and security, was killed while crossing a
river after nightfall with a group of guerrillas inside Mozambique. Although
FRELIMO claimed Magaia's death was an accidental shooting, it quickly
became a subject of controversy. Earlier that year, Magaia had allegedly criticized the leadership in Dar es Salaam for not heeding advice from the military commanders and for releasing boastful war communiqués that threatened
the guerrillas' safety, leading to mounting casualties. Rumors thus spread that
Magaia was murdered, a victim to a plot concocted by the "southerners" to

centralize their power over the military. In a move that seemed only to give credence to the rumors, Samora Machel, born in southern Gaza province, became the new chief of defense.[114]

Mondlane's deputy, Reverend Uria Simango, secretly encouraged such rumors because he too resented the dominance of southern *mestiço-assimilado* elites and wanted to replace Mondlane as president. One of Simango's allies was Mateus Gwenjere. A Roman Catholic priest, Gwenjere joined FRELIMO in Dar es Salaam in 1967 and started teaching at the Mozambique Institute. He caught Mondlane's eye due to his intelligence and was dispatched together with Simango to speak at the UN General Assembly. According to John Marcum, Simango and Gwenjere bonded in New York over what they believed was the racial nature of Portuguese colonial rule. Simango also shared his discontent with what he described as a power grab by the southern "mulatto-*assimilado*" group in the leadership.[115]

In March 1968, tensions exploded into the open when students at the Mozambique Institute openly rebelled against FRELIMO's leadership. The Mozambique Institute was a key project envisioned by Mondlane and his wife, Janet, to educate and train cadres for a future independent Mozambique. However, by 1967, it had become clear that educational priorities had given way to the needs of the revolution when FRELIMO required students to attend a military preparation course at the Nachingwea camp during the school holidays. The students, mostly Makonde from northern Mozambique, saw these changes as an imposition forced on them by the "southerners." With Gwenjere's support, students spoke out against the leadership and campaigned to remove the white professors from the institute. The standoff ended on March 5, 1968, when the FRELIMO leadership entered the students' dormitories and made sure they were arrested and dispatched to one of the refugee camps in Tanzania.[116]

However, the most formidable challenge to Mondlane's leadership was a regional rebellion led by Lázaro Nkavandame. A Makonde entrepreneur from Cabo Delgado province, Nkavandame initially joined FRELIMO because he became frustrated that the Portuguese were hindering his efforts to set up an agricultural cooperative in the north. When FRELIMO appointed Nkavandame the head of the civil administration in Cabo Delgado province in 1963, he continued to modernize Makonde agriculture based on the "free British capitalism" model he had experienced in Tanzania. Nkavandame was also responsible for FRELIMO-administered stores and trade in Cabo Delgado province, amassing a small fortune in the process. While FRELIMO's narrative always depicted Nkavandame as a "chief" who stood against progress, new research portrays him as someone who represented the rising class of rural African capitalists.[117]

The conflict came to a head in 1968 when FRELIMO decided to centralize its structures in the Cabo Delgado province. Fearing he would be sidelined, Nkavandame allied with Mateus Gwenjere to replace Mondlane with Uria Simango. On at least two occasions in May, Nkavandame's supporters entered FRELIMO's offices in Nkrumah Street, Dar es Salaam, and engaged in physical altercations with Mondlane's supporters. Then Nkavandame and Gwenjere called for FRELIMO's Second Congress to be convened and elections for new leadership. Nkavandame hoped that if a FRELIMO Congress could be held in Tanzania, he could amass enough support. However, Mondlane managed to undercut his opposition by holding the Congress in Mozambique in late July 1968. Nkavandame refused to attend, and Mondlane was reelected president. In an explicit statement of its revolutionary direction, the Congress asserted that the struggle stood for the "construction of a new society free from the exploitation of man by man and confirmed the basic principles of racial and gender equality."[118]

The crisis in FRELIMO was closely entangled with Tanzanian politics. Many Tanzanian politicians were of Makonde origin, like Nkavandame and the majority of rank-and-file recruits. Although Mondlane received strong support from Nyerere, Makonde Tanzanians often found common cause with those who opposed the FRELIMO president. Mondlane admitted as much in a series of conversations with Arkadii Glukhov, counselor at the Soviet embassy at Dar es Salaam, with whom he shared that Nkavandame and Gwenjere had received support from the Chinese and also "middle-ranking Tanzanian officials" who shared their "anti-white" line.[119]

The key figure who opposed Mondlane was Lawi Sijaona. A minister of state for refugees in the office of Vice President Rashidi Kawawa, Sijaona was a Makonde like Nkavandame and shared his dislike for Mondlane on racial grounds. As a chairman of the TANU Youth League, he was inspired by Maoist rhetoric and spearheaded the protests against the Soviet invasion of Czechoslovakia in August 1968.[120]

Mondlane seemingly emerged victorious from the Second Congress, but the conflict continued. At a meeting in Mtwara, Tanzania, in August 1968, Nkavandame and other Cabo Delgado leaders charged FRELIMO with executing military and civilian leaders who had opposed the leadership in Dar es Salaam. Nkavandame then issued orders to border committees to bar FRELIMO from entering Cabo Delgado. When Paulo Kankhomba, FRELIMO's deputy chief of operations, defied the ban and entered the province in December 1968, he was killed, allegedly by local Makonde militants. Gwenjere then pressed for new presidential elections. Once again, Mondlane managed to undercut the opposition. He persuaded the Tanzanian authorities to place Gwenjere under house arrest and suspended Nkavandame from his post. Nyerere's support for Mondlane undoubtedly allowed him to overcome opposition at crucial moments in the crisis. In the meantime, the Mozambique Institute was closed to avoid further conflict in the wake of the students' revolt.[121]

The Soviets received information about FRELIMO's internal politics through a variety of sources. One of the KGB's Mozambican contacts was Joaquim Chissano. A native of southern Gaza province like Mondlane, Chissano had participated in the student activist organization NESAM before pursuing a degree in medicine, first in Portugal and then in France. In 1962, he joined FRELIMO in Dar es Salaam. In 2016, the declassification of the Vasilii Mitrokhin archives in Cambridge led to the revelation that it was Chissano whom Mitrokhin and Christopher Andrew described as the "KGB confidential contact" codenamed TSOM. These (rather limited) records show that Chissano started collaborating with the KGB after receiving training in the USSR in 1965. In 1970, the KGB even tried to "promote" Chissano to the status of an "agent," but the International Department rejected the idea to avoid jeopardizing their official relationship.[122] Chissano denied he was ever a "spy" but confirmed exchanging information with the KGB for the benefit of FRELIMO.[123]

While recent revelations about Chissano's contacts with the KGB made quite a furor in the press, in reality, the Soviets had many sources of information about developments in the Mozambican liberation movement. They had regular conversations with the top leadership, especially with Mondlane, Santos, Simango, and Chissano. The Soviet intelligence services also cultivated clandestine contacts inside FRELIMO and, very likely, the Tanzanian government.[124] In October 1968, one such "trusted source" of the GRU submitted a full report on the situation inside the organization after the Second Congress and the August meeting in Mtwara. The source detailed the tense exchange between Mondlane and Nkavandame, noting that Simango was playing both sides in the standoff between the two men. The report also described the close connections between Lawi Sijaona and Nkavandame. However, there were no suggestions in the report that Mondlane's life was in danger.[125]

On the morning of February 3, 1969, Mondlane picked his mail at FRELIMO's offices at 201 Nkrumah Street in Dar es Salaam before driving to the house of his American friend Betty King. As he sat down to work and opened his mail, Mondlane was instantly killed by a parcel bomb, hidden in a book bearing a stamp from Moscow. As the investigation discovered, the stamp was a forgery, and the batteries in the detonators had been manufactured in Japan and sold by a firm in Lourenço Marques. The assassination had clear signs of Portuguese involvement, and evidence pointed to the so-called Aginter Press, a clandestine network of sleeper agents who fought against Portugal's enemies in Africa. Local collaboration was also likely, and most people pointed to Sijaona and Mondlane's key critics, including Nkavandame, Simango, and his ally Silvério Nungu. Although Sijaona was very likely involved, there is little evidence to suggest that either Simango or Nungu played a role. As George Roberts has argued in his detailed reconstruction of the various theories, the plan was most likely concocted by the Portuguese and executed with African collaboration. Still, Mondlane's murder remains unsolved.[126]

The Soviets did not seem to have any unique insights into the identity of the perpetrators. In a note on developments in FRELIMO after the murder, the KGB's deputy chairman Nikolai Zakharov argued that Mondlane's foreign policy, which included maintaining relations with both socialist and capitalist countries, had been sharply criticized by Algeria, Cuba, and especially China. Moreover, Mondlane had angered some among the Tanzanian establishment by maintaining a relatively independent stance since many of them still hoped to create a federation between Tanzania and Mozambique. With Mondlane gone, continued Zakharov, it was very likely the Chinese would intensify attempts to influence the organization leadership.[127]

The Czechoslovak intelligence service also tried to comprehend the mystery behind Mondlane's murder. In an overview of the situation in FRELIMO from February 1969, the StB declared that Mondlane's assassination was part of a wider trend of "political murders" to target the late president and his supporters. The men who potentially profited from the murder were Simango, Silvério Nungu, and Lázaro Nkavandame. The PIDE must have been involved as well as "elements in the Tanzanian government," in particular Lawi Sijaona. Overall, the StB described Mondlane as a "capable organizer" who was an anti-imperialist, influenced by Marxism, stating that his murder was a "huge loss" for FRELIMO.[128]

The report was clearly informed by information from Czechoslovak intelligence officers on the ground. One of them was Dr. Zdeněk Kirschner, an StB officer codenamed "Vilim." Kirschner had arrived in Dar es Salaam in 1966 and worked undercover, teaching civics at the Mozambique Institute. In his role, he had established friendly relations with the teachers at the Institute and FRELIMO's leadership. The StB had sources inside FRELIMO and even considered developing a special clandestine relationship with Marcelino dos Santos (whom they codenamed SLAO) and his wife, Pamela. They decided against pursuing the relationship, citing Pamela's friendly relations with Betty King, who was allegedly close to Bill Sutherland—the American Friends Service Committee representative in Dar es Salaam and Mondlane's close friend—who the StB suspected was a CIA agent.[129] The report shows the StB had a much more favorable evaluation of Mondlane than their Soviet counterparts. Although the documents do not reveal any explicit disagreements with the Soviets, differences were not uncommon.[130] Kirschner was recalled to Prague in October 1968 and subsequently "released" from his duties at the StB due to his opposition to the Soviet invasion of Czechoslovakia. He was nonetheless commended for his work in Dar es Salaam.[131]

Meanwhile, Mondlane's assassination intensified the power struggle within FRELIMO. In April 1969, Uria Simango, Samora Machel, and Marcelino dos Santos established the Council of the Presidency. Although Simango expected to occupy Mondlane's position after his death, he was forced to share power with the others. For about six months, the triumvirate managed to keep the appearance of unity. In July 1968, Simango and Chissano went to the Soviet Union. Once again, financial assistance was on the agenda, and Moscow allegedly approved the provision of at least a portion of the requested $100,000 in cash.[132]

However, the power-sharing arrangement did not last. In November, Simango released a pamphlet, "Gloomy Situation in FRELIMO," in which he accused Machel and Santos of usurping power, eliminating political rivals, and plotting to kill him. He also criticized the late Mondlane for allowing the Portuguese to dominate the Mozambique Institute and accused his widow Janet of conspiring with the CIA to infiltrate the organization. Simango denied he was racist at the time, as did his biographer Ncomo, who argued the vice president wanted to prevent FRELIMO's domination by southern elites.[133] Although such a narrow focus on ethnicity has been challenged, the crisis exposed differences between those like Mondlane and his allies, including Santos, who championed a cosmopolitan nationalism, and others like Simango, who defined the struggle in racial terms.[134]

Moscow closely followed these power struggles. In a lengthy analysis of the triumvirate in July 1969, Petr Ivashutin argued that FRELIMO was a weak organization, rooted in the "peasant masses," with little experience of armed struggle, and riven by intra-ethnic tensions. He described Simango, Santos, and Machel as "petit-bourgeoisie" who mistakenly shared the "pseudo-revolutionary" Maoist concept of popular partisan warfare. The only significant difference between the two factions was their attitudes toward white Mozambicans. Uria

Simango exhibited a more "racist and pro-Chinese line," while Samora Machel's faction seemed more interested in developing relations with the USSR. At the same time, Ivashutin acknowledged that the nationalist movement in Mozambique was important because of the country's location, bordering Southern Rhodesia and South Africa. Therefore, he proposed countering Chinese propaganda and dispatching a Soviet military adviser who could influence the course of guerrilla warfare.[135]

Ivashutin's mentioning of South Africa is noteworthy, since the end of Portuguese rule opened up possibilities for the ANC to use Mozambique as a launching pad for operations in South Africa. From the GRU's perspective, it also allowed for the possibility of expanding its signals intelligence capability. After independence in 1975, the Soviets did indeed prioritize southern Mozambique in their defense strategy they developed for FRELIMO, with an eye toward developments in Pretoria.[136]

As the conflict entered its final stage, Simango tried to win Moscow to his side. In a conversation with Arkadii Glukhov in Dar es Salaam on September 25, Simango outlined familiar arguments about the dominance of southerners in leadership positions. He also argued that Janet Mondlane was dangerous because she was a "white American," and the CIA could continue to exercise control over the movement through her. His friend Silvério Nungu had already been eliminated, continued Simango, and he was next on the hit list.[137] After the release of "the Gloomy Situation" in November, Simango approached the Soviets again with an explanation. He never wanted to make the criticisms public, but the inaction of the Tanzanian authorities left him no choice. Once again, he charged FRELIMO's leadership with corruption, "tribalism," and political killings. As for his attitude toward race, explained Simango, he was never against whites in the organization; he only resented foreign influence.[138]

By this point, the GRU did not trust any member of the FRELIMO leadership. In an overview of the situation in October 1969, the GRU's Aleksandr Predvechnov argued that neither Simango, nor Machel, nor Chissano, nor Santos were "consistent friends of the Soviet Union." While Simango was looking to improve relations with the USSR, the GRU doubted his intentions. In a striking passage, Predvechnov argued that FRELIMO had always been determined to lock Soviet influence out of the organization. He relayed the suggestions of "trusted sources" who insisted that Filipe Magaia and Paulo Kankhomba—FRELIMO military commanders allegedly close to the USSR—were assassinated by those who feared the strengthening of Soviet influence over the movement. Predvechnov described Simango as a more generally "acceptable figure," since the others were openly sympathetic to China.[139] In an evaluation of developments inside FRELMO one month later, Ivashutin mirrored Simango's assessment of Janet Mondlane, arguing the CIA could use her close relationship with Machel to influence internal politics. Although Ivashutin did not think that Simango had a clear political affiliation and that his influence was on the decline, he predicted that an internal party struggle would continue.[140]

In the end, Ivashutin overestimated Simango's strength. Shortly after the publication of "Gloomy Situation in FRELIMO," Simango was suspended from the Presidential Council and deported from Dar es Salaam. In May 1970, the Central Committee expelled him from the party and declared he would be subject to "the people's justice."[141] However, by that time, Simango had already fled Tanzania and later joined a rival splinter organization, COREMO. After Mozambique became independent in 1975, FRELIMO brought Simango and other critics like Nkavandame back to Mozambique. In May 1975, they were subjected to a show trial at Nachingwea, forced to confess to betrayal, dispatched to a "re-education camp," and subsequently executed.[142] After Simango fled in 1970, Machel was appointed president and Marcelino dos Santos the vice president. Machel would come to dominate FRELIMO until he died in a plane crash in 1986.

Conclusion

The Soviet view of developments in Africa was fundamentally ideological. Moscow believed the African military was a neocolonial institution, prone to Western influence and outright meddling. They were also concerned about the challenge posed by China, especially in East Africa. The Soviets thus attempted to correct what they considered their mistake of underestimating the role of African militaries in politics. They thus drew in allies by ramping up assistance and making new clandestine contacts with the eventual goal of extending the reach of Soviet navy and signals intelligence. At the same time, military training was meant to earn loyalty from young soldiers and convince them of the attractiveness of the socialist system. Thus, the Soviet military was increasingly drawn in as officials became involved in advising, training, and providing military supplies to allies.

The level of assistance depended on the vastly different dynamics of the Soviets' relationships with Cabral, Neto, and Mondlane. By the mid-1960s, the Soviets had developed a close relationship with Cabral, based on his personal associations with men like Evsiukov. Moscow was committed to facilitating a military victory in Guinea-Bissau and therefore continued to supply increasingly sophisticated weapons, training, and cash to the PAIGC. Since military advisers wanted to enable victory, heated disagreements emerged about guerrilla strategy. Although many details of these discussions are still unclear, Soviet, Czechoslovak, and Cuban advisers shared at least some criticisms of Cabral's military strategy. Still, Cabral managed to resist pressure and used contacts with Soviet liaisons to obtain new weapons systems. The majority of Cabral's guerrillas experienced Soviet modernity mainly during their time in military training. As interviews with trainees have indicated, the full extent of their exposure to Soviet realities is difficult to separate from a variety of influences and ideas that soldiers were exposed to before coming to the USSR. However, Soviet military technology, rather than ideology or organizing principles, seemed to most significantly impact rank-and-file soldiers, who felt that weapons equaled liberation.

The dynamics of guerrilla warfare also underpinned the Soviet relationship with the MPLA. Although we do not have the exact figures, it seems that the provision of arms was initially limited, mainly due to logistical challenges. Although Moscow did ramp up assistance to Neto after 1967, the Soviets became critical of the MPLA's campaign in Cabinda and southeast Angola. Fundamentally, the Soviets did not believe the MPLA was doing enough to create a truly broad movement and often questioned the efficacy and scope of military operations. Criticisms of this kind fed into their rocky relationship with Neto, who looked to Yugoslavia and elsewhere for alternative sources of military support. The new evidence does not shed light on any disagreements between the International Department and the Soviet military or the KGB and the GRU on the MPLA's progress. It is very likely, though, that the Soviet military played an important role in shaping views of developments on the ground, which contributed to the complicated relationship Neto had with Moscow.

Military strategy played less of an essential role in Soviet views of FRELIMO in the 1960s. The documents reveal a strikingly bleak view that the Soviets and especially the GRU developed of their relationship with the Mozambicans. The GRU had multiple sources inside the organization but still struggled to come to grips with its factionalism, becoming convinced the leadership was fundamentally anti-Soviet. On the one hand, the Soviets distrusted Mondlane because of his contacts in Washington and feared CIA influence. On the other, they resented what they believed was growing Chinese influence, which meant that even initial allies like Marcelino dos Santos were not seen favorably. Although a Soviet cadre like Evsiukov clearly respected Mondlane, the GRU seemed to buy into the misguided narrative of his critics that the CIA could exert influence over the movement via his wife, Janet.

The GRU initially saw Machel as a popular yet amenable figure who could be influenced by Mondlane's widow. As the crisis within the organization deepened, the Soviets were being pulled in different directions, as various factions all sought support from international patrons. Nevertheless, the GRU argued that the Soviet Union should increase its (rather limited) military support for FRELIMO to strengthen its foothold in the organization. Once Machel centralized power in 1970, the Soviets would proceed to court him with offers of new assistance packages for the guerrilla campaign.

The full story of cooperation between Prague, Havana, and Moscow is still buried in the archives. The level of Czechoslovak involvement with liberation movements such as the PAIGC, in particular, was extraordinary, and there clearly existed cooperation between advisers on the ground and those at higher levels. This collaboration did not preclude differences of opinion, and the StB evaluations of Mondlane point to one such example. The Soviet intervention in Czechoslovakia in 1968 did not seem to impact its relations with the nationalist movements in any significant way. The most considerable effect was on Czechoslovakia itself. By the mid-1960s, Prague was already seeking to limit its commitments to anticolonial movements for fundamentally economic reasons, and the events of 1968 only accentuated the trend. The evidence available shows that Havana, Prague, and Moscow were broadly aligned in terms of their view of the guerrilla struggle in the Portuguese colonies. As the next chapter shows, the often-heated discussions of military strategy would continue. However, the Soviets would have to square the ever-intensifying demands of the anticolonial movements with their burgeoning détente with the United States.

CHAPTER SIX

Disappointments

The Portuguese Offensives and Détente, 1970–1974

O N SEPTEMBER 27, 1968, Portugal's president Américo Tomás invited Marcelo Caetano, a sixty-two-year-old Lisbon law professor, to take over from Salazar, who had suffered a debilitating stroke. At first glance, Caetano had little in common with Salazar. Unlike his ascetic predecessor, Caetano was married with four children. Salazar had never ventured beyond Portugal's borders, while Caetano had traveled widely, spoke French, and fashioned himself as a moderate. However, his regime differed little from his predecessor's. As a legal adviser to Salazar in 1929, Caetano had been one of the architects of the Estado Novo, occupying several high-level government posts in the late 1950s.[1] Caetano also shared Salazar's resolve to retain the empire at any cost. In 1970, he authorized major military offensives against the nationalist movements in the colonies. The offensives put immense pressure on the liberation movements, intensifying internal divisions—to devastating effect.

Caetano found that the new incumbents of the White House—President Richard Nixon and his influential national security adviser Henry Kissinger—were fairly accommodating. In the face of domestic opposition to the Vietnam War, Nixon and Kissinger sought to reduce commitments in the Third World. In Africa, their strategy entailed relying on regional "policemen" like Joseph Mobutu in Zaire to contain communism. They also believed that white minority rule in southern Africa would continue and favored closer relations with Southern Rhodesia, South Africa, and Portugal. Washington thus came to an understanding with Caetano, which involved cutting off all aid to Holden Roberto's FNLA and expanding trade relations with Portugal.[2]

At the same time, Nixon and Kissinger's realpolitik foreign policy provided an opening for a rapprochement with the Soviet Union known as détente. Arguably a conservative reaction to the crises of 1968, détente started in Europe with West German chancellor Willy Brandt's *Ostpolitik* (eastern policy), which aimed to settle the status of East Germany to ensure a durable peace in Europe. Nixon and Kissinger believed that calculated agreements with the Soviet Union could restore U.S. power and leveraged their support for a settlement on West Germany for a negotiated peace deal in Vietnam. They also launched a parallel rapprochement with China and employed "triangular diplomacy" with the Soviets to encourage progress in ongoing talks on arms limitations.

In the 1970s, détente led to a number of breakthroughs. The 1970 Moscow Treaty recognized the postwar border in Europe, and the 1972 Strategic Arms Limitation Treaty (SALT I) limited the build-up of antiballistic missiles. Détente would have been impossible without CC CPSU general secretary Leonid Brezhnev. He believed rapprochement with the United States was essential to avoid another war, and his partnership with Brandt and Nixon, in particular, enabled some of the key agreements.[3] As Rui Lopes has argued, détente actually helped strengthen Portugal's Western alliances since it legitimized the notion of working with disreputable regimes and solidified divisions between the Global North and South.[4]

The impact of détente on Soviet policy in the Third World has been subject to substantial debate. Although there was a considerable relaxation of tensions in Europe in the 1970s, the Cold War in the Third World did not exhibit any signs of abating. The United States failed to constrain its ally, Israel, during the Yom Kippur War and backed a coup against Salvador Allende, Chile's socialist president, in 1973. Meanwhile, the Soviets and Cubans became involved in crises in Angola and Ethiopia, and in 1979, the Soviet Union invaded Afghanistan. In the United States, neoconservative critics of Nixon and Kissinger argued their strategy encouraged Soviet interventionism.[5]

New evidence has shown that Moscow never intended to use détente as a way to achieve world domination.[6] In fact, the Soviets saw events such as U.S. actions during the Yom Kippur War as evidence that Washington was still determined to exclude Moscow from engagements in the Third World. As Odd Arne Westad has argued, many younger cadres of the International Department advocated a more active Third World policy that would show that the Soviets were willing to protect revolutions abroad despite détente.[7] In Africa, the argument continues, the KGB developed a "new Soviet African strategy," which entailed greater support for liberation movements in southern Africa.[8]

This chapter argues that Soviet policy toward the liberation movements was shaped by perceived developments in the anticolonial campaigns rather than détente. As discussed in the previous chapter, by the mid-1960s, the Soviet intelligence services had come to believe that Western countries would not shy away from using military means and "subversion" to protect their interests in Africa.

Détente did not change this view. They saw Nixon's policy in Africa as a continuation of confrontation by other means and worried about the "reemergence" of China. The Soviets also faced a challenge posed by European social democracies, especially after the Nordic countries began providing humanitarian assistance to the liberation movements.

As this chapter demonstrates, Soviet relations with liberation movements were shaped by military considerations and personal connections to African revolutionaries rather than a "new Soviet Africa strategy." In the face of Portuguese offensives, guerrilla warfare strategy once again became a subject of significant discussion. The Soviets were willing to ramp up military assistance and provided new weapons systems, such as the modified portable rocket launcher Grad-P, but they also hoped their clients would heed their advice and devise a more ambitious military strategy. These expectations were largely unmet. In Angola, the Portuguese offensive wreaked havoc on the MPLA, resurrecting internal debates about political and military strategy. As these disagreements had exploded into a major internal crisis by 1973, the Soviets suspended assistance to the MPLA to put pressure on Neto to come to an agreement with his internal critics. Meanwhile, the Soviets increased assistance to FRELIMO, now centralized under the leadership of Samora Machel.

Guinea-Bissau was a theatre of particularly dramatic confrontations between the Portuguese and the PAIGC. In the early 1970s, the Portuguese tried to break the military stalemate with a number of daring operations to capture the PAIGC leadership in Conakry. Meanwhile, Cabral pressed the Soviets for new military technology to overcome Portugal's air superiority, obtaining the surface-to-air Strela-2 "Arrows" (SA-7 Grail) missile complex in 1972. However, the prolonged war exerted a toll, and in January 1973, Cabral was assassinated in a plot orchestrated by disgruntled members of the PAIGC. New evidence reveals how the Soviet military evaluated debates on guerrilla strategy in Guinea-Bissau, their differences with the Cubans, and their response to Cabral's murder. The chapter highlights that détente played only a limited role in Soviet relations with the liberation movements.

Cold War in Africa and Détente: A View from the Kremlin

In January 1970, the KGB chief Iurii Andropov warned the Central Committee about the Western "offensive in Africa." Andropov argued that the West viewed coups in Somalia, Libya, and Sudan with alarm and were determined to counter Soviet influence. While economic aid remained a critical tool, he continued,

Western countries did not shy away from applying military pressure. The key Western tactic was to rely on proxies, such as Morocco, Ethiopia, and Zaire in their attempts to subvert Soviet influence on the continent. All in all, Andropov concluded, it was likely that Western countries would provide support for "reactionary coups" in "progressive African countries" such as Libya and Sudan.[9] In another note to Boris Ponomarev, Andropov shared his view that the West believed the Soviet Union was not planning for a "broad offensive" in southern Africa. These warnings notwithstanding, the KGB made no explicit recommendations as to the Soviet response.[10]

In the context of the Western offensive against Soviet interests in Africa, the KGB also noted "growing contradictions" in the OAU. In a note to the Central Committee in April 1970, the KGB outlined several worrying trends vis-à-vis African attitudes toward the liberation movements. The OAU was split: many members had lost interest in national liberation and were failing to pay their share into the Liberation Committee's fund. Meanwhile, vital host states such as Tanzania and Zambia "constrained the development of nationalist liberation struggle" because they feared retaliation from white minority regimes while pocketing the military hardware designated for the liberation movements. A major symptom of the trend toward accommodation was the 1969 Lusaka manifesto, which prioritized "peaceful means of struggle" against white minority regimes. A number of "progressive African countries" wanted to activate national liberation movements with Soviet help.[11] Here again, the KGB did not make any concrete proposals.

Meanwhile, Soviet military intelligence highlighted Africa's central role should there be another war. In a sweeping overview of Western military relations with African countries, the GRU's Lev Tolokonnikov argued that Western countries were stepping up their military cooperation with African countries in exchange for permission to construct U.S. military bases. In particular, he emphasized the role of South Africa as a source of crucial minerals and resources, which grew in importance following the closure of the Suez Canal after the 1967 Six Day War. Further, the GRU's logic differed little from familiar arguments. The role of African armies was on the rise, and Western countries targeted the military to exert influence. Under such circumstances, coup attempts were likely in Sudan, Libya, Somalia, Congo-Brazzaville, and Tanzania.[12]

The breakthrough in Soviet-American relations after signing the SALT I treaty in 1972 did not do much to change the KGB's outlook on Western policy in Africa. In an overview of Nixon's policy from May 1973, the KGB argued that Washington still wanted to increase its military presence on the continent and expand political and economic cooperation with those countries that had "real possibilities of rapid development." Nixon was making serious efforts to weaken Soviet influence on the continent, and thus he was strengthening his cooperation with white minority regimes and Portugal. The United States was no longer interested in "direct interference" in African countries but believed that the development of long-term commercial and political relations would bring the desired benefits. At the same time, the KGB argued, the United States still did not believe the Soviet Union could pose a threat to its long-term interests due to the USSR's lack of experience in Africa and Sino-Soviet disagreements: "The Americans believe that general tendencies on the continent are favorable for the West. They believe that the economic necessity of the African countries would contribute to keeping these countries in the Western sphere of influence."[13]

The Soviets were also concerned with the resurgence of China. In the early 1970s, China emerged from the peak of the Cultural Revolution, and Beijing was eager to reconstruct its role on the international stage. In 1971, China's rapprochement with the United States enabled its admission to the United Nations. The CCP revived diplomatic relations with most African countries and pursued an increasingly active international agenda to win over allies at Moscow's expense. While China's militant anti-Soviet stance had derailed relations with the MPLA and the PAIGC, in the early 1970s, Beijing sought rapprochement. In 1971, Agostinho Neto and Samora Machel went to Beijing. To their satisfaction and surprise, they were received by China's premier Zhou Enlai and courted with promises of military assistance.[14] China's return to Africa alarmed the Soviets. The Soviet Solidarity Committee feared that China could return to international forums such as the AAPSO and derail Soviet influence.[15]

The GRU believed that China's growing influence could be countered with Soviet military assistance. In an October 1970 overview of China's activities in Africa, Petr Ivashutin and General Nikolai Dagaev argued that the key to China's success was the quick provision of economic and military aid on preferential terms. To tackle the challenge, the Soviet military should be allowed to make independent decisions about dispatching advisers quickly on request, expanding propaganda related to military assistance programs, and ensuring that military aid satisfied the requirements of the recipients. China's influence could be countered with more effective and swifter military assistance and by developing interpersonal relationships and contacts with African militaries.[16]

Another challenge to the Soviets in Africa stemmed from European social democracies. In 1968, Amílcar Cabral went to Stockholm and met the Swedish

Social Democratic Party leader, Olof Palme. After the meeting, Sweden became a significant donor of humanitarian assistance such as food, clothing, and medicine to the PAIGC. The governments of Norway, Denmark, and Finland followed with assistance programs to the MPLA, FRELIMO, and the PAIGC.[17] Assistance from the Nordic countries allowed for the provision of basic goods to the civilian population and decreased dependency on aid from the socialist countries.[18]

The response of the Nordic countries was at least partly shaped by changes in European public opinion. Since the late 1960s, a number of solidarity organizations in Europe and the United States had started to campaign against white minority rule in southern Africa. One notable campaign focused on Portugal's plan to construct a hydroelectric dam on the Zambezi River at Cabora Bassa in Mozambique's Tete province. Solidarity groups believed the scheme served to attract white settlers and entrench Portuguese rule and thus they campaigned vigorously against the participation of Western capital. In 1969, the Swedish firm ASEA withdrew from the project due to widespread opposition. The clearest indication of a change in public opinion came in 1970 when Pope Paul VI held a brief audience with Marcelino dos Santos, Agostinho Neto, and Amílcar Cabral at the Vatican. The papal reception was a public relations disaster for Caetano's conservative Catholic regime, which had consistently branded the liberation movements as "terrorists."[19]

The Soviets never publicly voiced opposition to the support from the Nordic countries. In the early 1970s, Vladimir Shubin was involved in developing contacts with European solidarity groups at the Soviet Solidarity Committee, and he has always insisted that Moscow did not have a negative attitude toward the Nordic countries' involvement in Africa.[20] In internal communications, attitudes were more complex. As the Soviet ambassador to Tanzania Viacheslav Ustinov argued in a letter to the CC CPSU from April 1972, contacts with social-democratic governments could increase the popularity of "bourgeois-liberal reformist" views about the role of "Western democracies" in national liberation and could promote ideas about reaching a compromise with the colonial authorities.[21] At the Rome Conference, held in solidarity with the struggles in the Portuguese colonies in 1970, Vasilii Solodovnikov, the director of the Institute of African Studies in Moscow, acknowledged that the Soviet Union was supplying arms to the liberation movements in an interview with *Pravda*.[22] Soviet military support was an open secret, but public acknowledgment demonstrated that Moscow wanted credit for supporting the anticolonial campaigns.

The Soviet military and intelligence services did not believe détente had a significant effect on the Cold War in Africa. Rather accurately, the KGB saw Nixon's policy in Africa as a continuation of confrontation by other means, and there were no suggestions that détente would lead to the withering away of competition. The USSR's solutions to challenges from the West and China were familiar and included expanding aid and contacts with African militaries. The Soviet military and the GRU wanted greater involvement and more "independence" to provide a viable alternative to Western and Chinese assistance. However, there is little evidence to suggest that Soviet policy in Africa added up to a new, coordinated strategy.

As Vladislav Zubok has argued, the Soviet military's lobbying for more international assistance might have been at least partly motivated by material gain. The 1970s saw the emergence of what has been described as Brezhnev's "little deal," which involved a system of perks and privileges, which often functioned via the shadow economy, allowing certain sections of society to enjoy daily comforts. Soviet military advisers working in Africa were often well paid, which allowed them to buy goods and commodities in short supply back home.[23] While these motivations are impossible to discern from the documents, they were not incompatible with the strategic considerations that fitted into a fundamentally ideological worldview shared by the Soviet military. As far as the liberation movements were concerned, the early 1970s saw the expansion of military assistance from the socialist countries. The impetus for such developments came as the Soviets observed the changes in military strategies adopted by the Lusophone nationalist movements.

Moscow Loses Trust in Neto

The war in the vast, sparsely populated hinterland of southeast Angola has been described as a "war for people."[24] The Portuguese and the MPLA used similar, often violent, methods to force people to abandon their villages and move to the bush or Portuguese-run protected villages. In 1970, the Portuguese launched a major offensive against the MPLA. Its architect, General Francisco da Costa Gomes, borrowed from the French in Algeria, employing a *quadrillage* garrisoning system, which divided the country into sectors, each permanently controlled by troops, to isolate the guerrillas. The army launched a renewed bombing campaign and started dropping industrial chemicals on the fields to destroy crops.[25] These tactics caused widespread deprivation and starvation in the MPLA-controlled zones, while transportation problems hindered resupply. As people fled to Portuguese-held areas, the numbers of those accused of betrayal and witchcraft and executed as traitors in MPLA territory increased dramatically.[26]

Neto tried to adapt by devising a more ambitious military strategy. In a conversation with Dmitrii Belokolos, the Soviet ambassador to Zambia, on September 14, 1970, Neto admitted that the war had stalled, which was terrible for morale, and carried the risk of losing support from the civilian population.[27] Neto's plan included establishing larger guerrilla units of roughly 100 men each, equipped with heavy artillery, to destroy fortified Portuguese posts. He also prepared to intensify military activity in the economically important regions in the west of the country.[28] Neto's plan might have originated in conversations between himself, Tito, and Yugoslav military advisers in the late 1960s.[29] However, it was also consistent with what the Soviets and the Cubans had been advising for some time. In a lengthy report to Moscow, Belokolos argued that the Soviets should support Neto's plan by providing necessary logistical assistance and advice on operations.[30]

The Soviets saw the adoption of a more ambitious strategy of guerrilla strategy as a positive development. In a progress report from April 1972, the Soviet ambassador to Tanzania, Viacheslav Ustinov, noted that guerrilla campaigns were limited to mainly sporadic hit-and-run tactics in the border areas. The liberation movements did not prioritize extending the geographical reach of military operations and did not build "underground cells" across the country. Now, continued Ustinov, the MPLA and FRELIMO understood that they had to reorganize small guerrilla detachments into a regular army and set up a network of cells to create a clandestine underground movement, including in the cities. The Soviets supported the expansion of military operations, and in the early 1970s, the MPLA received new pieces of heavy artillery and the Grad-P weapons system.[31]

Neto's plans did not materialize, however. In February 1972, Costa Gomes launched Operation Attila, a large-scale offensive in southeast Angola that included aircraft dropping defoliants to destroy crops and communication lines. Gomes also made a secret deal with Jonas Savimbi to join forces against the MPLA. Having established UNITA in 1966, Savimbi had built up his following among the Ovimbundu of southeast Angola. However, the MPLA was much better trained and equipped and thus represented a direct challenge to UNITA. Costa Gomes and Savimbi agreed that they would not fight each other but would cooperate to eliminate the MPLA with intelligence support from UNITA, including on locations of the MPLA bases. By late 1972, the colonial authorities estimated that the offensive had reduced the insurgents' strength by more than half of the total number of men recorded in 1970.[32]

The renewed offensive exacerbated preexisting inequalities inside the MPLA. The majority of the MPLA's top-level commanders and the political leadership were of Mbundu or multiracial origins and came from Luanda and northwest Angola. The commanders thus often had little in common with the rank-and-file soldiers, many Ovimbundu, in southeast Angola. As Neto's close MPLA associate Lúcio Lara later acknowledged, some commanders in southeast Angola did indeed "abuse their positions" by ordering the rank-and-file soldiers to carry heavy loads on long marches from Zambia to the southeast. There was also discrimination in allocating food.[33] Such inequalities brewed discord among rank-and-file members. As Neto acknowledged in a conversation with Ambassador Belokolos on March 18, 1972, the MPLA experienced incidents of "tribalism," but reassured that these would not impact the armed struggle.[34]

New evidence shows that in 1972, Neto's critics portrayed growing rifts within the MPLA in Cold War terms. In May 1972, a group of MPLA activists approached the Soviet embassy in Brazzaville, complaining that the MPLA's *mestiço* leadership, including Lúcio Lara, had denied scholarships for military training in the USSR to rank-and-file members. Brazzaville-based recruits also criticized Neto and Lara for misappropriating funds and matériel from the socialist countries.[35] According to MPLA vice president Domingos da Silva, the crux of the conflict lay in disputes over relations with the Soviet Union. He contended that the MPLA was split between pro-Soviet and pro-Chinese factions. Silva argued that Neto secretly belonged to the pro-Chinese faction and wanted to limit Soviet influence.[36] While little is known about the real reasons behind the dispute these events perhaps predated the formation of *Revolta Activa* (Active Revolt), a Brazzaville-based group critical of Neto for setbacks on the battlefield and an undemocratic, "presidential" leadership style. Although *Revolta Activa* became particularly prominent in 1974, discord was clearly fomenting for some time.[37]

In the meantime, Neto started talks to reach an accommodation with Holden Roberto. Neto always believed that northern Angola should be the core base of operations for the guerrilla movement. As Neto explained to his Soviet interlocutors, an agreement with Roberto would mean the Zairean authorities would allow the MPLA to cross into northern Angola.[38] On December 13, 1972, the MPLA and the FNLA signed a unity agreement, creating the Supremo de Libertação de Angola (Supreme Council for the Liberation of Angola) to oversee joint military command. However, the merger never translated into any practical form of unified actions, despite recurrent attempts at further talks in 1973.[39]

The Soviets were skeptical of the rapprochement between Neto and Roberto. As the Soviet embassy in Kinshasa (formerly Léopoldville) argued in a telegram to Moscow, the agreement could mean much greater Zairean and, therefore, U.S. influence on the Angolan liberation movement. The outcome could mean a "pro-Western" regime in the country after independence.[40] Petr Evsiukov recalled that the nature of the agreement was "confusing" to them as well as the MPLA's rank-and-file members.[41] It is true that Neto's agreement with Roberto did little to calm growing discord inside the organization.

In April 1973, the MPLA made a dramatic announcement that some of its members had conspired to assassinate Neto. The MPLA leadership proceeded to arrest the plotters and imprisoned them in the Kalombo camp in western Zambia. Under interrogation, the men confessed that their ringleader was Daniel Chipenda. The forty-three-year-old son of a prominent Protestant clergyman and activist, Jesse Chipenda, Daniel Chipenda became involved in politics as a student at the University of Coimbra, Portugal. After fleeing Portugal in 1961, he joined the MPLA, was elected the youth leader, and became a popular commander on the eastern front, no doubt partly because of his Ovimbundu heritage. As Chipenda recalled to an interviewer much later, in May 1973, the MPLA's Henrique "Iko" Carreira arrived in Lusaka with orders for him to depart for the front in Angola. Chipenda refused and asked Zambia's president Kenneth Kaunda for protection.[42] He then remained in Lusaka and maintained an uneasy standoff with Neto. By June, grievances in Eastern Angola erupted into a major rebellion, known as *Revolta do Leste* (Eastern Revolt). MPLA camps in western Zambia became divided between Neto's and Chipenda's supporters and were shaken by outbursts of violence.[43]

Chipenda denied his allegedly central role in the Eastern Revolt. He argued that Neto had mishandled complaints about arbitrary executions of civilians and other abuses committed by MPLA field commanders in southeast Angola. Then, in 1971, the MPLA began a process known as "readjustment," which called on party cadres to examine their actions in the light of military failures and engage in "criticism and self-criticism." Chipenda claimed that he had opposed the Chinese-inspired campaign because it would only stir up "racist accusations" against the leadership, and he maintained that a "fundamental structural adjustment" was required to address underlying issues. He also denied that there was ever any coup against Neto, arguing that the arrest and subsequent torture of the Kalombo detainees sparked the Eastern Revolt.[44] Speaking on behalf of the MPLA, Lúcio Lara argued that the "readjustment" movement was productive.

Chipenda was the one who did not want to be accountable to the people and therefore was expelled.[45] One way or another, the Eastern Revolt presented a significant challenge to Neto's leadership and drastically curtailed the MPLA's attempts to organize military operations in southeastern Angola.

As the crisis within the MPLA unfolded, the Soviets tried to mediate between Neto and Chipenda. In September 1973, Petr Evsiukov and GRU's Ivan Plakhin arrived in Dar es Salaam for talks. In conversation with Neto on September 14, 1973, the newly appointed Soviet ambassador in Tanzania, Sergei Slipchenko, informed Neto that 112 tons of Soviet weapons—AKs, Grad-P rocket launchers, and 82mm mortars—would be shipped to Dar es Salaam before end of the month. Evsiukov, Plakhin, and Slipchenko also discussed the "situation in the Angolan liberation movements." Although a record of the conversation is not available, the schism with Chipenda was likely on the agenda. Further, the presence of Plakhin, who was responsible for coordinating aid to the liberation movements, attests to the seriousness of the matter.[46]

Soon it became clear that Neto was unwilling to accommodate Chipenda. On October 18, Neto wrote directly to Leonid Brezhnev, describing the schism in the MPLA as part of an "imperialist plan" to derail the Angolan nationalist movement. The opposition, argued Neto, were "counterrevolutionaries" who were stoking the fires of "tribalism" and "racism," and he urged the Soviets to intervene with the Zambian authorities to restore support for the MPLA.[47]

However, the Soviet military did not share Neto's version of events. On December 21, 1973, Viktor Kulikov, the chief of the Soviet General Staff, presented a damning evaluation of Neto's actions during the crisis. Neto had disregarded "ethnic considerations" in creating the MPLA's leadership structure; he had also imposed a dictatorial leadership style and underestimated the importance of "political work." Instead of understanding the causes behind the crisis, continued Kulikov, Neto used brute force and executed alleged plotters when confronted with criticism. When the majority of guerrillas in the Zambian base camps rebelled in August 1973, Neto responded by cutting supplies. The outcome of all these mistakes, concluded Kulikov, was the almost complete cessation of MPLA military operations. Therefore, he proposed that Moscow impress upon Neto and Chipenda the contingency of Soviet aid on their ability to overcome the internal crisis.[48] The International Department backed Kulikov's assessment. On January 7, 1974, Petr Manchkha cabled Ambassador Belokolos in Zambia to tell Neto about the decision to suspend support because of the conflict with Chipenda.[49]

It is not clear whether the decision to suspend assistance was unanimous. Although the military adopted Chipenda's version of the crisis, the KGB might have seen the conflict differently. Neto's first KGB contact from Zaire in the early 1960s, Oleg Nazhestkin, recalled that he and his superiors never trusted Chipenda. He argued that the decision originated with the International Department: its cadres disliked Neto and were duped by Chipenda's "revolutionary rhetoric."[50] The KGB and the GRU were notoriously competitive, and their evaluation of developments on the ground often differed—a fact that Evsiukov acknowledged in his memoirs.[51]

Another piece of evidence comes from Marga Holness, a British activist who worked as Neto's interpreter in Dar es Salam. According to her recollections, around the time of Chipenda's revolt, she was approached by an official she recognized as a Soviet embassy staff member in Dar es Salaam. The man told her that he did not share the views of the Soviet embassy in Zambia. She was surprised because the USSR was always presented as a monolith.[52] Unfortunately, it is impossible to discern if the said official was a KGB officer. However, Vladimir Shubin's recollections support the contention that a highly negative view of Neto might have been perpetuated by the Soviet embassy in Zambia, mainly by GRU's Vladimir Bezukladnikov, a World War II veteran who served as the counsellor at the embassy in Lusaka.[53]

One way or another, the suspension of assistance came unexpectedly to Neto. In a conversation with Ambassador Slipchenko on March 20, 1974, Neto complained there was "much confusion" in the MPLA's relations with the Soviet Union, which was "playing into the hands of the enemy." He argued that the Soviets followed the conclusion reached by the Zambian authorities, who were prejudiced in Chipenda's favor. Soviet financial assistance was the primary source of cash for the organization, and therefore the termination of aid was putting the organization in an extremely difficult position. It was a "shock" to the MPLA.[54]

In many ways, the Soviet decision was a logical if not an inevitable outcome of a very rocky relationship with Neto. Since the mid-1960s, the Soviets believed that Neto's dictatorial leadership style and reliance on *mestiços* was preventing the organization from fully connecting with rank-and-file recruits across Angola. The MPLA was elitist and non-representative of all ethnicities, they believed, which prevented substantial progress in the guerrilla campaign. The Soviet military and the International Department saw Neto's conflict with Daniel Chipenda in the same light. To them, Chipenda represented the Ovimbundu and a chance to make the MPLA genuinely popular in the southeast. The lack of trust between

Neto and members of the International Department such as Evsiukov hastened the decision. By suspending assistance, the Soviets wanted to put pressure on Neto to come to an accommodation with Chipenda. As 1974 approached, the Angolan nationalist movement was deeply divided, and Portuguese pressure seemed to have worked. In Mozambique, however, the situation was quite different.

Moscow Courts Samora Machel

In June 1970, the newly appointed commander-in-chief of Mozambique, General Kaúlza de Arriaga, initiated a massive military offensive against FRELIMO. A strong supporter of the dictatorship and a three-star general when he arrived in 1970, Arriaga vowed to crush the insurgency by the end of the year. His plan for the offensive, *Operação Nó Górdio* (Operation Gordian Knot), was to strike FRELIMO's stronghold in Cabo Delgado province in northern Mozambique and cut supply links with Tanzania, supported by heavy bombardment. He also initiated the expansion of strategic hamlets to deprive FRELIMO of its base of support, deployed "search and destroy" operations to paralyze supply routes, and carried out preemptive hit-and-run strikes to weed out nationalist sympathizers.[55]

Arriaga's offensives pushed the guerrillas out of Cabo Delgado, but it failed to end the war. The guerrillas did not directly engage the armed forces but fled to the bush. FRELIMO also started to build new bases along the Zambian border, moving from Cabo Delgado to Tete province. Arriaga shifted his offensive to Tete and claimed victory, which he celebrated by staying at one of the captured bases with his wife for Christmas in 1970 (see map 6.1). The celebrations were premature since Lisbon canceled all further offensives because of spiraling costs and mounting casualties. Then, Arriaga reinforced the deployment of African troops in *Grupos Especiais* (Special Groups) and created units of African commandos (known as *flechas*) in the local security service. The bombing raids were devastating for the local population, but FRELIMO managed to survive and adapt.[56]

Samora Machel, who was now firmly in charge of FRELIMO, realized he needed a more significant commitment from international patrons to overcome the effects of Arriaga's offensives. In the summer of 1971, Machel left for a tour of Eastern Europe, the USSR, and China. His first stop was Moscow. FRELIMO leadership had long been dissatisfied with the extent of the Soviet commitment. One contentious issue was the lack of financial assistance. Another was persistent shortages of ammunition for Soviet-made arms.[57] Machel

MAP 6.1. Mozambique

was also sensitive that the Mozambicans were never accorded the privilege of meeting Leonid Brezhnev and were "reduced" to passing requests via middle-ranking cadre.[58] He was also irritated about the importance that the Soviets accorded to the Portuguese Communist Party.[59]

Machel's first trip to the USSR in 1971 brought him closer to Moscow. He took part in the Twenty-Fourth Congress of the CPSU, held from March 30 to April 9, but the real purpose of Machel's trip was to obtain modern arms. Machel's close associate, Sérgio Vieira, recalled that Machel complained to General Kulikov that FRELIMO had not received any of the modern arms on display in Moscow. Kulikov was allegedly impressed with Machel's "honest and direct manner" and agreed to review the military allocations for the Mozambican nationalist movement.[60]

It is not clear whether Kulikov was that impressed, as Machel claimed. As discussed in the previous chapter, the Soviets had a complicated view of FRELIMO's new president, his close relationship with Janet Mondlane, and what they believed was his "pro-Chinese" stance. As the Soviets frequently observed, Machel was eager to play Moscow against Beijing in a bidding war for more aid.[61] Still, as FRELIMO's guerrillas moved into Tete province, the Soviets acknowledged that the organization was making progress. As the Soviet embassy in Tanzania reported to Moscow in June 1972, the guerrillas managed to subvert the construction of the important Cabora Bassa project and achieved some military successes in Cabo Delgado, Niassa, and Tete provinces. These developments showed that the Portuguese had failed to crush the national liberation movement by military means.[62]

The introduction of modern Soviet weapons systems into FRELIMO's arsenal would dominate the USSR's relations with Machel for the remainder of the war. In 1972, the Soviets delivered their first portable rocket launchers, Grad-P, to FRELIMO. The operation to introduce the weapons meant that Soviet arms experts were dispatched to a camp near Arusha in Tanzania to provide training on the spot. A group of FRELIMO recruits was also selected to receive specialized training in the Soviet Union. In a conversation with Ambassador Ustinov on June 20, 1972, in Dar es Salaam, Machel emphasized that FRELIMO was betting on the new weapon, which they hoped to use against Portuguese tanks in Tete province.[63]

In another meeting with Ustinov, Machel praised the Soviet military instructors teaching the recruits how to operate Grad-P in Arusha. These instructors effectively passed on advanced skills quickly, unlike those in the Soviet Union, who wasted a lot of time teaching the men how to operate rudimentary weapons. FRELIMO combatants dispatched to the Soviet Union, continued Machel,

Samora Machel (left) and Armando Guebuza (right) laying a wreath at
Lenin's mausoleum in Red Square, Moscow, 1971. Runov/Sputnik.

should focus on learning how to operate Grad-P only, and all the other classes,
including the political ones, should be limited.[64] At that point, Machel clearly
saw the Soviet Union primarily as an essential provider of advanced military
technology.

The Soviets also supported FRELIMO's campaign to attract international
attention to Portuguese conduct during the colonial war in Mozambique. On
July 10, 1973, *The Times* in London published an article by a British priest named
Adrian Hastings detailing a massacre perpetrated by the Portuguese army in
Wiriyamu, a collection of villages in the vicinity of Cabora Bassa, in Central
Tete province. In 1972, the Portuguese had discovered that FRELIMO men and
supplies were coming through Wiriyamu. After FRELIMO launched a number
of assaults against the military units protecting the construction of the site, the

Portuguese had assumed the villages were aligned with the insurgents. On December 16, 1972, they launched a punitive operation, slaughtering hundreds of men, women, and children.[65]

Hastings's account of the massacre caused an international uproar, and FRELIMO was eager to capitalize on the repercussions of these revelations. As Machel shared with Ambassador Slipchenko, the Vatican had gotten ahead of FRELIMO in publicizing the Portuguese atrocities. He did not want the Vatican to gain political capital and asked Slipchenko to support several measures at the UN in order to seize the initiative.[66] Machel's request was not unusual—the Soviets had consistently supported the liberation movements at the UN since the early 1960s.[67] After learning about Wiriyamu, the Soviets started a campaign in the press. They also supported attempts to condemn Portugal at the United Nations.[68] Marcelino dos Santos testified about the events in Wiriyamu at the United Nations, comparing them Nazi death camps, Sharpeville in South Africa, and Pidjiguiti in Guinea-Bissau. As Mustafah Dhada has argued, Wiriyamu was significant because it "advanced the nationalist narrative" and helped the Portuguese disengage from Mozambique.[69]

In the final years of the war, FRELIMO slowly expanded its operations south of the Zambezi River. By 1972, the guerrillas had moved into the Beira region of Central Mozambique and started attacking the railway carrying goods from Southern Rhodesia to the port of Beira on the Indian Ocean coast (see map 6.1). In the early 1970s, FRELIMO developed a close relationship with the Zimbabwe African National Union (ZANU), one of the two movements claiming to represent the liberation movement in Southern Rhodesia (the other was ZAPU, supported by the Soviet Union). FRELIMO's alliance with ZANU was more than matched by Portugal's close relationship with Southern Rhodesia and South Africa, which secretly included agreements on cooperation in fighting nationalist movements in southern Africa. As part of the military alliance, cryptically referred to as "Exercise ALCORA," Portugal allowed Southern Rhodesian forces to cross into Mozambique to pursue ZANU and FRELIMO guerrillas.[70]

In 1973, the Soviets decided to deliver the Strela-2 surface-to-air missile complex to FRELIMO.[71] The decision was significant. The weapon was potentially a game-changer in the context of the colonial wars in the Portuguese colonies because it could strike much more effectively at low-flying aircraft, thus eliminating Portugal's key advantage over the guerrillas. As will be discussed shortly, the PAIGC was the first to receive Strela-2 from Moscow. The fact that the Soviets extended the offer to FRELIMO showed that they remained committed to the organization. However, the acquisition of Strela-2 did not significantly impact the progress of the guerrilla war in Mozambique because its first deployment did not take place until April 1974.[72]

The Soviets hoped that military technology would be the winning card in their competition with Beijing in East Africa. In a lengthy report on China's influence in Tanzania, made in February 1973, Slipchenko argued that Dar es Salaam had started to look toward closer cooperation with the Soviet Union. Among the many reasons for this was Tanzania's disappointment with Chinese military technology and training, making the country vulnerable in its developing conflict with neighboring Uganda. The Tanzanians also realized that they did not have a modern air force or an anti-aerial defense system and had to turn to the Soviet Union for the latter. In addition, Dar es Salaam realized that the Soviet weapons supplied to the liberation movements were more effective than what China had delivered to the Tanzanian army. Besides, Slipchenko continued, the Tanzanians were wary of China's rapprochement with the United States because they feared Beijing would no longer have the same foreign policy priorities.[73]

Overall, the Soviets stepped up their support for FRELIMO in the early 1970s. Although competition with China might have played a role, the main reason for the delivery of modern weapons was the extension of guerrilla warfare beyond the remote Cabo Delgado province. Although the Portuguese offensive was devastating for the civilian population and slowed the insurgency in northern Mozambique, FRELIMO managed to survive and solidify alliances with international patrons. The Soviets provided the Mozambicans with support over its international strategy, highlighting Portuguese atrocities such as Wiriyamu. However, their most important role was as the supplier of weapons for guerrilla warfare. In fact, the Soviets realized that by transferring military technology and providing training, they could effectively compete with rivals "on the left," such as China. In 1974, FRELIMO managed to extend its operations into the central Manica and Sofala provinces. However, there were reverses in Tete province, and overall, there was some modest progress rather than any significant breakthrough.[74] The military stalemate with the Portuguese would only be broken in Guinea-Bissau.

Breaking the Stalemate in Guinea-Bissau: Cubans, Soviets, and the PAIGC

Back in west Africa, the Portuguese campaign against the PAIGC in Guinea-Bissau was led by General Antonio de Spínola. A talented commander,

Spínola arrived in Guinea-Bissau in 1968 only to discover the Portuguese counterinsurgency strategy on the brink of collapse.[75] He asked urgently for reinforcements, eventually building the army's fighting capacity up to 40,000 men—its highest level ever. Spínola also sped up the Africanization of the Portuguese army, eventually employing up to 10,000 African commandos, many from the Fula ethnic group, to fight alongside white army officers. He also decided to abandon some forts and focused on defending only those crucial for cutting the guerrillas' supply lines to Guinea. Perhaps most importantly, he initiated a new program to win over the "hearts and minds" of the locals known as *Guiné Melhor* (Better Guinea). These measures included building schools and hospitals in rural areas and providing better access to food and water. African farmers received improved access to credit, while loyal chiefs were given sponsored trips to Portugal and Mecca. He also established the Council of Guinea, which allowed chiefs a measure of political participation.[76] As previously discussed, the war in Guinea-Bissau had stalled, but the PAIGC managed to make some progress, such as at Madina do Boé in 1969.

The stalemate made Spínola increasingly impatient, and in 1970, he gambled on a bold scheme to attack the PAIGC's headquarters in Guinea. The plan, codenamed *Operação Mar Verde* (Operation Green Sea), included sending a raiding party to free Portuguese prisoners of war held at a PAIGC detention center in Conakry and arresting Cabral and other high-ranking party members. The Guinean exiles who participated in the operation were also supposed to topple Guinean president Sékou Touré. On November 22, 1970, at around two o'clock in the morning, six vessels with approximately 400 men disembarked on the beaches of Conakry. They succeeded in freeing the Portuguese prisoners of war and inflicting some damage on the PAIGC's buildings and vehicles. However, lacking accurate intelligence and poorly organized, they failed to locate Touré or Cabral (the latter was out of the country). The plan thus quickly unraveled, and the men withdrew from Conakry. However, the men who failed to escape were questioned and quickly identified their real sponsors. The botched operation was a public relations disaster for Portugal and was swiftly condemned at the UN.[77]

The failed coup also heightened Sékou Touré's insecurity. He seemed to believe the unsubstantiated rumors that the West German intelligence service was involved in the failed coup, and thus he broke off diplomatic relations with Bonn.[78] The Soviet position in Guinea was also strengthened in the aftermath of Mar Verde. The day after the attempted coup, a Soviet naval ship entered Conakry's harbor with one battalion of marines on board in an apparent show of support for Touré's regime. In the aftermath of these events, Touré requested that Soviet naval ships remain near Conakry harbor to come to the rescue in the event of another coup attempt.[79]

The Cubans also stepped up their support for Touré. After the attack on Conakry, Havana revived their program to train the local police force and provided additional weapons and ammunition—all at a whopping cost of $2 million. The Cubans believed that the survival of Touré's regime was at stake, especially since the status of the PAIGC in Guinea could be endangered in the event of a successful coup.[80]

As the military stalemate in Guinea-Bissau continued, the Cubans grew increasingly impatient with Cabral's military strategy. On December 17, 1971, Raúl Díaz Argüelles arrived in Conakry. Argüelles was the head of Décima Dirección, the special task force in charge of all Cuban military missions abroad. He came to discuss the new training for Touré's militia, but the war in Guinea-Bissau was also on his agenda. During a meeting with the Soviet ambassador to Guinea, Anatolii Ratanov, on December 17, 1971, Argüelles criticized Cabral for prioritising diplomacy and giving only minimal attention to military operations. Soviet assistance and modern weapons were being used ineffectively, argued Argüelles, since Cabral did not plan for any large-scale operations and limited the war to ambushes. Cuba was ready to step up assistance to the PAIGC, but Cabral's tactics were increasingly frustrating some popular military commanders like "Nino" (João Bernardo Vieira). In his report to Moscow, Ratanov disagreed with Argüelles's assessment. The Cubans were too critical of Cabral, relying extensively on military commanders like Vieira. One reason for Cubans' criticism, speculated Ratanov, might be that Cabral did not want an even closer relationship with Cuba.[81]

In late 1971, a high-ranking Soviet delegation arrived in Conakry to discuss the stalemate in Guinea-Bissau. The delegation included Petr Evsiukov, the GRU's general Ivan Plakhin, and Nikolai Tiazhev, who had recently been appointed to coordinate questions related to military assistance in Guinea. The delegation stayed in Conakry, but also made a trip to "liberated areas" inside Guinea-Bissau. In his memoirs, Evsiukov remembered sailing past a Portuguese military post at Guiledge, in southern Guinea-Bissau, without any precautions. While Evsiukov thought Portuguese inaction was "strange," Cabral explained it as a result of the clandestine contacts he had with some officers among the Portuguese high command in Guinea-Bissau. They apparently had regular meetings and discussed the unwritten "rules of war."[82] What Evsiukov did not mention was the content of discussions that Evsiukov, Plakhin, and Tiazhev had with Cabral during their trip to Guinea-Bissau.

Although the details of these negotiations are still unavailable, new evidence suggests that Cuban criticisms of Cabral's military strategy was on the agenda. The specifics come from conversations between Tiazhev and members of the Cuban military mission in Guinea. As Cabral's Cuban adviser, Eduardo César, informed Tiazhev on December 31, 1971, there still existed major differences among the PAIGC's leadership on military strategy. Some military leaders were unhappy that Cabral was mainly focused on politics and diplomacy and did not pursue a more aggressive military strategy. Talks with the Soviet delegation, César continued, seemed to convince Cabral of the need to crush the enemy at its fortified posts. Still, continued César, Cabral argued that the FARP lacked heavy weaponry and more assistance from the socialist countries was necessary to a renewed offensive.[83] One month later, César sounded a much different note. In another conversation with Tiazhev, he explained that after talks with the Soviet delegation, the Cuban leadership finally realized it was "unreasonable to demand" that the PAIGC engage in large-scale operations because these could lead to multiple casualties and result in a decline in morale.[84] These conversations show that the Soviet military probably tried to persuade the Cubans to accept Cabral's approach.

It is not clear, though, whether the Soviet efforts to persuade the Cubans change their stance were entirely successful. In May 1972, Fidel Castro stopped in Conakry on his way to the Soviet Union and Eastern Europe. He arrived to discuss economic and military aid to Guinea as well as the war in Guinea-Bissau. On May 7, Castro had a long meeting with Soviet ambassador Anatolii Ratanov. As the conversation reveals, Castro remained critical of Cabral's military strategy. In his report to Moscow, Ratanov argued that Castro was wrong to criticize Cabral because the Cuban leader had underestimated the difficulties of the war in Guinea-Bissau. Ratanov was particularly aghast at Castro's suggestion that the Guineans should help by sending troops—Cabral regularly expressed anxiety about Touré's meddling.[85]

As battles raged over military strategy in Guinea-Bissau, Cabral continued pushing the Soviets for more advanced weapons. In 1972, his strategy focused on obtaining Strela-2 missiles for the PAIGC. During a meeting with Ratanov and Tiazhev on May 9, Cabral shared his irritation about some Cuban advisers who wanted him to accept some "premature decisions" on military strategy. The FARP was preparing for the "intensification of armed struggle," but they still lacked anti-aerial defense. He shared that he had recently learned about the

Soviet officials with Amílcar Cabral and PAIGC combatants during their trip to Guinea and Guinea-Bissau in late 1971/early 1972. Amílcar Cabral (sunglasses) is in the center. Petr Evsiukov is fourth from the left in the back row. Next to him is GRU's Ivan Plakhin (glasses). Czechoslovak-trained Otto Schacht is first from the left in the first row, holding a gun. The Soviet delegation travelled to Guinea-Bissau and engaged in consultations with the PAIGC leadership in Conakry and the Cubans. Fundação Mário Soares e Maria Barroso/Arquivo Amílcar Cabral.

Strela complex while reading news articles about the Vietnam War and argued that the new weapon could provide the solution to breaking Portuguese aerial power.[86] Negotiations continued in Moscow throughout 1972, and by November, the Soviets approved Cabral's request.[87] Cabral rightly assumed that the complex would be decisive in ending the military stalemate. However, he was not destined to see the outcome of his life's work.

"Shots Fired in Minière": Cabral's Murder and the Soviet Response

On January 20, 1973, Amélia Araújo and her daughter Teresa stayed late at Escola Piloto. Run by the Cape Verdean Maria da Luz "Lilica" Boal, the school educated the children of PAIGC commanders and others selected from the interior to prepare them for further education in the Soviet Union. That night, many children and their parents stayed at the school, as they hosted a

FRELIMO delegation. Lilica Boal recalled that suddenly their meeting was interrupted by reports of "shots fired" at Minière—the location of PAIGC headquarters in Conakry.[88]

Recollections of those who lived through the night paint a picture of the chaos that ensued. After hearing about the shots, Teresa remembered that they drove off in a car with her parents in the direction of Minière. As they approached the location where Cabral's house was located, they were told they could not proceed any further. The children were taken to a safe house, and Amélia went out. She recalled: "I went to find out what had happened. People were saying, 'Cabral has been murdered.' None of us could believe it."[89]

The only eyewitness account we have of Cabral's murder comes from his wife, Anna Maria, as she relayed it to the Soviet journalist Oleg Ignatev. A good friend of Cabral's, Ignatev happened to be in Guinea-Bissau in January 1973, covering the war for the Soviet daily *Pravda*. When he heard the news, he rushed back to Conakry to record her version of events, published in *Pravda* on March 6, 1973. According to the account, Cabral and Anna Maria had almost reached their apartment after returning from a reception at the Polish embassy when they noticed a group of armed men approaching their car. They recognized them instantly. One was Inocêncio Kani. Another was Mamadou Ndjai. Kani ordered Cabral to get out of his car and tried to tie him up with a piece of rope. Cabral resisted, and the rope fell to the ground, after which Kani panicked and shot Cabral.[90]

Cabral's murder was the opening salvo of another coup attempt organized by the Portuguese, this time with participation from inside the PAIGC. Once Cabral was dead, the assassins seized his right-hand man, Aristides Pereira, drove him to the port, threw him onto a barge, and sailed away. Another group of conspirators arrested other Cape Verdeans in the PAIGC leadership and incarcerated them in La Montagna prison in Conakry. However, the plot unraveled after Sékou Touré learned about the coup and ordered his soldiers to release the incarcerated PAIGC leaders and arrest the conspirators. He also asked Ambassador Ratanov to help locate Pereira. Ratanov agreed to help and drove to the port, where a Soviet navy vessel was docked. He then convinced the Soviet captain to chase the vessel—a risk since he was acting without official approval from Moscow. Ratanov's intervention paid off: the Soviet ship managed to find the vessel and rescue Pereira.[91] The inquiry that followed found forty-three individuals guilty of participating in the plot, and ten were subsequently shot.[92]

Most commentators agree that the plot was the outcome of a Portuguese secret operation. In 1970, Spínola made several overtures to Cabral via the Senegalese president Léopold Senghor in an attempt to negotiate an end to the war. However, Caetano rejected any prospect of a negotiated solution. Frustrated by the stalemate and fearful that the PAIGC might proclaim independence in 1973, the Portuguese secret police exploited what they saw as long-standing tensions among Cape Verdeans and the Guinean-Bissauans.

Indeed, the plotters were party members. The ringleaders, Momo Turé and Rafael Barbosa, had been captured by the Portuguese several years earlier and subsequently turned against the PAIGC. Their links with the PIDE were discovered, and the men were detained. In September 1972, Cabral amnestied those who had been accused of plotting against the party. Some were released; others were put under house arrest. Somewhat ironically, Mamadou Ndjai was temporarily put in charge of security at the PAIGC headquarters. Inocêncio Kani was a naval commander who had studied at Poti in the USSR. He had been fired for personal misconduct but then restored to his post since Cabral believed in the rehabilitation of party members. As Patrick Chabal has argued, the Portuguese tapped into the war-weariness and grievances of such men, potentially with the proposal that with the Cape Verdeans in the leadership gone, they could negotiate an end to war, solely for Guinea-Bissau.[93] While this theory remains unproven, the coup clearly targeted Cape Verdeans. According to Alvaro Dantas Tavares, a naval commander, the coup was a "big shock," and some Cape Verdeans even started to question whether it would be possible to continue with the binationalist project.[94]

In the meantime, Cabral's followers were mourning his death. Júlio de Carvalho was deployed in the south of the country when he heard the news on the radio. He and another commander, Umaro Djaló, immediately went out to tell the soldiers. They gathered everyone, and Umaro Djaló began to speak. He was then quickly interrupted by one of the rank-and-file guerrillas who said they had already heard about Cabral's death and that the fight would continue Carvalho recalled: "That was exactly what we wanted to hear. It was, without question, the most painful moment for me."[95] Cabral loyalists like Carvalho relayed stories of resilience among the rank-and-file soldiers, but the actual situation was much more complicated.

In reality, the PAIGC faced an acute crisis in the aftermath of Cabral's death. Almost immediately, the Portuguese started to drop propaganda leaflets saying, "Cabral is dead, the war is over. Come out!" Villages everywhere held *tchur* (funeral proceedings), and people were crying and saying that now the Portuguese would come and take the land. In some parts of the country, morale was low, and there was talk about how it was high time to desert the army before the Portuguese started a new offensive. The Political Bureau in Conakry realized they had to convince people that Cabral's murder did not mean an end to the struggle for independence. Since Aristides Pereira was still recovering from his injuries, Pedro Pires sent radio messages and emissaries to explain that the war would continue. The political commissars were instructed to deliver the same message. Then, supplies started coming in, and, in a major policy shift, the PAIGC lifted all limits on the use of ammunition against property and human targets.[96]

Oleg Ignatev was one of the foreign journalists who helped shape the narrative around Cabral's death and its consequences. In his reports for *Pravda*, he emphasized Cabral's bravery in dealing with his assassins, reinforcing his image as a slain revolutionary hero. In his commentary, Ignatev stressed that Cabral was murdered by mere criminals who worked for the Portuguese. His reports were meant to help ensure the PAIGC's success and provide support for an organization in crisis. He further developed this narrative in a book-length study of Cabral's murder, published in Portuguese and Russian a few years later.[97]

Cabral's murder was a significant loss for the Soviets. Over many years, he had developed close personal relations with many Soviet liaisons, including Evsiukov. He recalled that he was emotional during Cabral's funeral in Conakry: "It was incredibly difficult to see an intelligent man, who had recently been very energetic, lying in a coffin with a bullet hole in his head." Evsiukov then appealed to the CC CPSU to rename a square in Moscow after Amílcar Cabral. His proposal was soon approved.[98] In January 1974, "Amílcar Cabral Square" was inaugurated in East Moscow with a rally. Vladimir Shubin participated on behalf of the Soviet Solidarity Committee.

The Soviet military also feared that with Cabral gone, the PAIGC could be vulnerable to outside interference. In a striking report on the aftermath of Cabral's death, General Kulikov argued that the Guineans and the Cubans were trying to exert control over the organization. The Guinean authorities in Conakry kept the PAIGC leadership under arrest for several days, seizing control of the warehouses and taking over all communications and transport. They also proposed that Guinean soldiers join FARP to fight in Guinea-Bissau—an offer that Cabral had always rejected because he feared the loss of autonomy. The Cubans were also guilty of putting pressure on Cabral for stepping up operations "at all costs" and maintained direct contact with the military leadership. Cabral did not allow the Cubans direct involvement in planning military operations, which caused dissatisfaction. With Cabral gone, continued Kulikov, the Guineans and the Cubans were quick to publicly denounce Cabral's "so-called mistakes." He

Rally to mark the naming of a square in the Veshnyaki District in Moscow "Amílcar Cabral Square," 1974. Vladimir Shubin from the Soviet Solidarity Committee is third from left in the front row. Sikorskiy/Sputnik.

thus recommended the expansion of Soviet military assistance to restore confidence in the organization.[99]

The CC CPSU quickly approved the proposal. Between 1963 and 1973, Moscow provided military funding and matériel in the sum of 21.7 million rubles and 4.4 million rubles in humanitarian aid. Almost 2,000 men—40 percent of the military force, the FARP—had been trained in the Soviet Union.[100] After Cabral's death, Soviet military assistance almost doubled, rising to 3.8 million rubles in weapons and other support in 1973 alone.[101]

The strategy worked. The influx of Soviet arms and the removal of all limits on the use of ammunition led to more aggressive offensive tactics. In the autumn of 1972, a group of twenty-four men led by commander Manuel "Manecas" dos Santos was selected to undergo a three-month course to learn how to operate the Stela-2 complex. After their return to Guinea-Bissau in early 1973, Santos led the first anti-aircraft group, christened after one of Cabral's pen names, "Abel Djassi." The men then started targeting Portuguese aircraft. On March 28, 1973, the PAIGC shot down the Fiat G-91 that belonged to Almeida Brito, the chief of the Portuguese air force. The Portuguese did not expect the arrival of Strela missiles and canceled all aerial operations after Brito's death. In May, FARP took

Guiledge, a strategic Portuguese post on the border with Guinea.[102] As Pedro Pires recalled, Strela-2 was the "fatal weapon" that liquidated Portuguese air superiority, thus effectively ending the war.[103] These victories gave the Soviets confidence that the crisis had been overcome.[104]

These military advances also created a favorable moment for the PAIGC to declare the independence of Guinea-Bissau on September 24, 1973. A year earlier, the party had organized an election to the "National Assembly" in the so-called liberation zones. On September 24, the 120 elected deputies convened at Madina de Boé to approve the formation of the Republic of Guinea-Bissau in a highly publicized ceremony. Oleg Ignatev once again covered the event for *Pravda*.[105] The declaration of independence was quickly recognized by more than forty states, including the USSR. In a show of international support for the PAIGC, on November 2, 1973, the UN General Assembly passed a motion, which "welcomed the recent accession to independence of the people of Guinea-Bissau" and condemned Portugal's continuous presence in the country.[106]

By early 1974, it had become clear that the endgame in Guinea-Bissau was close. Contacts between the Portuguese military and the PAIGC already existed, but in early 1974, Marcelo Caetano started looking for a way out of the war. In March 1974, a three-person mission went to London to discuss a negotiated settlement with Caetano's envoy. One member was Silvino da Luz. The meeting, he recalled, did not go well because the Portuguese negotiators refused to discuss Cape Verde's independence. They left London but agreed to continue the conversation in May.[107] That meeting never took place because only a month later, Caetano would be gone, swept away in the process of democratic transformation in Portugal.

Conclusion

This chapter shows that superpower détente and the Cold War in Africa ran along two parallel tracks. While détente negotiations were overseen by senior Soviet diplomats and Brezhnev personally, the cadres of the International Department and the Soviet military held sway over day-to-day relations with the liberation movements. The Soviet military and the KGB believed that the West remained committed to countering Soviet influence in Africa and would not shy away from using "subversion" and sponsoring coups to maintain a strategic advantage. These views did not change as détente progressed, and in fact, the Soviet military believed Nixon's appeasement of white minority regimes and Portugal only confirmed the ongoing competition in the Third World.

The chapter also reveals the significance of military developments in understanding Soviet relations with the liberation movements. Since the late 1960s, the Soviet military had propagated a more active approach to guerrilla strategy because they believed that hit-and-run operations would not impact the well-trained and well-equipped Portuguese army. By 1971, the MPLA, FRELIMO, and PAIGC had made new plans to ramp up the intensity of attacks, and thus they received new weapons systems, such as the Grad-P and Strela-2 complexes from Moscow. In Guinea-Bissau, the Strela-2 complex had a particularly decisive impact on the war. The Soviets had also come to believe that the provision of advanced military technologies would play an important role in their continuing competition with China in East Africa.

The Soviets' personal relations with African revolutionaries were also important. The Soviet military and the *mezhdunarodniki* were receptive to the narrative put forward by Neto's critics, who argued that the MPLA leadership was failing because they would not listen to Soviet advice or rely on those trained in the USSR. As viewed from Moscow, the fundamentally intra-MPLA conflict between the *mestiço* leadership and the Ovimbundu rank-and-file was closely tied to debates about relations with the socialist countries and failures in the military field. Since the 1960s, the Soviets believed that under Neto, the MPLA was not representative enough of the Black majority in Angola and thus failed to achieve military progress. The Eastern Revolt in Zambia only confirmed such fears. That is why it was unsurprising that the Soviets accepted Chipenda's version of events in 1973 and opted to suspend assistance. As of 1974, Soviet relations with the MPLA were at a new low, and the Portuguese were in the driver's seat from a military perspective. These factors would prove crucial for the way events unfolded in Angola after the Carnation Revolution in Portugal.

Simultaneously, the Soviets' close relationship with Cabral led to a very different reaction to military developments in Guinea-Bissau. As was also the case in Angola, the Soviet military believed the PAIGC could have carried out a much more active guerrilla campaign. Still, new evidence shows they disagreed with Havana's harsh criticism of Cabral's strategy. In the end, Cabral engaged in a delicate and ultimately successful balancing act, arguing that only Soviet military technology could make possible the necessary breakthrough against the Portuguese. In the aftermath of Cabral's murder, the Soviets ramped up military support to help overcome the crisis and maintain its special relationship with the PAIGC. Cabral's long-term strategy worked—the acquisition of Strela-2 missiles in 1973 led to a tipping point in the war. In contrast to the MPLA, by 1974, the PAIGC was well positioned to take advantage of any changes in Portugal.

The difficult campaign in Guinea-Bissau also had a significant impact on the Portuguese military. By 1974, the army was war weary, unwilling to keep fighting a war that increasingly looked unwinnable. In 1974, a clandestine organization known as the Armed Forces Movement (MFA; Movimento das Forças Armadas) emerged. The MFA was composed mainly of junior military officers who were initially dissatisfied with the army's new system of promotions and privileges. Their agenda soon became more radical, and they started plotting a coup to overthrow the dictatorship. Dissatisfaction also spread to the top military ranks. In September 1973, General António de Spínola returned to Portugal, exhausted with the war in Guinea-Bissau. Haunted by what had transpired in Goa in 1961 when Salazar had blamed the military for the loss of Portuguese India, he spent the following months writing *Portugal e o futuro* (Portugal and the future), a book in which he described a negotiated solution to the colonial wars. Caetano would not have any of it. In response to the publication, he ordered Spínola and 120 army generals to pledge allegiance publicly to his policy in Africa. The generals refused.[108] For the MFA, the time had come to seize the initiative.

CHAPTER SEVEN

Triumph to Tragedy

Revolution in Portugal and the Angolan Civil War, 1974–1975

ON APRIL 24, 1974, at 10:55 p.m., the Armed Forces Movement (MFA) launched a military coup. First, the MFA seized all the key strategic locations in Lisbon, including radio and television stations, the airport, and bridges. Once the first stage of the coup was complete, detachments loyal to the MFA rolled into the capital, encountering little resistance. They soon learned that Prime Minister Marcelo Caetano had fled to the Carmo barracks, the headquarters of the National Republican Guard. The MFA surrounded the barracks, and after several hours of negotiation, Caetano agreed to surrender to General António de Spínola. Meanwhile, jubilant crowds swamped the city, festooning soldiers with red carnations. In less than twenty-four hours, the coup developed into a popular movement for democracy, commonly referred to as the "Carnation Revolution" that led to momentous political changes in Portugal.[1] On April 25, the MFA Coordinating Committee appointed the Junta of National Salvation, which abolished censorship and freed political prisoners. In May, it established the first Portuguese provisional government, comprised of a broad coalition of political parties.

The Carnation Revolution offered an opportunity for rapid decolonization, which was a priority for the MFA. In May, the leader of Portuguese Socialists, Mário Soares, was appointed foreign minister and immediately entered into talks with the PAIGC. The MFA Coordinating Committee preferred quick transfers of power to the liberation movements. Thus, in 1974, Lisbon struck deals to transfer control to the PAIGC in Guinea-Bissau and to FRELIMO in Mozambique. In Angola, however, the transition was much more complicated because the liberation movement was split between three nationalist organizations—FNLA, MPLA, and UNITA—with each relying on regional allies and international donors for support.

In January 1975, the Portuguese negotiated a power-sharing agreement between the three movements with independence set for November 11, 1975. However, the peace did not last, and by June, armed clashes among rival organizations on the streets of Luanda turned into a full-scale civil war. As the violence intensified, the Soviet Union and Cuba stepped up their support for the MPLA, while the United States and South Africa threw their weight behind the FNLA and UNITA. In October, South Africa invaded Angola to shore up the FNLA and UNITA, and Havana responded by sending Cuban troops in support of the MPLA.

This chapter argues that the Soviet response to decolonization was more significantly shaped by the evolution of events in Portugal than previously thought. The Soviets saw events in Portugal and its colonies in ideological terms. Shortly after the coup, the leader of the Portuguese Communists, Alvaro Cunhal, returned to Lisbon to a hero's welcome after many years in exile and was appointed minister without portfolio in the first provisional government. The Soviets believed that these developments signified a major victory for the so-called progressive forces, but they were also anxious about a counter-coup in Portugal. To bolster Cunhal's position, the Soviets established diplomatic relations with Portugal and urged the liberation movements to moderate their pressure on Lisbon during decolonization talks in the spring-summer of 1974.

The Soviets also initially hoped for a diplomatic solution in Angola. It has already been established that Moscow denied aid to Neto and pushed for the unification of various MPLA factions in the aftermath of the coup in Lisbon. New evidence shows precisely why the Soviets resumed military assistance to the MPLA by January 1975. It details how Agostinho Neto lobbied the Soviets, arguing his close connections to the MFA made him the clear candidate for the top job in independent Angola. The Soviets decided to restore military support for the MPLA because they perceived events in Luanda as part of an international conspiracy backed by Zaire and the United States, and they believed Soviet arms could maintain the military equilibrium.

Though they hoped the Portuguese could ensure relative peace in Angola before independence, an escalation of armed clashes between MPLA and FNLA loyalists in Luanda in the spring of 1975 shook their confidence in a diplomatic solution. The new documents provide the details of the Soviet decision to arm the MPLA and the logistics of arms transfers via Congo-Brazzaville. These records also confirm that Soviet cooperation with the Cubans in Angola was minimal until independence on November 11. Building on the works of Arne Westad, Vladimir Shubin, and Piero Gleijeses, and recently declassified documents in Russia and Eastern Europe, the discussion that follows builds a more nuanced narrative account of Soviet involvement and resolves a number of lingering questions about early Soviet-Cuban cooperation in Angola.[2]

The Carnation Revolution and Negotiations for Independence in Guinea-Bissau and Mozambique, April–September 1974

The guerrillas received news of the coup in Portugal with mixed feelings. On the one hand, many rejoiced that now, at last, negotiations and peace might be possible. The revolution also meant an end to the Portuguese dictatorship. As Amelia Araújo recalled, they were also happy for the Portuguese people, who were now free from the "clutches of dictatorship."[3] Nonetheless, many remained cautious, skeptical that the coup would actually lead to a major policy change. The Mozambican Mateus Oscar Kido was in training at Perevalnoe when he heard the news about the fall of the dictatorship. He remembered there was much uncertainty—the guerrillas were divided about whether this would lead to an end to the war in Mozambique.[4]

Since uncertainty was high, the PAIGC responded with a propaganda drive and other mobilizational measures to demonstrate strength. In April, the organization invited its close allies to establish formal diplomatic relations. The Soviets appointed their ambassador to Guinea, Leonid Musatov, to act as a diplomatic representative with the PAIGC, and on May 9, he traveled from Conakry across the border into Guinea-Bissau to present his diplomatic credentials to Luís Cabral.[5] The PAIGC also began rallying support among population in the urban areas, de facto taking over the towns in Guinea-Bissau. Cape Verdeans in the PAIGC were particularly concerned about the status of the archipelago since there had been no fighting there. They thus started to organize their supporters and ferried arms to the islands.[6]

Much of the initial uncertainty stemmed from the fact that the first MFA pronouncements on decolonization lacked clarity. The MFA manifesto on decolonization, published on April 26, 1974, urged "peace" and "dialogue" to obtain a "political rather than military solution" in the colonies, but there were no direct references to self-determination. Another source of mistrust was the appointment of General Spínola as president of Portugal. Although Spínola had criticized Caetano's colonial policy, he preferred moderate political change and pushed for a referendum to decide the future relationship with the colonies. Although the MFA's policy on decolonization, drafted by Major Melo Antunes, had entailed rapid transfers of power to the "dominant" liberation movements, the junior military officers who were behind the coup accepted a "watered down" version of the manifesto as a concession to Spínola.[7]

When the foreign minister Mário Soares began talks with the PAIGC in May, Spínola's agenda shaped the Portuguese negotiating position. First, it became

apparent that Soares only had the mandate to negotiate a ceasefire and thus de-
clined to accept de jure independence of Guinea-Bissau—a major sticking point
for the PAIGC. Second, the Portuguese negotiators refused to accept self-determination for Cape Verde, which was fundamental to the PAIGC's binational
project. Another sticking point was the Portuguese offer to hold a referendum
on the future of Guinea-Bissau. As Aristides Pereira recalled much later, the
PAIGC could not accept the referendum because it would have set a precedent
for Mozambique and Angola, where outcomes would be much less certain.[8] The
PAIGC's tough negotiating stance was reinforced when the OAU called on the
liberation movements not to accept a ceasefire before Portugal committed to independence. Realizing that his position was unworkable, Mário Soares flew to
Lisbon in the middle of negotiations, trying to persuade Spínola to be more accommodating. However, the president refused, and talks broke down on June 14.[9]

Spínola then launched a diplomatic offensive to gain support for his decolonization strategy. He tried to convince the British government to support his
referendum plan publicly and approached Senegal's president Léopold Senghor,
who promised to try to sway the PAIGC leadership. In a meeting with U.S. president Richard Nixon in the Azores on June 19, Spínola tried to get the president
to publicly back his plan. He warned Nixon about the threat of communism in
Portugal and argued that the Soviets were responsible for the breakdown of talks
because they wanted to establish military bases in Cape Verde. His campaign
was not successful. There was limited international support for his plan, and
Nixon's administration was tied up in the Watergate scandal.[10]

New evidence shows that Spínola's claim about the Soviet role was not true
because Moscow actually exercised great caution when reacting to events in Portugal. On the one hand, the Carnation Revolution offered the prospects of a
revolutionary transformation in Portugal. The PCP had dominated the underground resistance against the dictatorship, thus acquiring many followers among
the professional middle class, the army, and the workers. As a senior cadre in the
International Department, Anatolii Cherniaev, noted in his diary at that time,
Cunhal's return to Lisbon could be compared to Lenin's arrival to Petrograd in
April 1917.[11] On the other hand, the PCP remained highly insecure, fearing a
right-wing counter-coup in Portugal. As a member of the first provisional government, Cunhal adopted a moderate position. The PCP urged restraint in labor
disputes and compromised on the minimum wage, hoping to cement an alliance
with the urban middle class. The Soviets wanted to reinforce Cunhal's position
in the provisional government, which precluded them from putting excessive
pressure on Lisbon over decolonization.

The Soviet decision to establish diplomatic relations with Portugal reveals that Moscow's agenda prioritized the Portuguese Communists. On June 4, the PCP advised the Soviets against establishing formal diplomatic relations with Portugal. The Portuguese Communists argued that the timing was not right—recognition could strengthen Spínola, thus delaying decolonization.[12] However, only days later, the PCP recommended that Moscow establish diplomatic relations with Portugal as soon as possible. The request had come directly from Spínola, and Cunhal believed that by acting as intermediaries with Moscow, the PCP could solidify their position within the provisional government.[13] The USSR launched formal diplomatic relations with Portugal only four days later, on June 10, 1974.

The Soviet decision revealed a clash of priorities with the liberation movements, which wanted to maintain constant pressure on Lisbon. In July, Petr Manchkha and Andrei Urnov from the International Department went to Dar es Salaam for informal talks. In one particularly heated meeting on July 6, FRELIMO's president Samora Machel criticized the Soviets for establishing diplomatic relations with Portugal, arguing it could negatively affect the ongoing negotiations. While the guerrilla campaign played a significant role in the collapse of the dictatorship, argued Machel, there were no positive results from the coup. Manchkha and Urnov countered that Soviet recognition would strengthen the "progressive forces" within the provisional government and thus help resolve the colonial issue.[14] Sérgio Vieira, a senior FRELIMO member, wrote in his memoir that the Soviets wanted the Mozambicans to assume a more conciliatory stance during negotiations, which was "like a splash of cold water for us."[15]

Despite this rocky start, domestic developments in Portugal favored the agenda of the liberation movements. On July 8, the first provisional government led by Palma Carlos resigned. In the political battle that ensued, the MFA's Coordinating Committee managed to replace Carlos with its preferred candidate: Colonel Vasco dos Santos Gonçalves. A key figure in the MFA, Gonçalves was close to Cunhal, and his appointment was deemed a leftist victory. In addition, one of the key architects of the MFA's decolonization policy, Major Melo Antunes, became the minister responsible for decolonization.

Events then moved swiftly. On July 27, the MFA Coordinating Committee forced Spínola to sign Constitutional Law 7/74 (Decolonization Law), which recognized the right to self-determination for the colonies. These developments paved the way for UN secretary-general Kurt Waldheim to visit Portugal to discuss decolonization. On August 4, the Portuguese government and the UN confirmed the commitment to self-determination and outlined a roadmap for decolonization. Spínola's plan for a gradual transition was dead in the water.[16] In August, Mário Soares resumed talks with the PAIGC in Algiers, quickly reaching a settlement and an agreement on the withdrawal of troops. Guinea-Bissau became an independent country under the PAIGC government on September 10, while the future of Cape Verde would be settled in a referendum.

Mário Soares then turned his attention to the settlement in Mozambique. Initially, Soares signaled to Western diplomats that he did not want to directly transfer power to FRELIMO because the organization did not have country-wide support.[17] However, after talks with Samora Machel in Dar es Salaam in mid-August, Soares changed course. In private conversations with U.S. officials in Lisbon, Soares argued that Lisbon could either agree to a direct transfer of power or the war would continue, eventually leading to an independent Mozambique governed by a FRELIMO hostile to Portugal.[18]

As Samora Machel expressed to the Soviet ambassador in Dar es Salaam, Sergei Slipchenko, it was FRELIMO's hardball negotiating strategy that led to the fall of the first provisional government and a quick transfer of power in Mozambique.[19] On September 7, the Portuguese publicized an agreement to form a provisional government that would govern during a transition period, with full independence set for June 25, 1975. FRELIMO would assume the dominant role in the provisional government, paving the way for single-party rule after the proclamation of independence in 1975.

Negotiations for the independence of Guinea-Bissau and Mozambique took place in record time after an initial delay. The main reason behind the quick transfers of power was the stance of the MFA Coordinating Committee, which favored rapid decolonization. Although General Spínola claimed the Soviets wanted to derail the process, the opposite was, in fact, the case. Moscow viewed developments in Portugal through the lens of PCP priorities and thus urged accommodation between liberation movements and the provisional government. Their strategy did not align with that of the independence leaders, and thus the Soviets had limited influence over the negotiating process.

The early stage of decolonization conveyed important lessons to the leadership of the liberation movements. The first lesson was that Lisbon was indeed willing to negotiate quick transfers of power, especially after Vasco Gonçalves became the prime minister. The one obstacle to speedy decolonization was General António de Spínola. He remained unhappy with the outcome of the talks, and in September, he announced that he was taking charge of the transition in Angola personally and called on the "silent majority" to support his policies. As Spínola and the MFA were set on a collision, communists, socialists, and the MFA united to barricade Lisbon against what looked like a rightist coup. On September 30, after two days of unrest in the capital, Spínola resigned. His replacement, General Costa Gomes, announced the government would immediately proceed with decolonization in Angola. The final obstacle to the MFA's strategy was therefore removed.

Another lesson was the importance of military strength. The liberation movements believed the threat to resume hostilities sped up the negotiating process and excluded potential local rivals. In Angola, events in Portugal created a power vacuum, which reinforced rivalries among the MPLA, FNLA and UNITA. Shortly after the coup in Lisbon, all three appealed to regional and international donors to reinforce their bids for a dominant position in Angola. These rivalries would make a peaceful transition increasingly challenging to achieve, but a violent outcome was neither predetermined nor predictable from the perspective of 1974.

The Search for Unity in Angola, April 1974–January 1975

The revolution in Portugal led to new attempts to unite the Angolan nationalist movement. In July 1974, Agostino Neto, Holden Roberto, and Jonas Savimbi met in Bukavu, Zaire, and pledged to act as a common front in negotiations with the Portuguese. The meeting took place with the support of four African presidents: Marien Ngouabi of Congo-Brazzaville, Kenneth Kaunda of Zambia, Joseph-Désiré Mobutu of Zaire, and Tanzania's Julius Nyerere. None were neutral observers in the conflict. Kaunda favored Savimbi's UNITA and was also sheltering Daniel Chipenda and his Eastern Revolt faction in Zambia. Mobutu had been a long-time supporter of Holden Roberto, and soon after the revolution in Portugal, he began to build up the FNLA's military wing with the support of Chinese instructors. Ngouabi harbored sympathies for Active Revolt, an MPLA splinter group based in Brazzaville and led by the MPLA's former president, Mário Pinto de Andrade, and his older brother Joaquim. Both Mobutu and Ngouabi also had their eyes on the oil-rich Cabinda enclave and courted the leaders of FLEC, the Cabindan separatist movement. Such a constellation of conflicting interests would not bode well for unity.

Neto's top priority was to restore Soviet support, which had been suspended in early 1974 due to his conflict with Chipenda. In a meeting with the Soviet chargé d'affaires in Dar es Salaam on May 22, 1974, Neto relayed his request to the CC CPSU to urgently clarify their stance on the MPLA. The termination of financial and military support placed the MPLA in a difficult situation, argued Neto, and it was essential to know if he could rely on Soviet assistance.[20] We do not know the exact wording of the Soviet response, but Moscow did give a modicum of reassurance. When Neto spoke to the Soviet ambassador to Brazzaville Evgenii Afanasenko on June 8, he expressed gratitude for the Soviets' response and their trust in him personally. The Soviets also invited Neto for talks in Moscow.[21]

Soviet reassurances, however, did not lead to any concrete action. The International Department was still committed to putting pressure on Neto to reconcile with Chipenda before resuming support. When Petr Manchkha and Andrei Urnov spoke to Neto during their trip to Dar es Salaam in July, they told him that future Soviet assistance depended on the outcome of the MPLA Congress and the resolution of internal divisions.[22] The Soviets also continued to maintain relations with Chipenda. In a meeting with the Soviet ambassador in Zambia Dmitrii Belokolos on May 6, Chipenda argued that Neto's unwillingness to compromise with the opposition had already alienated Kaunda and Nyerere. In fact, Zambia was prepared to help organize the MPLA Congress and support his claim to leadership of the MPLA.[23]

The MPLA Congress finally opened near Lusaka on August 12, but it failed to achieve unity. During the first week, the conflict became apparent—members loyal to Agostinho Neto insisted the delegates confirm him as the MPLA's president. Others refused. When one of Chipenda's supporters openly proclaimed his loyalty to the FNLA, Neto and his followers withdrew from the meeting and announced they would hold their own congress inside Angola. The Zambian authorities objected, warning Neto they would "lock the border" if he decided to go forward with the plan. Then, Kaunda, Ngouabi, and Nyerere tried to broker an agreement between Neto and Chipenda. On September 3, Neto reached a compromise, appointing himself as president and Chipenda and Mário de Andrade as vice-presidents in the new Central Committee.[24] However, no real unity was achieved. In fact, in September, Chipenda moved to Kinshasa (formerly Léopoldville), where he formed a tentative alliance with Holden Roberto.

In late September, Neto held a new regional conference in southeast Angola. With Chipenda in Zaire, the conference represented a gathering of Neto loyalists, who elected a new ten-member politburo and revived the MPLA's military wing, the Popular Armed Forces for the Liberation of Angola (FAPLA; Forças Armadas Popular para Libertação de Angola).[25] Arne Westad has argued that it was after the MPLA's regional conference that the Soviets decided to throw their weight behind Neto.[26] In a meeting with Ambassador Afanasenko in Brazzaville on October 10, the MPLA's José Eduardo dos Santos used the convocation of the conference and Chipenda's move to Luanda as evidence that the movement was united under Neto's leadership and again asked for military and financial assistance. Afanasenko seemed unconvinced, responding that it was the "lack of candor on the part of the MPLA's leadership" that caused ongoing problems.[27] Nevertheless, Soviet attitudes toward Neto began to shift, not least due to Chipenda's decision to move to Zaire and align with the FNLA.

One of Neto's regular contacts in Brazzaville was Boris Putilin, a GRU officer who had arrived in the country a year earlier to liaise with the MPLA's leadership. As Putilin told a Polish diplomat, Chipenda's group was "compromised" once they started to cooperate with the FNLA and Mobutu. Meanwhile, Neto enjoyed support from the OAU, Mário Soares, and the PCP, identifying him as the most suitable candidate for negotiations with the Portuguese because he stood above race and "tribal considerations" and could thus unite the country.[28] In his report to the International Department from November 25, 1974, Putilin reiterated that Chipenda's group could "no longer be called the MPLA" because of their alliance with the FNLA, while Neto had gained widespread international support and undertook measures to "politicize and organize the masses" in Angola. The MPLA also wanted to reorganize its armed forces inside Angola, but, warned Putilin, they had neither the weapons nor the finances to do so.[29]

Another major factor in the change in Soviet attitudes was the MFA's support for Neto. In July, the MFA Coordinating Committee appointed one of their own, Admiral António Alva Rosa Coutinho, as the new governor-general of Angola. Coutinho liked the MPLA for their explicitly nonracist ideology and believed they enjoyed broad support among the Angolan bureaucracy and intelligentsia. At the same time, he intensely disliked the FNLA, whom he considered "black racists."[30] It is well known that Coutinho backed the MPLA's bid for power in Angola, even using Portuguese troops to assert control over the oil-rich Cabinda province for the MPLA's benefit. On November 2, the MPLA and the Portuguese troops entered Cabinda city, secured critical communications sites, and arrested the district governor, who was known for his sympathies toward the local secessionist movement, FLEC.[31]

While enjoying Coutinho's support on the ground in Angola, Neto also presented himself as the MFA's preferred partner during the transition. In conversations with Manchkha, Urnov, and Soviet ambassador Sergei Slipchenko in Dar es Salaam in July, Neto flaunted his backchannel communications with Mário Soares and close contacts with the Portuguese Communists. The Soviets indeed believed that Neto could lead the Angolan delegation during negotiations with the Portuguese.[32] In fact, the extent of MFA support for Neto apparently went much further.

The newly released documents reveal that Neto claimed to have struck a secret deal with the MFA that guaranteed him wide-ranging Portuguese support on the ground in Angola during the transition. On December 1, 1974, Neto met ambassador Slipchenko for lunch in Dar es Salaam. In a striking exchange, Neto revealed that the MPLA and MFA had struck a secret agreement to coordinate their policies and prevent the FNLA from coming to power in talks with the Portuguese delegation in Algeria. As Neto put it to Slipchenko, the MFA's key negotiator, Major Melo Antunes, fully supported the MPLA because behind the FNLA stood Mobutu and the United States, who were "attracted to the smell of Angolan oil." Thus, he claimed, the Portuguese agreed to hand over access to military airfields, roads, and army vehicles in Angola to the MPLA. As a result, the MPLA could quickly receive Soviet military assistance, which was urgently required to reinforce its military wing, the FAPLA. The president of Congo-Brazzaville, Marien Ngouabi, was also apparently on board with the plan.[33]

In late December, MPLA defense minister Iko Carreira and Pedro van Dúnem arrived in Moscow for talks. Their message was similar to Neto's. According to Carreira, the MPLA had entered into an alliance with the MFA, but the FNLA held a much stronger military position and could seize power by force. The Portuguese army was war-weary and would not intervene. The implication was that to overcome the MPLA's vulnerability, Soviet assistance was crucial.[34]

Soviet fact-finding trips to Luanda confirmed the MPLA's narrative. In late September 1974, the Soviet journalist Oleg Ignatev visited Luanda. In his report, he emphasized that Holden Roberto had been building up his armed forces, and 3,000 of his soldiers had already entered northern Angola. Ignatev thus advised Moscow to increase "all kinds of assistance" to the organization, which would play a "key role in independent Angola."[35] He was followed by another *Pravda* correspondent, Mikhail Zenovich, who arrived in Luanda in early December. Zenovich confirmed that the MPLA enjoyed support among the "urban proletariat, the students and a large section of the intelligentsia," while the FNLA had an 8,000-strong army "well equipped with Chinese arms and trained with Chinese instructors." Thus, the future of Angola hinged not only on the parties' capabilities to disseminate propaganda and train political cadres but also on their "ability to form military detachments trained for combat in urban and rural areas."[36]

As Moscow pondered over Neto's requests for military assistance, ambassador Afanasenko was tasked to negotiate a route for Soviet arms via Congo-Brazzaville. In early December, Afanasenko first spoke to President Marien Ngouabi, asking for permission to deliver military assistance to the MPLA. The timing reveals the decision to resume aid to the MPLA was on the Soviet agenda if not fully finalized by that point. In late January 1975, Afanasenko spoke to Ngouabi again, seeking approval. On both occasions, Ngouabi made no objections to the request and promised logistical cooperation with the Soviet transfers via the port cities of Point-Noire on the Atlantic coast and the capital Brazzaville.[37] Having received Ngouabi's approval, Afanasenko could inform the MPLA about the resumption of Soviet military assistance.

On January 30, 1975, Afanasenko relayed to José Eduardo dos Santos the Soviet decision to deliver weapons and war matériel to the MPLA via Congo-Brazzaville without charge. Dos Santos was elated: "The cooling down of relations between the CPSU and the MPLA had been overcome."[38] The first shipment of Soviet arms reached Luanda on March 18, 1975.[39] The Soviets also agreed to provide additional training for the MPLA's armed force, the FAPLA. In March, a large group of Angolans left for the Soviet Union. Around twenty to thirty underwent a crash training course at the famous "Vystrel" Higher Officer courses, while another approximately two hundred men would be dispatched to Perevalnoe in Soviet Crimea. These men would constitute the so-called Ninth Brigade of the FAPLA, who later played an important role in countering FNLA attacks on Luanda.[40]

The decision to resume military assistance to the MPLA was apparently controversial. Georgii Kornienko, then the head of the Africa desk at the Ministry of Foreign Affairs, recalled that the CC CPSU Politburo initially only agreed to provide "political and some material support for the MPLA" but refused to become militarily entangled in Angola. However, "only a few days later," Kornienko recalled, the International Department drafted a resolution to give the MPLA a limited number of weapons. Kornienko was worried that the escalation of support could jeopardize ongoing arms limitation talks with the United States and tried to persuade the foreign minister Andrei Gromyko not to endorse the resolution. Gromyko still signed, grudgingly, since support for the liberation movements was the realm of Boris Ponomarev, the head of the International Department.[41]

By the end of January 1975, the Soviets had recommitted to Agostinho Neto's MPLA for three main reasons. Much more than previously realized, Chipenda's alliance with Mobutu and the FNLA made Soviet insistence on reconciliation between the two factions redundant. The Soviets felt that Mobutu represented U.S. imperialism and thus Moscow saw Chipenda's move as a betrayal. In contrast, Neto emerged as the key partner for negotiations with the Portuguese. As the new documents reveal, Neto claimed he enjoyed a special clandestine relationship with the MFA, which would ensure a quick transition to MPLA control in Angola. Only a military challenge by the FNLA, backed by Zaire and the United States, could prevent such an outcome.

Neto's interpretation of events matched that of the Soviets, who saw developments in Angola and Portugal through an ideological lens. Still, it took Moscow nine months to renew military support for the MPLA, testifying to ongoing distrust of Neto and possibly an unwillingness to damage the détente with the United States. The Soviet decision was fundamentally a defensive measure, meant to fortify the MPLA in the case of a possible showdown with the FNLA. However, the MPLA and the Soviets still believed the transition to independence could be peaceful. That perception would change in the course of the following six months.

From Urban Violence to Civil War, January–July 1975

On January 15, the Portuguese government, Agostinho Neto, Jonas Savimbi, and Holden Roberto signed the Alvor Agreement outlining the transition to independence in Angola. The three organizations would form a transitional government, which would be run jointly by the Portuguese high commissioner and a three-person presidential council. Elections would be held in October with de jure independence to follow on November 11, 1975. The agreement also called for the creation of a mixed military force to compensate for the withdrawal of Portuguese troops. However, the Alvor Agreement did not limit the number of troops the liberation movements were allowed to maintain outside the joint military force. In addition, MPLA, FNLA and UNITA were allowed to maintain their separate barracks and installations in the city. As a result, the MPLA and FNLA continued to increase their number of loyal soldiers in Luanda.[42] The peace in Angola thus hinged on the success of the power-sharing agreement. In private conversations with the Cubans, Neto expressed dissatisfaction with the Alvor Agreement and conceded that he accepted power-sharing due to the "growing influence of the FNLA and UNITA in Angola."[43] Indeed, such a peace proved elusive.

The violence on the streets of Luanda had been festering since November 1974. In the city, the FNLA had been amassing stocks of weapons, which could be easily transported from Zaire via northern Angola, and assembling men.

Signatories of the Alvor Agreement, January 1975. Left to right: Admiral Rosa Coutinho, Agostinho Neto, Francisco da Costa Gomes, Holden Roberto (sunglasses), Jonas Savimbi (with a cane) and Mario Soares. The Keystone Press/Alamy Stock Photo.

Meanwhile, the MPLA established its headquarters in the city, with crowds cheering when Neto's right-hand man Lúcio Lara arrived in the capital on November 8. Shortly afterward, Tom Killoran, the U.S. consul general in Luanda, reported the first violent outburst in the city, which left fifty dead and a hundred wounded. As he cabled to Kissinger on November 13, "a siege complex began to take over Luanda in the past two days, and many people are hoarding food and supplies."[44]

The Alvor Agreement did not end the violence. On January 25, the FNLA kidnapped and assaulted the deputy director of a local radio station, whom they believed was an MPLA sympathizer.[45] Next, shooting started after the inauguration of the provisional government on January 31, provoking a series of belligerent communiqués from the FNLA.[46] The situation remained tense on the eve of Neto's scheduled return to the capital, February 4, 1975.

To showcase support for Neto in anticipation of his return, the MPLA invited representatives of the socialist countries to visit Luanda. The head of the Soviet delegation was Aleksandr Dzasokhov, the general secretary of the Soviet Solidarity Committee. As Dzasokhov recalled in his memoirs, the International

Department instructed him to "reconnect with Neto" and evaluate the situation on the ground in Angola. When he and Sergei Vydrin, a researcher at the Institute of African Studies, arrived in Luanda, they did not feel safe and decided to hide their real identities, registering at the hotel as "experts in citrus fruit." Once he was back in Moscow, he shared his observations with interested parties, including the GRU. Dzasokhov wrote that GRU's chief Petr Ivashutin was very interested in Angola because the issue had "significant implications" for the future of South West Africa (now Namibia), South Africa, and the region as a whole.[47]

Although the available records do not tell us about the contents of Neto's talks with Dzasokhov, in meetings with representatives of the socialist countries around the same time, the MPLA president highlighted the FNLA's military dominance. As the Polish ambassador to Zaire, Lucjan Wolniewicz, reported to Warsaw after visiting Luanda at the same time as Dzasokhov, the MPLA leadership argued that the FNLA had already smuggled well-trained guerrilla units into Luanda and would liquidate their competition unless they encountered a resolute response. The MPLA thus required weapons, cash, and means of transportation to safeguard the coastline and move arms from Cabinda and Congo-Brazzaville to Luanda. Neto also urged the socialist countries to open consulates in Luanda for ease of communications.[48]

The KGB seemed to buy the MPLA's version of events. According to a report from March 21, the KGB reported that the FNLA continued to strengthen its military in the capital, with "Air Zaire" delivering large arms shipments to Angola. The United States, according to the KGB, approved of Zaire's plans to strengthen the FNLA by popularizing Roberto and aiming to transfer large amounts of weapons, equipment, and cash to his followers before independence.[49]

While Holden Roberto and the FNLA provided an explicit and increasingly violent challenge to the MPLA in Luanda, Jonas Savimbi's endgame was less clear. Although Savimbi had been building support in Ovimbundu-dominated southeast Angola since the late 1960s, UNITA had only 1,500 trained soldiers in 1974. This was a relatively small number, especially compared to the strength of the FNLA. In July, the Paris-based magazine *Afrique-Asie* published documents revealing UNITA had collaborated with the Portuguese military to wipe out the MPLA in southeast Angola in 1972. Although Savimbi denounced these as forgeries, the documents were genuine, most likely leaked by MPLA supporters in the Portuguese military.[50] To overcome the reputational damage and compensate for his organization's lack of military strength, Savimbi adopted the role of peacemaker in the run-up to the Alvor Agreement, publicly urging all three nationalist movements to unite.[51]

Behind the scenes, however, Savimbi used the prospect of Zairean intervention in Angola to push for a tactical alliance with the MPLA. New documents reveal that in January 1975, Savimbi approached President Marien Ngouabi and warned that Zaire had drafted a plan to intervene militarily in Angola, which would start with Chipenda's followers attacking Neto's in Luanda. He also promised that UNITA would back the MPLA in case of intervention.[52] Although we do not know if Mobutu actually entertained any such plans at that point, the message was characteristic of Savimbi's balancing act. Ngouabi favored an MPLA-UNITA alliance, not least because the idea was appealing to Joaquim Pinto de Andrade, the leader of the MPLA's Active Revolt faction, who was close to Brazzaville.[53] By July, Neto in principle agreed to a "tactical alliance" with UNITA, but it would never work in practice.[54] In the meantime, Savimbi's backchannel communications might have reinforced the specter of a possible showdown between the MPLA and FNLA in Luanda.

Neto's return to Luanda and talk of a Zairean intervention led to a more aggressive MPLA strategy to build up its presence in the capital. They organized "popular power" and "neighborhood" committees consisting of supporters in the suburbs of Luanda. In February, the MPLA also launched a military operation to dislodge Chipenda's faction from the capital.[55] On March 27, Killoran informed Kissinger about renewed violence on the outskirts of the city. In that particular incident, FNLA patrols stopped trucks allegedly carrying MPLA soldiers and civilians on the road from Luanda to Caxito. They were allegedly herded together and shot. The situation in Luanda remained tense, and sporadic shooting between FNLA and MPLA supporters was commonplace.[56]

Despite the rising violence, MPLA leaders believed that with the arrival of Soviet arms, they could avoid a full-blown civil war. During a conversation with the Soviet chargé d'affaires in Brazzaville on April 16, 1975, Iko Carreira and José Eduardo dos Santos shared that the timely arrival of Soviet weapons on March 18 had allowed the MPLA to counter the FNLA's attempts to surround their barracks in Luanda. As Carreira observed, "after the MPLA successfully repulsed an FNLA attack against its barracks, its popularity among the population has grown." The pair argued that a military confrontation with the FNLA was probably "inevitable," but open civil war would not begin, at least until the declaration of independence on November 11. However, warned Carreira and Santos, more weapons—82 mm mortars, rocket-propelled grenades, anti-aerial weapons—were urgently required to maintain a favorable military balance.[57] Still, as of mid-April, Neto maintained that the Zaireans were building up the FNLA with U.S. assistance and still retained military preponderance, counting 20,000 men under arms, with 4,000 only in Luanda.[58]

A similar view of developments in Angola came from Igor Uvarov. A GRU officer who was dispatched to Luanda in January 1975, Uvarov was a regular source of information for developments on the ground.[59] In a report from March 28, Uvarov argued that the Alvor Agreement did little to resolve disagreements among the competing nationalist organizations because of its very distinctive approaches to Angola's future. The FNLA was a proxy for the United States, which was trying to establish several areas as "buffers" against the spread of the MPLA's "communist" ideas and influence. Meanwhile, the MPLA was the "most progressive, popular and mass organization." The Portuguese, in general, supported the MPLA because they stood no chance of having any economic influence in Angola if the FNLA came to power. The Portuguese military presence also contributed to peace in the country, and it was unlikely that significant fighting between the MPLA and FNLA would occur before elections in October 1975.[60] These predictions of a relatively peaceful transition would soon change.

On the eve of Labor Day (May 1) celebrations, a violent conflict between the supporters of the MPLA and FNLA once again erupted in Luanda. On April 28, heavy mortar and machine-gun fire started at night in the city's poverty-stricken areas. The following day, fighting spread into the European sector when MPLA forces launched an attack on the headquarters of the Angolan militia, which the FNLA had recently occupied. The fighting caused multiple casualties and appeals for blood donors were issued over the radio.[61]

It is not clear who initiated the violence. To some, the MPLA seemed to be the culprit. Tom Killoran reported to Kissinger that violence had been instigated by the MPLA, who, as rumor had it, wanted to start a "bloodbath" during the May Day parade, which would give them an excuse for a coup d'état. Such suspicions were only exacerbated by the arrival of the Yugoslav ship *Postoyna*, which was carrying weapons for the MPLA. Killoran also noted the arrival of "Russian and some bloc personnel, perhaps to direct the final stages of the coup."[62] According to Soviet sources, it was the FNLA that initiated the violence, attacking the headquarters of the MPLA-affiliated National Union of Angolan Workers (UNTA).[63] However, it was true that there were Soviets in Angola at the time because, on the eve of May 1, a three-man Soviet delegation—Petr Evsiukov, Eduard Kapskii, and Genadii Ianaev—flew to Luanda to participate in the Labor Day parade.

The experience of violence in Luanda seemed to be a key turning point for the Soviets. In his memoirs, Evsiukov recalled his landing in Luanda on the eve of

Labor Day, with the city pitch black. As they arrived, an airport clerk informed them that all rallies had been canceled due to the escalation of violence. They spent the night on the floor of their hotel, keeping away from the windows to avoid stray bullets. The following morning, they spoke to Agostinho Neto, who informed them that armed action was the only way forward because of the FNLA's recurrent provocations.[64]

Back in Moscow, the Soviet delegation submitted a lengthy report, arguing that armed conflict was inevitable, especially after the departure of the Portuguese. The Soviets also acknowledged that Lisbon was too consumed with domestic problems to act in defense of peace during the transition and therefore recommended increasing assistance to the MPLA.[65] The experience of violence in Luanda showed that the Portuguese would not and could not sustain peace before independence. On June 12, another load of arms for the MPLA docked at Pointe-Noire aboard the Soviet trawler *Captain Anistratenko*.[66]

The Soviets had come to believe the MPLA was up against not only the FNLA and UNITA, but also Zaire and the United States. As Petr Manchkha argued in a closed session of the Soviet Solidarity Committee on June 5, 1975, events in Angola were part of a "serious international imperialist conspiracy" that involved "imperialist circles" striking out against the Soviet Union in Africa after their defeat in Vietnam and Cambodia. To Manchkha, the shadow of the crisis in Zaire loomed large: "In this circle, I can say that there is a possibility of a Zairean scenario, when all of ours [our friends] will be beaten." The Soviet Union had invested "enormous material resources" in the MPLA, he continued, and these should not have been expended in vain. Nevertheless, it was about more than money. He argued: "The forces of socialism and capitalism are concentrated there now."[67]

In May and June, the MPLA and the FNLA engaged in intense fighting at Caxito, only 60km north of Luanda. From June 16–21, Kenya hosted Neto, Roberto, and Savimbi for a summit meeting in Nakuru. Hailed as the "Summit of Hope," this represented a last-ditch attempt to avoid a civil war. Although all sides reiterated their support for the provisional government and the Alvor Agreement, the peace did not last. A few weeks later, fighting in northern Angola resumed with new intensity, and the country descended into a full-blown civil war.

On June 21, 1974, the Soviet ambassador to Poland Stanislav Pilotovich delivered a message to the Central Committee of the Polish United Workers' Party:

The reactionary FNLA led by Holden Roberto acting with support from the Zairean President Mobutu, the United States, and China are striving to seize power by force. . .The MPLA has already received part of the

Soviet weaponry and other assistance via the People's Republic of Congo [Congo-Brazzaville]. In the nearest future, it will receive larger quantities of weapons and means of transport. The Soviet government has turned to leaders of several African countries with words of concern about the situation in Angola and has appealed for them to investigate whether they could offer the MPLA political and other assistance.[68]

This internal communiqué was a strong message of support for the MPLA and expressed a commitment to escalate assistance. Shortly afterward, Poland promised to provide 5 million złoty in equipment.[69] However, the largest provider of humanitarian aid was the GDR, which sent four ships with food, medicines, textiles, and clothing for the MPLA between January and June 1975.[70]

In Brazzaville, ambassador Afanasenko ramped up pressure on the Congolese government to support the logistics of the Soviet arms deliveries. In January, he had received confirmation from President Ngouabi that the Congolese authorities would facilitate the unloading of weapons and matériel for the MPLA at Pointe-Noire. However, it soon became apparent that Brazzaville was ambivalent about the MPLA when ships carrying weapons for the organization (Soviet, Algerian, and Yugoslav vessels) started encountering difficulties in gaining permission to dock at Pointe-Noire.[71]

In an emotional exchange with Afanasenko on June 14, Ngouabi confirmed he had a difficult relationship with Neto, who maintained "no contact" with Brazzaville and instead criticized the Congolese authorities for sheltering Joaquim Pinto de Andrade, the leader of the MPLA's Active Revolt faction. "We do not like Neto's stance," the president shared. "On one hand, he demands assistance, and on the other, he constantly accuses us of something." Ngouabi also warned he would not allow the transfer of weapons to the MPLA via Cabinda and threatened to withdraw cooperation if the Angolans continued to use that route.[72] Although Ngouabi's endgame for Cabinda was not fully certain, it was clearly endangering the logistics of Soviet supplies to the MPLA.

Moscow made it clear that the MPLA had to sort out relations with Brazzaville to ensure uninterrupted supplies. In early July 1974, Neto held talks with Ngouabi, who allegedly agreed that the MPLA could use Pointe-Noire to receive arms from the Soviet Union.[73] However, delays at the port continued, with the Congolese claiming logistical problems, that their warehouses were overflowing with weapons for the MPLA.[74] When Iko Carreira informed Afanasenko that he wanted to visit Moscow to discuss the deliveries of new military equipment, the Soviet ambassador countered that the trip might be "premature" because of ongoing problems with deliveries at Pointe-Noire. Carreira seemed surprised, believing the issue had been settled during Neto's talks with Ngouabi.[75] Only a week later, on August 6, the Congolese officials informed Afanasenko that all issues had been resolved after negotiations with the MPLA. Brazzaville was ready to receive "any quantity of assistance" from the Soviet Union and pass it on to the MPLA.[76]

It is still not fully clear why the Congolese eventually acquiesced. Arne Westad has argued that the Cubans facilitated Congolese cooperation after a Soviet request.[77] However, there is no direct evidence that the Soviets asked the Cubans to intervene at that point, even though it is not inconceivable that Moscow and Havana both applied backchannel pressure on Brazzaville. In a conversation with Putilin on July 29, the first secretary of the Cuban embassy in Brazzaville claimed that the Congolese changed their minds because of talks with the MPLA leadership.[78] Most likely, Ngouabi attempted to put pressure on Neto over Cabinda, only to realize that negotiating for some form of autonomy was probably unrealistic. However, they still refused to allow supplies to pass via Cabinda, and it would take the Cubans' intervention to convince Ngouabi to change his mind.

The Soviet assessment of outcomes in Angola changed dramatically between January and June 1975. In the aftermath of the Alvor Agreement, Moscow believed the delivery of Soviet arms would enable the MPLA to maintain an equilibrium with the FNLA and that relative peace was likely before the final withdrawal of Portuguese troops on November 11. However, the escalation of violence in Luanda in late April showed that the Portuguese army would not intervene to keep the peace. The documents have also confirmed the importance of Congo-Brazzaville for the logistics of arms deliveries, demonstrating their ability to slow down Soviet shipments to the MPLA. As we now know, the Soviets dispatched at least two shiploads of weapons to Pointe-Noire before the end of June, which allowed the MPLA to gain dominance in Luanda. By June, the Soviets had come to believe that events in Angola were part of a major international conspiracy, backed by the United States, and increased their military support to prevent a "Zairean scenario" in Angola, whilst still hoping for a negotiated solution. However, it was actually not until July 1975 that Washington intervened directly to support the FNLA via Zaire.

From Civil War to Cold War Hot Spot, July–November 1975

Washington did not pay much attention to Angola until early 1975. The U.S. presidency was battered by the Watergate scandal, which led to the resignation of President Richard Nixon in August 1974. Although Henry Kissinger retained a decisive role in the White House under Nixon's successor Gerald Ford, he was busy dealing with the crisis in South-East Asia as North Vietnamese troops overran Saigon in April. Only on January 22, 1975, did the National Security Council approve $300,000 for Holden Roberto.[79] However, the United States did not extend any additional military support to the FNLA or Zaire. Kissinger started to pay more attention to Angola in May when the Zambians and the Chinese lobbied Washington for greater involvement.[80] His support for the intervention grew due to his fear that a win for the "Soviet-backed MPLA" would be another severe reputational blow to the United States after Vietnam.[81]

Around the same time, Mobutu stepped up pressure on Washington. On June 15, the Zairean daily *Elima* accused the United States of involvement in a coup against Mobutu, and U.S. ambassador Deane Hinton was ordered to leave the country. Mobutu's message to Washington was clear: he wanted the United States to increase funding for Roberto and to provide arms via Zaire. To Kissinger, Mobutu's action showed that U.S. allies were losing faith following the Vietnam debacle. The National Security Council remained split about the wisdom of greater U.S. support for the FNLA because some feared international criticism and doubted Roberto's potential as a military leader. With Ford's support, Kissinger prevailed, and on July 18, the CIA launched a covert operation in Angola codenamed IAFEATURE.[82]

The CIA-led operation involved airlifting weapons to Kinshasa to resupply the Zairean army, which would subsequently transfer weapons to Roberto's FNLA. First, the CIA was assigned $14 million to cover expenses. In August, Ford approved another $11 million, and he signed off on another $7 million in November.[83] The CIA also recruited white mercenaries to help organize Roberto's forces. To oversee the operation, the CIA hastily compiled an Angola Task Force headed by John Stockwell. As he later recalled, by early August, Mobutu's army had transferred "enough arms for two infantry battalions" as well as nine armored cars to the FNLA base at Ambriz, only seventy miles north of Luanda. Stockwell himself flew down to Kinshasa to oversee the operation.[84]

The escalation of U.S. involvement in Angola paralleled South Africa's. South Africa was deeply concerned about the security of South West Africa (Namibia), which could potentially be attacked by the guerrillas of the South West African People's Organization (SWAPO) from Angola if the MPLA came to power.[85] In February 1975, South African Defense Force (SADF) and Bureau for State Security (BOSS) officers made the first overtures to the FNLA and UNITA. In talks with officials, Holden Roberto, Daniel Chipenda, and Jonas Savimbi promised they would refuse to allow SWAPO to establish bases in Angola in exchange for South African support. Then, on July 14, Prime Minister John Vorster approved 20 million rand in weapons, supplies, and equipment for the FNLA and UNITA. Another step in the escalation of Pretoria's involvement occurred in early August, when the SADF seized control of the Pretoria-funded Calueque Dam and the Ruacana hydroelectric installations across the Angola-Namibia border, citing security concerns. The move led to the entrenchment of the South African army in southern Angola, and in September, the SADF started training UNITA and Chipenda's branch of the FNLA.[86]

As violence escalated over the summer, the MPLA seemed confident in their ability to push back against the FNLA and UNITA. In early August, Neto passed a message to Moscow that the military situation had become more favorable for the MPLA. The FAPLA had managed to stop the FNLA's offensive and "blockade" them in northern Angola. They also defeated the FNLA's detachments who had landed to the south of Luanda at Novo Redondo and Port Amboim. In fact, according to Neto, the USA had decreased their support for Roberto in favor of Savimbi. Given the situation, the MPLA was no longer willing to share power and was hoping to "clear the FNLA out of Angola by force."[87]

To solidify their gains, in late August, Iko Carreira and Pedro van Dúnem went to the socialist countries, seeking more assistance. In Moscow, Carreira and Dúnem painted a fairly optimistic about the military situation. The MPLA managed to counter the FNLA advance on Luanda in July, and they hoped to push the FNLA back from the coastal areas and the northern provinces with Soviet assistance.[88] During talks in Warsaw, the pair explained that the MPLA had managed to retain control of Luanda, key strategic ports, and Cabinda, but they would need a 40,000-strong, well-trained, and well-equipped army to decisively turn the military situation in their favor.[89]

The outcome of the trip was successful. The Soviets offered additional military assistance, while Warsaw agreed to provide uniforms, means of communication, and medicine. Bulgaria allocated 1,243,882 leva worth of weapons and $50,000 as a one-off payment for the MPLA.[90] The most generous contribution came from the GDR, which approved the delivery of 6 million marks ($2,290,000) of military aid to the MPLA in September.[91]

It was at this point—August 1975—that Cuba became involved in Angola. Cuba was initially slow to respond to events there, and Gleijeses has cited several reasons for its delayed engagement. First, Fidel Castro might have been unwilling to jeopardize the chance of a rapprochement with the United States. The Cubans were busy with preparations for the First Congress of the Cuban Communist

Party, scheduled for December 1975. Further, Cuba's relations with the MPLA had been complicated since the 1960s, and Castro might have felt there was no need for intervention. In early August, the head of the Cuban Décima Dirección (Tenth Directorate), Diaz Argüelles, led a mission to Luanda for talks with Neto. In response to Neto's request, Castro proposed dispatching weapons and 480 instructors who would train FAPLA at four training centers inside Angola. Most of the Cuban instructors arrived in Luanda by the end of September, and Diaz Argüelles became the head of the Cuban military mission in Angola.[92]

The Portuguese and Congolese supported the Cuban military mission. When a top MFA commander, Major Otelo Saraiva de Carvalho, visited Havana in August, he gave tacit approval for the introduction of special advisers and even encouraged Castro to send regular troops to support the MPLA.[93] The Congolese authorities also finally granted permission to transport weapons and supplies via Cabinda after talks between Marien Ngouabi and Fidel Castro in mid-September.[94] According to Arne Westad, Castro also sought Brezhnev's support for the Cuban mission, asking for transport assistance and the use of Soviet staff officers to help with planning military operations.[95] The newly released documents do not shed any further light on communications between Moscow and Havana at this point. However, as we will see, it is clear there were no Cuban troops in Angola before November, only military instructors.

Despite the increase in support, the MPLA's fortunes on the battlefield deteriorated throughout September. Much of the fighting in northern Angola focused on Caxito, a small town located only forty-two miles north of Luanda. In early September, around 100 Soviet-trained FAPLA fighters from the Ninth Brigade attacked the FNLA forces there, forcing them to hastily withdraw. The Cubans looked upon these developments positively and expected the MPLA to prevail.[96] By the end of the month, however, the FNLA had retaken Caxito, while UNITA managed to surround Luso (Luena) in Eastern Angola, which threatened Lunda province (see map 7.1).

The MPLA also feared a right-wing coup in Portugal and its potential implications for the course of the civil war.[97] Boris Putilin recalled that the MPLA leadership was generally unhappy with the extent of Soviet assistance. In one particularly passionate exchange on the street in Brazzaville, Lara charged: "You have divided the world with the United States, and Angola is not under your sphere of influence. You are not helping us properly."[98]

Then, on October 14, South Africa initiated a direct invasion of Angola from Pretoria-controlled South West Africa (Namibia), codenamed Operation Savannah. The South African invasion force, codenamed Zulu, consisted of about

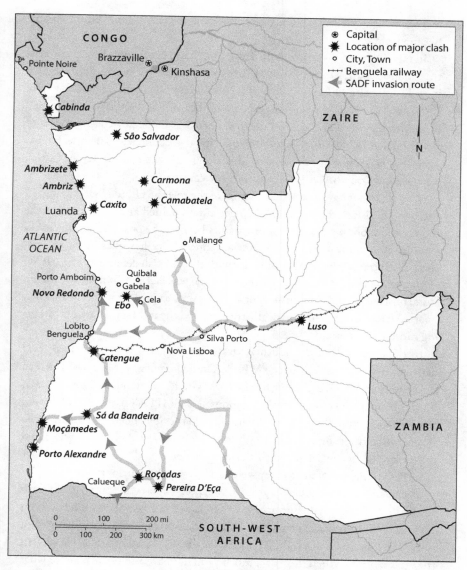

MAP 7.1. Fighting in Angola, 1975

1,000 men, including Daniel Chipenda's FNLA and so-called *flechas*, Angolan soldiers who had fought with the Portuguese during the anticolonial wars. The group was initially led by a small group of white South African officers. A separate column, task force Foxbat, was assembled from UNITA's men and SADF instructors at Savimbi's headquarters at Silva Porto (Cuíto) in Central Angola (see map 7.1).

In mid-October, task force Zulu drove from Namibia-Angola border towards the Atlantic coast, capturing the MPLA controlled towns in southern Angola, including Pereira D'Eça (N'Giva), Roçadas (Xangongo), and Sá da Bandeira (Lubango). On October 28, Zulu captured Moçâmedes (Namibe), a major port in southern Angola and pushed northwards towards the key coastal towns of Benguela and Lobito in a race towards the capital—Luanda. Meanwhile, Foxbat drove inland from Silva Porto toward Malange. By the end of October, there were around 1,000 SADF soldiers inside the country.[99]

We still do not have a complete picture of the role the United States played in Pretoria's decision to intervene. Kissinger always denied any knowledge of the intervention, but many early commentators believed he pushed for it via back-channel communications with Pretoria. Jamie Miller has questioned this as-sumption, arguing the responsibility lay with the hawkish defense minister P. W. Botha, who believed that the apartheid regime was facing a communist-driven "total onslaught" and thus pushed for a military solution.[100] One way or another, South Africa's invasion dramatically transformed the military balance, prompt-ing Moscow to respond.

In the aftermath of the South African invasion, the Soviets sped up their delivery of heavy weapons to the MPLA. On September 25, Moscow agreed to send additional arms, including five BM-21s "Grad," to Luanda by November 11. The Cubans agreed to operate the weapons at the MPLA's request.[101] However, the deterioration of the military situation led to the Soviet decision to airlift the BM-21s directly to Brazzaville. On November 2, Soviet AN-22 "Antei" cargo planes landed in Brazzaville with the weapons on board. Then, a Soviet pilot flew them to Pointe-Noire as they were too heavy to be transported by rail.[102]

The Soviets also dispatched a group of weapons experts to Brazzaville to train the FAPLA to operate the surface-to-air Strela-2 in the case of bombing raids on Luanda. The group did not proceed to Luanda, staying in Brazzaville instead. One of the interpreters, Andrei Tokarev, recalled: "We spent around a week in the capital [Brazzaville]; Moscow probably did not have a concrete plan for what to do with us."[103] The Soviets did not want to ramp up its intervention before November 11.

In fact, Moscow was still hoping for a last-minute accommodation among the three nationalist movements before November 11. As Oleg Nazhestkin recalled, in late October, the chief of the KGB's First Directorate, Vladimir Kriuchkov, instructed him to fly to Luanda to "reconnect with Neto." As he was stunned to learn, he was to advise Neto to "make peace with Roberto and Savimbi." Having established a rapport with Neto during his time in Léopoldville in the 1960s, Nazhestkin believed the Soviet Union should provide all-out support for the MPLA. However, when he landed in Brazzaville around November 1, he received new instructions. Nazhestkin was to relay to Neto that the USSR would unilaterally recognize the MPLA as the government of Angola on November 11, exchange embassies, and open negotiations on mutual cooperation and military assistance.[104]

Indeed, the Soviets favored for the MPLA to forge some kind of temporary accommodation with their rivals, especially with Savimbi's UNITA. Back in July, the KGB had welcomed the Nakuru agreement as a way for the "progressive forces" (read: the MPLA) to obtain "breathing space" to extend their influence in the country.[105] Some talks with Savimbi had been ongoing over the summer and autumn, only to fail over what the MPLA called UNITA's "unacceptable demands."[106] As independence day approached, pressure for last-minute accommodation was coming from other quarters. As Uvarov relayed to Vladimir Shubin much later, in late October, Angola's high commissioner Lionel Cardoso had apparently approached Uvarov, asking him to influence the MPLA so that the forthcoming handover could be of "joint nature."[107] Uganda's Idi Amin was negotiating a last-minute attempt at a ceasefire agreement in Angola, and, as Cardoso told Tom Killoran, the MPLA had allegedly agreed.[108]

In fact, not only the Portuguese but also Tanzania's Julius Nyerere consistently pushed for Neto to come to some kind of agreement with his rivals, especially Savimbi. As late as November 3, 1975, Nyerere urged Ambassador Slipchenko to try to persuade the MPLA to include rival nationalist movements in the new government. However, continued Nyerere, this was not a "principled position," and it would "no longer matter" for most African countries if the FNLA and UNITA had to withdraw from the government after November 11.[109] Given such efforts at last-minute accommodation, it makes sense that the Soviets would use recognition as a tactic to put pressure on the MPLA to negotiate.

Why did the Soviets then reverse course and accept unilateral recognition of the MPLA? Nazhestkin hints that the International Department and the KGB held somewhat different positions, and the latter gained the upper hand.[110] There may have been differences of opinion, but the key reason must have been a dawning realization that the MPLA would no longer accept an agreement with the FNLA and even UNITA. In conversation with Ambassador Slipchenko on October 30 in Dar es Salaam, the MPLA's Augusto Lopes Teixeira ruled out any unity or agreement with either the FNLA or UNITA because these organizations were "pro-imperialist puppets" armed by Zaire and the United States and connected to the "CIA, Brazilian fascists, and South Africans." The FNLA had engaged in torture, rape, and even "acts of cannibalism" in Luanda, argued Teixeira, and thus a "return to the past" was not possible. He urged the Soviets to fly the weapons directly to Luanda since time was of the essence at "such a critical hour for our people."[111]

It was also apparent that many African countries favored the MPLA, especially after Pretoria's intervention. For example, Brazzaville pressed the Soviets not to push for accommodation. As the spokesperson for the Congolese government, Pierre Nzé, conveyed to the Soviet chargé d'affaires at Brazzaville on October 30, the MPLA should not compromise with "puppets, cooperating with the Americans." African countries had made many mistakes, he continued, allowing Mobutu to turn into a "gigantic snake." The time had come to do everything to "roll back Zaire's aggression" and "avoid the penetration" into Central Africa of the United States and France.[112]

Neto recognized that the Soviet decision to unilaterally recognize the MPLA as the government of Angola on November 11 was an unmistakable sign of its commitment. On November 2, Nazhestkin flew to a besieged Luanda with new instructions. He, alongside Oleg Ignatev and Igor Uvarov, then drove to Neto's residence to deliver the message. Thus, Nazhestkin recalled Neto's reaction: "On Neto's face—surprise, which turned to happiness, exhilaration. 'Finally, we have been understood. This way, we will cooperate and fight together. The Cubans and other friends are helping us, but it was very difficult without the Soviet Union. Now we will certainly win.'"[113]

We do not know the exact wording of the message, but according to Nazhestkin, Neto expected the Soviets to work with the Cubans to step up military support. The following day, Nazhestkin met with the head of the Cuban mission in Luanda. The Cubans, recalled Nazhestkin, told them that they were waiting for a special message from Havana about assistance to the MPLA and said that a battalion of Cuban Special Forces had already been dispatched to Luanda. The Cubans then handed over a list of weapons for him to request from Moscow as a matter of urgency.[114]

Nazhestkin arrived in Luanda at a critical juncture. On October 28, the South African Zulu force overran Moçâmedes (Namibe) and was racing toward Benguela and Lobito, two major ports on the Atlantic coast. On November 2, the FAPLA and around forty Cuban instructors ambushed the advancing South African column with heavy artillery fire at the town of Catengue on the way to Benguela. That was the third time the Cuban military instructors had participated in a battle to support the FAPLA, but it was the first time they suffered casualties (fourteen dead and seven wounded). After a grueling battle, FAPLA and the Cubans retreated from Benguela and Lobito. Meanwhile, Holden Roberto's FNLA also intensified attacks against Quifangondo on the outskirts of Luanda. The capital seemed within grasp (see map 7.1).

Gleijeses has argued that Fidel Castro decided to dispatch regular Cuban troops to Angola, launching Operation Carlota on November 4. FAPLA and the Cuban instructors had already discussed the need for troops, and after Catengue, Diaz Argüelles asked for reinforcements. The first battalion of elite Special Forces would fly directly to Luanda, and an artillery regiment would follow by boat. The first plane with about 100 Cuban Special Forces on board left Havana the same day.[115] Meanwhile, Westad has argued that Cuban soldiers had already been fighting with FAPLA before November.[116]

Newly available records of conversations between Fidel Castro and the Soviet ambassador to Cuba Nikita Tolubeev confirm Gleijeses's timeline. On November 3, Tolubeev informed Castro about the Soviet decision to provide unilateral recognition of the MPLA as the government of Angola on November 11. Castro responded that Cuba had already dispatched 500 Cuban officers, who had been training FAPLA soldiers at three military schools and participating in military operations. He also expressed concern that FAPLA was still weak and lacking in military experience. As a result, Angolan soldiers often abandoned their positions, leaving the Cubans alone on the battlefield. Castro expressly referred to a recent battle in "the area of Cabinda city [sic]," where 150 Cubans participated in a battle against a South African column. What Castro referred to was most likely the battle over Catengue (the reference to Cabinda must have been a mistake in the document), where the Cubans had suffered their first casualties. Castro also emphasized the need to coordinate Soviet and Cuban military assistance: "The Soviet Union can deliver weapons, and Cuba—military personnel who could train the MPLA fighters, and if required [could] be used in a military operation."[117]

Then, on November 5, Castro informed Tolubeev about the decision to dispatch regular troops—the start of Operation Carlota. The South African troops had advanced almost "halfway" between Namibia and Luanda and taken over many cities and ports. As a result, continued Castro, "We have made a decision to dispatch 500 [men] armed with anti-tank weapons within two days. In addition, another artillery unit of 600 will be deployed to Angola by ship before November 15." To further explain the decision, Castro argued that unlike the Zaireans, the South African force was much more effective. Castro also speculated that the proclamation of independence could occur on November 5 and that Congo-Brazzaville might become involved in military clashes with Zaire if the latter invaded Cabinda. Two days later, Castro informed Tolubeev that the Cubans had already departed for Angola the previous day and that he wanted to dispatch another 1,200 troops in November–December. He suggested the Soviet Union should supply BM-21s and once again expressed the hope that there would be cooperation. Coordination between Moscow and Havana, argued Castro, would make military assistance much more effective.[118]

We already know that Castro's decision took the Soviets by surprise. Georgii Kornienko recalled that he and other Soviet leaders found out about Castro's decision by chance when a Soviet ambassador requested landing rights in Conakry. Andropov and Grechko drafted an urgent letter to Castro in an attempt to dissuade him, but it was too late. The Cuban troops had already departed from Havana.[119] Indeed, Castro informed Tolubeev of his decision on November 5, a day after the first plane with Cuban Special Forces onboard had departed from Havana for Luanda.

The new records show that the Soviets undoubtedly preferred an "African solution" to the Angolan conflict. On November 8, the Soviet ambassador to Guinea-Bissau, Viacheslav Semenov, informed Luís Cabral that Moscow had decided to recognize the MPLA as the official government of Angola. In a telling passage, Semenov emphasized that Moscow believed that support from "friendly African countries above all" would be "the most effective" in helping Angola "reach true national independence." Guinea-Bissau was clearly such a country since, as Cabral relayed to Semenov, the PAIGC had already dispatched a group of experienced commanders who would help organize the defense of Luanda and operate the STRELA-2.[120] The Soviets hoped the Soviet-trained FAPLA could hold onto Luanda with support from African allies, like the PAIGC.

The newly released documents thus resolve several questions about the buildup of Cuban troops and Soviet-Cuban cooperation. It seems the Soviets were in the driver's seat in the first six months of 1975. Only in August did Castro start pushing the Soviets to coordinate military assistance. Although the Soviets and Cubans exchanged opinions and shared information on developments in Angola throughout 1975, there is no evidence that military cooperation took place before November, when Castro decided to dispatch regular troops without asking the Soviets. The decision was made after Moscow had agreed to extend official diplomatic recognition to the MPLA on November 11 and increased military support. Castro would likely have launched Operation Carlota either way, but the Soviet decision to recognize the MPLA might have been a contributing factor. There were no Cuban troops in Angola before November, but military instructors participated in slightly larger numbers than previously thought.

After the official declaration on November 11, 1975, the numbers of Cuban troops in Angola increased quickly. As Cuban ambassador to Congo-Brazzaville, Arquimedes Columbié, told Afanasenko on December 4, an artillery regiment had already arrived in Luanda, ready to fight alongside the FAPLA.[121] When Castro decided to send in regular troops, he probably calculated that the Soviets would not refuse to help if presented with a fait accompli. He was not wrong—in the following months, Soviet-Cuban cooperation would grow into a full-blown strategy to support the MPLA.

The Soviet-Cuban Intervention in Angola and Its Consequences

The first urgent task was the defense of Luanda in the run-up to the declaration of independence. On November 6, the first plane, carrying a hundred Cuban Special Forces troops, arrived in Brazzaville: one group went to Pointe-Noire for training, while most of them flew to Luanda.[122] Soviet weapons specialists, who had arrived in Brazzaville on November 1, were also dispatched to Pointe-Noire. There, they would train the Cubans to handle the Strela-2M man-portable air defense system.[123] On November 7, the Cuban ship *La Plata* transported six Soviet BM-21s from Pointe-Noire to Luanda. With only a few days to go before official independence, FAPLA and the Cubans prepared to defend the city against Holden Roberto's forces, stationed only a few dozen kilometers north of Luanda.

On November 10, Roberto initiated a frontal assault on Luanda. The decision allegedly met with strong opposition from his South African advisers, who pointed out that the terrain was unsuitable: the only viable approach to the city ran along a narrow stretch of road surrounded by marshes but exposed by the view from the hills of Quifangondo. Eager to reach Luanda in one last push before the Portuguese withdrawal—scheduled for the following day—Roberto took charge. The attack began with a bombing raid of Luanda. There were no casualties, and by the time the FNLA military column set out to march toward Quifangondo, the FAPLA had managed to reassemble their heavy artillery behind the hills, augmented by about 120 Cubans from the Special Forces. Then, the FAPLA unleashed heavy artillery fire on the advancing column, forcing Holden Roberto to retreat to his temporary headquarters at Ambriz.[124]

As the battle for Luanda was raging, the remainder of the Portuguese garrison departed from the capital on November 11. That night, huge crowds gathered in Luanda's stadium to celebrate Angolan independence. As the new black-and-white Angolan flag was placed on the mast and raised, soldiers started firing rounds of ammunition into the night sky. Celebrations continued the following day with a military parade and speeches.[125] Ambassador Afanasenko and Putilin attended celebrations in Luanda in a clear show of support. Once the MPLA was officially the government of Angola, the Soviet-Cuban operation began in earnest.

Cooperation between the Soviet instructors and the Cuban troops was very close, and relations were amicable. On November 16, a group of Soviet instructors, which had increased in size due to reinforcements from Moscow, flew to Luanda. Alexander Grigorovich, one of the interpreters, recalled the extent of uncertainty in the capital upon their arrival: "Nobody was there to meet us. We had a feeling that we would be captured. For two hours we were inside the plane. The engines were on, we were ready to take off any minute." The Soviet instructors set up mini learning centers at the Luanda airport to provide weapons training to FAPLA soldiers. The Soviet General Staff had not sent enough provisions for their group, and for the first three weeks, the Cubans shared their food with the Soviet experts.[126]

Another key aspect of Soviet-Cuban cooperation in Angola included Moscow's support for the airlift of Cuban troops using long-range IL-62 flights to Angola. Piero Gleijeses has argued that the first IL-62 left Havana on January 9, 1976, after high-level negotiations between the Cubans and the Soviet leadership in late December, while Westad suggested the airlift started shortly after November 11.[127] The actual date could have been somewhere in-between. At least one report, from the U.S. consul in Ponta Delgada in the Azores, claims the United States detected "Cuban aircraft" flying IL-62s on December 20, 21, 24, and 27, 1975.[128] Grigorovich also recalled that IL-62s started arriving almost every night at the end of December, with Cuban airhostesses and Cuban soldiers in full military gear. They would be driven off to their detachments, armed, and dispatched to the front in the cover of darkness.[129]

The story of how FAPLA and the Cubans managed to halt the advance of the South African troops is well known. Initially, the MPLA's position seemed precarious. On November 13, the South African Zulu force took Novo Redondo and was pushing toward Port Amboim, a major port only 250 kilometers from Luanda. The Cubans managed to stop South Africa's advance toward Port Amboim by blowing up the bridge over the Queve River. Then, Zulu turned eastwards to find an alternative route toward Luanda, but Cuban and FAPLA troops managed to hold them off around the town of Quibala. Another South African column, Foxbat, was racing toward Gabela, but on November 24, Díaz Argüelles staged an ambush at the village of Ebo, and the South Africans suffered significant casualties (see map 7.1).[130]

The battle allowed the Cubans and FAPLA to receive reinforcements and supplies. In the following weeks, the bulk of the Cuban troops (numbering 1,254 overall) arrived in Luanda. Meanwhile, the Soviets dispatched hundreds of tons of heavy weapons, including BM-21s, 76-mm artillery pieces, 82-mm and 120mm mortars, T-34 tanks, and several Mig-21 fighter jets.[131] By the end of 1974, FAPLA and the Cubans managed to stop South Africa's advance. Meanwhile, in the north, the FAPLA's Ninth Brigade pushed Holden Roberto's forces beyond Caxito.[132] Increasingly isolated and under international pressure, on December 23, Pretoria decided to withdraw its forces from Angola.

Washington initially responded to South Africa's defeats by escalating support. Kissinger believed that the United States could still reverse the losses if they could match the Cuban effort and bring allies on board. On November 28, President Ford approved another $7 million for the CIA operation in Angola, bringing the total funding to $31.7 million.[133] In early December, Kissinger engaged in frantic shuttle diplomacy, trying to gain support from the Chinese and the French. However, his plans were cut short on December 19 when U.S. Congress refused to approve any additional funding for a covert operation in Angola. Kissinger then approached the Shah of Iran, the Saudi Arabian government, and Egyptian president Anwar Sadat to provide additional funds for Zaire. The central problem was that there could be no substitute for South Africa, yet association with Pretoria became a significant problem, as news of direct SADF involvement hit the press. Once South Africa decided to withdraw, Kissinger tried to apply diplomatic pressure on the Soviets to force the withdrawal of Cuban troops and arrange a form of power-sharing among the MPLA, FNLA, and UNITA, using détente as a bargaining chip.[134]

The strategy backfired. The Soviets believed that Kissinger was using Angola as an excuse to roll détente back. After all, détente had proceeded apace in the early 1970s, despite rivalry in the Middle East, Chile, and elsewhere. As Boris Ponomarev, the head of the International Department, told Anatolii Dobrynin, the Soviet ambassador to the United States, détente did not prevent the United States from consolidating its positions in Egypt and overthrowing a legitimate government in Chile.[135] Brezhnev felt similarly. As Anatolii Cherniaev noted in his diary, Brezhnev believed that Kissinger and Ford were attempting to use Angola as one of the pretexts to derail détente.[136] Rather than pushing for the Cubans to withdraw as Kissinger had proposed, on January 16, 1976, Havana and

Members of the MPLA's armed forces, the FAPLA, atop a Soviet armored
patrol car BRDM-2 in Angola, 1975. The MPLA subscribed to gender
equality and thus both men and women were often portrayed as fighters in
the struggle for national liberation. November 1975. Ignatev/Sputnik.

Moscow signed a military protocol in which the Soviets pledged to transport 35
million rubles ($25 million) worth of weapons directly to the Cubans in Angola.
The agreement officially launched long-term Soviet-Cuban cooperation there.[137]

Conclusion

The Cold War deeply impacted the dissolution of the Portuguese Empire. Eleven
years of anticolonial wars led to the rise of dominant armed movements, which
claimed to represent the people of Guinea-Bissau and Mozambique. Although
the modernization projects of FRELIMO and the PAIGC were not universally
accessible to their constituents, Soviet military support had allowed these organizations to obtain enough resources to demand quick transfers of power and

then suppress any internal rivals. The MPLA also claimed to represent the nation but did not acquire the equivalent preponderance in Angola. At its outset, the Angolan Civil War was a complex, regional African conflict with multiple stakeholders.

The new documents recreate Soviet views on the decolonization of the Portuguese Empire. The Soviets took a somewhat "Portugal-centric" view of decolonization, relying on the PCP and left-wing members of the MFA to push for rapid transfers of power in the colonies. As seen from Moscow, events in Portugal and the colonies were closely linked, and they believed that strengthening the left wing within the provisional government would endow it with greater power and result in success for the liberation movements. While FRELIMO used the threat of military force to push for negotiations, under Neto, the MPLA embraced a diplomatic route in close cooperation with the MFA.

We already knew that the MFA favored the MPLA during negotiations, but new documents show that Neto harnessed his unique relationship with the MFA and their "clandestine agreements" to convince the Soviets to resume military assistance. Neto also perpetuated a conspiratorial version of events in Angola, arguing that the FNLA was a puppet for Zaire and the United States. Neto's interpretation matched the Soviets' worldview. The Soviet decision to restart military assistance in January 1975 was thus meant to restore military parity between the MPLA and its rivals, putting it in a position of dominance, given MFA support. We also know now that the Soviet weapons that first arrived in Luanda in March of that year made it possible to maintain the balance of military force in Luanda and keep the FNLA at bay. However, the strategy faltered when it became clear that the Portuguese army could not keep the peace in Angola. The Labor Day violence was a critical turning point, convincing the Soviets that the Portuguese were incapable of preventing a civil war before independence. Moscow thus stepped up their commitment to the MPLA to avoid a "Zairean scenario" in Angola *before* the CIA launched its operation to supply the FNLA via Zaire in July.

The new documents also resolve some key questions about Soviet relations with Cuba. Although we still do not have access to the majority of Soviet-Cuban discussions, it is clear that Moscow fundamentally wanted an "African solution" in Angola. The Soviets rested their hopes on Soviet-trained FAPLA members and, as we know, preferred that the MPLA's African allies, like the PAIGC, intervene to help defend Luanda. They held off until November 3 to unilaterally recognize the MPLA government, perhaps leaving the door open for a last-minute negotiated solution. The documents confirm that Castro argued for closer coordination with the Soviets after Havana escalated its involvement in August, but we still do not know what the Soviets envisioned in terms of their cooperation with the Cubans after independence. On November 4, Castro decisively seized the initiative with the introduction of Cuban troops. The story from then on is familiar. With the support of Soviet weapons and Cuban troops, the FAPLA managed to hold onto Luanda and subsequently roll back the South African invasion. By 1976, the lines had been drawn and the stage set for another round of violence that would last, intermittently, until Jonas Savimbi's death in 2002.

Conclusion

THE COLD WAR HAD a profound impact on the course, strategies, and outcomes of anticolonial movements in Portuguese Africa. The global competition over the meaning of modernity was at the core of the projects pursued by African revolutionaries. The first generation of African leaders adopted "African socialism" as a strategy of "indigenous modernization." However, by the early 1970s, those elites who would come to lead the MPLA, FRELIMO, and the PAIGC became weary of "African socialism." This was partly due to the perceived failure of "African socialism" in countries such as Ghana or Guinea and partly following outbreaks of ethno-nationalism that the liberation movements experienced during their struggle for independence. In the context of societies that were often highly diverse and frequently divided, socialism served as a unifying, nation-building framework. The African revolutionaries who led the MPLA, FRELIMO, and the PAIGC thus favored socialist-inspired modernization for fundamentally internal reasons, but ideological competition provided both the ideational framework and served as a key source of external legitimacy.

The contacts forged during the years of armed struggle were important, too. While only a small minority of African nationalist leaders traveled to the socialist countries in the 1950s, the onset of military campaigns led to an expansion of exchanges and interactions, as increasing numbers of Africans came to the USSR, mainly as students. The majority of rank-and-file men traveled to the Soviet Union, China, Cuba, and state socialist Eastern Europe for military training. Although Africans' experiences in socialist countries were not uniform, they were often impressed by what they saw.

While China and Cuba provided inspiration due to the perceived dynamism of their revolutions, the Soviet Union represented a kind of advanced technological modernity embodied in its military technology. Although China, Cuba, and the Eastern European countries could provide weapons, only the Soviet Union could contribute the kind of arms required to change the outcomes of war. The importance of military technology was evident not only to the leadership of the liberation movements but also to rank-and-file soldiers, for whom Soviet weapons formed part of their daily material world. In the context of the Vietnam War, Soviet military technology often signified liberation from colonial rule.

The Cold War also shaped the diplomatic strategies pursued by African revolutionaries. The fundamental reality facing African nationalists was the refusal of the Portuguese to proceed toward self-government. By the early 1960s, it had become clear that whichever political force could engage in armed struggle against the Portuguese would acquire the legitimacy to represent "the nation" on both domestic and international levels. From the start, the MPLA, FRELIMO, and PAIGC all faced internal rivals that claimed leadership of the liberation movement. The ability to harness international support and legitimacy thus became crucial to overcoming domestic competitors. In the context of the Cold War, the Soviet Union and the socialist countries became key to sustaining armed struggle. This book has shown how African revolutionaries from the Portuguese colonies used diplomacy to initiate and increase Soviet support and deny similar assistance to their rivals. The MPLA, FRELIMO, and the PAIGC all leveraged the Cold War, but their strategies differed.

In Guinea-Bissau, Amílcar Cabral used personal diplomacy to forge close relations with his foreign patrons. In the Soviet Union and Czechoslovakia, Cabral managed to establish trust with his interlocutors, based on their shared view of colonialism and imperialism. As the story of his relationship with Czechoslovak intelligence shows, Cabral also exhibited substantial flexibility, leveraging his influence and authority—including with African leaders—to obtain support for the PAIGC. In the guerrilla campaign, Cabral followed a cautious military strategy that relied upon the receipt of advanced military technology from the Soviet Union to put pressure on the Portuguese. This book shows that the Cubans disputed this strategy much more persistently than previously known and demonstrates that Soviets and Czechoslovak advisers were closely involved in such discussions. In the end, Cabral managed to maintain his line of support from the Soviets and maintain his independence. Between 1961 and 1974, the PAIGC received around 25.5 million rubles worth of Soviet military aid.[1] The Soviets also allocated $50,000 to $100,000 in yearly cash allocations.[2] According to PAIGC estimates, total Soviet aid before independence in 1974 amounted to thirty million U.S dollars.[3]

We know now that Cabral's death triggered a major crisis in the immediate term and that the Soviets responded with a massive injection of military hardware to maintain the prestige and autonomy of the PAIGC. In the end, Cabral's "technological solution" worked. Once the PAIGC received the Strela missile complex from the Soviet Union, the Portuguese started to lose their military advantage. In the course of the anticolonial struggle, external aid helped Cabral establish the

PAIGC as the only alternative to Portuguese rule. After the Carnation Revolution therefore, there was little that the Portuguese could do but negotiate a speedy transfer of power to the PAIGC in Guinea-Bissau and Cape Verde.

After Guinea-Bissau gained independence in 1974, the PAIGC government pursued a pragmatic foreign policy, encouraging diverse sources of assistance to sponsor a modest program of import-substitution industrialization. According to Soviet estimates, after 1974, the USSR became the most significant foreign aid donor to Guinea-Bissau.[4] However, Portugal remained its primary trading partner.[5] The Soviets' impact was perhaps most pronounced in the army. The majority of the officer corps was trained in the USSR and equipped with Soviet weapons. Close military cooperation thus continued after independence.

However, Cabral's vision of unity for Guinea-Bissau and Cape Verde did not last. On November 14, 1980, João Bernardo Vieira toppled Luís Cabral's government, citing grievances over the dominance of Cape Verdeans at the highest level of government. The coup put an end to the formal union of Cape Verde and Guinea-Bissau, splitting the PAIGC into two national branches. João Vieira's government proceeded to accept a structural adjustment program from the IMF and greatly expanded the cultivation of cashews for export. In 1985, the Soviets lost the right to fish in Guinea-Bissau's waters because the government complained about the unfair conditions governing its joint venture, the *Estrela do Mar*.[6] However, Soviet military cooperation with Guinea-Bissau continued right up to the collapse of the USSR in 1991.

While Cabral relied on personal connections, FRELIMO leadership leveraged the Sino-Soviet split. In East Africa and especially Tanzania, the "China factor" was crucial for the Soviets because Beijing remained influential, even throughout the Cultural Revolution. Nevertheless, FRELIMO managed to secure Soviet support, first through personal contacts and then by leveraging their relations with Beijing. The strategic significance of Mozambique for the struggle in South Africa mattered, too, especially for the GRU and the Soviet military. As we know now, the Soviets maintained a high degree of mistrust toward the FRELIMO leadership and believed the top cadres were profoundly "anti-Soviet." Only after the consolidation of leadership around Samora Machel and what they regarded as "progress" in military operations did Moscow increase assistance to FRELIMO and dispatch new weapons systems. In Mozambique, too, the Portuguese had little option but to transfer power to FRELIMO after a brief transition period.

Similar patterns emerged in Soviet relations with FRELIMO after independence. The Soviets remained skeptical of what they termed Machel's "left-wing extremism," mainly due to what they believed was his preference for China's models and prescriptions. The Soviets treated Machel's economic policies with skepticism and disapproved of FRELIMO's drastic citizenship rules, which led to the mass exodus of Portuguese citizens after independence.[7] Military assistance dominated. Out of 1.184 million rubles in credits provided to Mozambique between 1975 and 1987, almost half (576 million) accounted for military equipment.[8]

The matériel was required to train the Mozambican army, which now faced violent opposition from the Mozambican National Resistance (RENAMO; Resistência Nacional Moçambicana), a paramilitary organization that received support from South Africa. Machel would come to resent the priority that the Soviets accorded to the struggle against apartheid South Africa rather than the development and defense of Mozambique.[9] Meanwhile, Soviet economic assistance to Mozambique remained paltry, especially in comparison to Western donors.[10] FRELIMO's application to join the Soviet-led Council for Mutual Economic Assistance (CMEA) was also unsuccessful, demonstrating the limits of socialist internationalism.

In one of the most controversial acts of his entire career, on March 16, 1984, Samora Machel signed the Nkomati Accord with South Africa. According to terms of the agreement, Mozambique agreed to curtail the ANC's activities in South Africa in exchange for Pretoria ending its support for RENAMO. By 1985, FRELIMO also abandoned "Marxism-Leninism" as its official ideology and proceeded toward market reforms. On October 19, 1986, Machel's Tu-34 plane, operated by a Soviet pilot, crashed en route from Mbala, Zambia, to Maputo, killing the president. There was no love lost between Samora Machel and the cadres of the CPSU, especially after Nkomati, and thus news of his death led to much speculation, including (fairly unsubstantiated) allegations of Soviet involvement.[11] The civil war in Mozambique continued intermittently until a peace agreement was signed in 1992.

The Soviet relationship with Agostinho Neto was similarly complex because he never established close relations with the International Department cadres or the Soviet military. The Soviets believed the MPLA under Neto was not representative of rank-and-file members and thus lacked the support required to expand military operations. Thus, the Soviet bureaucratic and military elite was consistently critical of Neto's military and political strategy, and those opposed to him often found a sympathetic ear among the Soviets. Nonetheless, Neto's contacts with the Portuguese Communist Party, his ideological credentials, and, ultimately, his "staying power" meant the Soviets had to contend with him over the long term.

Although Neto was never Moscow's "preferred candidate" to lead the MPLA, he emerged as the most favored partner for the MFA in the aftermath of the coup in Portugal. Once again, Neto leveraged his contacts with the PCP and the left wing of the MFA to obtain a commitment of military assistance from Moscow. As this book has shown, Soviet military assistance was decisive in the MPLA's battle for the control of Luanda in 1975. This book also confirms that the Soviets preferred an "African solution" to the Angolan problem. Although we still do not know the full extent of Soviet plans for Angola after the declaration of independence on November 11, it would likely have been much more limited without Cuba's involvement.

The consequences of Soviet-Cuban intervention are well known. The most immediate was the rapid expansion of the Soviet commitment to Angola. Although economic aid was modest compared to Western assistance, Soviet military support was crucial to the regime's survival.[12] Although the MPLA emerged victorious in 1976, UNITA continued its insurgency, using Namibia as its launching pad. By 1983, Pretoria launched a massive military invasion of southwestern Angola. We do not know if the MPLA would have been able to stay in power without the support of Cuban troops and the influx of Soviet arms. From 1976 to 1988, the Soviet Union dispatched 3.4 billion rubles worth of weapons to Angola to supply local and Cuban troops.[13] The Soviets also maintained a large military mission in Angola, with around 1,000 Soviet advisers training the Angolan military, the FAPLA, at any given time.[14]

While the Cold War was winding down by the late 1980s, it was arguably the shift in the balance of power following the successful Cuban defense at Cuito Cuanavale in 1987 that pushed Pretoria to agree to peace talks.[15] In December 1988, Cuba, Angola, and South Africa signed the New York Accords, which provided for Namibia's independence and the gradual withdrawal of Cuban troops from Angola. The Soviet-Cuban involvement in Angola thus fundamentally shaped the Cold War endgame in southern Africa.

While "successes" in Angola and elsewhere in the Third World were events driven by regional and local factors, many Soviet cadres interpreted these as signs of U.S. structural weakness. According to the often-quoted line from Karen Brutents, the deputy head of the International Department, it seemed like the world "was turning in our direction."[16] New advances in the Third World added to the jubilant and confident mood at the Twenty-Fifth CPSU Congress, held in February–March 1976. A growing sense of optimism for socialism's prospects in the Third World arguably contributed to Soviet interventionism in the 1970s.[17] In September 1977, the Soviets threw their weight behind the Marxist revolutionary regime in Ethiopia, helping it fight against a Somali offensive during the Ogaden War. In December 1979, the Politburo authorized the deployment of Soviet troops to Afghanistan to install a government friendly to Moscow. These interventions were all meant to be temporary measures, yet Moscow was inevitably pulled into local power struggles with unpredictable results. In most cases, an escalation of commitments ensued.

This book has shown that the origins of Soviet interventions were deeply rooted in the 1960s. One outcome was the rise of a Soviet bureaucratic and military elite with a stake in African affairs. These changes were a direct result of the expansion of the Soviet foreign policy bureaucracy under Nikita Khrushchev. The main thrust of Khrushchev's policy in the Third World was to revive Soviet socialism based on an idealist notion of "Leninist principles," which included a commitment to socialist internationalism. The expansion of the CC CPSU International Department and the establishment of the Institute of African Studies and the Soviet Solidarity Committee, among other bodies, led to the emergence of a new cast of *mezhdunarodniki* whose job was to expand Soviet engagement with Africa, Asia, and Latin America.

The people who would come to "manage" Soviet relations with Africa were a mixed bunch. There were men like Ponomarev, Ulianovskii, and Potekhin, who still held memories of the Comintern and the debates surrounding African liberation. However, the most populous group was made up of men from a younger generation, whose formative experiences were shaped by World War II and the optimism of the postwar years. The younger cohort also initially believed that socialism would bring prosperity to developing countries. Many of them would become dedicated supporters of the anticolonial struggles in the course of the 1960s, as they forged personal relationships with African revolutionaries. Since Africa was never among the Soviet leadership's priorities, these men came to influence decisions at the top. One such man, and one of the key protagonists in this story, was Petr Evsiukov, who grew to play an essential role as a liaison, but also as someone who could influence information flows, and ultimately decision-making at the top. Men like Evsiukov would continue to sustain the Soviet commitment to Africa in a variety of roles.

Another consequence of the 1960s was the militarization of the Soviet engagement with the African continent. By the mid-1960s, it had become clear that Soviet-inspired development initiatives did not lead to rapid economic growth. Soviet economic assistance proved costly and was often a source of conflict rather than cooperation with African partners. At the same time, a series of military coups in the mid-1960s highlighted the lasting power of the military in postcolonial Africa. The Soviets thus concluded that training armies and supplying them with weapons would probably be a more effective way to gain influence and allies among these powerful groups. In addition, the military believed that soldiers and officers trained in the USSR would become friends of the Soviet Union. By gaining new friends and allies in Africa, Asia, and Latin America, the Soviet military hoped to gain access to port facilities and airfields, thus increasing their reach.

This book has also highlighted the role of the GRU which was instrumental in providing information on internal developments and coordinated the distribution of arms and advice to anticolonial movements. Although the roles of the Soviet military in general and specific individuals require further research, GRU chief Petr Ivashutin was clearly interested in the Third World for strategic, Cold War reasons. The collapse of the Portuguese Empire in Africa opened up new military intelligence and reconnaissance opportunities in the Atlantic and the Indian Oceans. According to CIA files, the GRU maintained signals intelligence posts in Angola and Mozambique after independence. The military also gained access to airfields and port facilities.[18]

However, there were additional considerations. For example, the Third World provided a "training ground" for thousands of Eastern Bloc military advisers who were usually paid in foreign currency, in amounts significantly larger than the average Soviet salary.[19] This system of benefits does not mean that the military was solely motivated by material gain. Similar to bureaucratic cadres, many in the military felt a sense of affinity with African revolutionaries and were motivated by their "internationalist duty."

However, by the early 1980s, a significant sector of the Soviet elite started to voice criticism about the prospects for revolutionary transformation in the Third World. Criticism came from the International Department and the KGB, who complained about corruption, economic mismanagement, and double-dealing with the West. There were also ever-increasing concerns about the economic and human costs of Soviet intervention, especially in Afghanistan. For Vadim Kirpichenko, a KGB officer who had spent many years managing intelligence activities in the Third World, the experience of Soviet intervention in Afghanistan convinced him that local problems could not be solved via foreign interventions.[20]

The Ministry of Foreign Affairs also became increasingly vocal, arguing that interventions in the Third World had damaged relations with the West. According to Anatolii Adamishin, the deputy foreign minister from 1986 to 1990, Soviet economic decline in the 1980s made one "stop and think" in order to "determine which, fundamentally, are the national interests—to carry the ideals of socialism to the world, or to improve the economy of one's own country and the welfare of the people."[21]

These criticisms started to shift attitudes at the top, including policy on Africa. When Mikhail Gorbachev first came to power in 1985, there was little indication of a major policy change. In fact, Gorbachev reaffirmed Soviet commitments toward Third World allies. In 1986, the head of the International Department was replaced by Anatolii Dobrynin, the long-serving Soviet ambassador to the United States. Andrei Urnov, who had previously worked in the Africa section of the International Department, became Dobrynin's deputy, replacing Rostislav Ulianovskii. Although these were important changes, to Urnov, this indicated a strengthening of the International Department, which was supposed to become a new "coordinating center" for Soviet policy. However, two years later, Dobrynin, along with approximately a hundred "old" CPSU cadres, was replaced by people who shared Gorbachev's "new thinking." Urnov believed these changes happened because Dobrynin clashed with Foreign Minister Eduard Shevardnadze, who refused to accept the International Department's primacy.[22]

In fact, changes at the top generally reflected Gorbachev's broader reforms. In June 1988, the Nineteenth All-Union Conference of the CPSU ended the Communist Party's monopoly on power in the USSR, opening up Soviet policy to public scrutiny. As figures of Third World debt became public, there was increasing pressure to scale down overseas commitments. In 1990, the newly independent national assembly, the Supreme Soviet, ordered spending cuts for Third World assistance.[23]

However, not all *mezhdunarodniki* applauded the changes in Soviet policy in the Third World. Many of those involved in Africa policy were distraught about compromises between the new leadership and the United States and Pretoria, often at the expense of their traditional allies, such as SWAPO and the ANC. One source of discontent concerned the transition to independence in UNTAG's Namibia and the role of the United Nations Transition Assistance Group (UNTAG), which was supposed to oversee the transition after the New York Peace Accord was signed in 1988. In 1989, the United States proposed that the UN reduce the size of UNTAG's military contingent, allegedly to cut costs. As the deputy head of the International Department, Andrei Urnov was involved in the negotiations but was troubled when Shevardnadze agreed to the reduction "behind SWAPO's back." Such a compromise, argued Urnov, led to a tragedy in April 1989 when South African forces started attacking SWAPO guerrillas who had crossed the border into Namibia in anticipation of a ceasefire.[24]

Another source of disagreement concerned the way that Gorbachev and She-vardnadze handled relations with the ANC. By 1989, South Africa's government had started talks with the ANC, but Gorbachev and Shevardnadze sought ways to have a direct rapprochement with Pretoria. One of the most vocal critics of such an approach was Vasilii Solodovnikov who occupied the position as direc-tor of the Institute of African Studies before serving as Ambassador to Zambia from 1976 to 1981. In a series of memoranda to Shevardnadze in 1989 and 1990, he warned the Soviet leadership against developing relations with the South Af-rican regime "at the expense of the ANC." After a meeting with Nelson Mandela shortly after his release from prison in 1991, Solodovnikov recommended that the Soviet Union continue supporting the ANC because they were destined to play a leading role in post-apartheid South Africa. When it became apparent that Gorbachev would not meet Mandela in Moscow, Solodovnikov vigorously defended Soviet commitments to the ANC in the press.[25]

Such criticism was unified by a sense that the Soviet leadership was "betray-ing old friends" for the sake of a rapprochement with the United States "at any cost." In his memoirs, Evsiukov underscored how the Cubans had made con-siderable sacrifices in Africa and criticized Russia's reformers for "betraying the ideas of internationalism."[26] Although Evsiukov did not spell out precisely what he meant, he was most likely referring to the scaling down of assistance to Cuba under Gorbachev.

The debate about Soviet policy in Africa raged up to the dissolution of the Soviet Union, mainly in academic circles and the press. A meeting held by the Soviet Solidarity Committee in June 1991 to discuss its future reflected sharp divisions between those who defended sustained engagement in Africa on an economic and political basis and others who argued for the "de-ideologization" of Soviet policy. Unsurprisingly, Solodovnikov was among those who insisted that Gorbachev's policy in Africa was contrary to the "national interest." Behind his assessment stood a fundamentally Marxist understanding of the world: "Our foreign policy is rooted in the mistaken view of world trends and the aims of the Western countries, especially the USA, on the world stage. We often take tactical proclamations of Western leaders as matters of strategic principle. We underestimate the aggressiveness of imperialism, its pursuit of world domination and enrichment at the expense of exploiting other peoples, its unacceptability to the socialist choice, made by our people."[27]

Men like Solodovnikov, Evsiukov, and Urnov criticized Gorbachev's approach for several reasons, but at its core, their critique was a moral one. It was wrong to abandon "old friends" to improve relations with the United States at all costs.

Reflecting on Soviet support for liberation movements in 2015, Solodovnikov argued that Soviet policy was motivated by historical and moral considerations aligned with a communist ideology. "It was our sacred duty," he argued.[28] Gorbachev's critics also appealed to the notion of "national interest." To them, disengagement from Africa meant losing hard-earned political capital and potential profits, which could become a source of income for the flagging Soviet economy. Urnov argued that ideology chimed with geopolitics since the Soviet Union, as a great power, was interested in expanding "our sphere of influence."[29]

In the end, what united those who criticized disengagement from Africa was a fundamental understanding of the USSR as a global power and Africa as an important area for economic and political gains. They also shared a particular worldview, an ideology based on a Marxist reading of history. The sudden collapse of the Soviet Union rendered these disagreements obsolete. However, the debate about Russia's role in the world in general and in Africa more specifically was never resolved. Under President Vladimir Putin, Russia has tried to "return to Africa," often using military and security cooperation as the basis of constructing new partnerships. Although the motivations behind Russia's involvement are very different today, these cannot be understood without delving into the past.

NOTES

Introduction

1. Putilin, "My obespechivali," 24.
2. "Angola: A Brief Ceremony, A Long Civil War," *Time*, November 24, 1975.
3. Putilin, "My obespechivali," 23–24.
4. Smith, "New Bottles," 568.
5. Westad, *Global Cold War*. A few examples of this new scholarship include: Nguyen, *Hanoi's War*; Miller, *African Volk*; Harmer, *Allende's Chile*; Friedman, *Shadow Cold War*; Lüthi, *Cold Wars*.
6. A typical example is Davidson, *No Fist is Big Enough*. On the history of the resistance literature, see Cooper, "Conflict and Connection."
7. Most of this research focused on southern Africa as a whole. See Onslow, *Cold War in Southern Africa*; Sapire, "Liberation Movements"; Sapire and Saunders, *Southern African Liberation Struggles*; White and Larmer, "Mobile Soldiers and Un-National Liberation"; Alexander, McGregor, and Tendi, "Transnational Histories"; Dallywater, Saunders, and Fonseca, *Southern African Liberation Movements*.
8. For two very different perspectives, see Ellis, *External Mission*; Macmillan, *The Lusaka Years*.
9. Peterson, *Dubois, Fanon, Cabral*; Lopes, *Africa's Contemporary Challenges*; Manji and Fletcher, *Claim No Easy Victories*; Rabaka, *Africana Critical Theory*; Saucier, *A Luta Continua*.
10. Exceptions include Sousa, *Amílcar Cabral*.
11. For a recent study on FRELIMO in Mozambique, see Banks, "Socialist Internationalism."
12. For example, see Schlesinger, "Origins of the Cold War."
13. A number of Cold War historians have revised their interpretations of the Cold War conflict. John Lewis Gaddis first focused on "national interest" but later acknowledged the role of ideas in *We Now Know*.
14. Westad, *Global Cold War*.
15. Friedman, *Shadow Cold War*.
16. Radoslav Yordanov revives the juxtaposition of "revolutionary" and "statist" lines in Soviet foreign policy, arguing that the "statist" or pragmatic line often prevailed, thus contradicting current historiographical trends. See Yordanov, *Between Ideology and Pragmatism*.
17. Natufe, *Soviet Policy in Africa*, 31–49.

18. Eran, *Mezhdunarodniki.*

19. Rupprecht, *Soviet Internationalism after Stalin,* 230–84. Also see Friedman, *Shadow Cold War,* 22.

20. Shubin, "Unsung Heroes," 154–77.

21. For an overview of the state of the field, see Richterova and Telepneva, "An Introduction: The Secret Struggle for the Global South."

22. Some of the early works include Legum, *After Angola*; Klinghoffer, *The Angolan War*; Somerville, *Angola*; Kempton, *Soviet Strategy toward Southern Africa.*

23. Gaddis, *We Now Know,* 187. A similar interpretation is pursued by Melvyn P. Leffler in *For the Soul of Mankind,* 255.

24. Haslam, *Russia's Cold War,* 286–87.

25. Zubok, *A Failed Empire,* 251.

26. Westad, *Global Cold War,* 228–49; Gleijeses, *Conflicting Missions,* 246–73.

27. Shubin, *Hot "Cold War,"* 32–57.

28. Some of these records were initially made available only to a select number of scholars in the 1990s. Since then, they have been reclassified, only to be reopened around 2015 after undergoing a special declassification process.

29. Bowen, *State against the Peasantry*; Brinkman, *War for People*; Moorman, *Intonations*; Pearce, *Political Identity and Conflict.*

Chapter One

1. Marx and Engels, *Manifesto of the Communist Party.*

2. Suny, "'Don't Paint Nationalism Red!,'" 2. For a summary of debates on the national question, see Löwy, "Marxists and the National Question."

3. This argument is most forcefully pursued in Manela, *Wilsonian Moment.*

4. Matusevich, "Journeys of Hope." On the role of African Americans in the Comintern, see Adi, *Pan-Africanism and Communism.*

5. The main exception for Stalin was the status of Italian colonies, over which Stalin bickered with the Allies at the Yalta conference. See Mazov, "USSR and the Former Italian Colonies."

6. Tomlinson, "What was the Third World?"

7. On Nkrumah's ideology of non-alignment, see: Gerits, "When the Bull Elephants Fight."

8. This paragraph is based on Uhl, "Nikita Khrushchev."

9. Zubok, *Failed Empire,* 86–92; Roberts, "A Chance for Peace?"

10. Quoted in Fursenko and Naftali, *Khrushchev's Cold War,* 57; Taubman, *Khrushchev,* 354.

11. Iandolo, "Rise and Fall," 692.

12. Mirskii, "Na znamenatelnom rubezhe," 132.

13. On the Czechoslovak-Egyptian arms deal and its impact, see Muehlenbeck, *Czechoslovakia in Africa,* 91–95.

14. "Soviet Foreign Ministry Notes on Current Issues in Soviet Global Policy," January 4, 1956, in Békés, Byrne, and Rainer, *The 1956 Hungarian Revolution*, 106–13.

15. Békés, "Cold War, Detente and the Soviet Bloc," 251. On the transformation of the Eastern Bloc, see Jersild, "The Soviet State as Imperial Scavenger."

16. Taubman, *Khrushchev*, 270–77.

17. Zubok, *Failed Empire*, 168–69; Taubman, *Khrushchev*, 286–87.

18. For a summary, see Békés, "East Central Europe."

19. Westad, *Cold War*, 243.

20. For connections between Soviet decision-making on Hungary and the Suez, see Fursenko and Naftali, *Khrushchev's Cold War*, 114–38.

21. There were two "Congos" during colonial times. The Belgian Congo became the "The Democratic Republic of the Congo (DRC)" upon independence in June 1960. The neighboring "French Congo" became "Republic of the Congo." In 1971, the Democratic Republic of the Congo was renamed "Zaire," a name it retained until 1997 before re-gaining its name from 1960. To avoid confusion, I have consistently used "Zaire" to refer to the former Belgian Congo and DRC. I use "Congo-Brazzaville" to refer to Republic of the Congo.

22. On CIA in Zaire, see Devlin, *Chief of Station*.

23. Quoted in Khrushchev, *Nikita Khrushchev*, 405.

24. Namikas, *Battleground Africa*, 107.

25. Iandolo, "Imbalance of Power."

26. Telepneva, "Cold War on the Cheap."

27. Khrushchev, *Nikita Khrushchev*, 436.

28. I borrow this term from Roman, *Opposing Jim Crow*, 1–2.

29. Khrushchev, *Memoirs of Nikita Khrushchev*, 3:877.

30. Taubman, *Khrushchev*, 317–18.

31. One of them was Ivan Maiskii, a long-serving Soviet diplomat. See Davidson, Mazov, and Tsypkin, *SSSR i Afrika*, 132.

32. For biographical details, see Dazyshen, "Potekhin."

33. On the founding of the institute and controversy surrounding its affiliation, see Davidson, "Osnovatel."

34. Quoted in Skorov, "Ivan Potekhin."

35. Personnel file of Boris Ponomarev, Rossiiskii Gosudarstvennyi Arkhiv Sotsial'no-Politicheskoi Istorii (Russian State Archive of Socio-Political History, hereafter RGASPI), fond (f.) 495, opis (op.). 65a, delo (d.) 330.

36. Brutents, *Tridtsat let*, 130–283; Shubin, *Hot "Cold War,"* 9.

37. On the relationship between Gromyko and Ponomarev, see Brutents, *Tridtsat let*, 166–67.

38. Brutents, *Tridtsat let*, 189–93.

39. Vasilkov and Sorokina, *Liudi i sudby*.

40. Mazov, *Distant Front*, 19; Dzasokhov, *Chelovek i politika*, 28–34.

41. For a detailed bibliography of Aleksandr Shelepin, see Mlechin, *Zheleznyi Shurik*.

42. Vadim Zagladin, interview, in Tolts, "Pamiati Vadima Zagladina."

43. Kolpakidi and Prokhorov, *Imperiia GRU.*

44. Haslam, *Near and Distant Neighbours*, 210–13; Pringle, *Historical Dictionary*, 148.

45. Davidson, "Osnovatel," 128–29.

46. For an in-depth study of the postwar generation, see Fürst, *Stalin's Last Generation.*

47. Mirskii, "Na znamenatelnom rubezhe," 132.

48. Solodovnikov interview.

49. Mitrokhin, "Elita 'Zakrytogo Obshchestva,'" 155.

50. Leonov, *Likholetie*, 7–39.

51. Mitrokhin, "Elita 'Zakrytogo Obshchestva,'" 159.

52. Shubin interview.

53. Golden, *Long Journey*, 168.

54. Shubin, *Hot "Cold War,"* 3; Shubin interview.

55. Kirpichenko, *Razvedka*, chapter: "Afrika grez i deistvitelnosti [Africa of Dreams and Reality]."

56. Kirpichenko, *Razvedka*, chapter: "Afrika grez i deistvitelnosti"

57. The festival has been researched extensively, see in particular Zubok, *Failed Empire*, 174–76; Roth-Ey, "'Loose Girls' on the Loose?"; Koivunen, "Friends."

58. Davidson, *Pisma s Mysa Dobroi Nadezhdy*, 61–64.

59. Urnov, "Sovetskii Soiuz i borba protiv kolonializma."

Chapter Two

1. Ferraz de Matos, *Colours of the Empire*, 176–89; Cairo, "Portugal is Not a Small Country."

2. Disney, *History of Portugal*, 27–44, 119–44.

3. Disney, *History of Portugal*, 65–83, 172–203.

4. For a detailed study of forced labor in São Tomé, see Higgs, *Chocolate Islands.*

5. On the First Republic's colonial policies, see Clarence-Smith, *Third Portuguese Empire*, 116–46.

6. For a detailed summary of the early years and the road to power, see Meneses, *Salazar*, ch. I.

7. There is still a debate about whether politics or economics was fundamental to Salazar's conception of the Portuguese Empire. For the two sides of the debate, see Clarence-Smith, *Third Portuguese Empire*, and Pitcher, *Politics.*

8. Newitt, "Portuguese African Colonies," 223.

9. Newitt, "Portuguese African Colonies," 225–30.

10. Mateus, *A luta*, 22–23.

11. Spencer, *Toward an African Church*, 77.

12. Mondlane, *Struggle for Mozambique*, 60.

13. Mateus, *A luta*, 27.

14. Disney, *History of Portugal*, 101–9.

15. Sapega, *Consensus and Debate*, 127.

16. Carreira, *People of the Cape Verde Islands*, 166.

17. Keese, "Managing the Prospect of Famine," 57.

18. Quoted in Ball, *Angola's Colossal Lie*, 8.

19. Birmingham, *Short History*, vii–xi.

20. Clarence-Smith, *Third Portuguese Empire*, 134.

21. Cahen, "Anticolonialism and Nationalism," 14.

22. For further discussion, see Corrado, *Creole Elite*; Havik and Newitt, *Creole Societies*, 102–3.

23. Around 1,703 Cape Verdean immigrants appear in the 1950 census of Guinea-Bissau. See Keese, "Role of Cape Verdeans," 498.

24. Chabal, *Amílcar Cabral*, 29–31.

25. Norman Araujo, "West African Area," 280.

26. Funada-Classe, *Origins of War*, 149.

27. Birmingham, *Short History*, 65–66. The terms "creole" and "Luso-African" have been subject to much debate, particularly when used to enhance the racist narrative of "Lusotropicalism." A number of historians still have found it useful to employ these terms, especially in reference to the complex cultural milieu of interwar Luanda. See Corrado, *Creole Elite*.

28. Laban, *Mário Pinto de Andrade*, 34.

29. Laban, *Mário Pinto de Andrade*, 29–33.

30. See "Statement of Bishop Ralph E. Dodge, Washington D.C.," in U.S. Senate, *Hearings before the Subcommittee on African Affairs*, 202.

31. Marcum, *Angolan Revolution*, 1:37–38; Lara, *Um amplo movimento*, 1:13.

32. On Neto's poetry, see Marques, "Postcolonial African Consciousness"; Mata, "Projective Nostalgia."

33. For an overview of the role of religion, see Péclard, "Moral Economy of Exclusion," 153–58.

34. Amélia and Teresa Araújo interview.

35. For a summary of different alternatives to statehood, see Cooper, *Africa since 1940*, 38–65.

36. On economic measures, see Pitcher, *Politics*, 147.

37. For an overview, see Antunes, "Kennedy, Portugal, and the Azores Base."

38. Other important members included the Mozambican poetess Noémia de Sousa, Lúcio Lara from Angola, Vasco Cabral from Guinea-Bissau, Francisco José Tenreiro from São Tomé, and Guilherme Espírito Santo.

39. Mateus, *A luta*, 66–79; Chabal, *Cabral*, 45.

40. Gruffydd Jones, "Race, Culture and Liberation;" Reza, "African Anti-colonialism."

41. Moorman, *Intonations*, 56–80.

42. Laban, *Mário Pinto de Andrade*, 34, 51, 67.

43. For an overview, see Akyeampong, "African Socialism."

44. Laban, *Mário Pinto de Andrade*, 105–8.

45. On the PCP's stance on the colonial question, see José Neves, "Role of Portugal." On African students' reactions, see Laban, *Mário Pinto de Andrade*, 105–8; Lara, *Um amplo movimento*, 1:39.

46. Laban, *Mário Pinto de Andrade*, 108. Other founders of the PCA were António Jacinto, Mário António de Oliveira, and Ilídio Machado; Laban, *Angola*, 155–56.

47. Lara, *Um amplo movimento*, 1:23–29.

48. Gruffydd Jones, "Race, Culture and Liberation."

49. Rabaka, *Concepts of Cabralism*, 208.

50. Laban, *Mário Pinto de Andrade*, 105–8.

51. Sousa, *Amílcar Cabral*, 178.

52. Gould-Davis, "Logic of Soviet Cultural Diplomacy."

53. Katsakioris, "L'union soviétique."

54. "Information about the results of the conference of Asian and African writers in Tashkent," Rossiiskii Gosudarsvennyi Arkhiv Literatury i Iskusstva (Russian State Archive of Literature and Arts, hereafter RGALI), f. 631, op. 26, d. 6104, 5.

55. Djagalov, *From Internationalism to Postcolonialism*, 77.

56. Transcript of the SKSSAA presidium meeting, November 20, 1958, Gosudarstvennyi Arkhiv Rossiiskoi Federatsii (State Archive of the Russian Federation, hereafter GARF), f. 9540, op. 1, d. 13, 12–17, 28.

57. Laban, *Mário Pinto de Andrade*, 145.

58. Djagalov, *From Internationalism to Postcolonialism*, 71.

59. Andrade, "Appel aux écrivains du monde."

60. Laban, *Mário Pinto de Andrade*, 120.

61. Andrade, "L'esprit de Tachkent."

62. "Report on the results of the Tashkent conference," undated, RGALI, f. 631, op. 26, d. 6104, 11.

63. Lara, *Um amplo movimento*, 1:209.

64. Lara, *Um amplo movimento*, 1:206.

65. Santos, *Pesnia istinnoi liubvi*.

66. Shmelkov, "Obshchestvennye sviazi s Afrikoi," 1:28–29.

67. This paragraph is based on Westad, *Cold War*, 233–61.

68. On the early stage of Sino-Soviet competition, see Friedman, *Shadow Cold War*, 25–42.

69. See the chapter on Marcelino dos Santos in Mateus, *Memórias*.

70. Laban, *Mário Pinto de Andrade*, 147–48.

71. Marcum, *Angolan Revolution*, 1:61–62.

72. Quoted in Marcum, *Angolan Revolution*, 1:68.

73. Marino, "America's War in Angola," 34.

74. See the second chapter in Antunes, *Kennedy e Salazar*.

75. "National Security Council Report 5719/1," *Foreign Relations of the United States* (FRUS), Document 24. On Eisenhower's policy, see Borstelmann, *Cold War and the Color Line*, 85–134.

76. Rakove, *Kennedy, Johnson, and the Nonaligned World*, 31–45.

77. Antunes, "Kennedy, Portugal, and the Azores Base," 152.

78. Messiant, "Angola," 161–63.

79. Birmingham, *Frontline Nationalism*, 44–46.

80. On Cabral's ideas on agriculture, see César, "Reading Amílcar"; Neves, "Ideology, science, and people in Amílcar Cabral."

81. Lopes, *Aristides Pereira*, 40.

82. Sousa, *Amílcar Cabral*, 185–89.

83. On the impact of events in Algeria on anticolonial movements, see Connelly, Connelly, *Diplomatic Revolution*; Byrne, *Mecca of Revolution*.

84. Lara, *Um amplo movimento*, 1:239.

85. Schmidt, "Cold War in Guinea."

86. Friedman, *Shadow Cold War*, 48–51.

87. Laban, *Mário Pinto de Andrade*, 160.

88. Friedman, *Shadow Cold War*, 54.

89. Laban, *Mário Pinto de Andrade*, 162.

90. Ellis, *External Mission*, 13.

91. Ellis, "Nelson Mandela, the South African Communist Party." On reactions to Ellis's argument, see Macmillan et al., "Debating the ANC's External Links"; Stevens, "The Turn to Sabotage." Also see Simpson, "Nelson Mandela."

92. "A note on Angola," 1963, Arkhiv Vneshnei Politiki Rossiiskoi Federatsii (Foreign Policy Archive of the Russian Federation, hereafter AVPRF), f. 658, op. 3, papka (p.) 1, d. 1, 38.

93. Quoted in Shubin, *Hot "Cold War,"* 8.

94. Lara, *Um amplo movimento*, 1:407.

95. Marcum, *Angolan Revolution*, 1:124–26.

Chapter Three

1. "Portugal: Revolt on the High Seas," *Time*, February 3, 1961. Galvão later confirmed in his memoirs that engineering a coup in Angola was part of his plan. See Galvão, *Santa Maria*.

2. For a discussion of the figures, see Neves, "Frantz Fanon," 11, 14.

3. "Angola: Lawless Terror," *Time*, May 19, 1961.

4. Antunes, "Kennedy, Portugal, and the Azores Base."

5. On the reasons behind the 1961 Berlin Crisis, see Harrison, *Driving the Soviets up the Wall*, Ch. 4.

6. On Kennedy's decision-making, see Schneidman, *Engaging Africa*, 22–28; Muehlenbeck, *Betting on the Africans*, 103–104; Rakove, *Kennedy*, 123–24.

7. "Angola: Land of Brotherly Love," *Time*, February 17, 1961.

8. Dalila Cabrita Mateus and Álvaro Mateus, *Angola 61—Guerra Colonial*.

9. Lara, *Um amplo movimento*, 1:426–27.

10. Laban, *Mário Pinto de Andrade,* 165–66.

11. Marcum, *Angolan Revolution,* 1:135–42.

12. Schneidman, *Engaging Africa,* 25.

13. Marcum, *Angolan Revolution,* 2:160–61.

14. Lara, *Um amplo movimento,* 2:106.

15. On Czechoslovak motivations, see Richterova, Pešta, and Telepneva, "Banking on Military Assistance"; Muehlenbeck, *Czechoslovakia in Africa,* 2–17.

16. In the USSR and Czechoslovakia, the KGB and the StB contained under its umbrella domestic security and foreign intelligence branches. Foreign intelligence operations were run by the KGB and the StB's "First Directorate." In the context of this book, I refer to "KGB" and "StB" when speaking about foreign intelligence and not internal security.

17. On Barák, see Blažek and Žáček, "Czechoslovakia," 154–56.

18. "Záznam o návštěvě představitelů národně-osvobozeneckého hnutí Angoly [Record of a visit by representatives of the Angolan National Liberation Movement]," January 28, 1961, Národní Archiv (The National Archives, hereafter NA), Archiv ÚV KSČ, fond (f.) 1261/0/44, Kancelář 1. tajemníka ÚV KSČ Antonína Novotného-II. Část, (KSČ/ÚV/ANII), inventární číslo (inv. č.) 75, karton (ka.) 71, 1–3.

19. "Usnesení: 143 politického byra ÚV KSČ ze dne 18. dubna 1961 [Resolution 143of the CC CPC Political Bureau of April 18, 1961]," NA, f. 1261/0/44, KSČ/ÚV/ANII, inv. č. 394, ka. 166.

20. "Důvodová zpráva [Explanatory Memorandum]," NA, f. 1261/0/44, KSČ/ÚV/ANII, inv. č. 394, ka. 166, 9.

21. V. Tereshkin (deputy, International Department) to CC CPSU, May 30, 1961, Rossiiskii Gosudarsvennyi Arkhiv Noveishei Istorii (Russian State Archive for Contemporary History, hereafter RGANI), f. 5, op. 50, d. 360, 72; D. Dolidze to CC CPSU, May 23, 1961, RGANI, f. 5, op. 50, d. 360, 71.

22. Lara, *Amplo movimento,* 2:104–105; Conversation with Pascoal Luvualu, June 9, 1961, GARF, f. 9540, op. 2, d. 40, 81–82.

23. "Sitsuatsiia v Angole: Deklaratsiia sovetskogo pravitelstva [The Situation in Angola: Declaration of the Soviet Government]," *Pravda,* May 27, 1961.

24. "Vienna Meeting Between the President and Chairman Khrushchev," Vienna, June 3, 1961, 3 p.m., doc. 85, FRUS/1961-1963/V.

25. "Record of proceedings between the Soviet KGB and the Interior Ministry of the Czechoslovak Socialist Republic," June 1961.

26. Alter (Conakry) to Barák (Ministry of the Interior), June 21, 1961, Archiv Bezpečnostních Složek (Security Services Archive, hereafter ABS), 43197/000, 3–5.

27. Alter (Conakry), July 7, 1961, ABS, 43196/000, 29–30. I thank Mikuláš Pešta for sharing this document.

28. RGANI, f. 89, op. 38, d. 4, 5.

29. For a full analysis of the document, see Zubok, "Spy vs. Spy." The author could not locate the document that Zubok refers to in the archive.

30. On the various rival organizations, see Dhada, *Warriors at Work*, 6–12. For the part Cape Verdeans played, see Keese, "Role of Cape Verdeans."

31. Bangura interview.

32. Cabral to Ivanov, September 26, 1960, Fundação Mário Soares/Arquivo Amílcar Cabral (FMS/AC), Pasta: 07057.011.003

33. Lev Sukhanov (Soviet Solidarity Committee) to Amílcar Cabral (Conakry), November 4, 1960, FMS/AC, Pasta: 07066.090.023.

34. Telepneva, "Code Name SEKRETÁŘ," 4–5.

35. Bangura interview.

36. Ivanov (Soviet Solidarity Committee), March 8, 1961, GARF, f. 9540, op. 2, d. 40, 50–56.

37. Václav David to Antonín Novotný, July 20, 1961, NA, f. 1261/0/44, KSČ/ÚV/ANII, inv. 394, k.166.

38. Lopes, *Aristides Pereira*, 96–97.

39. Miller (chief, First Directorate of the StB) to Barák, March 27, 1961, ABS, 43197/000, 30–34.

40. David to Novotný, July 20, 1961, NA, f. 1261/0/44, KSČ/ÚV/ANII, inv. 394, k.166.

41. Alter (Conakry) to StB, August 14, 1961, ABS, 43197/000, 16. The first to uncover the connections between the StB and Amílcar Cabral (and conduct archival research into Czechoslovak policy in the Third World) were historians-turned journalists Petr Zídek and Karl Sieber. See: Zídek and Sieber, *Československo a Subsaharská Afrika*.

42. For further discussion, see Telepneva, "Code Name SEKRETÁŘ."

43. This paragraph is based on Cahen, "Mueda Case," 29–46.

44. Early figures cited 600 people killed. Cahen has argued that the real number of people killed in those events fell between 9 and 36. See Cahen, "Mueda Case"; Israel, "Mueda Massacre."

45. Marcum, *Angolan Revolution*, 1:197.

46. Quoted in Shubin, *Hot "Cold War,"* 120.

47. RGANI, f. 89, op. 38, d. 4.

48. Budakov (ambassador, Ethiopia) to Mezhdunarodnyi Otdel (International Department, hereafter MO), February 3, 1961, RGANI, f. 5, op. 50, d. 416, 63–68.

49. Cabrita, *Mozambique*, 5–12.

50. Cabrita, *Mozambique*, 6.

51. "Memorandum of Conversation," Dar es Salaam, April 25, 1976," doc. 194, FRUS/1969–1976/ XXVIII.

52. The third smaller organisation was UNAMI (the African Union for Independent Mozambique). It was organized by migrant workers in British Nyasaland, later independent Malawi.

53. Cahen, "Mueda Case," 43.

54. Dolidze to CC CPSU, August 9, 1962, GARF, f. 9540, op. 2, d. 53, 131–35.

55. Gafurov to CC CPSU, August 7, 1962, GARF, f. 9540, op. 2, d. 53, 119–22.

56. Shubin, *Hot "Cold War,"* 120; Evsiukov, "Iz vospominanii," 1:231.

57. Wheeler, "African Elements," 234–37.

58. Ruaridh Nicoll, "The Great Escape that Changed Africa's Future," *The Guardian*, March 8, 2015; Harper and Nottingham, *Escape from Portugal*.

59. Amélia and Teresa Araújo interview.

60. For an overview, see Mazov, *Distant Front*, 227–51.

61. Katsakioris, "Students from Portuguese Africa," 7.

Chapter Four

1. The Office of Current Intelligence Special Report, "The Angolan Rebellion and White Unrest," April 1963, CIA Records, FOIA, CIA-RDP79-00927AO04000030002–5.

2. Wheeler, "African Elements," 237.

3. Meneses, *Salazar*, ch. X.

4. Marino, "America's War in Angola," 71–86.

5. Fonseca and Marcos, "Cold War Constraints," 209–26.

6. I borrow the phrase from Burton, "Hubs of Decolonization."

7. Bjerk, "Postcolonial Realism," 231–32.

8. Friedman, *Shadow Cold War*.

9. Laban, *Mário Pinto de Andrade*, 177.

10. Neumann (first secretary, Guinea) to MfAA, September 12, 1961, Politisches Archiv des Auswärtigen Amt–Ministerium für Auswärtige Angelegenheiten der Deutschen Demokratischen Republik (Political Archive of the GDR's Foreign Ministry, hereafter PAAA-MfAA), A15964, 16–24.

11. Telepneva, "Cold War on the Cheap," 133–37.

12. Nazhestkin, "Superderzhavy," 31.

13. "Work plan: Angola," January 10, 1962, ABS, 11611/000, 103–9.

14. Marcum, *Angolan Revolution*, 1: 243–48.

15. Gafurov (Soviet Solidarity Committee, deputy chairman) to CC CPSU, August 7, 1962, GARF, f. 9540, op. 2, d. 53, 112–16.

16. Marino, "America's War in Angola," 67–68.

17. Marcum, *Angolan Revolution*, 2: 76–80.

18. Guimarães, *The Origins of the Angolan Civil War*, 212.

19. Marcum, *Angolan Revolution*, 2: 85–92.

20. "Memorandum from the Assistant Secretary of State for African Affairs (Williams) to Secretary of State Rusk," Washington, October 23, 1962, doc. 360, FRUS/1961–1963/XXI.

21. Laban, *Mário Pinto de Andrade*, 180–81; Lúcio Lara, interview, in Barber and Hélder, *Angola*, 50.

22. For further discussion of Viriato da Cruz and the reasons for the split, see Marcum, *Angolan Revolution*, 1: 85–92; Guimarães, *Origins*, 67–69. On Viriato Cruz and his relationship with Maoism, see Sun, "Viriato da Cruz and His Chinese Exile."

23. Rocha, "Conflitos."

24. Laban, *Mário Pinto de Andrade*, 182–83.

25. Shubin, *Hot "Cold War,"* 10–11.

26. Nazhestkin, "Superderzhavy," 239.

27. Nazhestkin, "V ognennom koltse," 240–41.

28. Prague (first directorate, 4th department), 7 January 1966, "D.S. KONÍK," ABS, 11611/114.

29. Nazhestkin, "Gody kongolezskogo krizisa," 160–64.

30. Holden Roberto (Léopoldville) to the President, November 27, 1962, Papers of John F. Kennedy, Bowles, Chester, 1963, JFKPOF-062-015, 33–35.

31. Azimov (Soviet representative, UN) to CC CPSU, December 4, 1963, RGANI, f. 5, op. 50, d. 604, 1–4.

32. Bazanov (Soviet Solidarity Committee, secretary) to CC CPSU, January 27, 1964, GARF, f. 9540, op. 2, d. 64, 282–84.

33. Bashev (foreign minister, Sofia) to the Central Committee of the Bulgarian Communist Party (CC BCP), December 1963, Tsentralen D'rzhaven Arkhiv (Central State Archives, hereafter TsDA), f. 1b, op. 64, a.e. 322; Dimo Dichev to the Secretariat of the CC BCP, January 30, 1964, TsDA, f. 1b, op. 64, a.e. 322.

34. "Telegram from the Embassy in the Congo [Zaire] to the Department of State," Léopoldville, March 27, 1964, 7 p.m., doc. 162, FRUS/1964–1968/ XXIII.

35. Marino, "America's War in Angola," 71–78.

36. Bridgland, *Jonas Savimbi*, 58.

37. Klein (CSSR third secretary, USSR) to Prague, conversation between R. Klein and N. Bazanov on January 22, 1964, Archiv Ministerstva Zahraničních Věci (Archive of the Ministry of Foreign Affairs, hereafter AMZV), TERITORIÁLNÍ ODBORY TAJNÉ (TO-T)/IV/4, sign. 274, 125.

38. Scholz (GDR ambassador, Cairo) to Schwab (deputy foreign minister, Berlin), February 25, 1964, PAAA-MfAA, A15964, 75–76; Lessing to Schwab, February 25, 1964, PAAA-MfAA, A1596, 77; Schwab to Scholz, February 25, 1964, PAAA-MfAA, A15964, 78–79; Scholz to Schwab and Lessing, April 6, 1964, PAAA-MfAA, A17416, 1–2.

39. Dolidze to CC CPSU, May 21, 1964, RGANI, f. 5, op. 50, d. 603, 32–41.

40. Prague, reception of the FNLA delegation by the Czechoslovak Solidarity Committee on April 14, 1964, AMZV, TO-T/IV/4, sign. 274, 1–7; Berlin, April 22, 1964, Information about the visit of Dr. Jonas Savimbi and Florentino Duarte in the GDR from April 19 to April 21, 1964, Bundesarchiv–Stiftung Archiv der Parteien und Massenorganisationen der DDR (Federal Archive of Parties and Mass Organizations of the GDR, hereafter BA-SAPMO), DY 30/IV, A 2/20/948, 163–66.

41. Nazhestkin, "Superderzhavy," 31.

42. Bridgland, *Jonas Savimbi*, 66.

43. "Research Memorandum from the Director of the Bureau of Intelligence and Research (Hughes) to Secretary of State Rusk," Washington, November 5, 1963, doc. 372, FRUS/1961–1963/XXI.

44. East Berlin, September 8, 1964, conversation with Baya on May 27, 1964, PAAA-MfAA, A15964, 47–49; Belskii (USSR chargé d'affaires, Algeria) to Ministerstvo Inostrnnykh Del (Soviet Ministry of Foreign Affairs, hereafter MID), January 21, 1964, AVPRF, f. 658, op. 4, p. 1, d. 1, 7–8.

45. Shubin, *Hot "Cold War,"* 18. The timing of the incident is still not entirely clear, but there are several indications it took place in March 1964. Khrushchev was in Pitsunda and Neto was in Moscow at the same time. Midtsev's article in *Pravda* appeared on March 17, 1964. See Veniamin Midtsev, "Angola: Za edinstvo patriotov" [Angola: For the unity of patriots], *Pravda*, March 17, 1964.

46. Nazhestkin to Moscow, June 15, 1964, AVPRF, f. 658, op. 4, p. 1, d. 1, 51–53.

47. Maksudov to CC CPSU, July 30, 1964, RGANI, f. 5, op. 50, d. 603, 103–112.

48. Bridgland, *Jonas Savimbi*, 64–65.

49. Marino, "America's War in Angola," 78–86.

50. Patolichev (second secretary, Czechoslovakia) to Moscow, October 22, 1962, RGANI, f. 5, op. 50, d. 603, 160–169. The document is Patolichev's summary of the notes Provazník passed to the Soviet embassy in Czechoslovakia.

51. Midtsev, "Bortsy i politikany" [Fighters and politicians], *Pravda*, December 16, 1964, 3.

52. Brutents, *Tridtsat let*, 205.

53. Alter and Farsky to StB, November 1, 1961, ABS, 43197/000, 134–35.

54. Bakhitov (Soviet Solidarity Committee) to CC CPSU, December 19, 1961, GARF, f. 9540, op. 2, d. 40, 165–72.

55. Evsiukov, "Natsionalno-osvoboditelnaia borba," 5:140.

56. Evsiukov, "Natsionalno-osvoboditelnaia borba," 5:140–43.

57. RGANI, f. 89, inv. 38, d. 5 and d. 6.

58. Katsakioris, "Students from Portuguese Africa," 9.

59. Dhada, *Warriors at Work*, 13.

60. Houska (chief of intelligence) to Štrougal (minister of the interior, Czechoslovakia), February 21, 1963, ABS, 43197/020, 43–45.

61. Lopes, *Aristides Pereira*, 97–98.

62. Gorbunov, "Dva goda v Gvinee"; Mazov, *Distant Front*, 188–89.

63. Václavíc (Conakry) to Prague, November 10, 1962, ABS, 43197/020, 24–27.

64. Lopes, *Aristides Pereira*, 100.

65. Dhada, *Warriors at Work*, 13–14.

66. Ignatev, *Syn Afriki*, 40.

67. Houska to Štrougal, February 26, 1963, ABS, 43197/020, 40–42.

68. Sousa, "Amílcar Cabral, the PAIGC and the Relations with China," 12–15.

69. Marcum, *Conceiving Mozambique*, 40–42.

70. Marcum, *Conceiving Mozambique*, 43–55.

71. Timoshchenko (ambassador, Tanzania) to Dolidze, November 15, 1963, GARF, f. 9540, op. 2, d. 70, 146–47.

72. Record of a conversation between Second Secretary Hruzy and David Mabunda on December 15, 1962, AMZV, TO-T/IV/8. sign. 273, inv. č. 67.

73. Telepneva, "Mediators of Liberation," 9–10.

74. Maksudov (Soviet embassy in the UAR, Cairo) to the Soviet Solidarity Committee, June 5, 1963, GARF, f. 9540, op. 2, d. 68, 63–65.

75. Houska to Štrougal, Prague, April 2, 1962, ABS, 11690/305, 115.

76. Ustinov (counselor, Tanzania) to Moscow, September 24, 1963, GARF, f. 9540, op. 2, d. 70, 53–65.

77. Muehlenbeck, *Betting on the Africans*, 105.

78. Schneidman, *Engaging Africa*, 46; Roberts, "Assassination of Eduardo Mondlane," 8.

79. Cabrita, *Mozambique*, 18.

80. Timoshchenko (ambassador, Tanzania) to Dolidze, November 15, 1963, GARF, f. 9540, op. 2, d. 70, 146–47.

81. Cabrita, *Mozambique*, 27.

82. Telepneva, "Mediators of Liberation," 13.

83. Václavic, Prague, May 28, 1964, ABS, 11690/312, 9–15.

84. Mondlane (Dar es Salaam) to the Soviet Government, March 11, 1965, AVPRF, f. 659, op. 2, p. 1, d. 1, 1–2.

85. Shubin, *Hot "Cold War,"* 121.

86. Cabrita, *Mozambique*, 207.

87. Petr Manchkha's intervention in Stenogram of SKSSAA Presidium session on October 13, 1964, GARF, f. 9540, op. 1, d. 155, 38–44.

88. Mondlane, *The Struggle for Mozambique*, 12.

89. Lal, "Maoism in Tanzania," 96–116. For an overview of Maoism in Africa, see Lovell, *Maoism*, ch. 6. Also see Burgess, "Mao in Zanzibar."

90. Sousa, "Amílcar Cabral, the PAIGC and the Relations with China," 5.

91. Luz interview.

92. Silva interview.

93. Silva interview.

94. There exists a rich and growing literature on African students in the USSR. See, in particular, Guillory, "Culture Clash"; Matusevich, "Probing the Limits of Internationalism"; Matusevich, "An Exotic Subversive"; and Katsakioris, "Burden or Allies."

95. See Hessler, "Death of an African Student," 33–63.

96. On African students in Eastern and Central Europe, see Muehlenbeck, *Czechoslovakia in Africa*, 168–73; Slobodian, "Bandung in Divided Germany," 654; Branch, "Political Traffic"; and Burton, "Decolonization."

97. Katsakioris, "Students from Portuguese Africa," 14–16. On the 'antiparty plot' and da Silva's involvement, also see Santos, *Amílcar Cabral*, 367–88.

98. Katsakioris, "Students from Portuguese Africa," 14–16; Da Silva interview.

99. Hevi, *An African Student in China*.

100. Liu, "Petty Annoyances?"

101. Katsakioris, "Students from Portuguese Africa," 14–16.

102. Timoshchenko (ambassador, Tanzania) to Moscow, "Conversation with Eduardo Mondlane on August 25, 1967," RGANI, f. 5, op. 59, d. 394, 172–74.

Chapter Five

1. Zubok, *Failed Empire*, 193–201.

2. Iandolo, "Rise and Fall," 699–704; Legvold, *Soviet Policy in West Africa*, 335–44; Natufe, *Soviet Policy in Africa*, 282–84. In his overview of Soviet relations with southern Africa, Westad focuses mainly on the 1970s. See his *Global Cold War*, 207–18.

3. Iandolo, "Rise and Fall," 683–704.

4. Pikhoia, *Moskva, Kreml, Vlast*, 469; Doklad Prezidiuma TsK KPSS.

5. Darame interview; Pires interview.

6. Václav David (CSSR foreign minister) to Antonín Novotný (CSSR general secretary), May 7, 1966, Národní Archiv, KSČ-ÚV-ANII, f. 1261/0/44, inv. č. 2, ka. 3.

7. Information Given to Angel Solakov on the Visit of a Bulgarian CSS delegation to the Soviet Union and their Meetings with the Leadership of the KGB First Chief Directorate, March 18, 1966, *The KGB and the Bulgarian State Security Service*, 126–38, 130.

8. On Soviet-Czechoslovak cooperation in Ghana after 1966, see Telepneva, "Saving Ghana's Revolution."

9. Consultation between representatives of the solidarity committees of the European socialist countries on June 28 and 29, 1966, BA-SAPMO, DZ8/32, 54.

10. On Poland in Africa, see Gasztold, "Lost Illusions."

11. Muehlenbeck, *Czechoslovakia in Africa*, 173–76; Muehlenbeck, "Czechoslovak Assistance to Kenya and Uganda."

12. Richterova, Pešta, and Telepneva, "Banking on Military Assistance."

13. Kaňák, Dvořáková, Jurová, *Československá rozvědka*, 45–84.

14. Spitskii, "Obrazovanie afrikanskikh otdelov," 2:35.

15. Startsev (ambassador, Conakry) to MO, RGANI, f. 5, op. 60, d. 453, 172–74, 173.

16. George Roberts, "Assassination of Eduardo Mondlane," 13.

17. Lal, "Maoism in Tanzania," 110.

18. Mordvintsev (embassy counselor, Guinea) to MO, June 28, 1967, RGANI, f. 5, op. 59, d. 390, 105–11; Sousa, "Amílcar Cabral, the PAIGC and the Relations with China," 12–18.

19. Jackson, "China's Third World Policy."

20. Vasilii Solodovnikov, in Transcript of the SKSSAA Presidium session on October 1, 1968, GARF, f. 9540, op. 1, d. 240, 12–13.

21. Transcript of the SKSSAA Presidium session on February 19, 1969, GARF, f. 9540, op. 1, d. 255, 85.

22. Bangura interview, March 30, 2019.

23. Sousa, *Amílcar Cabral*, 338–40.

24. Work Plan: Portuguese Guinea, January 8, 1962, ABS, 11853/000, 40.

25. Václavic (Conakry) to Prague, November 10, 1962, ABS, 43197/020, 15–19.

26. Houska to Štrougal, December 29, 1962, ABS, 11853/103, 36–38.

27. Houska to Štrougal, February 26, 1963, ABS, 43197/020, 40–42.

28. Na Nhakpba interview.

29. Camará interview.

30. MacQueen, *Decolonization of Portuguese Africa*, 38.

31. Cann, *Flight Plan Africa*, 250–56.

32. Na Nhakpba interview; Bangura interview. On the experiences of women in the struggle, see Galvão and Laranjeiro, "Gender Struggle in Guinea-Bissau."

33. Dhada, *Warriors at Work*, 18–20.

34. Chabal, *Amílcar Cabral*, 81–82.

35. Amílcar Cabral to Nikita Khrushchev, May 26, 1964, FMS/AA, Pasta: 07057.011.007.

36. Polda's personnel file, see ABS-6125-František Polda (13.6.1925).

37. Mané, interview.

38. Antonín Janovec (Felix Dzerzhinsky Central School, director) to StB, December 22, 1961, ABS, 11853/102, 56–59.

39. Janovec to StB, November 6, 1963, ABS, 11853/102, 104–9.

40. Camará interview, March 29, 2019.

41. Zubarev, "Kursanty."

42. Mané interview; Na Nhakpba interview.

43. Epishev to CC CPSU, April 12, 1966, RGANI, f. 5, op. 47, d. 496, 108–109; Epishev to CC CPSU, July 18, 1966, RGANI, f. 5, op. 58, d. 177, 21.

44. Gorbunov, "Partizany dlia Afriki."

45. See, for example, "Shkola Terroristov."

46. Na Nhakpba interview.

47. Cassama interview; da Matta interview.

48. Mané interview.

49. Silva interview.

50. For further discussion, see Fonseca, "The Military Training of Angolan Guerrillas"; Alexander and McGregor, "African Soldiers in the USSR."

51. Houska to Kudrna, May 25, 1965, ABS, 43197/000, 204–11.

52. CCP Politburo Resolution, June 1, 1965, NA, f. 1261/0/44, KSČ/ÚV/ANII, inv.č. 394, ka.166.

53. Lopes, *Aristides Pereira*, 118–26.

54. Prashad, *Darker Nations*, 105–19.

55. Amílcar Cabral, "Weapon of Theory."

56. Gleijeses, *Conflicting Missions*, 187–89.

57. Lopes, *Aristides Pereira*, 140–41.

58. Bangura interview, March 30, 2019.

59. Cassama interview, March 22, 2019.

60. Mendy and Lobban, *Historical Dictionary*, 353–54.

61. Josef Janouš (4th department of the StB's first directorate, chief), Prague, February 13, 1967, ABS, 43197/020, 157–69, 160.

62. Gleijeses, *Conflicting Missions*, 196–99.

63. Janouš, "The PAIGC—a brief summary of the consultations," November 15, 1966, ABS, 11853/011, 61–62.

64. Peták to Prague, May 17, 1967, "Consultations about the PAIGC with Cubans on May 8 and 17.5," ABS, 43197/020, 151–53.

65. Peták to Prague, March 7, 1967, ABS, 43197/020, 141.

66. Peták to Prague, February 10, 1968, ABS, 43197/020, 240.

67. On the aborted mission to Cape Verde, see Lopes, *Aristides Pereira*, 130.

68. Silva interview.

69. Carvalho interview.

70. Luz interview, January 14, 2017.

71. Pires interview; Darame interview.

72. Evsiukov, "Natsionalno-osvoboditelnaia borba," 5:144–45.

73. Silva interview.

74. Predvechnov to CC CPSU, August 11, 1969, RGANI, f. 5, op. 61, d. 542, 107–11.

75. Pires interview; Cassama interview.

76. Gleijeses, *Conflicting Missions*, 174–78.

77. Gleijeses, *Conflicting Missions*, 178–84.

78. Slipchenko (ambassador, Zambia) to MO, conversation with Neto and Anibal de Melo, June 1, 1966, RGANI, f. 5, op. 58, d. 302, 104–106.

79. Slipchenko to MO, conversation with Anibal de Melo on June 6 and 8, 1966, RGANI, f. 5, op. 58, d. 302, 116–18; Slipchenko to CC CPSU, August 22, 1966, RGANI f. 5, op. 58, d. 302, 200–202.

80. Slipchenko to CC CPSU, September 23, 1966, RGANI, f. 5, op. 58, d. 302, 259–77, 272.

81. RGANI, f. 89, inv. 38, d. 8; Algiers to Prague, January 21, 1965, AMZV, TO-tajné, IV/6, sign. 274/111.

82. W. B. Rychlowski, Warsaw, April 2, 1966, Record of conversation with Manchkha, Archiwum Akt Nowych (Central Archive of Modern Records, hereafter AAN), Polska Ziednoczona Partia Robotnicza/Komitet Centralny w Warszawe (hereafter PZPR), 237/XXII-1354.

83. Shubin, *Hot "Cold War,"* 15.

84. Telepneva, "Letters from Angola," 137–40.

85. Telepneva, "Letters from Angola," 141–49.

86. Simonov (counselor, Congo-Brazzaville) to MO, February 15, 1967, RGANI, f. 5, op. 59, d. 388, 41–54.

87. Putiatov (second secretary, Tanzania) to MO, February 11, 1967, RGANI, f. 5, op. 59, d. 388, 34–40.

88. Kirpichenko, *Razvedka*, Chapter: "Tantsy v Angole [Dancing in Angola]."

89. Lessing to MfAA, February 24, 1967, February 18, 1967, PAAA-MfAA, M3/136, 1–8. The author thanks George Roberts for providing access to this document.

90. Quoted in Shubin, *Hot "Cold War,"* 16.

91. Glukhov (embassy counselor, Tanzania) to MO, conversation with Daniel Chipenda, April 19, 1968, RGANI, f. 5, op. 60, d. 454, 168–69.

92. Čavoški, "'Yugoslavia's Help was Extraordinary,'" 134–39.

93. Slipchenko to MO, September 4, 1969, RGANI, f. 5, op. 61, d. 542, 141–44.

94. A. Malygin (KGB, deputy chairman) to CC CPSU, June 4, 1970, RGANI, f. 5, op. 62, d. 536, 73–76.

95. Mondlane, *Struggle for Mozambique*, 139.

96. Christie, *Samora Machel*, 34; Marcum, *Conceiving Mozambique*, 49.

97. Czechoslovakia allocated weapons worth one million Czech crowns, while Bulgaria sent 170,000 leva worth of weapons as well as humanitarian assistance and scholarships. See Resolution of the 115th meeting of the Presidium of the Czechoslovak Communist Party on June 29, 1965, Prague, NACR, KSČ/ÚV/ANII, č. f. 1261/0/44, inv. č. 328, ka. 138; Dimo Dichev to CC BCP, April 21, 1965, Tsentralen D'rzhaven Arkhiv (TsDa), f. 1b, op. 64, d. 332.

98. Mondlane to CPSU, March 11, 1965, AVPRF, f. 659, op. 2, p. 1, d. 1.

99. Ustinov (counselor, Tanzania) to MO, March 17, 1965, March 16, 1965, RGANI, f. 5, op. 50, d. 699, 116–20, 118.

100. Ulianovskii to CC CPSU, 29 March 29, 1966, RGANI, f. 5. Op. 50, d. 767, 183–84.

101. Information about the stay of Uria Simango and Marcelino dos Santos as guests of the GDR's Solidarity Committee from December 6–13, 1963, BA-SAPMO, DZ8/163.

102. Marcum, *Conceiving Mozambique*, 103; see the entry for "Simango, Uria Timoteo" in Darch, *Historical Dictionary of Mozambique*.

103. R. Malinovskii and M. Zakharov to CC CPSU, March 30, 1966, RGANI, f. 5, op. 50, d. 767, 185–90.

104. M. Domogatskikh to M. V. Zimianin (*Pravda*, chief editor), December 27, 1965, Conversation with Samuel Moyana, RGANI, f. 5. op. 50, d. 767; M. Domogatskikh to M. V. Zimianin (*Pravda*, chief editor), Conversation with George Chilambe, commander of the FRELIMO training camp in Lindi, Tanzania, February 28, 1968, 91–94.

105. Altorfer-Ong, "Old Comrades and New Brothers," 119–40.

106. Lal, "Maoism in Tanzania," 96–116.

107. Isaacman and Isaacman, *Mozambique's Samora Machel*, 88, 150.

108. Evsiukov, "Iz vospominanii," 1:231.

109. Epishev to CC CPSU, RGANI, f. 5, op. 57, d. 177, 21–23.

110. Banks, "Socialist Internationalism," 38.

111. Dolidze to CC CPSU, December 6, 1966, RGANI, f. 5. op. 58, d. 335.

112. Seiferth (attaché, Moscow) to Ministerium für Auswärtige Angelegenheiten (GDR's Ministry of Foreign Relations, hereafter MfAA), November 30, 1966, November 26, 1966, PAAA-MfAA, A1166, 147.

113. Lessing to MfAA, February 24, 1967, February 18, 1967, PAAA-MfAA, M3/136, 5.

114. Marcum, *Conceiving Mozambique*, 104–106; Cabrita, *Mozambique*, 47; Opello Jr., "Pluralism and Elite Conflict," 74–75.

115. Marcum, *Conceiving Mozambique*, 102–3.

116. For details, see Panzar, "Pedagogy of Revolution," 803–20.

117. Derluguian, "Social Origins"; Cahen, "Mueda Case," 46.

118. Quoted in Isaacman and Isaacman, *Mozambique*, 98.

119. Glukhov to MO, June 14, 1968, conversation with Mondlane on May 21, 23, and 28, 1968, RGANI, f. 5, op. 50, d. 460, 11–15.

120. Roberts, "Assassination of Eduardo Mondlane," 12.

121. Marcum, *Conceiving Mozambique*, 131–33.

122. Mitrokhin and Andrew, *The Mitrokhin Archive II*, 445; Papers of Vasilii Mitrokhin, Churchill Archives Centre, Churchill College, Cambridge, K-12, 269.

123. Rui Duarte Silva, "Chissano confirma colaboração com o KGB" [Chissano confirms collaboration with the KGB], *Expresso*, April 8, 2016.

124. One of the Czechoslovak clandestine contacts was Dennis Phombeah, a close ally of Oscar Kambona. Brennan, "Secret Lives of Dennis Phombeah."

125. Ivashutin to CC CPSU, November 13, 1968, RGANI, f. 5, op. 60, d. 460, 147–52.

126. This paragraph is based on Roberts, "Assassination of Eduardo Mondlane."

127. Zakharov (KGB, deputy chief) to CC CPSU, February 13, 1969, RGANI, f. 5, op. 61, d. 542.

128. Čestmír Podzemný (chief of foreign intelligence) to Vašek (deputy interior minister, CSSR), February 5, 1969, ABS, 11616/101, 7–15.

129. Prague, February 18, 1969, ABS, 11690/312, 67.

130. Telepneva, "Mediators of Liberation."

131. Kirschner's personnel file, ABS-896-Kirschner Zdeněk (15.1.1924).

132. Glukhov to MO, September 3, 1969, conversation with Simango and Chissano, RGANI, f. 5, op. 61, d. 542, 134–37, 135.

133. Ncomo, *Uria Simango*, 183–253, 331–42.

134. Macamo, "Violence and Political Culture," 91; Marcum, *Conceiving Mozambique*, 138–40. On contemporary understanding of Simango and his legacy in Mozambique, see Pearce, "Simango."

135. Ivashutin to CC CPSU, July 28, 1969 RGANI, f. 5, op. 61, d. 542, 90–102.

136. Alves Gomes interview.

137. Glukhov to MO, September 25, 1969, RGANI, f. 5, op. 61, d. 542, 173–76.

138. Glukhov and Samsonov to MO, November 14, 1969, RGANI, f. 5, op. 61, d. 542, 264–68.

139. Tolokonnikov to CC CPSU, October 13, 1969, RGANI, f. 5, op. 61, d. 542, 215–19.

140. Ivashutin to CC CPSU, November 24, 1969, RGANI, f. 5, op. 61, d. 542, 246–49.

141. Marcum, *Conceiving Mozambique*, 140.

142. Cabrita, *Mozambique*, 180–84. FRELIMO never officially confirmed that Simango was executed.

Chapter Six

1. Gallagher, *Portugal*, 165–73.

2. Marino, "America's War in Angola," 97–103.

3. On the U.S. side, see Garthoff, *Détente and Confrontation*, 279–87; Hanhimäki, *Flawed Architect*, 85–91. For Brezhnev's role in détente, see Zubok, *Failed Empire*, 201–26.

4. Lopes, *West Germany and the Portuguese Dictatorship*, 237–48.

5. For a summary, see Westad, "Fall of Détente."

6. Zubok, *Failed Empire*, 223.

7. Westad, *Global Cold War*, 194–206.

8. Westad, *Global Cold War*, 214.

9. Andropov to CC CPSU, January 26, 1970, RGANI, f. 5, op. 62, d. 535, 1–4.

10. Andropov to Ponomarev, May 6, 1970, RGANI, f. 5, op. 62, d. 535, 32–35.

11. Chebrikov to CC CPSU, April 16, 1970, RGANI, f. 5, op. 62, d. 535, 10–31.

12. Tolokonnikov to CC CPSU, September 22, 1970, RGANI, f. 5, op. 62, d. 535, 71–90.

13. Tsvigun to CC CPSU, May 30, 1973, RGANI, f. 5, op. 66, d. 1040, 33.

14. Jackson, "China's Third World Foreign Policy," 401–22; Vieira, *Participei*, 618–19.

15. See the arguments made by Latip Maksudov, Georgii Kim, and Mirzo Tursun-Zade in Stenogram of SKSSAA Presidium session on August 10, 1971, GARF, f. 9540, op. 1, d. 287, 26, 30, 33.

16. Ivashutin and Dagaev to MO, October 5, 1970, RGANI, f. 5, op. 62, d. 535, 95–101.

17. For overviews of Nordic countries' support for African liberation movements, see Soiri and Peltola, *Finland and National Liberation*; Eriksen, *Norway and National Liberation*; Morgenstierne, *Denmark and National Liberation*. On Cabral's trip to Sweden, see Lopes, *Onésimo Silveira*, 119–23.

18. Lúcio Lara and Joaquim Chissano, interviewed in Sellström, *Liberation in Southern Africa*, 19, 39.

19. Tornimbeni, "Nationalism and Internationalism"; Lopes, *Aristides Pereira*, 149.

20. Shubin, interview, in Sellström, *Liberation in Southern Africa*, 247.

21. Ustinov (ambassador, Tanzania) to MO, April 27, 1972, RGANI, f. 5, op. 64, d. 549, 93–107.

22. Solodovnikov, *Tvorcheskii put*, 91.

23. Zubok, *Failed Empire*, 249–50; Urnov interview. On the "Little Deal," see Millar, "The Little Deal."

24. I borrow this term from Brinkman, *War for People*.

25. Clayton, *Frontiersmen*, 46.

26. Brinkman, "War, Witches and Traitors," 311.

27. Belokolos (ambassador, Zambia) to MO, September 14, 1970, RGANI, f. 5, p. 62, d. 536, 195–200.

28. Belokolos to MO, November 26, 1970, RGANI, f. 5, p. 62, d. 536, 241–43.

29. Cavoški, "'Yugoslavia's Help was Extraordinary,'" 141; see also Lazic, "Comrades in Arms," 151–81.

30. Belokolos to MO, October 19, 1970, RGANI, f. 5, p. 62, d. 536, 219–28.

31. Ustinov to MO, April 27, 1972, RGANI, f. 5, op. 64, d. 549, 93–107.

32. Marcum, *Angolan Revolution*, 2:201; Weigert, *Angola*, 41.

33. Lúcio Lara, interview, in Jaime and Barber, *Angola*, 41.

34. Belokolos to MO, March 18, 1972, RGANI, f. 5, op. 64, d. 549, 62–67.

35. Pavlov (counselor, Congo-Brazzaville) to MO, May 26, 1972, May 29, 1972, RGANI, f. 5, op. 64, d. 549, 136–37.

36. Pavlov to MO, August 12, 1972, RGANI, f. 5, op. 64, d. 549, 193–96.

37. Marcum, *Angolan Revolution*, 2:248–49.

38. Rymko (charge d'affaires, Congo-Brazzaville) to MO, June 10, 1972, RGANI, f. 5, op. 64, d. 549, 141–44.

39. Marcum, *Angolan Revolution*, 2:209–10.

40. V. Kulikov, V. Egorov (counselors, Kinshasa) to MO, January 16, 1973, RGANI, f. 5, op. 66, d. 843, 4–9; V. Kulikov (secretary of the consulate, Kinshasa) to MO, April 12, 1973, RGANI, f. 5, op. 66, d. 843, 53–57.

41. Quoted in Shubin, *Hot "Cold War,"* 19.

42. Daniel Chipenda, interview, in Jaime and Barber, *Angola*, 146–47.

43. Wilkowski (U.S. ambassador, Zambia) to Secretary of State (SecState), November 9, 1973, doc. 1973LUSAKA02040, Central Foreign Policy Files, 1973–1979, National Archives and Records Administration, Access to Archival Databases (hereafter CFPF/1973-79/NARA-ADD).

44. Daniel Chipenda, interview, in Jaime and Barber, *Angola*, 146–47; Marcum, *Angolan Revolution*, 2:201–3.

45. Lúcio Lara, interview, in Jaime and Barber, *Angola*, 41–42.

46. Slipchenko (ambassador, Tanzania) to MO, September 14, 1973, RGANI, f. 5, op. 60, d. 865, 162–63.

47. Agostinho Neto (Lusaka) to Leonid Brezhnev, October 18, 1973, RGANI, f. 5, op. 60, d. 865, 187–89.

48. Kulikov to MO, December 21, 1973, RGANI, f. 89, op. 46, d. 104, 33–35.

49. Ulianovskii to MO, January 7, 1974, RGANI, f. 89, op. 46, d. 104, 32; Manchkha to Lusaka, RGANI, f. 89, op. 46, d. 104, 29.

50. Nazhestkin, "Superderzhavy," 33.

51. Evsiukov, "Iz vospominanii," 28.

52. Holness interview.

53. Shubin, *Hot "Cold War,"* 33, 272.

54. Slipchenko to MO, March 20, 1974, RGANI, f. 5, op. 67, d. 758, 48–51.

55. West, *Kupilikula*, 145–46.

56. Newitt, *History of Mozambique*, 531–32. For a detailed study of Flechas, see Cann, *The Flechas*.

57. Eduardo Mondlane's conversation with members of the Soviet Solidarity Committee during their stay in Dar es Salaam, GARF, f. 9540, op. 1, d. 243a, 14–16; Peter Spacek (GDR journalist, Tanzania) to Berlin, April 1, 1970, BA-SAPMO, DZ8/163, 6.

58. Vieira, *Participei*, 597.

59. Mota-Lopes interview.

60. Vieira, *Participei*, 598–99.

61. Ustinov to MO, RGANI, April 27, 1972, RGANI, f. 5, op. 64, d. 549, 93–107.

62. I. Granin (first secretary, Tanzania) to MO, May 12, 1972, RGANI, f. 5, op. 64, d. 549, 109–19.

63. Ustinov to MO, June 20, 1972, RGANI, f. 5, op. 64, d. 549, 150–51.

64. Ustinov to MO, August 16, 1972, RGANI, f. 5, op. 64, d. 549, 184–86.

65. For a detailed account of the Wiriyamu massacre, see Dhada, *Portuguese Massacre*.

66. Slipchenko to MO, conversation with Machel, Santos, and Chissano, July 17, 1973, RGANI, f. 5, op. 60, d. 865, 110–14.

67. On the issue of Portuguese colonialism at the UN, see Santos, *A Organização das Nações Unidas*.

68. Shanigmatov (counselor, Tanzania) to MO, conversation with Joaquim Chissano, July 20, 1973, RGANI, f. 5, op. 60, d. 865, 108–9.

69. Dhada, *Portuguese Massacre*, 8.

70. Meneses and McNamara, "Last Throw of the Dice," 201–15.

71. Slipchenko to MO, conversation with Julius Nyerere, February 7, 1973, RGANI, f. 5, op. 60, d. 865, 4–9.

72. Cann, *Flight Plan Africa*, 338–39.

73. Slipchenko to MO, May 26, 1973, RGANI, f. 5, op. 60, d. 865, 55–100.

74. Hall and Young, *Confronting Leviathan*, 32–35.

75. Memorandum of Conversation, "The Secretary's Visit to Madrid and Lisbon," Lisbon, November 19, 1968, 9:30 a.m., doc. 174, FRUS/1964–1968/XII.

76. Chabal, *Amilcar Cabral*, 94.

77. Cann, *Brown Waters of Africa*, 232–56; Marinho, *Operação Mar Verde*.

78. There is some evidence to suggest the rumors were engineered by East German intelligence. On the consequences of Mar Verde for West German-Guinean relations, see Lopes, *West Germany and the Portuguese Dictatorship*, 25–30.

79. Danilov, "Trevozhnye mesiatsy," 2:72–78.

80. Ratanov (ambassador, Guinea) to MO, conversation with Raúl Díaz Argüelles and Cuban ambassador Oscar Oramas Oliva, December 17, 1971, RGANI, f. 5, op. 64, d. 528, 12–18; Gleijeses, *Conflicting Missions*, 448.

81. Ratanov to MO, December 17, 1971, RGANI, f. 5, op. 64, d. 528, 12–18.

82. Evsiukov, "Iz vospominanii," 150–51.

83. Tiazhev to MO, January 6, 1972, December 31, 1971, RGANI, f. 5, op. 64, d. 528, 1–2.

84. Tiazhev to MO, January 27, 1972, RGANI, f. 5, op. 64, d. 528, 15–16.

85. Ratanov to MO, May 7, 1972, RGANI, f. 5, op. 64, d. 529, 213–17.

86. Ratanov to MO, May 9, 1972, RGANI, f. 5, op. 64, d. 528, 34–37.

87. Ratanov to MO, May 15, 1972, RGANI, f. 5, op. 64, d. 528, 32–33; Ratanov to MO, November 18, 1972, RGANI, f. 5, op. 64, d. 528, 65–72.

88. Boal interview.

89. Amélia and Teresa Araújo interview.

90. Oleg Ignatev, "Kto ubil Amilkar Kabrala: Reportazh iz Gvinei [Bisau] [Who killed Amílcar Cabral: A report from Guinea (Bisseau)]," *Pravda,* March 6, 1973, 4.

91. Danilov, "Trevozhnye mesiatsy v Konakri,"2:81–83.

92. Chabal, *Amílcar Cabral,* 133.

93. Chabal, *Amílcar Cabral,* 132–42.

94. Tavares interview.

95. Carvalho interview.

96. Na Nhakpba interview; Matta interview.

97. Ignatev, *Tres tiros da PIDE.* See also Telepneva, "'Letters from Angola,'" 129–51.

98. Evsiukov, "Natsionalno-osvoboditelnaia borba," 5:147.

99. Kulikov to CC CPSU, February 14, 1973, RGANI, f. 5, op. 66, d. 1190, 48–54.

100. Kulikov to CC CPSU, September 28, 1973, RGANI, f. 5, op. 66, d. 1190, 210–13.

101. Kulikov to CC CPSU, July 18, 1973, RGANI, f. 5, op. 66, d. 1190, 133.

102. Dhada, *Warriors at Work,* 50.

103. Pires interview.

104. Ogarkov to CC CPSU, May 30, 1973, RGANI, f. 5, op. 66, d. 1190, 92–95.

105. For Soviet coverage of the ceremony, see Oleg Ignatev, "Tak sozdavalos' gosudarstvo [This is How a State was Created]," *Pravda,* November 13, 1973, 4.

106. MacQueen, "Belated Decolonization," 51.

107. Luz interview.

108. Maxwell, *Making of Portuguese Democracy,* 35.

Chapter Seven

1. Maxwell, *Making of Portuguese Democracy,* 55–60.

2. On events in Angola in 1974–75, see Westad, *Global Cold War,* 228–49; Gleijeses, *Conflicting Missions,* 246–73; Shubin, *Hot "Cold War,"* 32–57.

3. Amélia and Teresa Araújo interview; Na Nhakpba interview; Matta interview; Carvalho interview; Leite interview.

4. Kido interview.

5. Musatov, "Afrikanskie Marshruty," 1:121–22.

6. Luz interview.

7. Reis, "Decentering the Cold War," 9–10.

8. Lopes, *Aristides Pereira,* 211.

9. Rodrigues, "International Context of Portuguese Decolonization," 104.

10. Haslam, *Russia's Cold War,* 282; Rodrigues, "International Context of Portuguese Decolonization," 108–10.

11. Cherniaev, *Sovmestnyi iskhod,* 96.

12. Drozdov (Soviet embassy in France) to MO, June 4, 1974, RGANI, f. 5, op. 67, d. 830.

13. Drozdov to MO, June 6, 1974, RGANI, f. 5, op. 67, d. 830, 26–27.

14. Slipchenko to MO, July 6, 1974, RGANI, f. 5, op. 67, d. 784, 4.

15. Vieira, *Participei,* 589.

16. Quoted in Haslam, *Russia's Cold War*, 282; Rodrigues, "International Context of Portuguese Decolonization," 108–10.

17. Post (U.S. embassy, Lisbon) to SecState, August 16, 1974, doc. 1974LISBON03328, CFPF/1973-79/NARA-ADD.

18. Post (U.S. embassy, Lisbon) to SecState, August 19, 1974, doc. 1974LISBON03523, CFPF/1973-79/NARA-ADD.

19. Slipchenko to MO, conversation with Samora Machel on September 11, 1974, RGANI, f. 5, op. 67, d. 784.

20. Iukalov (chargé d'affaires, Tanzania) to MO, May 22, 1974, RGANI, f. 5, op. 67, d. 758, 70–71.

21. Afanasenko to MO, June 8, 1974, RGANI, f. 5, op. 67, d. 758, 78–81.

22. Slipchenko to MO, RGANI, f. 5, op. 67, d. 758, 114. This document is a record of a conversation between Neto and Slipchenko on September 30, 1974, during which Neto refers to the talks with Manchkha and Urnov in July.

23. Belokolos to MO, May 6, 1974, RGANI, f. 5, op. 67, d. 758, 63–68.

24. Dzasokhov to CC CPSU, September 17, 1974, RGANI, f. 5, op. 67, d. 758, 101–10. This document is a record of conversation with Angolan students José Neluba de Carlmo and Sebastian Correira. It is not clear if any Soviet representatives actually took part in the failed MPLA Congress.

25. Marcum, *Angolan Revolution*, 2:252.

26. Westad, *Global Cold War*, 224.

27. Afanasenko to MO, 1974, October 10, 1974, RGANI, f. 5, op. 67, d. 758, 122.

28. "Notatka z rozmowy z I Sekretarzem Ambasady ZSRR w Brazzaville tow. Putilinem [Conversation with the first secretary of the Soviet embassy in Brazzaville, comrade Putilin]," September 11, 1974, Archiwum Ministerstwa Spraw Zagranicznych (Archive of the Foreign Ministry, hereafter AMSZ), 19.77.W1.

29. Putilin (first secretary, Brazzaville) to MO, November 25, 1974, RGANI, f. 5, op. 67, d. 758, 131–38.

30. Rosa Coutinho interview in Barber and Hélder, Angola, 270.

31. Marcum, *Angolan Revolution*, 2:253–54; Porter (U.S. consul, Luanda) to SecState, November 4, 1974, doc. 1974LUANDA00942, CFPF/1973-79/NARA-ADD.

32. Slipchenko (ambassador, Tanzania) to MO, July 4, 1974, RGANI, f. 5, op. 67, d. 758, 84–86.

33. Slipchenko (ambassador, Tanzania) to MO, December 1, 1974, RGANI, f. 5, op. 67, d. 758, 144–50.

34. Shubin, *Hot "Cold War,"* 34–35. The author could not locate the document detailing meetings with Iko Carreira and Dúnem in the Russian archives.

35. Dzasokhov to CC CPSU, October 18, 1974, Report on O. Ignatev's trip to Cape Verde, Guinea-Bissau, Angola, and Mozambique, RGANI, f. 5, op. 67, d. 897, 201.

36. Information about a visit to Angola, December 27, 1974, AVPRF, f. 658, op. 14, p. 62, d. 1, 69–72.

37. Afanasenko to MO, December 4, 1974, 1974, RGANI, f. 5, op. 68. d. 1962, 11–12; Afanasenko to MO, January 26, 1975, RGANI, f. 5, op. 68. d. 1962, 37–38.

38. Afanasenko to MO, January 30, 1975, RGANI, f. 5, op. 68. d. 1962, 26.

39. Zverev (chargé d'affaires, Brazzaville) to MO, conversation with Iko Careira and José Eduardo, April 16, 1975, RGANI, f. 5, op. 68. d. 1962, 100–104, 100.

40. Shubin, *Hot "Cold War,"* 40.

41. Kornienko, *Kholodnaia voina*, 210–11.

42. Killoran (U.S. consul general, Luanda) to SecState, January 16, 1975, doc. 1975LUANDA00050, CFPF/1973-79/NARA-ADD. According to Portuguese army estimates, by February, Holden Roberto had mustered about 20,000 men, Agostinho Neto had 10,000, and Jonas Savimbi could count on 8,000. These numbers were probably exaggerated.

43. Afanasenko (ambassador, Brazzaville) to MO, conversation with the Cuban ambassador to Congo-Brazzaville Arquimedes Columbié Alvarez, January 10, 1975, RGANI, f. 5, op. 68. d. 1962, 17.

44. Killoran to SecState, November 13, 1974, doc. 1974LUANDA00970, CFPF/1973-79/NARA-ADD.

45. Killoran to SecState, January 30, 1975, doc. 1975LUANDA00117, CFPF/1973-79/NARA-ADD.

46. Killoran to SecState, February 4, 1975, doc. 1975LUANDA00143, CFPF/1973-79/NARA-ADD.

47. Dzasokhov, *Chelovek i politika*, 39. The author could not locate the record of Dzasokhov's trip to Luanda in February 1975.

48. Wolniewicz (ambassador, Kinshasa) to Lucjan Piatkowski, February 13, 1975, AAN, PZPR, LXXVI.541; Lavrov (ambassador, Zaire) to MO, conversation with L. Wolniewicz on February 8, 1975, RGANI, f. 5, op. 68, d. 1954, 17–20; Egorov (counselor, Zaire) to MO, conversation with Neto on February 24, 1975, RGANI, f. 5, op. 68, d. 1954, 25-29.

49. Tsinev (KGB, deputy chief) to CC CPSU, March 21, 1975, RGANI, f. 5, op. 68, d. 2320, 14–17.

50. In an internal report about his trip to Luanda, Oleg Ignatev mentioned that the documents were genuine and that the Soviets could request photocopies from "friends" in the Portuguese military if necessary. Dzasokhov to CC CPSU, October 18, 1974, RGANI, f. 5, op. 67, d. 897, 200.

51. Bridgland, *Savimbi*, 111–15.

52. Afanasenko to MO, conversation with the Cuban ambassador to Congo-Brazzaville Arquimedes Columbié Alvarez, January 10, 1975, RGANI, f. 5, op. 68. d. 1962, 17.

53. Predvechnov (councilor, Brazzaville) to MO, conversation with Joaquim Pinto de Andrade, June 10, 1975, RGANI, f. 5, op. 68. d. 1962, 132–33.

54. Afanasenko (ambassador, Brazzaville) to MO, conversation with Agostinho Neto, July 4, 1975, RGANI, f. 5, op. 68. d. 1962, 157–59.

55. Killoran to SecState, February 14, 1975, doc. 1975LUANDA00185, CFPF/1973-79/NARA-ADD.

56. Killoran to SecState, March 27, 1975, doc. 1975LUANDA00326, CFPF/1973-79/NARA-ADD.

57. Zverev to MO, conversation with Iko Careira and José Eduardo, April 16, 1975, RGANI, f. 5, op. 68. d. 1962, 100–104.

58. Aldoshin (temporary charge d'affaires, Tanzania) to MO, conversation with Neto on April 20, 1975, RGANI, f. 5, op. 68. d. 1982, 153–56.

59. Shubin, *Hot "Cold War*," 37.

60. Uvarov (TASS representative, Luanda) to MO, March 28, 1975, GARF, f. 4459, op. 45, d. 7, 24–28.

61. Killoran SecState, April 30, 1975, doc. 1975LUANDA00493, CFPF/1973-79/NARA-ADD.

62. Killoran to SecState, May 5, 1975, doc. 1975LUANDA00518, CFPF/1973-79/NARA-ADD.

63. Shubin, *Hot "Cold War*," 41.

64. Shubin, *Hot "Cold War*," 41–42. The author could not obtain a copy of Evsiukov's unpublished memoirs on Angola or locate the record of the meeting in the archives.

65. Shubin, *Hot "Cold War*," 43. The author did not have access to Evsiukov's unpublished memoir on Angola or the documents to which Shubin refers.

66. Zverev to MO, June 12, 1975, RGANI, f. 5, op. 68. d. 1962.

67. Transcript of the SKSSAA presidium meeting, June 5, 1975, GARF, f. 9540, op. 1, d. 387, 24–25, 26.

68. "Informacja o Sytuacji w Angoli Przekazana Czlonkowi Biura Politycznego, Sekretarzowi KC - Janowi Szydlakowi przez Ambasadora ZSRR-St. Pilotowicza [Information on the situation in Angola provided to a member of the Political Bureau Jan Szydlak by the USSR ambassador—S. Pilotovich]," June 21, 1975, AAN, PZPR, LXXVI.679.

69. Kwiryn Grela do Jan Czapla, undated, "Dot. Pomocy dla Ruchow Narodowo-wyzwolenczych w Afryce [Assistance to the National-Liberation Movements in Africa]," AAN, PZPR, LXXVI.541.

70. Gleijeses, *Conflicting Missions*, 349.

71. Zverev to MO, conversation with Iko Carreira and José Eduardo, April 16,1975, RGANI, f. 5, op. 68. d. 1962; Zverev to MO, conversation with Pascal Muasiposso, June 4, 1975, RGANI, f. 5, op. 68. d. 1962, 143; Zverev to MO, conversation with André Obami Itou, June 6, 1975, RGANI, f. 5, op. 68. d. 1962.

72. Afanasenko to MO, June 14, 1975, RGANI, f. 5, op. 68. d. 1962, 137–38.

73. Afanasenko to MO, conversation with Agostinho Neto, July 4, 1975, RGANI, f. 5, op. 68. d. 1962, 157–59.

74. Putilin to MO, conversation with MPLA's representative in Congo-Brazzaville Jean-Mari Lutumba, July 21, 1975, RGANI, f. 5, op. 68. d. 1962, 176; Putilin to MO, conversation with Pierre Nzé, July 14, 1975, RGANI, f. 5, op. 68. d. 1962, 147–48.

75. Afanasenko to MO, conversation with Iko Carreira, August 1, 1975, RGANI, f. 5, op. 68. d. 1962, 180–81.

76. Afanasenko to MO, August 6, 1975, RGANI, f. 5, op. 68. d. 1962, 179.

77. Westad, *Global Cold War*, 231.

78. Putilin to MO, conversation with first secretary of the Cuban embassy in Congo-Brazzaville Reinaldo Calviac, July 29, 1975, RGANI, f. 5, op. 68. d. 1962, 172–73.

79. "Memorandum for the Record," Washington, January 23, 1975, doc. 102, FRUS/1969–1976/XXVIII.

80. "Memorandum of Conversation," Washington, April 19, 1975, 3 p.m., doc. 103, FRUS/1969–1976/XXVIII; Hanhimäki, *Flawed Architect*, 408–9.

81. "40 Committee Meeting," Washington, June 5, 1975, 10:00 a.m., doc. 106, FRUS/1969–1976/XXVIII.

82. "Minutes of a National Security Council Meeting," Washington, June 27, 1975, 2:30–3:20 p.m., doc. 113, FRUS/1969–1976/ XXVIII; Memorandum for the Record, Washington, July 14, 1975, 10:30 a.m.," doc. 118, FRUS/1969–1976/XXVIII; Bechtolsheimer, "Breakfast with Mobutu," 132–49.

83. Hanhimaki, *Flawed Architect*, 413.

84. Stockwell, *In Search of Enemies*, 87.

85. South West Africa was originally a German colony and was placed under a South African mandate by the League of Nations. The UN terminated the mandate in 1966, but Pretoria refused to relinquish control.

86. Miller, "Yes, Minister," 27–31.

87. Naumov (counselor, Tanzania) to MO, conversation with MPLA representative José Condesse on August 2, 1975, RGANI, f. 5, op. 68, d. 1982, 226–27.

88. Shubin, *Hot "Cold War,"* 47. The author could not locate the records of Carreira's meeting with the Soviets in late August in the Russian archives.

89. "Informacja o Wizycie w Polsce Delegacji Ludowego Ruchu Wyzwolenia Angoli [Information about the MPLA's visit to Poland]," AAN, PZPR, LXVI.682.

90. Grigorov (International Department, Sofia) to Central Committee of the Bulgarian Communist Party, TsDA, f. 1B, op. 64, a.e. 459; Politburo CC BCP Resolution "B" No. 7, September 3, 1975, TsDA, f. 1b, op. 64, a.e. 458; Politburo CC BCP Resolution "B" No. 8, September 4, 1975, TsDA, f. 1B, op. 64, a.e. 459.

91. Gleijeses, *Conflicting Missions*, 350.

92. Gleijeses, *Conflicting Missions*, 254–57, 259–61.

93. Reis, "Decentering the Cold War," 9–10.

94. Musatov (ambassador, Guinea) to MO, conversations with Cuban chargé d'affaires in Guinea Dario de Urra Torriente, October 8, 1975, RGANI, f. 5, op. 68. d. 1949, 465–69; Gleijeses, *Conflicting Missions*, 264.

95. Westad, *Global Cold War*, 232.

96. Badalian (consul, Santiago de Cuba), conversation with Víctor Dreke, September 15, 1975, RGANI, f. 5, op. 68. d. 1646, 204; Gleijeses, Conflicting Missions, 268–69.

97. Putilin (first secretary, Brazzaville) to MO, conversation with Lúcio Lara, September 27, 1975, RGANI, f. 5, op. 68. d. 1962, 204.

98. Putilin, "My obespechivali," 26.

99. Gleijeses, *Conflicting Missions*, 301; George, Cuban Intervention, 71.

100. Gleijeses, *Conflicting Missions*, 294–99; Butler, "Into the Storm," 446–52; Miller, "Yes, Minister," 27–31.

101. Gleijeses, *Conflicting Missions*, 265–66.

102. Zverev to MO, Record of conversation with Pierre Nzé, October 30, 1974, RGANI, f. 5, op. 68. d. 1962, 220–221; Zverev to MO, November 3, 1975, RGANI, f. 5, op. 68. d. 1962, 218–19; Putilin, "My obespechivali," 21–22.

103. Tokarev, "Komandirovka v Angolu."

104. Nazhestkin, "V ognennom koltse," 248.

105. Tsinev (KGB, debuty chief) to CC CPSU, July 11, 1975, RGANI, f. 5, op. 68, d. 2320, 103–4.

106. Naumov (chargé d'affaires, Tanzania) to MO, record of conversation with MPLA's representative, Makuntima, on October 3, 1975, RGANI, f. 5, op. 68. d. 1982, 270.

107. Shubin, *Hot "Cold War,"* 48. The author could not locate documents with these discussions in the archives.

108. Killoran to SecState, October 31, 1975, doc. 1975STATE258473, CFPF/1973-79/NARA-ADD.

109. Slipchenko to MO, conversation with Nyerere on November 3, 1975, RGANI, f. 5, op. 68. d. 1982, 305–7.

110. Nazhestkin, "V ognennom koltse," 248.

111. Slipchenko to MO, October 30, 1975, RGANI, f. 5, op. 68. d. 1982, 313–20.

112. Zverev to MO, October 30, 1974, RGANI, f. 5, op. 68. d. 1962, 221.

113. Nazhestkin, "V ognennom koltse," 251.

114. Nazhestkin, "V ognennom koltse," 253.

115. This is based on Gleijeses, *Conflicting Missions*, 301–8. Jorge Risquet gives a figure of 628 men in the first battalion. See Jorge Risquet, interview, in Jaime and Barber, *Angola*, 343.

116. Westad, *Global Cold War*, 234–35.

117. Tolubeev (ambassador, Cuba) to MO, conversation with Fidel Castro on November 3, 5, and 7, 1975, RGANI, f. 5, op. 68. d. 1645, 216.

118. Tolubeev to MO, RGANI, f. 5, op. 68. d. 1645, 217–18.

119. Kornienko, *Kholodnaia voina*, 211–12.

120. Semenov (ambassador, Guinea-Bissau) to MO, 1975, RGANI, f. 5, op. 68, d. 1950, 187–818; Semenov to MO, November 10, 1975, RGANI, f. 5, op. 68, d. 1950, 184–85.

121. Afanasenko to MO, December 4, 1975, RGANI, f. 5, op. 68. d. 1962, 230–31. The date of the conversation between the two ambassadors has been the subject of some controversy. The newly released documents show the meeting took place on December 4. Also see, Gleijeses, *Conflicting Missions*, 270–71.

122. Gleijeses, *Conflicting Missions*, 308.

123. Tokarev, "Komandirovka v Angolu."

124. Steenkamp, *Borderstrike!*, 104–7; George, *Cuban Intervention*, 88–90.

125. Holness interview.

126. Grigorovich, interview, in Shubin, *Ustnaia istoriia zabytykh voin*, 22.

127. Gleijeses, *Conflicting Missions*, 368; Westad, *Global Cold War*, 235.

128. Lisbon to SecState, December 31, 1975, doc. 1975LISBON07720, CFPF/1973-79/NARA-ADD.

129. Grigorovich, interview, in Shubin, *Ustnaia istoriia zabytykh voin*, 24.

130. Gleijeses, *Conflicting Missions*, 312–19.

131. Westad, *Global Cold War*, 236; Jorge Risquet, interview, in Jaime and Barber, *Angola*, 344. It is still not possible to determine exactly how much weaponry was passed to the Cubans and FAPLA in Angola during this period.

132. Gleijeses, *Conflicting Missions*, 312–19.

133. Hanhimäki, *Flawed Architect*, 418.

134. "Transcript of a Telephone Conversation between Secretary of State Kissinger and the Soviet Ambassador (Dobrynin)," Washington, December 10, 1975, 10:15 a.m., doc. 146, FRUS/1969–1976/XXVIII; "Minutes of a National Security Council Meeting: SALT (and Angola)," Washington, December 22, 1975, 9:30–11:30 a.m., doc. 163, FRUS/1969–1976/XXVIII.

135. Dobrynin, *In Confidence*, 362.

136. Cherniaev, *Sovmestnyi iskhod*, 200.

137. Gleijeses, *Conflicting Missions*, 369.

Conclusion

1. Kulikov to CC CPSU, July 18, 1973, RGANI, f. 5, op. 66, d. 1190, 133.

2. We do not have the full figures. The PAIGC received $35,000 in 1962, $50,000 in 1963, $70,000 in 1965 and 1966, and $100,000 in 1970. The figures for later dates are not available. See RGANI, f. 89, d. 5, d. 6, d. 8, d. 9, d. 12.

3. Semenov (ambassador, Guinea-Bissau) to the Ministry of Foreign Affairs, record of conversation with Vasco Cabral on September 11, 1976, AVPRF, f. 661, op. 13, p. 3, d. 2, 143.

4. According to Soviet estimates, by 1979, the Soviet Union had provided $57.3 million in foreign assistance to Guinea-Bissau, with $35.3 million provided gratis. These figures exclude military assistance. I. Aliabiev and S. Skripnichenko, Rossiiskii Gosudarsvennyi Arkhiv Ekonomiki (Russian State Archive for Economy, hereafter RGAE), f. 363, op. 9, d. 2834, 32–33.

5. According to Soviet estimates, by 1977, Portugal accounted for 60 percent of all exports from Guinea-Bissau and 40 percent of all its imports. See T. Britaev, RGAE, f. 365, op. 9, d. 2608, 58.

6. Brooke, "Soviet Is Losing Rights to Fish off West Africa."

7. Evsiukov, "Iz vospominanii," 231.

8. Banks, "Socialist Internationalism," 58. I would like to thank Elizabeth Banks for drawing my attention to these figures.

9. Alves Gomes interview.

10. According to CIA estimates, the Soviet Union and Eastern Europe provided $122 million in economic assistance, while members of the OECD countries gave $1.102 million / over $1.1 billion to Mozambique between 1975 and 1982. See "Comparison of

Western Economic and Military Aid with Soviet Economic and Military Aid," June 15, 1983, doc. CIA-RDP85B00652R000100060046-9, CIA Records/FOIA.

11. Jacinto Veloso has argued that the Soviets sided with South Africa to eliminate Samora Machel because of the latter's "pro-Western orientation." Shubin staunchly denied Soviet involvement, citing the change of leadership in Moscow as evidence there was no reason for Moscow to plot Machel's murder. See Veloso, *Memórias em Voo Rasante*; Shubin, *Hot "Cold War,"* 145–47.

12. According to CIA estimates, the Soviet Union and Eastern Europe provided $52 million in economic assistance, while the OECD countries gave $413 million to Angola between 1975 and 1982. See Memorandum: "Comparison of Western Economic and Military Aid" June 15, 1983, General CIA Records/FOIA.

13. "On the issue of Soviet compensation for the Cuban weapons that can remain in Angola," January 31, 1989, RGANI, f. 89, op 7, d. 7.

14. Gleijeses, *Visions of Freedom*, 71.

15. On the importance of Cuito Cuanavale, see Saunders, "Ending of the Cold War"; Onslow with Bright, "Battle of Cuito Cuanavale"; Gleijeses, *Visions of Freedom*, 393–421.

16. Quoted in Westad, "Moscow and the Angolan Crisis," 21.

17. For discussion, see Westad, *Global Cold War*, 241–49; Leonov, *Likholetie*, 137.

18. See the CIA research paper "Soviet Arms: Third World Attraction and Soviet Benefits," February 1, 1985, doc. CIA-RDP86T00586R000100110004-4, General CIA Records/FOIA.

19. Adamishin, *White Sun of Angola*, 95; Urnov interview.

20. Kirpichenko, *Razvedka: Litsa i lichnosti*, Chapter: "Pravda ob Afganistane [Truth about Afghanistan]."

21. Adamishin, *White Sun of Angola*, 92. For a discussion, see Filatova and Apollon Davidson, *Hidden Thread*, 369–99.

22. Urnov, *Vneshnaia politika SSSR*, 656–58; Urnov interview.

23. For an overview, see Westad, *Global Cold War*, 364–96.

24. Urnov, *Vneshnaia politika SSSR*, 626–27.

25. Solodovnikov, *SSSR i Iuzhnaia Afrika*, 100.

26. Evsiukov, "Natsional'no-osvoboditel'naia bor'ba," 152.

27. *Sovremennyi etap razvitiia*, 22.

28. Solodovnikov interview.

29. Urnov interview.

BIBLIOGRAPHY

Archives

Bulgaria

Tsentralen D'rzhaven Arkhiv (TsDa) [Central State Archives, Sofia]

Czechia

Archiv Ministerstva Zahraničních Věci (AMZV) [Archive of the Ministry of Foreign Affairs, Prague]
Archiv Bezpečnostních Složek (ABS) [Security Services Archive]
Národní Archiv (NA) [National Archive]

Germany

Bundesarchiv–Stiftung Archiv der Parteien und Massenorganisationen der DDR (BA-SAPMO) [Federal Archive of Parties and Mass Organizations of the GDR]
Politisches Archiv des Auswärtigen Amt–Ministerium für Auswärtige Angelegenheiten der Deutschen Demokratischen Republik, (PAAA-MfAA) [Political Archive of the Foreign Ministry]

Poland

Archiwum Akt Nowych (AAN) [Central Archive of Modern Records]
Archiwum Ministerstwa Spraw Zagranicznych (AMSZ) [Archive of the Foreign Ministry]

Russia

Arkhiv Vneshnei Politiki Rossiiskoi Federatsii (AVPRF) [Archive of Foreign Policy of the Russian Federation]
Gosudarstvennyi Arkhiv Rossiiskoi Federatsii (GARF) [State Archive of the Russian Federation]
Rossiiskii Gosudarsvennyi Arkhiv Noveishei Istorii (RGANI) [Russian State Archive for Contemporary History, Moscow]
Rossiiskii Gosudarsvennyi Arkhiv Sotsialno-Politicheskoi Istorii (RGASPI) [Russian State Archive of Socio-Political History, Moscow]

Rossiiskii Gosudarsvennyi Arkhiv Ekonomiki (RGAE) [Russian State Archive for Economy, Moscow]

Rossiiskii Gosudarsvennyi Arkhiv Literatury i Iskusstva (RGALI) [Russian State Archive of Literature and Art, Moscow]

United Kingdom

National Archives at KEW, London

Oral History Interviews Conducted by the Author

Cape Verde

Araújo, Amélia and Teresa, January 12, 2017, Praia

Boal, Maria da Luz "Lilica," January 10, 2017, Praia

de Carvalho, Júlio, February 13, 2018, Sal

Leite, Antonio, January 13, 2017, Mindelo

Luz, Silvino da, January 14, 2017, Mindelo

Pires, Olívio, January 13, 2017, Mindelo

Pires, Pedro, January 11, 2017, Praia

Reis, Carlos, January 10, 2017, Praia

Silva, Osvaldo Lopes da, January 9, 2017, Praia

Silva, João Pereira, January 6, 2017, Praia, Cape Verde

Tavares, Alvaro Dantas, February 19, 2017, Praia, Cape Verde

Guinea-Bissau (all interviews held in Bissau)

Badganny, Afonso Manga, March 24, 2019

Bangura, Dauda, March 30, 2019

Biague, Jorge, March 25, 2019

Camará, Mamadu, March 20, 2019

Cassama, Alanso, March 31, 2019

Cassama, Fode, March 22, 2019

Correia, Carlos, April 1, 2019

Dabo, Emfamara, April 2, 2019

Darame, Lassana, March 21, 2019

Django, Serifo, April 3, 2019

Djassi, Ladja, April 1, 2019

Gomes, Carlos, March 3, 19, 2019

Gomes, Mário, March 23, 2019

Mane, Arafan, April 1, 2019

Matta, Brandão Bull da, March 25, 2019
Na Nhakpba, Sae Breia, March 22, 2019
N'Bana, Omba, March 21, 2019
Pereira, Francisca, April 3, 2019
Reis, Quentino Napoleon dos, March 19, 2019
Santos, Manuel dos, March 18, 2019
Sisse, Lamine, April 2, 2019
Soares, Anna Maria, March 23, 2019

Mozambique

Gomes, António Alves, August 2020, Skype
Kido, Mateus Oscar, September 19, 2015, Maputo
Mota Lopes, José, September 21, 2015, Maputo
Santos, Marcelino dos, September 14, 2015
Vieira, Sérgio, September 19, 2015, Maputo

Russia and Western Europe

Draisma, Jan and Frouke, March 2, 2017, Amsterdam, Netherlands
Dzasokhov, Aleksander, March 24, 2015, Moscow, Russia
Graf, Herbert, 2015, Berlin, Germany
Holness, Marga, February 12, 2016, London, UK
Minter, William, October 15, 2015, Skype
Schleicher, Hans-Georg and Ilona, December 9, 2015, Berlin, Germany
Shubin, Vladimir, April 8, 2015, Moscow, Russia
Solodovnikov, March 26, 2015, Moscow, Russia
Urnov, Andrei, April 14, 2015, Moscow, Russia

Newspapers

The Guardian
The New York Times
Pravda
The Time

Online Documents

Adamshin, Anatoly. "The White Sun of Angola." Translated by Gary Goldberg
   and Sue Onslow. Cold War International History Project report. https://www
   .wilsoncenter.org/publication/the-white-sun-angola.

Andrade, Mário Pinto de. "Appel aux écrivains du monde [Appeal to the writers of the world]," 1958, Fundação Mário Soares/Arquivo Mário Pinto de Andrade. http:// hdl.handle.net/11002/fms_dc_83413.

————. "L'esprit de Tachkent [The spirit of Tashkent]," *Voies Nouvelles*, no. 8 (April 1959), Fundação Mário Soares/Arquivo Mário Pinto de Andrade. http://hdl.handle .net/11002/fms_dc_83415.

Dazyshen, Vladimir. "Potekhin-Osnovatel Sovetskoi Afrikanistiki [Potekhin-the Founder of Soviet African Studies]," *Novaia Universitetskaia Zhisn*, 26, no. 38 (2008): 4. https://gazeta.sfu-kras.ru/node/1242.

Brooke, James. "Soviet Is Losing Rights to Fish off West Africa," *New York Times*, January 13, 1988. https://www.nytimes.com/1988/01/13/world/soviet-is-losing-rights-to-fish-off-west-africa.html.

Cabral, Amilcar. "The Weapon of Theory." Speech given at the First Tricontinental Conference of the Peoples of Asia, Africa, and Latin America, Havana, January 1966. Marxists Internet Archive. https://www.marxists.org/subject/africa /cabral/1966/weapon-theory.htm.

Central Foreign Policy Files, 1973–1979, National Archives and Records Administration, Access to Archival Databases (NARA-ADD). https://aad.archives.gov/aad/.

CIA Records, Freedom of Information Act Electronic Reading Room (FOIA). https:// www.cia.gov/library/readingroom/document/cia-rdp85b00652r000100060045-0.

"Doklad Prezidiuma TsK KPSS na Oktyabrskom Plenume TsK KPSS [Report of the Presidium of the CC CPSU]" *Istochnik: Vestnik Arkhiva Prezidenta Rossiiskoi Federatsii*, no. 2 (1998): 102–25. http://on-island.net/History/1964.htm.

Foreign Relations of the United States, 1961–1963. Vol. V: Soviet Union. https:// history.state.gov/historicaldocuments/frus1961-63v05.

Foreign Relations of the United States, 1964–1968. Vol. XII: Western Europe. https:// history.state.gov/historicaldocuments/frus1964-68v12.

Foreign Relations of the United States, 1961–1963. Vol. XXI: Africa. https://history .state.gov/historicaldocuments/frus1961-63v21.

Foreign Relations of the United States, 1964–1968. Vol. XXIII: Congo, 1960–1968. https://history.state.gov/historicaldocuments/frus1964-68v23/comp1.

Foreign Relations of the United States, 1969–1976. Vol. XXVIII: Southern Africa. https://history.state.gov/historicaldocuments/frus1969-76v28.

Ilinskii, Igor. "Filipp Bobkov: SSSR pogubili trotzkisty Khrushchev i Gorbachev" [Filipp Bobkov: The Trotskyites Khrushchev and Gorbachev killed the USSR]. *Znanie. Ponimanie. Umenie*, no. 2 (2007): 6–20. http://www.zpu-journal.ru /zpu/2007_2/cold_war/2.pdf.

Fundação Mário Soares/Arquivo Amílcar Cabral (FMS/AC). http://casacomum.org /cc/arquivos?set=e_2617.

Fundação Mário Soares/Arquivo Mário Pinto de Andrade (FMS/AMPA). http:// casacomum.org/cc/arquivos?set=e_3944.

Fundação Mário Soares/Documentos Viriato da Cruz/Monique Chajmowiez (FMS/DVCMC). http://casacomum.org/cc/arquivos?set=e_9012

Iurii Gorbunov, "Partizany dlia Afriki [Partisans for Africa]," *Voennoe obozrenie*, December 16, 2013. https://topwar.ru/37347-krym-i-afrika-165-y-uchebnyy-centr -podgotovki-partizan-chast-3.html.

Marques, Irene. "Postcolonial African Consciousness and the Poetry of Agostinho Neto." *Comparative Literature and Culture* 5, no. 4 (2003). https://doi .org/10.7771/1481-4374.1199.

Marx, Karl, and Frederick Engels. *Manifesto of the Communist Party*. In *Karl Marx and Frederick Engels: Selected Works*, vol. 1. Moscow: Progress Publishers 1969. Marxists Internet Archive. https://www.marxists.org/archive/marx/works/ download/pdf/Manifesto.pdf.

Papers of John F. Kennedy. Presidential Papers. President's Office Files, John F. Kennedy's Presidential Library and Museum Online. https://www.jfklibrary.org /asset-viewer/archives/JFKPOF/062/JFKPOF-062-015.

Rocha, Edmundo. "Conflitos de personalidade entre Viriato da Cruz e Agostinho Neto [Personality clashes between Viriato da Cruz and Agostinho Neto]," *Agora*, September 23, 1999. FMS/DVCMC. http://casacomum.org/cc /visualizador?pasta=10461.006.014.

"Record of proceedings between the Soviet KGB and the Interior Ministry of the Czechoslovak Socialist Republic on the expansion of intelligence cooperation," June, 1961, History and Public Policy Program Digital Archive, Archiv Bezpečnost-ních Složek. https://digitalarchive.wilsoncenter.org/document/113217.

"Shkola Terroristov S Marksistskim Uklonom [School for Terrorists with a Marxist Specialization]," *Segodnya*, April 22, 2005. https://www.segodnya.ua/oldarchive /c22567130043f33f5c2256fea00516140.html.

Tolts, Vladimir. "Pamiati Vadima Zagladina [In Memory of Vadim Zagladin]," *Radio Svoboda*, November 28, 2006. https://www.svoboda.org/a/316631.html.

Tokarev, Andrei. "Komandirovka v Angolu [A Work Trip to Angola]," Union of Ango-lan Veterans website, http://www.veteranangola.ru/main/vospominaniya/tokarev.

Vasilkov, Ia., and M. Sorokina, *Liudi i sudby: Bibliograficheskii slovar vostokovedov-zhertv politicheskogo terrora v sovetskii period* [Men and Destiny: A bibliographic dictionary of Asianist victims of political terror during the Soviet period]. St. Petersburg: Peterburgskoe Vostokovedenie, 2003. http://memory.pvost .org/pages/ulianovskij.html.

Zubarev, Dmitrii. "Kursanty dlya bor'by za sotsializm vo vsem mire [Cadets for the socialist struggle]"; *Indeks* 19 (2003). http://index.org.ru/journal/19/zubar19.html.

Memoirs and Collated Documents

Békés, Csaba, Malcolm Byrne, and M. János Rainer, eds. *The 1956 Hungarian Revolu-tion: A History in Documents*. Budapest: Central European University Press, 2002.

Brutents, Karen. *Tridtsat let na Staroi Ploshchadi* [Thirty years on Staraia Ploshchad']. Moscow: Mezhdunarodnye otnosheniia, 1998.

Cabral, Amilcar. *Unity and Struggle: Speeches and Writings of Amilcar Cabral.* Translated by Michael Wolfers. New York: Monthly Review Press, 1979.

Davidson, Apollon, Sergei Mazov, and Georgii Tsypkin, eds. *SSSR i Afrika, 1918–1960: Dokumentirovannaia istoriia vzaimotnoshenii* [USSR and Africa, 1918–1960: A Documentary History]. Moscow: IVI RAN, 2002.

Cherniaev, Anatolii. *Sovmestnyi iskhod: Dnevnik dvukh epoch, 1972–1991* [Joint outcome: A diary of two epochs]. Moscow: ROSSPEN, 2008.

Danilov, Pavel. "Trevozhnye mesiatsy v Konakri" [Anxious months in Conakry]." In Vasilev, *Afrika v Vospominaniiakh,* 70–85.

Devlin, Larry. *Chief of Station, Congo: A Memoir of 1960–67.* New York: Public Affairs, 2007.

Dobrynin, Anatoly. *In Confidence: Moscow's Ambassador to America's Six Cold War Presidents (1962–1986).* New York: Times Books, 1995.

Dzasokhov, A. S. *Chelovek i politika* [The person and politics]. Moscow: Rossiiskaia gazeta, 2009.

Evsiukov, Petr. "Iz vospominanii o rabote v Mozambike" [From reminiscences about work in Mozambique]. In Vasilev, *Afrika v Vospominaniiakh,* 223–44.

———. "Natsionalno-osvoboditelnaia borba v Gvinee-Bissau i ee lider Amilkar Kabral" [The national liberation struggle in Guinea-Bissau and its leader, Amilcar Cabral]. In Vasilev, *Afrika v vospominaniiakh,* 139–53.

Golden, Lily. *My Long Journey Home.* Chicago: Third World Chicago Press, 2002.

Karpov, Vladimir, ed. *Vneshniaia razvedka* [Foreign Intelligence]. Moscow: XXI Vek-Soglasie, 2000.

Kornienko, Georgii M. *Kholodnaia voina: Svidetelstvo ee uchastnika* [The Cold War: A participant's testimony]. Moscow: Olma-Press, 2001.

Kiryakova, Tatyana, ed. *The KGB and the Bulgarian State Security Service—Connections and Dependences.* Sofia: COMDOS, 2009.

Lara, Lúcio, ed. *Um amplo movimento: Itinerário do MPLA através de documentos e anotações* [A broad movement: MPLA's itinerary through documents and notes]. 3 vols. Luanda: Lúcio e Ruth Lara, 1997–2008.

Laban, Michel. *Angola: Encontro com escritores* [Angola: Encounter with writers]. Vol. 1. Porto: Fundação Eng. António de Almeida, 1991.

———. *Mário Pinto de Andrade: Uma entrevista dada a Michel Laban* [Mário Pinto de Andrade: An interview given to Michel Laban]. Translated by Sócrates Daskalos. Lisbon: Edições João Sá da Costa, 1997.

Leonov, Nikolai. *Likholetie: Sekretnye missii* [Turbulent times: Secret missions]. Moscow: Mezhdunarodnye otnosheniia, 1995.

Lee, Christopher J., ed. *Making a World after Empire: The Bandung Moment and Its Political Afterlives.* Athens: Ohio University Press, 2010.

Lopes, José Vicente. *Aristides Pereira: Minha vida, nossa história* [Aristides Pereira: My life, our History]. Lisbon: Spleen, 2012.

————. *Onésimo Silveira, Uma vida, um mar de histórias* [Onésimo Silveira: A Life, a Sea of Stories]. Lisbon: Spleen, 2016.

Mateus, Dalila Cabrita. *Memórias do colonialismo e da guerra* [Memoirs of colonialism and war], Cordova: Edições ASA, 2012. Kindle.

Mirskii, Georgii. "Na znamenatelnom rubezhe [A significant turning point]" *Vostok*, no. 6 (1996): 128–40.

Musatov, Leonid. "Afrikanskie marshruty" [African routes]. In Vasilev, *Afrika v vospominaniiakh,*116–23.

Nazhestkin, Oleg. "Gody kongolezskogo krizisa, 1960–1963: Zapiski razvedchika [The years of the Congolese Crisis, 1960–1963: Notes of an Intelligence officer]." *Novaia i Noveishaia Istoriia*, no. 6 (2003): 154–64.

————. "Superderzhavy i sobytiia v Angole, 1960–1970-e gody [The superpowers and events in Angola, 1960s–1970s]." *Novaia i noveishaia istoriia*, no. 4 (2005): 30–50.

————. "V ognennom koltse blokady" [Inside the burning ring of a blockade]. In Karpov, *Vneshnaia razvedka*, 234–56.

Putilin, Boris. "My obespechivali MPLA oruzhiem [We supported the MPLA with weapons]." In Shubin and Tokarev, *Vospominaniia neposredstvennykh uchastnikov*, 16–30.

Santos, Daniel dos. *Amílcar Cabral: Um Outro Olhar* [Amílcar Cabral: A Different Perspective]. Lisbon: Chiado Editora, 2014.

Santos, Marcelino dos. *Pesnia istinnoi liubvi* [A song of true love]. Translated by Lidiia Nekrasova. Moscow: Biblioteka "Ogonek," 1959.

Shubin, Gennadii, ed. *Ustnaia istoriia zabytykh voin: Vospominaniia veteranov voiny v Angole* [The oral history of forgotten wars: Memoirs of the veterans of the Angolan War]. Moscow: Memories, 2007.

Shubin, Gennadii and Andrei Tokarev, eds. *Vospominaniia neposredstvennykh uchastnikov i ochevidtsev grazhdanskoi voiny v Angole: Ustnaia istoriia zabytykh voin* [Memories of direct participants and eyewitness of the civil war in Angola: The oral history of forgotten wars]. Moscow: Memories, 2009.

Solodovnikov, Vasilii. *SSSR i Iuzhnaia Afrika, 1987–1991: "Ia vystupal protiv politiki Gorbacheva-Shevardnadze v Iuzhnoi Afrike"* [The USSR and South Africa, 1987–1991: "I stood up against the politics of Gorbachev and Shevardnadze in South Africa"]. Moscow: Institut Afriki RAN, 2002.

————. *Tvorcheskii put v afrikanistiku i diplomatiiu* [My career as an Africanist and a diplomat]. Moscow: Institut Afriki RAN, 2000.

Sovremennyi etap razvitiia stran Azii i Afriki i Dvizhenie solidarnosti: Materialy diskussii [The modern stage of development of the countries of Asia and Africa and the Solidarity Movement: Minutes of discussion]. Moscow: Nauka, 1991.

Spitskii, Ivan. "Obrazovanie afrikanskikh otdelov v MID i moi opyt raboty v Narodnoi Respublike Kongo v 1964–1969 [The formation of the African sections of the Ministry of Foreign Affairs and my experiences working in the

People's Republic of Congo, 1964–1969]." In Vasilev, *Afrika v Vospominani-iakh,* 13–47.

Stockwell, John. *In Search of Enemies: A CIA Story.* New York: Norton and Company, 1978.

Urnov, Andrei. "Sovetskii Soiuz i borba protiv kolonializma i rasizma na iuge Afriki [The Soviet Union and the struggle against colonialism and racism in southern Africa]." *Afrika i Aziia Segodnia,* no. 3 (2009): 55–61.

———. *Vneshniaia politika SSSR v gody "kholodnoi voiny" i "novogo myshleniia"* [Soviet foreign policy during the "cold war" and the "new thinking"]. Moscow: RFK-Imidzh Lab, 2014.

Vieira, Sérgio. *Participei, por isso testemunho* [Participated, so I testify]. Maputo: Ndjira, 2011.

Veloso, Jacinto. *Memórias em Voo Rasante* [Memories at Low Altitude]. Lisbon: Papa-Letras, Lisboa, 2007.

U.S. Congress. Senate. Committee on Foreign Relations. *Hearings before the Subcommittee on African Affairs on U.S. Involvement in Civil War in Angola.* 94th Cong., 2nd sess. 1976. Washington, D.C.: Government Printing Office, 1976.

Secondary Literature

Adi, Hakim. *Pan-Africanism and Communism: The Communist International, Africa and the Diaspora, 1919–1939.* Trenton, N.J.: Africa World Press, 2013.

Akyeampong, Emmanuel. "African Socialism; Or, the Search for an Indigenous Model of Development." *Economic History of Developing Regions* 33, no. 1 (2018): 69–87.

Alexander, Jocelyn, and JoAnn McGregor. "African Soldiers in the USSR: Oral Histories of ZAPU Intelligence Cadres' Soviet Training, 1964–1979." *Journal of Southern African Studies* 43, no. 1 (2017): 49–66.

Alexander, Jocelyn, JoAnn McGregor, and Miles Tendi. "The Transnational Histories of Southern African Liberation Movements: An Introduction." *Journal of Southern African Studies* 43, no. 1 (2017): 1–12.

Altorfer-Ong, Alicia N. "Old Comrades and New Brothers: A Historical Re-Examination of the Sino-Zanzibari and Sino-Tanzanian Bilateral Relationships." PhD diss., London School of Economics, 2014.

Antunes, José Freire. *Kennedy e Salazar—O leão e a* raposa [Kennedy and Salazar—The Lion and the Fox]. Alfragide, Portugal: Dom Quixote, 2013. Kindle.

———. "Kennedy, Portugal, and the Azores Base, 1961." In Brinkley and Griffiths, *John F. Kennedy and Europe,* 148–68.

Araujo, Norman. "The West African Area: Cape Verde, Guinea-Bissau, Sao Tome e Principe." In Gerard, *European-Language Writing,* 268–89.

Babiracki, Patryk and Austin Jersild, eds. *Socialist Internationalism in the Cold War: Exploring the Second World.* Basingstoke, UK: Palgrave Macmillan, 2016.

Ball, Jeremy. *Angola's Colossal Lie: Forced Labor on a Sugar Plantation, 1913–1977*. London: Brill, 2015.

Banks, Elizabeth. "Socialist Internationalism Between the Soviet Union and Mozambique, 1962–91." PhD diss., New York University, 2019.

Barber, Drumond, and Jaime Hélder, eds. *Angola: Depoimentos para a história recente* [Angola: Testimonials on recent history]. Luanda: Edição dos Autores, 1999.

Békés, Csaba. "Cold War, Detente and the Soviet Bloc: The Evolution of Intra-Bloc Foreign Policy Coordination, 1953–1975." In Kramer and Smetana, *Imposing, Maintaining and Tearing Open the Iron Curtain*, 247–78.

———. "East Central Europe, 1953–1956." In Westad and Leffler, *The Cambridge History of the Cold War* 334–52.

Bechtolsheimer, Götz. "Breakfast with Mobutu: Congo, the United States and the Cold War, 1964–1981." PhD diss., The London School of Economics and Political Science, 2012.

Bender, Gerald J. *Angola under the Portuguese: The Myth and the Reality*. Berkeley: University of California Press, 1978.

Birmingham, David. *Frontline Nationalism in Angola and Mozambique*. Trenton, N.J.: Africa World Press, 1992.

———. *A Short History of Modern Angola*. New York: Oxford University Press, 2015.

Bjerk, Paul. "Postcolonial Realism: Tanganyika's Foreign Policy Under Nyerere, 1960–1963." *International Journal of African Historical Studies* 44, no. 2 (2011): 215–47.

Blažek, Peter, and Pavel Žáček. "Czechoslovakia." In Persak and Kamiński, *A Handbook of the Communist Security Apparatus*, 87–161.

Borstelmann, Thomas. *The Cold War and the Color Line: American Race Relations in the Global Arena*. Cambridge, Mass.: Harvard University Press, 2001. Kindle.

Bowen, Merle L. *The State against the Peasantry: Rural Struggles in Colonial and Postcolonial Mozambique*. Charlottesville: University of Virginia Press, 2000.

Branch, Daniel. "Political Traffic: Kenyan Students in Eastern and Central Europe," *Journal of Contemporary History* 53, no. 4 (2018): 811–31.

Brennan, James R. "The Secret Lives of Dennis Phombeah: Decolonization, the Cold War, and African Political Intelligence, 1953–1974." *International History Review* 43, no. 1 (2020): 153–69.

Bridgland, Fred. *Jonas Savimbi: A Key to Africa*. Edinburgh: Mainstream, 1986.

Brinkley, Douglas, and Richard Griffiths, eds. *John F. Kennedy and Europe*. Baton Rouge: Louisiana State University Press, 1999.

Brinkman, Inge. *A War for People: Civilians, Mobility, and Legitimacy in South-East Angola During the MPLA's War for Independence*. Cologne: Rüdiger Köppe, 2005.

———. "War, Witches and Traitors: Cases from the MPLA's Eastern Front in Angola (1966–1975)." *Journal of African History* 44, no. 2 (2003): 303–25.

Burgess, G. Thomas. "Mao in Zanzibar: Nationalism, Discipline and the (De)Construction of Afro-Asian Solidarities." In Lee, *Making a World after Empire*, 196–234.

Burton, Eric. "Decolonization, the Cold War, and Africans' routes to higher education overseas, 1957–65," *Journal of Global History* 15 (2020): 169–91.

———. "Hubs of Decolonization. African Liberation Movements and "Eastern Connections." In Dallywater, Saunders and Fonseca, *Southern African Liberation Movements*, 25–56.

Byfield, Judith A, et al., *Africa and World War II*. Cambridge: Cambridge University Press, 2015.

Byrne, Jeffrey James. *Mecca of Revolution: Algeria, decolonization, and the Third World Order*. New York: Oxford University Press, 2016.

Cabrita, João M. *Mozambique: The Tortuous Road to Democracy*. Basingstoke, UK: Palgrave, 2000.

Cahen, Michel. "Anticolonialism and Nationalism: Deconstructing Synonymy, Investigating Historical Processes; Notes on the Heterogeneity of Former African Portuguese Areas." In Morier-Genoud, *Sure Road?*, 1–28.

———. "The Mueda Case and Maconde Political Ethnicity." *Africana Studia* 2 (1999): 29–46.

Cairo, Heriberto. "'Portugal is Not a Small Country': Maps and Propaganda in the Salazar Regime." *Geopolitics* 11, no. 3 (2006): 367–95.

Cann, John P. *Flight Plan Africa: Portuguese Airpower in Counterinsurgency, 1961–1974*. Solihull, UK: Helion, 2015.

———. *The Flechas: Insurgent Hunting in Eastern Angola, 1965–1974*. Solihull, UK: Helion, 2013

Carreira, Antonio. *The People of the Cape Verde Islands*. London: Hurst, 1982.

Casey, Steven, and Jonathan Wright, eds. *Mental Maps in the Early Cold War Era, 1945–1968*. Basingstoke, UK: Palgrave Macmillan, 2011.

Čavoški, Jovan. "'Yugoslavia's Help was Extraordinary': Political and Material Assistance from Belgrade to the MPLA in Its Rise to Power, 1961–1975." *Journal of Cold War Studies* 21, no. 1 (Winter 2019): 125–50.

César, Filipa. "Reading Amílcar Cabral's Agronomy of Liberation," *Meteorisations*, Third Text, 32, nos. 2–3 (2018): 254–72.

Chabal, Patrick. *Amilcar Cabral: Revolutionary Leadership and People's War*. Cambridge: Cambridge University Press, 1983.

Chabal, Patrick, and Toby Green, eds. *Guinea-Bissau: Micro-State to "Narco-State."* London: Hurst, 2016.

Christie, Iain. *Samora Machel: A Biography*. 2nd ed. London: Panaf, 1989.

Clarence-Smith, Gervase. "The Impact of the Spanish Civil War and the Second World War on Portuguese and Spanish Africa." *Journal of African History* 25 (October 1985): 309–26.

———. *The Third Portuguese Empire, 1825–1975: A Study in Economic Imperialism*. Manchester: Manchester University Press, 1985.

Clayton, Anthony. *Frontiersmen: Warfare in Africa Since 1950*. London: UCL Press, 1999.

Connelly, Matthew J. *A Diplomatic Revolution: Algeria's Fight for Independence and the Origins of the Post-Cold War Era*. New York: Oxford University Press, 2002.

Cook, Alexander, ed. *Mao's Little Red Book: A Global History*. Cambridge: Cambridge University Press, 2014.

Cooper, Frederick. *Africa Since 1940: The Past of the Present*. Cambridge: Cambridge University Press, 2014.

———. "Conflict and Connection: Rethinking Colonial African History." *American Historical Review* 99, no. 5 (December 1994): 1516–45.

Corrado, Jacopo. *The Creole Elite and the Rise of Angolan Protonationalism: 1870–1920*. New York: Cambria Press, 2008.

Cunha, Carlos. "Nationalist or Internationalist? The Portuguese Communist Party's Autonomy and the Communist International." In Rees and Thorpe, *International Communism and the Communist International*, 168–87.

Dallywater, Lena, Chris Saunders, and Helder Adegar Fonseca, eds. *Southern African Liberation Movements and the Global Cold War 'East': Transnational Activism, 1960–1990*. Oldenbourg: De Gruyter, 2019.

Darch, Colin. *Historical Dictionary of Mozambique*. Lanham, Md.: Rowman & Littlefield, 2018. Kindle.

Davidson, Apollon. "Osnovatel Instituta Afriki (I. I. Potekhin) [The founder of the Africa Institute]." In Davidson, *Stanovlenie otechestvennoi afrikanistiki*, 116–35.

———. *Pisma s Mysa Dobroi Nadezhdy* [Letters from the Cape of Good Hope]. Moscow: Vysshaia shkola ekonomiki, 2017.

———, ed. *Stanovlenie otechestvennoi afrikanistiki* [The formative years of African Studies in Russia, 1920s–early 1960s]. Moscow: Nauka, 2003.

Davidson, Apollon, Irina Filatova, Valentin Gorodnov, and Sheridan Johns, eds., *South Africa and the Communist International: Socialist Pilgrims to Bolshevik Footsoldiers, 1919–1930*. London: Routledge, 2015.

Davidson, Basil. *In the Eye of the Storm: Angola's People*. Harmondsworth, UK: Penguin, 1975.

———. *No Fist is Big Enough to Hide the Sky: The Liberation of Guinea-Bissau and Cape Verde, 1963–74*. London: Zed, 1981.

Derluguian, Georgi. "The Social Origins of Good and Bad Governance: Re-Interpreting the 1968 Schism in Frelimo." In Morier-Genoud, *Sure Road?*, 79–102.

Dhada, Mustafah. *The Portuguese Massacre of Wiriyamu in Colonial Mozambique, 1964–2013*. New York: Bloomsbury Academic, 2017.

———. *Warriors at Work: How Guinea Was Really Set Free*. Niwot: University Press of Colorado, 1993.

Disney, Anthony. *The Portuguese Empire*. Vol. 2. *A History of Portugal and the Portuguese Empire: From Beginnings to 1807*. Cambridge: Cambridge University Press, 2009.

Djagalov, Rossen. *From Internationalism to Postcolonialism: Literature and Cinema between the Second and the Third Worlds*. Montreal: McGill-Queen's University Press, 2020

Domingos, Nuno, Miguel Bandeira Jerónimo, and Ricardo Roque, eds. In *Resistance and Colonialism: Insurgent People's in World History*. Cambridge, UK: Palgrave Macmillan, 2019.

Duara, Prasenjit, ed. *Decolonization: Perspectives from Now and Then*. New York: Taylor and Francis, 2004.

Ellis, Stephen. *External Mission: The ANC in Exile, 1960–1990*. London: Hurst, 2013.

———. "Nelson Mandela, the South African Communist Party and the origins of Umkhonto we Sizwe," *Cold War History*, 16, no. 1 (2016): 1–18.

Eran, Oded. *Mezhdunarodniki: An Assessment of Professional Expertise in the Making of Soviet Foreign Policy*. Tel Aviv: Turtle Dove Press, 1979.

Eriksen, Tore Linné. *Norway and National Liberation in Southern Africa*. Uppsala: Nordiska Afrikainstitutet, 2000.

Filatova, Irina, and Apollon Davidson. *The Hidden Thread: Russia and South Africa in the Soviet Era*. Johannesburg: Jonathan Ball, 2016. Kindle.

Ferraz de Matos. *The Colours of the Empire: Racialized Representations during Portuguese Colonialism*. Translated by Mark Ayton. New York: Berghahn Books, 2012.

Fonseca, Ana Mónica, and Daniel Marcos. "Cold War Constraints: France, West Germany and Portuguese Decolonization." *Portuguese Studies* 29, no. 2 (2013): 209–26.

Fonseca, Aldegar Helder. "The Military Training of Angolan Guerrillas in socialist Countries: A Rosopographical Approach, 1961-1974." In Dallywater, Saunders and Fonseca, *Southern African Liberation Movements*, 104–28.

Friedman, Jeremy. *Shadow Cold War: The Sino-Soviet Competition for the Third World*. Chapel Hill: University of North Carolina Press, 2015.

———. "Soviet Policy in the Developing World and the Chinese Challenge in the 1960s." *Cold War History* 10, no. 2 (Spring 2010): 247–72.

Funada-Classe, Sayaka. *The Origins of War in Mozambique: A History of Unity and Division*. Translated by Masako Osada. Somerset West, South Africa: African Minds, 2013.

Fursenko, Alexander, and Timothy Naftali. *Khrushchev's Cold War: The Inside Story of an American Adversary*. 1st ed. New York: W. W. Norton, 2006.

Fürst, Juliane. *Stalin's Last Generation: Soviet Post-War Youth and the Emergence of Mature Socialism*. New York: Oxford University Press, 2010.

Gaddis, John Lewis. *We Now Know: Rethinking Cold War History*. New York: Oxford University Press, 1998.

Gallagher, Tom. *Portugal: A Twentieth-Century Interpretation*. Manchester: Manchester University Press, 1983.

Galvão, Henrique. *Santa Maria: My Crusade for Portugal*. Translated by William Longfellow. London: Weidenfeld and Nicolson, 1961.

Galvão, Inês and Catarina Laranjeiro, "Gender Struggle in Guinea-Bissau: Women's Participation On and Off the Liberation Record." In Domingos, Jerónimo and Roque, *Resistance and Colonialism*, 85–122.

Garthoff, Raymond L. *Détente and Confrontation: American-Soviet Relations from Nixon to Reagan*. Washington, D.C.: Brookings Institution, 1994.

Gasztold, Przemysław. "Lost Illusions: The Limits of Communist Poland's Involvement in Cold War Africa." In Muehlenbeck and Telepneva, *Warsaw Pact Intervention in the Third World*, 197–220.

George, Edward. *The Cuban Intervention in Angola, 1965–1991: From Che Guevara to Cuito Cuanavale*. Cass Military Studies. London: Frank Cass, 2005.

Gerard, Albert S., ed. *European-Language Writing in Sub-Saharan Africa*. Amsterdam: John Benjamins Publishing Company, 1986.

Gerits, Frank. "'When the Bull Elephants Fight': Kwame Nkrumah, Non-Alignment, and Pan-Africanism as an Interventionist Ideology in the Global Cold War (1957–66)," *The International History Review*, 37, no. 5 (2015): 951–69.

Gleijeses, Piero. *Conflicting Missions: Havana, Washington, and Africa, 1959–1976*. Chapel Hill: University of North Carolina Press, 2002.

———. *Visions of Freedom: Havana, Washington, Pretoria, and the Struggle for Southern Africa, 1976–1991*. Chapel Hill: University of North Carolina Press, 2013.

Gorbunov, Oleg. "Dva goda v Gvinee" [Two years in Guinea]. In Vasilev, *Afrika v vospominaniiakh*, 45–64.

Gould-Davies, Nigel. "The Logic of Soviet Cultural Diplomacy." *Diplomatic History* 27, no. 2 (April 2003): 193–214.

Gruffydd Jones, Branwen. "Race, Culture and Liberation: African Anticolonial Thought and Practice in the Time of Decolonisation." *International History Review* 42, no. 6 (2020): 1238–56.

Guillory, Sean. "Culture Clash in the Socialist Paradise: Soviet Patronage and African Students' Urbanity in the Soviet Union, 1960–1965." *Diplomatic History* 38, no. 2 (April 2014): 271–81.

Guimarães, Fernando Andresen. *The Origins of the Angolan Civil War: Foreign Intervention and Domestic Political Conflict*. Basingstoke, UK: Palgrave, 2001.

Hall, Margaret, and Tom Young. *Confronting Leviathan: Mozambique Since Independence*. Athens, Ohio: Ohio University Press, 1997.

Hanhimäki, Jussi. *The Flawed Architect: Henry Kissinger and American Foreign Policy*. New York: Oxford University Press, 2004.

Harmer, Tanya. *Allende's Chile and the Inter-American Cold War*. Chapel Hill: University of North Carolina Press, 2011.

Harper, Charles R., and William J. Nottingham. *Escape from Portugal—the Church in Action: The Secret Flight of 60 African Students to France*. St. Louis, Mo.: Lucas Park Books, 2015.

Harrison, Hope M. *Driving the Soviets up the Wall: Soviet-East German Relations, 1953–1961*. Princeton, N.J.: Princeton University Press, 2003. Kindle Edition.

Haslam, Jonathan. *Near and Distant Neighbours: A New History of Soviet Intelligence*. New York: Farrar, Straus and Giroux, 2015.

———. *Russia's Cold War: From the October Revolution to the Fall of the Wall*. New Haven, Conn.: Yale University Press, 2011.

Hevi, Emmanuel John. *An African Student in China*. New York, NY: Praeger, 1963.

Havik, Philip J., and Malyn Newitt, eds. *Creole Societies in the Portuguese Colonial Empire*. Cambridge: Cambridge Scholars Publishing, 2015.

Hessler, Julie. "Death of an African Student in Moscow: Race, Politics, and the Cold War." *Cahiers du Monde russe* 47, nos. 1/2 (Jan.–June 2006): 33–63.

Heywood, Linda Marinda. *Contested Power in Angola, 1840s to the Present*. Rochester, N.Y.: University of Rochester Press, 2000.

Higgs, Catherine. *Chocolate Islands: Cocoa, Slavery and Colonial Africa*. Athens: Ohio University Press, 2013.

Iandolo, Alessandro. "Imbalance of Power: The Soviet Union and the Congo Crisis, 1960–1961." *Journal of Cold War Studies* 16, no. 2 (Spring 2014): 32–55.

———. "The Rise and Fall of the 'Soviet Model of Development' in West Africa, 1957–64." *Cold War History* 12, no. 4 (November 2012): 683–704.

Ignatev, Oleg. *Syn Afriki: Amilkar Kabral* [Son of Africa: Amilcar Cabral]. Moscow: Izdatel'stvo politicheskoi literatury, 1975.

———. *Tres tiros da PIDE: Quern, porque e como mataram Amilcar Cabral?* [Three shots of the PIDE: Who, why and how killed Amilcar Cabral?]. Lisbon: Prelo, 1975.

Ilič, Melanie, Susan E. Reid, and Lynne Atwood, eds. *Women in the Khrushchev Era*. New York: Palgrave, 2004.

Isaacman, Allen F., and Barbara S. Isaacman. *Mozambique: From Colonialism to Revolution, 1900–1982*. Boulder, Colo.: Westview Press, 1983.

———. *Mozambique's Samora Machel: A Life Cut Short*. Athens: Ohio University Press, 2020.

Israel, Paolo. "Mueda Massacre: The Musical Archive." *Journal of Southern African Studies* 43, no. 6 (December 2017): 1157–79.

Jackson, Steven F. "China's Third World Foreign Policy: The Case of Angola and Mozambique, 1961–93." *China Quarterly*, no. 142 (June 1995): 401–22.

Jersild, Austin. "The Soviet State as Imperial Scavenger: 'Catch Up and Surpass' in the Transnational Socialist Bloc, 1950—1960." *American Historical Review* 116, no. 1 (February 2011): 109–32.

Kaňák, Petr, Jiřina Dvořákov, Zdeňka Jurová, *Československá rozvědka a Pražské jaro* [Czechoslovak Intelligence and the Prague Spring]. Praha: ÚSTR, 2016

Katsakioris, Constantin. "Students from Portuguese Africa in the Soviet Union, 1960–74: Anti-colonialism, Education, and the Socialist Alliance." *Journal of Contemporary History* (2020): 1–24.

———. "L'union soviétique et les intellectuels africains: Internationalisme, panafricanisme et négritude pendant les années de la décolonisation, 1954–1964." *Cahiers du Monde russe* 47, no. 1/2 (Jan.–June 2006): 15–32.

———. "Burden or Allies? Third World Students and Internationalist Duty through Soviet Eyes." *Kritika: Explorations in Russian and Eurasian History* 18, no. 3 (2017): 539–67.

Keese, Alexander. "Managing the Prospect of Famine: Cape Verdean Officials, Subsistence Emergencies, and the Change of Elite Attitudes During Portugal's Late Colonial Phase, 1939–1961." *Itinerario* 36, no. 1 (April 2012): 49–70.

———. "The Role of Cape Verdeans in War Mobilization and War Prevention in Portugal's African Empire, 1955–1965." *International Journal of African Historical Studies* 40, no. 3 (2007): 497–511.

Kempton, Daniel. Soviet Strategy toward Southern Africa: the National Liberation Movement Connection. London: Praeger, 1989.

Khrushchev, Sergei. *Nikita Khrushchev: Creation of a Superpower.* University Park: Pennsylvania State University Press, 2000.

———, ed. *Memoirs of Nikita Khrushchev: Statesman, 1953–1964.* Vol. 3. University Park: Pennsylvania State University Press, 2007.

Kirpichenko, Vadim. *Razvedka: Litsa i lichnosti* [Intelligence: People and personalities]. Moscow: Geia, 1998. E-book edition.

Klinghoffer, Arthur Jay. *The Angolan War: a Study in Soviet Policy in the Third World.* New York: Routledge, 1980.

Koivunen, Pia. "Friends, 'Potential Friends,' and Enemies: Reimagining Soviet Relations to the First, Second, and Third Worlds at the Moscow 1957 Youth Festival." In Babiracki and Jersild, *Socialist Internationalism in the Cold War,* 219–47.

Kolpakidi, A. I., and D. P. Prokhorov. *Imperiia GRU: Ocherki istorii rossiiskoi voennoi razvedki: Dos'e* [The GRU empire: Studies in the history of Russian military intelligence; A dossier]. Moscow: Olma-Press, 2000.

Kozlov, Nicholas N., and Eric D. Weitz. "Reflections on the Origins of the 'Third Period': Bukharin, the Comintern, and the Political Economy of Weimar Germany." *Journal of Contemporary History* 24, no. 3 (July 1989): 387–410.

Kramer, Mark, and Vit Smetana, eds. *Imposing, Maintaining and Tearing Open the Iron Curtain: The Cold War and East-Central Europe, 1945–1989.* Lanham, Md.: Lexington Books, 2014.

Lal, Priya. "Maoism in Tanzania: Material Connections and Shared Imaginaries." In Cook, *Mao's Little Red Book,* 96–116.

Lazic, Milorad. "Comrades in Arms: Yugoslav Military Aid to Liberation Movements of Angola and Mozambique." In Dallywater, Saunders and Fonseca, *Southern African Liberation Movements,* 151–81.

Leffler, Melvyn P. *For the Soul of Mankind: The United States, the Soviet Union, and the Cold War.* New York: Hill and Wang, 2007.

Legum, Colin. *After Angola: The War over Southern Africa.* New York: Africana Publishing, 1976.

Legvold, Robert. *Soviet Policy in West Africa.* Cambridge, Mass.: Harvard University Press, 1970.

Liu, Philip Hsiaopong. "Petty Annoyances? Revisiting John Emmanuel Hevi's An African Student in China After 50 Years." *China: An International Journal* 11, no. 1 (2013): 131–45.

Lopes, Carlos, ed. *Africa's Contemporary Challenges: The Legacy of Amilcar Cabral*. London: Routledge, 2013.

Lopes, Rui. *West Germany and the Portuguese Dictatorship, 1968–1974: Between Cold War and Colonialism*, Palgrave Macmillan, 2014.

Lovell, Julia. *Maoism: A Global History*. London: Vintage, 2019. Kindle Edition.

Löwy, Michael. "Marxists and the National Question." *New Left Review*, no. 1/96 (March–April 1976): 81–100.

Lüthi, Lorenz M. *Cold Wars: Asia, the Middle East, Europe*. New York: Cambridge University Press, 2020.

Macamo, Elísio. "Violence and political culture in Mozambique." *Social Dynamics* 42, no. 1 (2016): 85–105.

Macmillan, Hugh, Stephen Ellis, Arianna Lissoni, and Mariya Kurbak. "Debating the ANC's External Links During the Struggle against Apartheid." *Africa* 85, no. 1 (2015): 154–62.

Macmillan, Hugh. *The Lusaka Years: The ANC in Exile in Zambia 1963–1994*. Johannesburg: Jacana Media (Pty), 2013.

MacQueen, Norrie. *The Decolonization of Portuguese Africa: Metropolitan Revolution and the Dissolution of Empire*. London: Longman, 1997.

———. "Belated Decolonization and UN Politics against the Backdrop of the Cold War: Portugal, Britain, and Guinea-Bissau's Proclamation of Independence, 1973–1974," *Journal of Cold War Studies*, no. 8 (2006): 29–56.

Manela, Erez. *The Wilsonian Moment: Self-Determination and the International Origins of Anticolonial Nationalism*. New York: Oxford University Press, 2007.

Manji, Firoze, and Bill Fletcher Jr., eds. *Claim No Easy Victories: The Legacy of Amilcar Cabral*. Lexington, Ky.: Daraja Press, 2013.

Marcum, John A. *The Angolan Revolution*. Vol. 1: *The Anatomy of an Explosion, 1950–1962*. Cambridge, Mass.: M.I.T. Press, 1969.

———. *The Angolan Revolution*. Vol 2: *Exile Politics and Guerrilla Warfare, 1962–1976*. Cambridge, Mass.: M.I.T. Press, 1978.

———. *Conceiving Mozambique*. Edited by Edmund Terry Burke III and Michael Clough. Cham: Palgrave Macmillan/Springer, 2018.

Marinho, António Luís. *Operação Mar Verde: Um documento para a história* [Operation Green Sea: A Document for History]. Lisbon: Temas e Debates, 2006.

Marino, Alexander Joseph. "America's War in Angola, 1961–1976." PhD diss., University of Arkansas, 2015.

Mata, Inocência. "Under the Sign of a Projective Nostalgia: Agostinho Neto and Angolan Postcolonial Poetry." *Lusophone African and Afro-Brazilian Literatures* 38, no. 1 (2007): 54–67.

Mateus, Dalila Cabrita. *A luta pela independência: A formação das elites fundadoras da FRELIMO, MPLA e PAIGC* [The struggle for independence: The formation of founding elites of FRELIMO, MPLA and PAIGC]. Mem Martins, Portugal: Editorial Inquérito, 1999.

Mateus, Dalila Cabrita, and Álvaro Mateus. *Angola 61—Guerra colonial: Causas e consequências: O 4 de Fevereiro e o 15 de Março* [Angola 61—Colonial War: Causes and Consequences: 4 February to 15 March]. Lisbon: Texto, 2011.

Matusevich, Maxim. "Probing the Limits of Internationalism: African Students Confront Soviet Ritual." *Anthropology of East Europe Review* 27, no. 2 (Fall 2009): 19–39.

———. "An Exotic Subversive: Africa, Africans and the Soviet Everyday." *Race and Class* 49, no. 4 (2008): 57–81.

———. "Journeys of Hope: African Diaspora and the Soviet Society," *Journal of African Diaspora*, vol. 1, no. 1–2 (2008), 53–85

Maxwell, Kenneth. *The Making of Portuguese Democracy.* Cambridge: Cambridge University Press, 1995.

Mazov, Sergey. *A Distant Front in the Cold War: The USSR in West Africa and the Congo, 1956–1964.* Stanford, Calif.: Stanford University Press, 2010.

———. "The USSR and the Former Italian Colonies, 1945–50." *Cold War History* 3, no. 3 (2003): 49–78.

McDermott, Kevin, and Jeremy Agnew. *The Comintern: A History of International Communism from Lenin to Stalin.* Basingstoke, UK: Macmillan, 1996.

Mendy, Peter Karibe and Richard Lobban, eds. *Historical Dictionary of the Republic of Guinea-Bissau.* Plymouth, UK: The Scarecrow Press, 2013.

Meneses, Ribeiro Filipe. *Salazar: A Political Biography.* New York: Enigma Books, 2010. Kindle.

Meneses, Ribeiro Filipe, and Robert McNamara. "The Last Throw of the Dice: Portugal, Rhodesia and South Africa, 1970–1974." *Portuguese Studies* 28 (2012): 201–15.

Messiant, Christine. "Angola, les voies de l'ethnisation et de la décomposition [Angola, the ways of ethnization and decomposition]." *Lusotopie* no. 1 (1994): 155–210.

Miller, Jamie. *An African Volk: The Apartheid Regime and Its Search for Survival.* New York: Oxford University Press, 2016.

———. "Yes, Minister: Reassessing South Africa's Intervention in the Angolan Civil War, 1975–1976." *Journal of Cold War Studies* 15, no. 3 (Summer 2013): 4–33.

Millar, James R. "The Little Deal: Brezhnev's Contribution to Acquisitive Socialism," *Slavic Review* 44, no. 4 (1985): 694–706.

Mitrokhin, Nikolai. "Elita 'zakrytogo obshchestva': MGIMO, Mezhdunarodnye otdely apparata TsK KPSS i prosopografiia ikh sotrudnikov" [The elite of a 'closed society': MGIMO, the International Section of the CC CPSS and a prosopography of their staffs]. *Ab Imperio*, no. 4 (2013): 145–86.

Mitrokhin, Vasilii, and Christopher Andrew. *The Mitrokhin Archive II: The KGB in the World.* London: Penguin, 2006.

Mlechin, Leonid. *Zheleznyi Shurik* [Iron Shurik]. Moscow: Eksmo, 2004.

Mondlane, Eduardo. *The Struggle for Mozambique.* Penguin African Library. Harmondsworth: Penguin, 1969.

Moorman, Marissa J. *Intonations: A Social History of Luanda, Angola, from 1945 to Recent Times.* New African Histories. Athens: Ohio University Press, 2008.

Morgenstierne, Christopher Munthe. *Denmark and National Liberation in Southern Africa: A Flexible Response*. Uppsala: Nordiska Afrikainstitutet, 2003.

Morier-Genoud, Eric, ed. *Sure Road? Nationalisms in Angola, Guinea-Bissau and Mozambique*. Boston: Brill, 2012.

Muehlenbeck, Philip E. *Betting on the Africans: John F. Kennedy's Courting of African Nationalist Leaders*. New York: Oxford University Press, 2012.

———. *Czechoslovakia in Africa, 1945–1968*. Basingstoke, UK: Palgrave Macmillan, 2015.

———. "Czechoslovak Assistance to Kenya and Uganda." In Muehlenbeck and Telepneva, *Warsaw Pact Intervention in the Third World*, 249–70.

Muehlenbeck, Philip E. and Natalia Telepneva, eds. *Warsaw Pact Intervention in the Third World: Aid and Influence in the Cold War*. London: IB Tauris, 2018.

Namikas, Lise. *Battleground Africa: Cold War in the Congo, 1960–1965*. Stanford, Calif.: Stanford University Press, 2013.

Natufe, O. Igho. *Soviet Policy in Africa: From Lenin to Brezhnev*. Bloomington, Ind.: iUniverse, 2011.

Ncomo, Barnabé Lucas. *Uria Simango: Um homem, uma causa* [Uria Simango: A Man and the Cause]. Maputo: Edições Novafrica, 2004.

Neves, Joao Manuel. "Frantz Fanon and the Struggle for the Independence of Angola: The Meeting in Rome in 1959." *Interventions: International Journal of Postcolonial Studies* 17, no. 3 (2015): 417–33.

Neves, José. "The Role of Portugal on the Stage of Imperialism: Communism, Nationalism and Colonialism (1930–1960)." *Nationalities Papers* 37, no. 4 (July 2009): 485–99.

———. "Ideology, science, and people in Amílcar Cabral," *História, Ciências, Saúde-Manguinhos* 24, no. 2 (2017): 333–47.

Newitt, Malyn D. *A History of Mozambique*. Bloomington: Indiana University Press, 1995.

———. "The Portuguese African Colonies During the Second World War." In Byfield, *Africa and World War II*, 220–37.

Nguyen, Lien-Hang T. *Hanoi's War: An International History of the War for Peace in Vietnam*. Chapel Hill: University of North Carolina Press, 2012.

Onslow, Sue, and Dimon Bright. "The Battle of Cuito Cuanavale: Media Space and the End of the Cold War in Southern Africa." In Radchenko and Kalinovsky, *The End of the Cold War*, 277–97.

Onslow, Sue, ed. *Cold War in Southern Africa: White Power, Black Liberation*. New York: Routledge, 2009.

Opello Jr., Walter. "Pluralism and Elite Conflict in an Independence Movement: Frelimo in the 1960s." *Journal of Southern African Studies* 2, no. 1 (October 1975): 66–82.

Panzer, Michael G. "The Pedagogy of Revolution: Youth, Generational Conflict, and Education in the Development of Mozambican Nationalism and the State, 1962–1970." *Journal of Southern African Studies* 35, no. 4 (December 2009): 803–20.

Pearce, Justin. *Political Identity and Conflict in Central Angola, 1975–2002.* New York: Cambridge University Press, 2015.

——. "Simango, Gwenjere and the Politics of the Past in Mozambique," *Journal of Southern African Studies* 47, no. 3. (May 2021): 387–404.

Péclard, Didier. "UNITA and the Moral Economy of Exclusion in Angola, 1966–1977." In Morier-Genoud, *Sure Road?*, 149–74.

Peterson, Charles F. *Dubois, Fanon, Cabral: The Margins of Elite Anti-Colonial Leadership.* Lanham, Md.: Lexington Books, 2007.

Persak, Krzysztof, and Łukasz Kamiński, eds. *A Handbook of the Communist Security Apparatus in East Central Europe, 1944–1989.* Warsaw: Institute of National Remembrance, 2005.

Pikhoia, Rudolf Germanovich. *Moskva, Kreml, vlast: Sorok let posle voiny, 1945–1985* [Moscow: Kremlin and Power: Forty years after the war, 1945–1985]. Moscow, Rus-Olimp, AST, 2007.

Pitcher, Anne. *Politics in the Portuguese Empire: The State, Industry, and Cotton, 1926–1974.* New York: Oxford University Press, 1993.

Prashad, Vijay. *The Darker Nations: A People's History of the Third World.* New York: New Press, 2008. Kindle.

Pringle, Robert W. *Historical Dictionary of Russian and Soviet Intelligence*, 2nd ed. Lanham, Md.: Rowman & Littlefield, 2015.

Rabaka, Reiland. *Africana Critical Theory: Reconstructing the Black Radical Tradition from W. E. B. Du Bois and C. L. R. James to Frantz Fanon and Amilcar Cabral.* Lanham, Md.: Lexington Books, 2009.

——. *Concepts of Cabralism: Amilcar Cabral and Africana Critical Theory.* Lanham, Md.: Lexington Books, 2014.

Radchenko, Sergey, and Artemy Kalinovsky, eds. *The End of the Cold War and the Third World.* London: Routledge, 2011.

Rakove, Robert B. *Kennedy, Johnson, and the Nonaligned World.* Cambridge: Cambridge University Press, 2013.

Reis, Bruno C. "Decentering the Cold War in Southern Africa: The Portuguese Policy of Decolonization and Détente in Angola and Mozambique (1974–1984)." *Journal of Cold War Studies* 21, no. 1 (Winter 2019): 3–51.

Rees, Tim, and Andrew Thorpe, eds. *International Communism and the Communist International, 1919–43.* Manchester: Manchester University Press, 1998.

Reza, Alexandra. "African Anti-colonialism and the Ultramarinos of the Casa dos Estudantes do Império," *Journal of Lusophone Studies*, 1, no. 1 (2006): 37–56.

Richterova, Daniela, Mikuláš Pešta, and Natalia Telepneva. "Banking on Military Assistance: Czechoslovakia's Struggle for Influence and Profit in the Third World, 1955–1968." *International History Review* 43, no. 1 (2021): 90–108.

Richterova, Daniela, and Natalia Telepneva. "An Introduction: The Secret Struggle for the Global South—Espionage, Military Assistance and State Security in the Cold War," *International History Review* 43, no. 1 (2021): 1–11.

Roberts, Geoffrey. "A Chance for Peace? The Soviet Campaign to End the Cold War, 1953–1955." Cold War International History Project Working Paper No. 57, Woodrow Wilson International Center for Scholars, Washington, D.C., December 2008, 35–61.

Roberts, George. "The Assassination of Eduardo Mondlane: Frelimo, Tanzania, and the Politics of Exile in Dar es Salaam." *Cold War History* 17, no. 1 (2017): 1–19.

Rocha, Edmundo, Francisco Soares, and Moisés Silva Fernandes. *Angola: Viriato da Cruz; O homem e o mito* [Viriato da Cruz; The man and the myth]. Luanda: Caxinde, 2008.

Roth-Ey, Kristin. "Loose Girls" on the Loose?: Sex, Propaganda and the 1957 Youth Festival." In Ilič, Reid, and Atwood, *Women in the Khrushchev Era*, 75–95.

Rodrigues, Luís Nuno. "António de Spínola and the International Context of Portuguese Decolonization." *Luso-Brazilian Review* 50, no. 2, (2013): 93–117.

Roman, Meredith. *Opposing Jim Crow: African Americans and the Soviet Indictment of U.S. Racism, 1928–1937*. Lincoln: University of Nebraska Press, 2012.

Rupprecht, Tobias. *Soviet Internationalism after Stalin: Interaction and Exchange between the USSR and Latin America During the Cold War*. Cambridge: Cambridge University Press, 2015.

Sachs, Jeffrey. *To Move the World: JFK's Quest for Peace*. New York: Random House, 2013. Google Play.

Santos, Marcelino [Lilinho Micaia]. *Pesnia istinnoi liubvi* [A song of true love]. Translated by Lidiia Nekrasova. Moscow: Biblioteka "Ogonek," 1959.

Santos, Aurora Almada. *A Organização das Nações Unidas e a Questão Colonial Portuguesa: 1960–1974* [The United Nations and the Questiono of Portuguese Colonialism, 1960–1974]. Liston: Instituto da Defesa Nacional, 2017.

Sapega, Ellen W. *Consensus and Debate in Salazar's Portugal: Visual and Literary Negotiations of the National Text, 1933–1948*. University Park: Pennsylvania State University Press, 2008.

Sapire, Hilary. "Liberation Movements, Exile, and International Solidarity: An Introduction." *Journal of Southern African Studies* 35, no. 2 (June 2009): 271–86.

Sapire, Hilary, and Chris Saunders, eds. *Southern African Liberation Struggles: New Local, Regional and Global Perspectives*. Claremont, South Africa: UCT Press, 2013.

Saucier, P. Khalil, ed. *A Luta Continua: (Re)introducing Amilcar Cabral to a New Generation of Thinkers*. Trenton, N.J.: Africa World Press, 2016.

Saunders, Chris. "The Ending of the Cold War and Southern Africa." In Radchenko and Kalinovsky, *The End of the Cold War*, 264–77.

Schlesinger Jr., Arthur M. "Origins of the Cold War." *Foreign Affairs* 46 (1967): 22–52.

Schmidt, Elizabeth. "Cold War in Guinea: The Rassemblement Démocratique Africain and the Struggle over Communism, 1950–1958." *Journal of African History* 48, no. 1 (2007): 95–121.

Schneidman, Witney W. *Engaging Africa: Washington and the Fall of Portugal's Colonial Empire*. Lanham, Md.: University Press of America, 2004.

Sellström, Tor. *Sweden and National Liberation in Southern Africa*. Vols 1, *Formation of Popular Opinion, 1950–1970*. Uppsala: Nordiska Afrikainstitutet, 1999.

———. *Sweden and National Liberation in Southern Africa*. Vol. 2, *Solidarity and Assistance*. Uppsala: Nordiska Afrikainstitutet, 2002.

———, ed. *Liberation in Southern Africa: Regional and Swedish Voices; Interviews from Angola, Mozambique, Namibia, South Africa, Zimbabwe, the Frontline and Sweden*. Uppsala: Nordiska Afrikainstitutet, 2002.

Shubin, Vladimir. *The Hot "Cold War": The U.S.S.R in Southern Africa*. London: Pluto Press, 2008.

———. "Unsung Heroes: The Soviet Military and the Liberation of Southern Africa." *Cold War History* 7, no. 2 (2007): 251–62.

Shmelkov, "Obshchestvennye sviazi s Afrikoi: Kak oni nachinalis [The beginning of public relations with Africa]," Vasilev, *Afrika v Vospominaniiakh*, 22–38.

Simpson, Thula. "Nelson Mandela and the Genesis of the ANC's Armed Struggle: Notes on Method." *Journal of African History* 44, no. 1 (2018): 133–48.

Skorov, George. "Ivan Potekhin—Man, Scientist, and Friend of Africa." *Journal of Modern African Studies* 2, no. 3 (November 1964): 446–47.

Slobodian, Quinn. "Bandung in Divided Germany—Managing Non-Aligned Politics in East and West, 1955–63," *The Journal of Imperial and Commonwealth History* 41, no. 4. (2013): 644–62.

Smith, Tony. "New Bottles for New Wine: A Pericentric Framework for the Study of the Cold War." *Diplomatic History* 24, no. 4 (2000): 567–91.

Soiri, Iina, and Pekka Peltola. *Finland and National Liberation in Southern Africa*. Uppsala: Nordiska Afrikainstitutet, 1999.

Somerville, Keith. *Angola: Politics, Economics and Society*. London: Pinter, 1986.

Sousa, Julião Soares. "Amílcar Cabral, the PAIGC and the Relations with China at the Time of the Sino-Soviet Split and of Anti-Colonialism: Discourses and Praxis." *International History Review* 42, no. 6 (2020): 1274–96.

———. *Amílcar Cabral (1924–1973): Vida e morta de um revolucionario africano* [Amílcar Cabral (1924–1973): The life and death of an African revolutionary]. Coimbra: Edição de Autor, 2016.

Spencer, Leon P. *Toward an African Church in Mozambique: Kamba Simango and the Protestant Community in Manica and Sofala, 1892–1945*. Mzuzu, Malawi: Mzuni Press, 2003.

Steenkamp, Willem. *Borderstrike! South Africa into Angola, 1975–1980*, 3rd ed. Durban: Just Done Productions, 2006.

Stevens, Simon. "The Turn to Sabotage by The Congress Movement in South Africa," *Past and Present* 245, no. 1 (2019): 221–55.

Sun, Jodie Yuzhou. "Viriato da Cruz and His Chinese Exile: A Biographical Approach," *Journal of Southern African Studies* 46, no. 5 (2020): 845–61.

Suny, Ronald Grigor. "'Don't Paint Nationalism Red!': National Revolution and Socialist Anti-Imperialism." In Duara, *Decolonization*, 176–98.

Taubman, William. *Khrushchev: The Man and His Era*. New York: W. W. Norton and Company, 2003.

Telepneva, Natalia. "'Code Name SEKRETÁŘ': Amílcar Cabral, Czechoslovakia and the Role of Human Intelligence during the Cold War." *International History Review* 42, no. 6 (2020): 1257–73.

———. "Cold War on the Cheap: Soviet and Czechoslovak Intelligence in the Congo, 1960–1963." In Muehlenbeck and Telepneva, *Warsaw Pact Intervention in the Third World*, 125–47.

———. "'Letters from Angola': Soviet Print Media and the Liberation of Angola, Mozambique, and Guinea-Bissau, 1961–1975." In Dallywater, Saunders and Fonseca, *Southern African Liberation Movements*, 129–51.

———. "Saving Ghana's Revolution: The Demise of Kwame Nkrumah and the Evolution of Soviet Policy in Africa, 1966–1972." *Journal of Cold War Studies* 20, no. 4 (Fall 2018): 4–25.

———. "Mediators of Liberation: Eastern Bloc Officials, Mozambican Diplomacy and the Origins of Soviet Support for FRELIMO 1958–1965," *Journal of Southern African Studies* 43, no. 1 (2017): 67–81

Tomlinson, B. R. 'What was the Third World?' *Journal of Contemporary History* 38, no. 2 (April 2003): 307–21.

Tornimbeni, Corrado. "Nationalism and Internationalism in the Liberation Struggle in Mozambique: The Role of the FRELIMO's Solidarity Network in Italy." *South African Historical Journal* 70, no. 1 (2018): 194–214.

Uhl, Matthias. "Nikita Khrushchev." In Casey and Wright, *Mental Maps in the Early Cold War Era*, 281–307.

Vasilev, Aleksei, ed. *Afrika v vospominaniiakh Veteranov Diplomaticheskoi Sluzhby* [Africa in the Recollections of the Veterans of the Foreign Office]. 5 vols. Moscow: Institut Afriki RAN, 2000–2006.

Weigert, Stephen L. *Angola: A Modern Military History, 1961–2002*. New York: Palgrave Macmillan, 2011.

West, Harry G. *Kupilikula: Governance and the Invisible Realm in Mozambique*. Chicago: University of Chicago Press, 2005.

Westad, Odd Arne. *The Global Cold War: Third World Interventions and the Making of Our Times*. Cambridge: Cambridge University Press, 2005.

———. *The Cold War: A World History*. London: Penguin UK, 2017.

———. "The Fall of Détente and the Turning Tides of History." In Westad, *The Fall of Détente* 4–33.

———, ed. *The Fall of Détente: Soviet-American Relations during the Carter Years*. Oslo: Scandinavian University Press, 1997.

Westad, Odd Arne, and Melvyn P. Leffler, eds. *The Cambridge History of the Cold War*. Cambridge: Cambridge University Press, 2010.

Wheeler, Douglas L. "African Elements in Portugal's Armies in Africa, 1961–1974," *Armed Forces and Society* 2 (February 1976): 237.

White, Luise, and Miles Larmer. "Introduction: Mobile Soldiers and the Un-National Liberation of Southern Africa." *Journal of Southern African Studies* 40, no. 6 (2014), 1271–74.

Yordanov, Radoslav A. *The Soviet Union and the Horn of Africa during the Cold War: Between Ideology and Pragmatism.* Harvard Cold War Studies. Lanham, Md.: Lexington Books, 2016.

Zídek, Petr and Karl Sieber. *Československo a Subsaharská Afrika v Letech 1948–1989* [Czechoslovakia and Sub-Saharan Africa, 1948–89]. Prague: Ústav Mezinárodních Vztahů, 2007.

Zubok, Vladislav M. *A Failed Empire: The Soviet Union in the Cold War from Stalin to Gorbachev.* Chapel Hill: University of North Carolina Press, 2007.

———. "Spy vs. Spy: The KGB vs. the CIA, 1960–1962." *Cold War International History Project Bulletin* 4 (Fall 1994): 22–33.

INDEX

Page numbers in *italics* refer to illustrations.

CPSIA information can be obtained
at www.ICGtesting.com
Printed in the USA
LVHW102307060622
720654LV00005B/268